The Rhetoric of Modernism

Graphic design and layout: Marine Gille and Line Martin-Célo
Adaptation for the English edition: Alexandra Zöller

Text of English edition by Tim Benton, with parts of chapter 3 and chapter 4 translated from French by Stefan Zebrowski-Rubin. The Le Corbusier texts in the Appendix translated by Clare Perkins, with the generous support of the Fondation Le Corbusier.

French edition published with the support of the Centre national du livre and the Ministère de la Culture et de la Communication (Direction de l'Architecture et du Patrimoine).

Photographic credits:
All illustrations by permission of Fondation Le Corbusier, Paris, with the exception of:
Avery Library, Columbia University, New York:
pp. 126-7, 129, 130-131
Tim Benton: pp. 17, 85, 151 left
Getty Research Institute, Los Angeles: pp. 38 left, 95, 101, 138-139, 144-145, 154, 156, 157, 159, 161 right, 164, 176, 186 bottom right, 188.
© Gotthard Schuh: cover and p. 13
© Willy Rizzo/Paris Match/Scoop: p. 92

Bibliographic information published by the German National Library
The Deutsche Nationalbibliothek lists this publication in the Deutsche Nationalbibliografie; detailed bibliographic data are available in the Internet at http://dnb.ddb.de.

Library of Congress Control Number: 2008943156

Basel · Boston · Berlin
P.O.Box 133, CH-4010 Basel, Switzerland
Part of Springer Science+Business Media

Printed on acid-free paper produced from chlorine-free pulp. TCF ∞

Printed in France

ISBN 978-3-7643-8944-4

www.birkhauser.ch

9 8 7 6 5 4 3 2 1

The Rhetoric of Modernism: Le Corbusier as a Lecturer

Tim Benton

Birkhäuser

Basel · Boston · Berlin

Acknowledgments

I would first like to thank the Open University which graciously afforded me the necessary time to pursue my research and which provided generous financial assistance in the production of the first edition.

I am very grateful to the Getty Research Institute, Los Angeles, for allowing me to consult the Le Corbusier material in their archives and for providing me with a Library Research grant. The Canadian Centre for Architecture generously allowed me access to their archives and the peace and quiet of the library while the book was being written.

Janet Parks, at the Avery Library, Columbia University, New York, made it possible to consult the vast and fragile drawings for Le Corbusier's lectures at Columbia.

The audiovisual department of Butler Library, Columbia University, provided me with a CD of Le Corbusier's two lectures in 1961.

The Fondation Le Corbusier in Paris provided me with the majority of the primary source material for this research and a home from home for my research. I would like to extend my warmest thanks to Michel Richard, the Director, to Arnaud Dercelles who was a constant source of assistance and Isabelle Godineau for her precise and detailed knowledge of the sources. They greatly helped in the creation of this book by their expertise, professionalism and patience. Stéphane Potelle transcribed several of the lecture notes included in the appendices of the book and I would like to thank him for his friendship and continuous intellectual support. I would also like to thank Jean-Louis Cohen and Joseph Rykwert for their encouragement and advice.

Grateful thanks to Frédéric Lenne and Valérie Thouard, of the publisher of the French edition, Le Moniteur, for supporting the project. This book would never have seen the light of day without the remarkable assistance of Stéphanie Grégoire, whose painstaking editing of my French text made the book readable.

Many thanks too to the graphic designers of the French edition, Marine Gille and Line Martin-Célo, who devised a means of presenting Le Corbusier's thought, in words and images, on the page.

This book is dedicated to Caroline Maniaque, with whom I have discussed every page and who translated much of it into French for the French edition.

Document references preceded by 'FLC', 'GRI' or 'CCA' indicate their origin:
FLC: Fondation Le Corbusier, Paris
GRI: Getty Research Institute, Los Angeles
CCA: Centre Canadien d'Architecture, Montreal

Cover: Le Corbusier delivering his lecture "Les relations entre l'architecture et la peinture", at Zurich on 12 January 1938 (Photograph: Gottfried Schuh, Arthur Rüegg Archive, Zurich)

Contents

226
183
113

Introduction

It goes without saying that Charles-Edouard Jeanneret (1887-1965) was one of the most persuasive architects of the twentieth century, both in theory and practice.[1] The influence he was able to exert on architects and public alike was in part due to his lectures, which he delivered continuously from 1924 until his death 41 years later. This book aims to trace the origins of this illustrous career as a lecturer and interrogate the way he deployed logic and rhetoric in support of his arguments.

Emergence of Le Corbusier as a public figure

It was shortly after leaving la Chaux-de-Fonds in Switzerland, where he was born, and establishing himself in Paris in 1917, that Charles-Edouard Jeanneret (he adopted the name Le Corbusier in 1920) began to establish his reputation based on his activities as painter, architect, and author.[2] The publication of the journal *L'Esprit Nouveau*, which he co-edited with Amédée Ozenfant and, for a short period, with Paul Dermée, gained him an international reputation.[3] Between October 1920 and May 1922, Jeanneret published twelve articles on architecture, under the pseudonym of Le Corbusier-Saugnier.[4] With the addition of a final chapter, these articles were published in October 1923 as the book *Vers une architecture*, one of the best known and the least understood books of the twentieth century. The book was quickly reprinted and translated into various languages. In 1925, further articles in *L'Esprit Nouveau* were put together to constitute three more books: *Urbanisme* (made up of articles published in June 1922 and between November 1923 and January 1925), *L'Art décoratif d'aujourd'hui* (with his articles published between November 1923 and January 1925) and *La Peinture moderne* (with his articles published between June 1922 and January 1925).[5] A fifth book, *Almanach de l'architecture moderne*, was published early in 1926, partly consisting of articles intended for a 29th issue of *L'Esprit Nouveau* which never appeared.[6] Therefore, by 1924, when Le Corbusier embarked on his regular career as a lecturer, many of his best known theoretical ideas had already been published.

Le Corbusier was also exhibiting regularly at the Salon d'Automne. In December 1922, he made a big public impression with a large plaster model of a standard housing unit which he called 'Citrohan' – named after the Citroën motor car – as well as a remarkable series of drawings representing a Contemporary City for Three Million Inhabitants. Notable among these were a large plan of one part of the city, several perspective views including a cavalier perspective of the city centre and a painted diorama 16.25 metres long and 5.25 metres high. Le Corbusier's cousin and associate Pierre Jeanneret designed a viewing platform from which the curved wall of the diorama could be seen in its entirety and with lighting diffused by a translucent sheet in the ceiling (Fig 1).[7]

A brief text and some slogans accompanied the exhibition as well as some diagrams explaining the problems of overcrowding and circulation produced by the crisis of the modern industrial city.[8]

Never had the press paid so much attention to Le Corbusier's work. Maurice Raynal, for example, described the contemporary city in glowing terms:

Previous page

Le Corbusier in his studio in the rue de Sèvres before a drawing of the Modulor (1950s).

1/This was the claim of the Hayward Gallery exhibition: Benton, T. et al. (1987). *Le Corbusier, Architect of the Century: a Centenary Exhibition Organized by the Arts Council of Great Britain*, London, Arts Council of Great Britain.

2/See de Smet, C. (2005). *Le Corbusier, Architect of Books*, translation from the French by Deke Dusinberre, Baden, Lars Müller Publishers.

3/Following a disagreement between Le Corbusier, Amédée Ozenfant and Paul Dermée in December 1920, the latter's participation ceased after the third issue. 28 volumes of *L'Esprit Nouveau* were republished by Da Capo Press, New York, in 1968. For more detailed information on *L'Esprit Nouveau* see von Moos, S., F. Ducros and T. Benton (1987). *L'Esprit Nouveau: Le Corbusier et l'industrie 1920-25*, Strasbourg; Colomina, B. (1987), 'L'Esprit nouveau: architecture and publicity', in Ockman, J., ed. (1998). *Architecture-Reproduction*, New York, Princeton Architectural Press, 1998, pp. 56-99; Eliel, C. (2001). *L'Esprit Nouveau; Purism in Paris 1918-1925*, Los Angeles, Los Angeles County Museum of Art, in association with Harry N. Abrams, New York.

4/Saugnier, one of the pseudonyms of Amédée Ozenfant, appeared on the cover of the first edition of *Vers une architecture*, and disappeared in the second edition, of January 1925.

Figure 1
Le Corbusier, diorama of the Contemporary City for Three Million Inhabitants, Salon d'Automne, 1922 (Glass transparency of the diorama used in the lectures, FLC).

> The architect Le Corbusier seems to hand us this formidable modern city ready made, like the bishops used to present models of their cathedrals in cathedral stained glass windows. We see this city as if in a dream, as a kind of paradise, but based on a most thoroughly and precisely researched reality, as a remedy to all the ills which present day cities are suffering from. [...] The architect's idea is remarkable for its precision and purity [...]. You have to admire this astonishing diorama which has so much to teach us of the highest interest and which undoubtedly holds the key to many urban problems for the future.[9]

The Swiss newspaper *La Tribune de Lausanne* noted:

> [...] and the crowd jostles before the diorama of Le Corbusier-Saulnier (a name familiar to us as a Swiss Romand). It represents a city of the future with huge houses, such as Gulliver might have seen at Brobdignac, lining well-defined avenues wider than rivers.[10]

André Gybal, writing in the *Journal du Peuple* on 8 November, said of the 'Cité contemporaine' that it was: '[...] the very heart of the Salon that symbolizes the whole of the future and constitutes a most noble and the most reassuring creation: this is Le Corbusier's work [...] Real beauty is not to be found in the picturesque but in absolute order.'

Others were less enthusiastic. René Chavance considered the 'Cité contemporaine' '[...] much less engaging. [...] Let us hope that progress will impose this barracks city only on much later generations.'[11] For Michel Maubeuge, it was a 'factory for living', whereas for the critic of *Le Journal*, the city looked like the ruins of Palmyra whose houses had lost theirs roofs in a squall.[12]

The left-wing press had its reservations as well. Jacques Mesnil, the critic of *L'Humanité*, was prepared to recognize that Le Corbusier's stand deserved close study, but regretted its lack of political understanding (only Communists could organize the collective life of the people...). He criticized the cubic and ori-

5/Le Corbusier (1966). *Urbanisme*, Paris, Editions Vincent, Fréal et Cie; Le Corbusier (1959). *L'Art décoratif d'aujourd'hui*, Paris, Editions Vincent, Fréal et Cie; and Charles-Edouard Jeanneret, and Amédée Ozenfant (1925). *La Peinture moderne*, Paris, Editions G. Crès et Cie.

6/Le Corbusier (1926). *Almanach d'architecture moderne; documents, théorie, pronostics, histoire, petites histoires, dates, propos standarts, apologie et idéalisation du standart, organisation, industrialisation du bâtiment*, Paris, Editions G. Crès et Cie; new ed. Paris, Editions Connivences, 1987.

7/This construction is documented in two plans: FLC 30832 and 30833.

8/Cf chapter 3.

9/Maurice Raynal in *L'Intransigeant*, 6 November 1922 (FLC X1(2)49). In *Montparnasse*, 1 November 1922, Charles Geo, believed that the Contemporary City expressed the 'desires and faith of a whole young generation turning its back more and more on the old fashion salon'. And if Emile Henriot, writing in *Paris-Midi* on 5 November, found the Diorama 'amusing', he nethertheless reproduced Le Corbusier's arguments sympathetically (FLC X1(2)47).

10/FLC X1(2)53.

11/Chavance, R. (1922). 'Le Salon d'Automne', in *Liberté*, 3 November (FLC X1(2)44).

ental aspects of the buildings, and the failure to indicate the shadows projected by the skyscrapers as well as the impracticality of the city centre with its many levels of dark, damp, and unhealthy basements.[13] Even the gallery owner and the journalist Waldemar George, after a close and respectful analysis of the diorama and the ideas behind it, judged the 'Cité contemporaine' 'a chimera', but added: 'Do not the chimeras of today become in effect the reality of tomorrow?'[14]

Writing to his parents on 2 November 1922, Le Corbusier noted:

> You would have been surprised at how this turnip worked out. And the ideas inscribed in it are hard and presented any how. The crowd presses forward […] open mouthed. They are respectful and interested. This is not painting any more and nobody is laughing. Am struck by the way architectural things catch people's attention. […] The problem posed is fundamental. It is neither futile nor minor. It is the great problem of the big city, and the conclusions arrived at in Les Châbles have been confirmed.[15] Here is a fundamental and durable study in urbanism. The newspapers have caught on to it; ink is going to flow about it.[16]

The French and Swiss newspapers asked for photographs, and even Pathé News showed an interest in the stand.[17]

Undoubtedly, Le Corbusier learned the lessons of this exhibition of 1922. The success of the Contemporary City depended as much on the controversy it provoked as on the admiration it produced. The shock factor certainly helped to galvanize public opinion, and Le Corbusier could not have failed to observe that it was the extremism of his project and the dramatic clarity of his images which captured the attention of the public. Similarly, it was the doctrinaire slogans in his articles, rather than their more nuanced arguments which had made an impact. Each time that the phrase: 'A house is a machine for living in' was repeated, his notoriety increased, whereas in every article he wrote he insisted on the importance of formal values and his belief in the high ideal of architecture.[18] Furthermore, every time Le Corbusier was criticized, his reputation with the young radicals increased. He came to understand that to extract a striking idea from his reasoning and push it to its extreme conclusion was much more effective that trying to argue for or against urban questions in all of their economic, social and technical complexity. So he learned that to propose radical solutions for transforming the city would have more impact on the public than debating more complicated architectural questions. Significantly, it was the exhibition of the Contemporary City which prompted the first requests for Le Corbusier to lecture to a wide public.

Le Corbusier held a first press conference in front of his stand on 8 November 1922, and gave a lecture there which was well received.[19] Shortly afterwards, Marcel Temporal, who was in charge of the architectural section of the Salon d'Automne, asked him on behalf of his committee to give one or more lectures on the Contemporary City.[20] This seems to have been one of the first invitations to give a prestigious public lecture, but there is no way of knowing if it really took place. In 1923, he was invited to contribute to an international conference in

12/Michel Maubeuge, in *Le Marbre*, 15 November 1922 (FLC X1(2)65) and anonymous critic in *Le Journal*, 19 November 1922 (FLC X1(2)71). The latter described the Citrohan house has 'a cubic villa aquarium […] enough to make you weep'.

13/Mesnil, J. (1922). 'Au Salon d'Automne', in *L'Humanité*, 11 November (FLC X1(2)58).

14/George, W. (1922). 'Chronique des arts modernes. L'urbanisme', in *L'Information*, 13 November (FLC X1(2)62).

15/Le Corbusier's parents rented a house in Les Châbles, waiting for the construction of the little lakeside house 'Le Lac' at Vevey, designed by Le Corbusier in 1923-24. It seems that Le Corbusier discussed his ideas with his parents there.

16/Le Corbusier, letter to his parents, 2 November 1922 (FLC R1(6)192).

17/For example, the *Schweizerische Bauzeitung* asked for photographs on 17 November 1922 (FLC A1(10)286). Le Corbusier replied to questions from Pathé News on 14 November 1922 (FLC R3(2)157).

18/Le Corbusier explained this distinction very clearly: 'The house is a tool: a purely technical matter. But feelings, which are always present, sometimes abundantly so, have made of the house the object of particularly close attention; to

Strasbourg on the theme: 'What is the state of urbanism in France and abroad?',[21] and from 1924 until the end of his life, he was in constant demand to lecture.

Although Le Corbusier gave lectures before 1924, this study will concentrate on the period 1924-1965 which constitutes the real laboratory for this aspect of his career.[22] This is partly because of the surviving documentation and partly because the lectures I have selected have a certain coherence. Although the form and style of Le Corbusier's ideas evolved over the years, the underlying concepts remained fairly constant. Chapters 2 and 3 will focus on the origins of the lectures on architecture and urbanism respectively in 1923-24, while chapter 4 is devoted to the lecture series in 1929 which draw together all the strength of Le Corbusier's teaching.

Le Corbusier as a lecturer

An indication of the importance that Le Corbusier attached to his activity as a lecturer can be found in the third volume of the *Complete works* (1938), in which he published a photograph of himself in the act of lecturing. Bearing his signature, it features as a frontispice of Max Bill's 'Introduction'.[23] It is as if the personal characteristic of the architect is that of drawing while lecturing. Towards the end of his life, Le Corbusier explained the importance of his lectures like this:

> I adopted my own very individual technique. I never prepared my lectures. […] This improvisation is a wonderful thing: I made drawings […] in the early days, I worked with chalk, coloured chalks on a blackboard, always assuming there was one. And when you draw on the basis of words, you draw with useful words, you create something. And my whole theory - my introspection and my reflection on the phenomena of architecture and urbanism, derives from these improvised and illustrated lectures.[24]

Figure 2
Le Corbusier photographed during a lecture in Switzerland, reproduced in *Oeuvre complète*, volume 3, p. 6.

Le Corbusier attached great importance to drawing during his lectures. This is partly because drawing was a means of enhancing his credibility both as orator and artist. The 'authority' thus obtained was an indispensable attribute of rhetoric. Secondly, instead of establishing a principle and then illustrating it with examples, Le Corbusier preferred to build up his arguments while drawing the examples which illustrated them. In order for this form of reasoning to appear convincing, it was necessary to suggest that the sketch was not *proposing* a general principle but instead was *illustrating* an already accepted principle. Consequently his commentary on the drawings was essential for his argument.

That Le Corbusier was embarking on a pedagogic mission appears clearly on a page on *La Ville radieuse* where he assembles a rather strange collage of sketches made during his lectures (Fig 3). In the caption, he described 'the improvisation in front of crowded lecture halls' where he made 'large coloured frescoes on great sheets of paper'. This is the work of a missionary: 'it was necessary to take the pilgrim's staff and leave, often very far away: preaching a crusade? Who knows! Already there are many encouraging signs.'[25] There are several reasons why Le Corbusier picked up the 'pilgrim's staff'. First, lecturing

identify the house with *oneself*, make it say "I exist", *radiate*. An expression of *my sentient being*: architecture. In the passage from one aim to the other, from the function of *utility* to the function of *radiating*, is located architecture.' in Le Corbusier (1926). 'Architecture d'époque machiniste', in *Journal de psychologie normale et pathologique*, vol. 23, pp. 18-19.

19/Le Corbusier's friend, Paul Lafollye, recalled the ideas, 'which you luminously put before our little meeting at the Salon d'Automne' (letter to Le Corbusier 6 January 1923 FLC 2(11)42) and asked him on behalf of the Chambre Syndicale des Propriétaires and in connection with a committee set up by the Minister of Hygiene to look into the construction of housing, to write a report or to give a lecture on the subject. Lafollye, like Le Corbusier, was a member of the technical committee of the group La Renaissance des Cités (Anon. (1935). *La Renaissance des Cités 1916-1935*, Paris).

20/Undated letter from Marcel Temporal to Le Corbusier, (FLC A2(11)14).

21/See chapter 3.

22/Le Corbusier himself dates the beginning of his lecturing career to 1925.

23/Le Corbusier and Pierre Jeanneret (1939). *Œuvre complète*, vol. 2, *1934-1938*, Zurich, 9th edition, 1964, p. 6.

broadened the field of his aquaintances and clients. Several clients came to him in fact thanks to his lectures. For example, the musician Paul Ternisien and his wife came to see him after his lecture at the Sorbonne on 12 June 1924 to commission from him the little studio house in Boulogne-sur-Seine.[26] Secondly, Le Corbusier saw in his invitations abroad an opportunity to establish himself as one of the leaders of the Modern Movement. The international contacts which he had obtained through the publication of *L'Esprit Nouveau* guaranteed him a steady

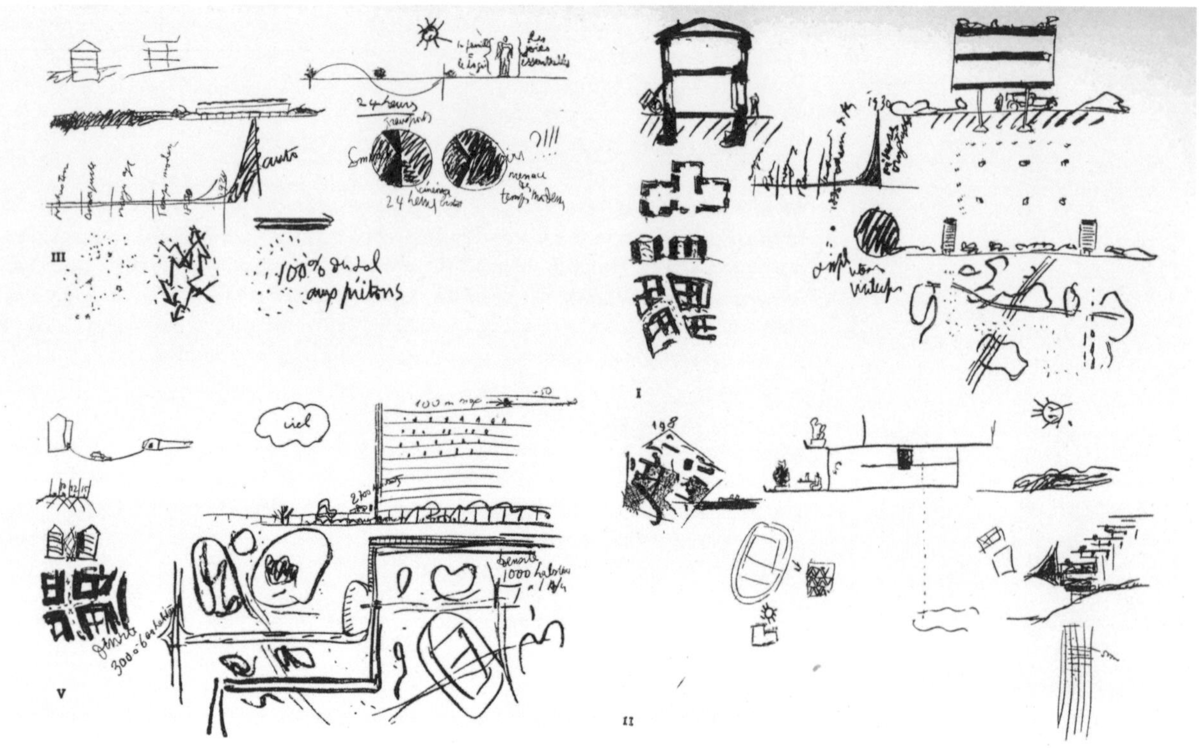

Figure 3
A selection of sketches made by Le Corbusier during his lectures and published in *La Ville radieuse* in 1935, p. 173.

stream of invitations from the European promoters of modern architecture.[27] Furthermore he was often received more warmly abroad than in Paris. From 1927, with the relative setback of his competition entry for the League of Nations building in Geneva, Le Corbusier's lectures became increasingly a pretext for waging war against academism.

Le Corbusier was invited to give lectures in all sort of places from university lecture halls to public theaters (Fig 4). He was proud of his ability to hold the attention of 3,000 or 4,000 people for two, three or even four hours. Most of his lectures were delivered to architectural students or an audience already sympathetic to modern architecture, and in these conditions Le Corbusier was listened to with respect. He often declared that he preferred talking to the young and not to their masters.[28] On the other hand, eager to change public opinion, he was not afraid to face up to a critical audience. Maximilien Gauthier, in his biography of Le Corbusier to which the master himself certainly contributed, recalled: 'he

24/Interview with rector Malet, 1951, extract from the recording, *L'Aventure Le Corbusier*, Fondation Le Corbusier.

25/Le Corbusier (1935). *La ville radieuse; éléments d'une doctrine d'urbanisme pour l'équipement de la civilisation machiniste*, Paris, Genève, Rio de Janeiro, Editions Vincent, Fréal et Cie, 1964, p. 173. Le Corbusier listed 23 cities in which he lectured between 1925-34.

26/This is reported by Le Corbusier in a letter to the adjudicating architect Vié on 8 July 1932: 'It was as a consequence of my lecture at the Sorbonne in 1923 [sic, should be 1924] that Mister and Mrs Ternisien insisted that we design them a house' (FLC H108(63, and 59)).

27/In 1926, Le Corbusier received invitations to lecture in Prague, Brussels, Lausanne, Zurich and Basel.

28/In his notes for a lecture at the Sorbonne on 19 October 1959, he wrote: 'I address myself to the young, not their elders' (FLC C3(8)89).

29/Gauthier, M. (1944). *Le Corbusier ou l'architecture au service de l'homme*, Paris, Editions Denoël, 1944, p. 142.

30/In his notes for a lecture at the Ecole Normale in Paris, he made repeated references to the 'whistles [at the Salle] Pleyel and at the Chambre du Cercle du F[aubour]g', which he attributed to 'the

Figure 4
In the great amphitheatre of the Sorbonne on 4 February 1960, Le Courbusier has a full house (FLC L4(7)88-001).

always spoke in front of a full house. The crowd, hostile or indifferent, resisted. It was this resistance which excited Le Corbusier to find either more clear, telling, endearing, striking, and unanswerable ways of expressing himself. To shift this inert mass, to break through barriers, it requires effort and stamina. Teaching his doctrine taught him to understand himself to focus on the key points.'[29] In the Pleyel auditorium, on 14 December 1931, nearly 3,000 people were there to greet him with applause but also with catcalls. Later he would refer to these hostile receptions with pride, flattering his sense of himself as the main protagonist of the revolutionary and outlaw avant-garde.[30] He enjoyed playing with the trope on revolution, contrasting the violence of political revolution with the peaceful transformation produced by modern technology.[31] In the underground amphitheatre of the Louvre, on 18 February 1930, he developed this idea further:

> A member of the audience has just remarked to me that this hall, in its form and its location in the basement, is an ideal place to plot a conspiracy and prepare the next revolution.[32]

reaction of the old masters' and 'the anxiety of the young' (FLC C3(8)208 to 211). In other notes, in January 1932, he wrote: 'whistles Salle Pleyel// and yet 3-4,000 people = interest.// 2 demonstrations: academic opposition from the old masters// a reaction: respect for architecture.' Further on, he returned to the theme: 'Whistles in the Salle Pleyel?// Pandemonium at the Cercle du Fg ?// = reaction of the old masters// anxiety of youth. Turning the page' (FLC C3(8)208).

31/See the introduction of his 1924 lectures: 'Revolutions are not only made by gun shots and spilled blood.' (FLC C3-06(29), preparatory notes for his lectures at Lausanne, Zurich and at the Sorbonne, February-June 1924). FLC C3(6)29,24,14.

32/FLC C3-08(118).

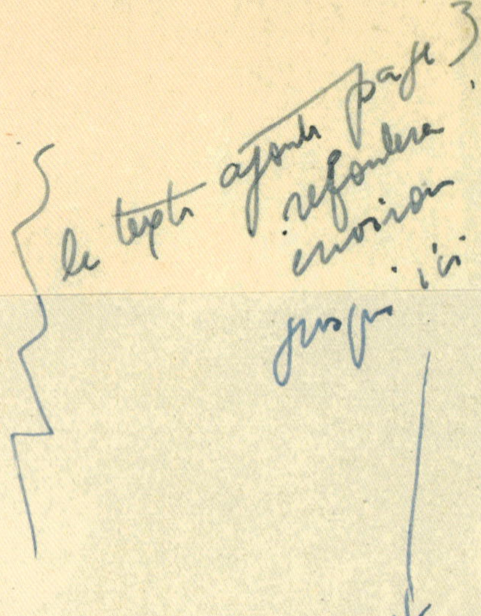

centaine de projections qui matérialisent les raisonnements précédents. Chaque ville que je visite m'apparaît sous un certain jour. J'y sens certains besoins. Je me fixe une certaine ligne de conduite appropriée à mon public; d'ailleurs, au cours de la conférence, cette ligne peut se modifier parfois. Et j'improvise, car le public aime à sentir que l'on crée pour lui. Ainsi ne s'endort-il pas.

A Buenos-Ayres, nous convînmes de diviser le sujet en dix conférences. L'initiative en fut prise par l'Association des « Amigos del Arte » que dirige magistralement Mme Helena Sansinéa de

Le Corbusier took the trouble to prepare his audience by inviting his friends and people of influence to participate. He was also precise about how he wanted the 'stage' organized. He needed a blackboard or a screen onto which large sheets of paper could be fixed with nails from which he could tear off drawings one by one. For his lectures in South America in 1929, he described the setting in detail, to the extent of providing an illustration. This is how he commented this illustration:

> I acquired a lecturing technique. I organized my stage: a block of a dozen large sheets of paper, on which I draw in black and coloured crayons; a line stretched from one end of the stage to the other, behind me, on which I peg out the sheets one by one, as I finish drawing on them. [...] Finally, a screen on which I project the hundred or so slides which turn the preceding theory into practice.[33]

Seventy-seven of the 100 or so lecture drawings he made on this trip have been conserved at the Fondation Le Corbusier in Paris.[34] Later in his career he preferred to draw on a roll of paper, several metres long. The longest of these to have been conserved, at the Avery Library at Columbia University, measures over 4 metres in length (see Fig 6).

Figure 5
Pageproof of page 20 of *Précisions sur un état présent de l'architecture et de l'urbanisme*, Paris, 1930, showing the organization of the stage for his lectures in South America in October 1929 (FLC B2(9)24).

Figure 6
Drawing made during a lecture at Columbia University on 19 November 1935 (Avery Library, Columbia University).

His other needs were modest. He asked for a glass of water, to drink at the end of his presentation, rather than at the beginning. He always insisted on the biggest possible screen, on which to project his transparencies and, after 1931, films.[35] A letter to a Dr Delore provides us with detail of his typical requests. Dr Delore was organizing a lecture in the Salle Rameau at Lyon, which was capable of seating 1,500 people, for 24 April 1937. He hoped that Le Corbusier would be able to interest 'a popular crowd' as well as 'the most cultivated classes'.[36] In answer to the speaker's request, Delore confirmed that the largest available

33/Le Corbusier (1960). *Précisions sur un état présent de l'architecture et de l'urbanisme avec un prologue américain et un corollaire Brésilien suivi d'une température Parisienne et d'une atmosphère Moscovite*, Paris, Editions Vincent, Fréal et Cie.

34/See chapter 4.

35/Le Corbusier screened the film by Pierre Chenal, *Architecture* (1930) in his lectures from 1931 to 1935 in Europe and in America.

36/Dr Delore to Le Corbusier, 6 February 1937 (FLC C3(13)52).

37/Dr Delore to Le Corbusier 16 March 1937 (FLC C3(13)50). Dr Delore also suggested to him that it would be a good idea to send a copy of one of Le Corbusier's recent books to the conference chairman, the Dean of the Faculty of Medicine, Professor Jean Lepine.

38/Le Corbusier to Dr. Delore, 17 April 1937 (FLC C3(13)48).

39/Le Corbusier (1946). *Propos d'urbanisme*, Paris, Editions Bourelier et Cie.

40/Sketches, notes and large drawings exist at the Museum of Modern Art, New York, the Canadian Centre for Architecture, Montreal, at Princeton University, Penn State University, the Avery Library at Columbia University, the Polytechnic of Milan, the Victoria & Albert Museum and many others.

screen was 3.75 m (12 ft 4 in).[37] A few days before the lecture, Le Corbusier, suffering from 'an inflammation of the left ear and raging neuralgia', explained that he would need an hour at the hotel before the lecture to prepare. He would welcome a cold meal at the hotel, never agreeing to dine before a lecture. 'After the lecture, whatever you like in the streets and bars of Lyons.'[38]

His aim, as he explained in the conclusion to his book *Propos d'urbanisme*, 'was to seduce, convince or wake up, if necessary, our contemporaries'.[39] He illustrated his arguments with a series of sketches which he deployed throughout his lecturing career and which he summarized in *La Ville radieuse* (Fig 3). These ideograms alone, once we understand how his lectures worked, are sufficient to allow us to reconstruct the content of his lectures.

The 'text' of Le Corbusier's lectures

Given that his lectures were improvised, what does the 'text' of the lectures consist of? Le Corbusier's score, closer to that of jazz than a sonata, presents the researcher with significant difficulties.

Nevertheless, there is no shortage of evidence. Thousands of documents are conserved at the Fondation Le Corbusier and elsewhere: manuscript notes, typescript transcriptions, sketches, large drawings in coloured chalk, glass lantern slides and transparencies.[40] And yet, the lectures themselves – unique human performances – remain elusive. The relationship between all these documents is not always clear, partly because they are often not identified or dated precisely but also because Le Corbusier tended to cannibalize his notes for one lecture while preparing another. He would often cut and paste sketches from one manuscript to another, regroup and annotate the notes for one lecture into a different order for another. In these circumstances, the original notes have often been damaged or lost, making reconstruction difficult.

Occasionally, a stenographer was asked to record Le Corbusier's lectures word for word – no easy task.[41] For example, there is a typescript of one of the lectures delivered on several occasions in 1924. Different from the version published in *Almanach de l'architecture moderne* (1925), which was transcribed stenographically from the lecture given at the Salle Rapp on 10 November 1924, this text can be compared to a page of manuscript notes prepared in advance of one of these lectures (Fig 7 and 8).[42] Where the stenographer had trouble following Le Corbusier's rapid exposition, gaps appear in the typescript. Comparing the manuscript notes with the transcript, it becomes possible to fill in these gaps precisely. This is what the stenographer could make out:

> One century (this last one) is in opposition to 400 previous centuries, the machine based on calculation ensures [...] the coherent system of the laws of physics; the machine imposes its consequences on our spirit towards purity [...] the gap and the [...] growing between two generations.[43]

41/Examples which will be analyzed in chapter 2 are those of the lectures at Lausanne and the Salle Rapp, in Paris (February and November 1924) (FLC C3(6)14-23 and C3(8)17-40). Another text 'stenotyped and mechanically reproduced' of Le Corbusier's lecture of 12 February 1944 at the Centre d'Etudes & d'Organisation, was attached to the letter from L. Guilloteau, on 5 March 1944. He hoped 'that you will not find its tenor too much modified and that it will interest you in this form' (FLC A2(18)24).

42/See chapter 2 and the technical appendix 1, for a detailed analysis of these documents.

43/FLC C3(6)14.

44/FLC C3(8)1.

45/Vincent, L. (pseud. of Vaillant) (1924), 'Divagations intempestives', *Paris-Journal*, 20 June (FLC C3(06)38).

46/The text printed in the *Bulletin de l'Ordre de l'Etoile d'Orient* and in *Almanach de l'architecture moderne* closely followed these two versions: 'Our century and the previous one stand in opposition to 400 previous centuries: the machine, based on calculation derived from the laws of the universe has established, by contrast with the possible wanderings of the mind the coherent system of the laws of physics. Imposing its consequences on our

Le Corbusier's preliminary notes fill in the gaps (missing text in italics):

> One century – the last one – is in opposition to 400 previous centuries. The machine, based on calculation *derived from the laws of the world, has created, in the face of the possible divagations of our spirit*, the coherent system of the laws of physics. The machine imposing its consequences *on our existence and forcing* our spirit towards purity, *modifies the basis of our life*. The gap is immense, *a chasm created today* between two generations.[44]

Perhaps the stenopgrapher had difficulty with the word 'divagations' (ramblings), a term considered sufficiently unusual to be used by Léandre Vaillant in the title of his review of one of these lectures, 'Divagations intempestives' (Intemperate ramblings).[45] It is clear that Le Corbusier had either learned by heart, or had read, the first pages of his notes, before launching off into a freer improvisation.[46]

From this point of view, the stenographer's transcription is extremely revealing. It seems that Le Corbusier would read a few pages of prepared text and then improvise based on tried and tested arguments, built around anecdotes or demonstrations drawn on the blackboard or on large sheets of paper. These arguments would appear in his notes as a keyword or little sketch, but could be developed at length in the lecture. The transcripts provide clear evidence of this. For example, the entry 'Eupalinos P. Valéry' in his notes was developed over a whole page in the printed transcription of the lecture at the Salle Rapp.[47] Similarly, a little sketch comparing Romanesque and Gothic buildings occupies two whole pages of the transcript. It is also in the first few minutes that his lectures vary most one from the other. Tantalizingly, there are only a few stenographic transcripts to work from, but these allow us to understand how Le Corbusier developed his oral presentations on the basis of a few pages of notes and some sketches. The lectures took the form of themes and variations, with some parts recurring many times in the lectures, while other parts were adapted specifically to each audience or to his state of mind at the time.

There are also a number of plans, often illustrated with sketches, which used headings to summarize the whole lecture.[48] Phrases included in these highly condensed summaries are repeated word for word in the stenographic transcript. In other cases, Le Corbusier would deliver a lecture on the basis of a few keywords only.

Occasionally, Le Corbusier asked his secretary to type out some text. This often happened when he was invited to lecture abroad and his hosts needed something to translate and publish in advance.[49] Sometimes, he typed phrases or keywords onto small index cards. He used these as an aide-memoire and a means of structuring his lectures. For example, a first attempt to accumulate ideas for the 1924 lectures took the form of a series of typed cards in the autumn of 1923 (Fig 9).[50]

Following pages

Figure 7

Stenographic transcript of Le Corbusier's lecture in Lausanne, 18 February 1924 (FLC C3(6)14).

Figure 8

Le Corbusier, extract from notes entitled 'Conférence Sorbonne, Prague', c. April 1924 (FLC C3(8)1).

existence and driving our minds towards a certain system of purity. It has already modified the framework of our existence; it really is a chasm formed between two generations' (*Bulletin de l'Ordre de l'Etoile d'Orient*, 1925, p. 29).

47/See his note (FLC C3(8)4) and the printed text of the Salle Rapp lecture (X1(3)84 p. 35). A simple sketch comparing Romanesque and Gothic buildings (C3(8)2) occupies two whole pages of the stenographic transcript (X1(3)84 pp. 30-31).

48/See Fig 12 of chapter 2. For a plan of a lecture consisting of little numbered sketches around an outline of headings, see FLC A2(18)34 (13/6/1945).

49/This is true of a typescript summarizing the main points of the 1924 lecture, entitled 'program for Prague, Brussels, Allendy' and 'Lecture Corbusier Sorbonne 1924' (FLC C3(8)10-12), marked up with the author's corrections and a corrected version of the same (FLC C3(8)13-15). I see this as the typescript sent to Prague in May 1924, the outline of a lecture that did not take place (see letter from the Architects' Club of Prague, on 5 May 1924, apologizing for the cancellation of the lecture and noting the arrival, too late, of Le Corbusier's text (FLC E1(16)354)). The lecture at Brussels, too, was postponed. 'Allendy' refers to the invitation by Le Corbusier's friend, the psychologist Dr. Allendy,

Mesdames, Messieurs,

Un Esprit Nouveau plus fort que celui des races et plus fort que les influences du milieu géographique passe par-dessus toutes les habitudes et les traditions et se répand sur le monde entier avec des caractères précis et unitaires.

Ces caractères sont universels et humains, pourtant jamais aussi que jamais le gouffre ne fut si grand, qui sépare l'ancienne Société de notre société machiniste.

Un siècle (ce siècle dernier) s'impose à 400 siècles antérieurs, la machine basée sur le calcul assure

le système cohérent des lois de la physique ; la machine impose ses conséquences à notre

notre esprit vers la pureté

l'écart et le croissants entre deux générations.

C'est devant cet écart que nous devons nous arrêter et réfléchir avant que de chercher à traverser la confusion dune crise pénible et générale.

Les révolutions ne se font pas qu'avec des fusils et dans le sang, on a pu voir maintes fois dans l'histoire des transformations totales, on a pu assister à l' anéantissement dun esprit et à l' avènement d'un autre esprit et d'une autre culture, par exemple, nous avons dans notre pays au XIème siècle la disparition de l' 'sprit méditerranéen chassé par l'esprit du Nord, on assiste aux conséquences de cet avènement et dans l'ordre des choses qui nous intéressent modification totale des formes qui constituaient le milieu.

Non seulement les formes usuelles ont été transformées par cet esprit, mais les conséquences ont été lointaines et sont allés jusque dans les objets de la vie ; le paysage lui même a changé.

Il a fallu la suite des siècles de travail de ce qu'on peut appeler de culture pour retrouver les éléments de la culture méditerranéenne, vers laquelle nous nous orientons à nouveau maintenant.

Vous voudrez bien me pardonner ce soir, je vous dessinerai très souvent des schémas au tableau estimant que le dessin

Conférence — Sorbonne — Prague 9

Un esprit nouveau plus fort que celui des races et plus fort que les influences du milieu géographique, passe par dessus toutes les habitudes et les traditions et se répand sur le monde entier avec des caractères précis et unitaires. Ces caractères sont aussi universels et humains que jamais. Pourtant jamais aussi le gouffre ne fut si grand qui sépare l'ancienne société de notre société machiniste. Un siècle, — le siècle dernier — s'oppose à 400 siècles antérieurs. La machine basée sur le calcul issu des lois du monde a dressé face aux divagations possibles de notre esprit, ~~les lois incontestables de notre univers~~ le système cohérent des lois de la physique. La machine ~~imposant~~ forçant ses conséquences à notre existence et ~~attirant~~ notre esprit vers la pureté, modifie le cadre de notre vie.

L'écart est immense, ~~creusant un gouffre~~ fossé creusé entre deux générations aujourd'hui.

C'est devant cet écart que nous devons nous arrêter et réfléchir avant que de chercher à traverser la confusion d'une crise pénible et générale

P. 2 C3- 6- 72

RENAISSANCE DES CITES

4 millions pour 100 maisons

16 Z

P. 1 C3- 6- 73

Trouble , ex: Barberine

PERENNITE .-

Religions mécanique , ex:
Citroen lumineux tue toute l'admiration d'hier du lumineux.

La loi d'économie .
L'anthropocentrisme ,

Un idéal nouveau, la précision
l'exactitude
la pureté
la géométrie
rencontrent des bases humaines fondamentales et des plus hautes joies spéculatives.

la notion parfaite (Renaissance Cité) manifestation humaine travail à la main

I D

P. 2 C3- 6- 74

Delloire Peugeot

Dessine une nouvelle usine
Le Conseil d'Administration a demandé : ce sera sheds , hangar
Fermes cintrés ,halls, etc .. ?

- Réponse : Je n'en sais rien j'étudie un organisme ,je l'organise , je dispose les manutentions successives et je les mets à la suite , je série , et crée des corps ,ces corps ,je les relierai à un moment donné ,suivant les possibilité de votre terrain. Puis je chercherai quelle sorte de toiture ,quelle sorte de mur .

Ici on procède du dedans au dehors .

Nov. 1923

16 Z

P. 1 C3- 6- 75

pour finir: Dans ex. d' E.N. la Revue, les moyens et son effort

15 Septembre 1923

Entretien avec Selder ,Directeur de Dial .

la première année perdu : 100.000 dollars ; maintenant quatrième année , réorganisation, n'en perdront que 30.000.

le dollar vaut : 17 Frs.-

12 D

Lectures and publications

The hybrid quality of the sources and the ephemeral nature of the performances created problems for the publication of these lectures. But Le Corbusier had no compunction creating books out of his lectures when he had a stenographic transcript to work from. When, in 1950, he was planning a publication for the Beaux-Arts museum at Rio de Janeiro, he reassembled the six lectures which he had given in Brazil in July and August 1936. He suggested a format in three parts, based on the preliminary manuscripts, the stenographic transcripts and the large drawings he had executed during the lectures.[51] It is as if he recognized that the three forms of his rhetoric – argumentation, exposition and illustration – could not be represented in its entirety by publishing the transcripts alone.

For this reason, in order to make the processes of Le Corbusier's thinking comprehensible as he prepared his lectures, and in order to reconstruct the quality of his oratory and the impact it had on different audiences, this book is illustrated by a large variety of documents: preparatory notes, sketches, stenographic transcripts, drawings produced during the lectures and transparencies projected at the beginning or the end of his lectures. I have also included some eyewitness accounts and reviews. The book focuses on the origins of Le Corbusier's lecturing career with occasional comparisons with later moments in the architect's life.

Figure 9

Typed notes on index cards, 1923-24 (FLC C3(6)72-5).

on 19 January 1924, to deliver a lecture at the Sorbonne before 'our study group for the examination of new ideas' which took place on 10 June 1924. It is difficult to imagine that these sheets could have been written after the cancellation of the lectures in Prague and Brussels in May 1924.

50/FLC C3(6)72-85. These typed index cards include many of the arguments of the 1924 lectures.

51/Tsiomis, Y. (2006). *Le Corbusier; Conférences de Rio*, Paris, Flammarion, pp. 10-11.

Chapter 1

Le Corbusier's logic

Le Corbusier the orator

Was Le Corbusier a good orator? For Demosthenes, the Greek fifth century politician, the necessary qualities for a good orator were 'eloquence, eloquence, eloquence' (*pronunciatio*[1]). Eloquence is the characteristic of rhetoric, distinguishing it from logic. According to Aristotle, logic is the search for truth whereas rhetoric has to do with opinion, subjective arguments and appeal to the emotions. There has been a revival of interest in rhetoric in the twentieth century, as a useful set of techniques for debating questions of value, about which logic has little useful to say.[2]

Does the strength of Le Corbusier's discourse reside in rhetoric or, as he himself often claimed, in the logic of his arguments? The architect often appeals to what he called 'the fearsome strides of logic'.[3] Strictly speaking, according to the classical terminology of argumentation, any public intervention must belong to rhetoric rather than logic. As Aristotle defines it, logical rules cannot be understood by the general public. According to him, the philosopher searches for truth on the basis of certain premises to which the strict rules of logic can be applied. A public lecture therefore must appertain to rhetoric rather than logic even if the rhetorician may appeal to logic as one of his weapons of persuasion.

Classical rhetoric includes three types of argumentation: logical proof (divided into inductive and deductive reasoning), ethical proof and the proof of *pathos*. Le Corbusier used all three.

The *logos*: logical proofs

One of the parts of classical rhetoric is the *logos*, made up of deductive logic (notably the syllogism and its derivative, the enthymeme) and inductive logic.

The classical form of deductive logic is the syllogism. Le Corbusier himself refers to it in his notes for a lecture in Brussels in 1926:

> This cast iron syllogism:
> our cities were conceived before the automobile
> the automobile has killed the great city
> the automobile must save the great city.[4]

But these three sentences do not constitute a syllogism in the real sense of the term. In the classic form there are very strict rules. For example: first premise 'all men are mortal'; second premise: 'Socrates is a man'; conclusion: 'Socrates is mortal'. Since Socrates belongs to the group 'men' it follows necessarily from the two premises that he is mortal. In Le Corbusier's 'syllogism', there is no necessary logical link between the three sentences.

This is a typical fragment of Le Corbusier's argumentation, from his lecture at the Salle Rapp on 10 November 1924:

> I want to establish that there is a hierarchy among the different systems of the mind, and that some are perhaps superior to others. At any rate, I can assert this because for me it is a certain truth (and I will demonstrate it to

Preceding page

Le Corbusier in front of a slide projection of the Voisin Plan for Paris (FLC photothèque).

1/Classical rhetoric is divided into 5 parts: *Inventio, dispositio, elocutio, memoria, pronunciatio*. *Elocutio* defines the style and ornaments of rhetoric, while *pronunciatio* corresponds to the modern term 'eloquence'.

2/Aristotle (in the *First* and *Second Analytics*) distinguishes analytical logic from dialectical reasoning (examined in the *Topics*, *Rhetoric* and the *Sophist Refutations*) and rhetoric is only one of its manifestations. The distinction between dialectical reasoning and rhetoric is purely one of audiences: rhetoric addresses a crowd rather than a single interlocutor. (Aristotle, *Rhetoric*, 1357 a 1-3), see Perelman, Ch. (1977, 3rd edition 1997). *L'Empire rhétorique; rhétorique et argumentation*. Paris, Librairie Philosophique J. Vrin, p. 21. Since the eighteenth century, rhetoric was restricted to the study of stylistic figures and literary tropes (see Perelman, *op. cit.*, pp. 10-11). The parallel between classical rhetoric and modern methods of persuasion (advertisements, political speeches and legal addresses) have interested researchers (see Robrieux, J.-J. (1993). *Eléments de rhétorique et d'argumentation*, Paris, Dunod, pp. 26-30.

3/Le Corbusier, 'Prologue Américain' in Le Corbusier (1960). *Précisions sur un état présent de l'architecture et de*

you), that the mind expresses itself through geometry. I deduce from this that when geometry is dominant it is a sign that the mind has progressed beyond a previous period of barbarism.[5]

The use of the verb 'deduce' implies the use of deductive logic. Clearly Le Corbusier understands by 'states of the mind' something very significant, close to the *Zeitgeist* (the spirit of the age which determines the style of the time, such as Neo Classical or Gothic). In this context, geometry refers to products of mechanization, based on calculation, which he thought tended to produce pure geometrical forms. Is there an underlying logic behind Le Corbusier's statement? If we transpose it into a syllogism, we might arrive at something like this:

A superior expression of the mind [in architecture] is through geometry.
Geometry is today dominant.
Therefore: there is a new superior spirit today [of architecture].

Without challenging the truth of the premises, this syllogism is false as an argument. Is the geometry expressed by the mind the same kind of thing as the geometry of machine-made goods? And, secondly, there is no necessary connection between geometry and the spirit. A surveyor or mathematician may employ geometry but not necessarily create a 'superior expression of the mind'. To translate this formula into a logical syllogism, we would have to put something like:

Everything geometrical is beautiful.
The modern works of engineering are geometrical.
Therefore: modern works of engineering are beautiful.

If you accept the premises, the conclusion is certainly true. But Le Corbusier would certainly not accept the first premise as it stands. His argument is both more subtle and more tendentious. He wants to persuade his audience that the spirit of calculation in the work of engineers could lead architects to discover anew the calm and formal perfection of the architecture of Greek and Roman antiquity. He works up to this conclusion bit by bit by accumulating examples and playing on the sensibilities of the audience. Logic alone could not achieve the desired result.

Since the rigour of the syllogism – 'all men are mortal; Socrates is a man; therefore Socrates is mortal' – has limited uses in ordinary discourse, the rhetoricians developed the enthymeme. The enthymeme allows you to leave out one of the premises. The famous enthymeme of Descartes – 'I think, therefore I am' – may be convincing but it is not logically certain. Furthermore, Aristotle explains that the premises of the enthymeme may be based on the probable rather than the true.

A feature of rhetoric is dialectical reasoning which can be used to mount arguments inaccessible to logic.[6] Dialectical reasoning depends on an understanding of the audience, its opinions and its ability to follow an argument. Aristotle distinguishes three types of opinion, that of 'everyone', that of 'the whole audi-

l'urbanisme avec un prologue américain et un corollaire Brésilien suivi d'une température parisienne et d'une atmosphère moscovite, Paris, Éditions Vincent, Fréal et Cie, p. 20 (first edition Paris, Editions G. Crès et Cie).

4/FLC C3(8)48.

5/Le Corbusier, 'L'esprit nouveau en architecture. Conférence donnée le 10 novembre 1924 à l'Ordre de l'Etoile d'Orient', published in *Bulletin de l'Ordre de l'Étoile de l'Orient*, c. March 1925 (FLC X1(3)64) and in *Almanach de l'architecture moderne*, Paris, Editions Connivences, 1987, p. 23 (First edition Paris, Editions G. Crès et Cie, 1926).

6/Perelman, *op. cit.*, p. 8 and pp. 18-25.

ence' and that of the 'best informed'. It is useless to deploy arguments which the audience is incapable of understanding or appreciating.

Classical rhetoric employs a number of 'quasi-logical' methods (divided into definitions and distinctions on the one hand and arguments derived from formal logic on the other) and empirical arguments (including those based on causality and succession, those based on confrontation and those of induction and analogy).[7] Le Corbusier was particularly fond of two kinds of 'quasi-logical' arguments: definitions (including condensed definitions or slogans) and the whole range of arguments based on causality and succession (with their many traps and ambiguities).[8]

In his lecture notes, Le Corbusier wrote down the kernel of his arguments in condensed form. For example, to refer to the argument of structural rationalism (every new constructional system leads to a new style of architecture), he wrote:

> With structure you make architecture
> " new " " " new " .[9]

The premise of this enthymeme is that architectural form is necessarily determined by the structural possibilities at any one time. The deduction is that if these possibilities change, architecture must change as well. This is the enthymeme reduced to its essential form, ignoring all possible objections. But Le Corbusier goes on to address the most obvious of the possible objections – that architecture and engineering do not occupy the same ethical and aesthetic domain – by continuing:

> But then we also have to understand what architecture is made of. I will try to define it. And since I maintain that architecture has nothing to do with ornament, drawing or the styles, I have to demonstrate to you how and why architecture comes about.[10]

We will see later how he did this. Let us examine another typical example of Le Corbusian logic. Le Corbusier often refers in these notes to the concept of *l'esprit nouveau* (the new spirit or the *Zeitgeist*).[11] His argument took the following form: 'We live in conditions transformed [by industrialization], and we must therefore completely revise our values.'[12] Reworking this argument into the form of an enthymeme (and replacing 'conditions' by 'the material world'), we arrive at the following formula:

> The material world has been transformed by industrialization.
> Therefore: values must be transformed by industrialization.

Figure 1

Page of notes for the lecture 'L'aventure du mobilier', Buenos Aires, 19 October 1929 (FLC C3(7)93).

Clearly, this argument is questionable. Do 'values' necessarily belong to the domain of the 'material world' transformed by industrialization or should we distinguish between 'values' and 'the material world'? To arrive at the logical form of the syllogism, we would need to add a second premise (the minor premise) – 'values are part of the material world' – which would be highly debatable.

Almost all of Le Corbusier's arguments turn on questions of value – beauty, dignity, judgement – rather than truth. And yet one of his favourite rhetorical argu-

7/Robrieux, *op. cit.*, pp. 97-150. Robrieux also explains the arguments of constraint and arguments in bad faith (pp. 155-178), which we will discuss later.

8/*Ibid.*, pp. 129-141

9/Notes ('Préambule') for the lecture in the great hall of the Bourse du Travail, 16 March 1927, p. 3.

10/*Ibid.*

11/This argument, quite different although related to that of structural rationalism, was defined by Le Corbusier in the *Déclaration de La Sarraz in 1928*: 'The destiny of architecture is to express the orientation of the times', cited in Steinmann, M. (1979a). *CIAM: Dokumente 1928-1939*, 1979, p. 30.

12/Le Corbusier, *op. cit.*, p. 29.

7] Le mobilier c'est des outils. 4

et aussi des domestiques.

Le mobilier sert nos besoins.

Nos besoins sont quotidiens, réguliers, toujours les mêmes,

nos meubles répondent à des fonctions constantes

quotidiennes régulières.

Tous les hommes ont les mêmes besoins aux mêmes heures, chaque jour, toute la vie.

Les outils de ces fonctions sont faciles à définir. Et le progrès nous apportant les techniques nouvelles nous fournit des moyens infiniment plus grands et plus précis qu'autrefois.

Et que l'intérieur de nos maisons ne ressemble plus à du Louis XIV voilà l'avertissement!

Ces besoins sont des besoins d'hommes.

ments is that of the definition, which looks as if it deals with fact and truth. These definitions turn out to be declarations of conviction:

> Geometry is the primary act. It is also the symbol by which we establish perfection, the divine.
> Geometry brings to our spirit the elevated satisfaction of mathematics. Machines work purely through geometry. This is a geometrical age: it orientates our dreams to the joys of geometry. Modern art and thought are moving away from the accidental, and geometry brings to them a mathematical order, a general aesthetic attitude which is new in the history of the arts.[13]

These sentences do not follow on from each other logically, even if, in Le Corbusier's mind, the statement 'This is a geometrical age' depends in a sense on the sentence before. This accumulation of declarations about the machine, geometry, perfection and order, all leading to 'a general aesthetic attitude', possesses a persuasive power impossible to explain in terms of logic. And yet Le Corbusier's appetite for declarations of principle gives his discourse the superficial appearance of a rigorous logic which is difficult to analyze.

Le Corbusier clearly derived great satisfaction from the use of definitions and the sense of power which they provide:

> Items of furniture are tools
> and also servants.
> Furniture meets our needs.
> Our needs are routine, regular, always the same.
> Our furniture serve constant, daily and regular functions.
> Everyone, with the same needs, at the same time, every day, throughout our lives.[14] **(Fig 1)**

Once again, a sequence of declarations and definitions, each one more or less plausible, prepares the listener, by dint of repetition, for the argument that furniture should be standardized and transformed into 'equipment'. Le Corbusier certainly did not believe that people are identical, above all in their thoughts and desires, but he wanted to persuade his audience that this individuality of thought and desire is best expressed in artistic or intellectual activity rather than in furniture.

Definitions may be 'exhaustive' (as in dictionary definitions), but more commonly they concentrate on certain aspects of a term, in order to emphasize what interests the orator. For example, an 'operative' definition draws attention to the effects produced by a thing whereas an 'explanatory' definition tries to get at the essence of an object. When Le Corbusier wants to contrast two ways of understanding furniture, he does it with the aid of 'operative' definitions:

> What is furniture?
> 'The means by which we make our social status known'
> This, precisely, is the mentality of royalty.
> Louis XIV was brilliant at it. Are we like Louis XIV […]

13/Typed text entitled 'Conférence Corbusier Sorbonne 1924' (FLC C3(8)11).

14/Preparatory notes for the lecture 'L'aventure du mobilier', Buenos Aires, 19 October 1929, sheet 4 (FLC C3(7)93).

Furniture consists of tools [...]
Furniture meets our needs.[15]

In the first definition, furniture has the effect of denoting social status while in the second it has the effect of meeting needs. By contrast, the formula: 'The house is a machine for living in' goes beyond an 'operative' definition. Of course, the word 'machine' implies mechanical operations, such as keeping out the rain or protection from intruders, which are uncontroversial. The sentence works much more powerfully as an 'explanatory' definition, with the implication that the essential characteristic of a house is its mechanical aspect (thus excluding considerations of sentiment, humanity, warmth etc.). It is only if understood in this sense that the dynamic impact of this slogan (both positive and negative) on succeeding generations of readers can be understood. Once again, the sentence juxtaposes the two worlds of the spiritual and material. Le Corbusier himself comments on the success of his most famous slogan in these terms:

> If this expression caused a stir it is because it includes both the word "machine", which obviously signifies to everyone notions of function, efficiency, work and product, and the word "living", which stands precisely for ideas of ethics, status and life-styles, about which there is the most perfect disagreement.[16]

The power of the definition lies precisely in its ambiguity. According to Chaïm Perelman, definitions – oratorical definitions – can be thought of as rhetorical figures when their purpose is not to clarify the meaning of an idea but rather accentuate one aspect of its meaning in order to produce the desired effect.[17]

Le Corbusier was a master of the selective explanatory definition: 'Architecture is illuminated floors'[18], 'Architecture is establishing moving relationships with raw materials'[19], 'Architecture is the knowledgeable, correct and magnificent play of volumes assembled in daylight'.[20] Evidently, none of these definitions can claim exhaustivity but each one serves its purpose in a particular context. Definition is a powerful rhetorical weapon.

Among the 'empirical' arguments, causality and succession have an important role. When Le Corbusier declares, 'the primary forms are the most beautiful forms because they can be easily read'[21], he is mounting an argument *ad consequentiam*, by indicating the *consequences* of the primary forms. In contrast, the causal arguments try to demonstrate the *causes* of a phenomenon. 'The engineer, inspired by the laws of economy and led by calculation, puts us in touch with the laws of the Universe. He achieves harmony'.[22] This time, we gather that the 'law of economy' and 'calculation' have harmony as a consequence.

Another kind of 'empirical' argument is that of succession. It is important not to confuse causality and succession. That something follows something else in time does not mean that the former determined the latter. Searching for the origin of a phenomenon (in order to deduce from it an 'essence' which in some sense defines its key characteristics), or tracing a sequence of phenomena (in order to predict its prolongation into the future) have been two deeply-rooted patterns of thought in architecture since antiquity. Vitruvius searched for the origins of architecture in a primitive wooden hut, and in doing so tried to tell us some-

15/*Ibid.*, sheet 3.

16/Le Corbusier, "Une cellule à l'échelle humaine" (fourth lecture in Buenos-Aires, 10 October 1929), in Le Corbusier (1991). *Precisions*, op. cit., pp. 86-87 (my translation).

17/Perelman, Ch. (1979). *The new rhetoric and the humanities*, Reidel, Boston, p. 20. I would like to thank Joseph Rykwert for kindly putting me on to Perelman's work.

18/*Ibid.*, p. 53.

19/Le Corbusier 1966). *Vers une architecture*, 2d edition, Paris, Editions Vincent, Fréal et Cie, p. xxv.

20/*Ibid.*, p. 16.

21/*Ibid.*, p. xxiii.

22/*Ibid.*, p. 3.

thing about the essential nature of architecture. For his part, Le Corbusier also describes the origins of the primitive temple as a tent constructed with simple means but following a pure geometric organization. He concluded, 'there are no primitive people, only primitive means. The idea [pure geometry] is constant, present from the outset'.[23] The implication is that because, as he claims, the first temples followed 'a pure geometric organization', this must be an essential feature of good architecture. Sequences developing over time also appear frequently in Le Corbusier's reasoning, often associated with the idea of 'progress' (and with the principle of Darwinian selection).

Le Corbusier's discussion of what he called the 'standart' (a non-standard French spelling) is exemplary. In a famous but frequently misunderstood comparison, he showed, in *Vers une architecture*, that the same process of formal refinement of a type (Doric temple or automobile) could lead from the primitive (Paestum, Humber) to the sophisticated (Parthenon, Delage Grand Sport). The Darwinian principle of natural selection demonstrates that species which cannot adapt to their changing environment die out, leading to an amelioration of the species.

> The Parthenon is the product of a process of selection applied to an established standart [sic] [...] Once a standart has been established, violent competition comes immediately into play. It's game on; to win, you have to outshine your adversary *in every field*, in the overall

106 VERS UNE ARCHITECTURE

PAESTUM, de 600 à 550 av. J.-C.

Le Parthénon est un produit de sélection appliquée à un standart établi. Depuis un siècle déjà, le temple grec était organisé dans tous ses éléments.

Lorsqu'un standart est établi, le jeu de la concurrence immédiate et violente s'exerce. C'est le match; pour gagner, il faut

Cliché de *La Vie Automobile*. HUMBERT, 1907.

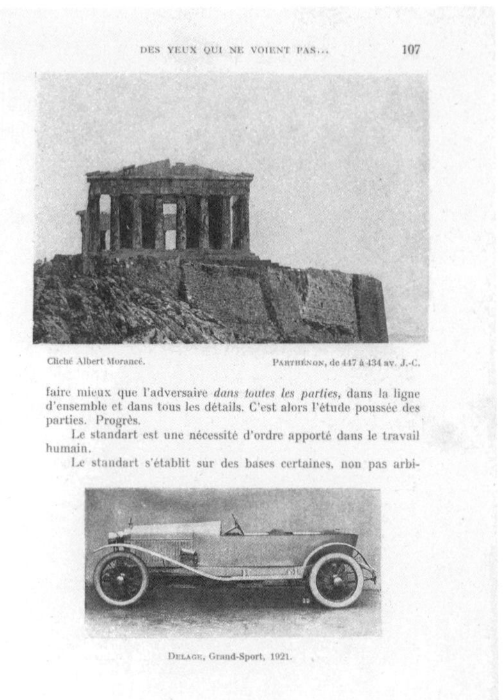

DES YEUX QUI NE VOIENT PAS... 107

Cliché Albert Morancé. PARTHÉNON, de 447 à 434 av. J.-C.

faire mieux que l'adversaire *dans toutes les parties*, dans la ligne d'ensemble et dans tous les détails. C'est alors l'étude poussée des parties. Progrès.

Le standart est une nécessité d'ordre apporté dans le travail humain.

Le standart s'établit sur des bases certaines, non pas arbi-

DELAGE, Grand-Sport, 1921.

Figure 2
Pages 106 and 107 of *Vers une architecture* setting up a comparison between the Doric temples of Paestum and the Parthenon on the one hand, and Humber and Delage automobiles on the other.

23/*Ibid.*, p. 53.

effect and in every detail. An intense study of every aspect follows. Progress.[24]

The argument compares the processes of 'selection' which lead to the perfection of the Parthenon compared to Paestum or the Delage Sport 1921 compared to the Humber of 1907. Each successive improvement appears to create a trend which points the way forward to new solutions.

Confusing succession and causality occurs frequently in Le Corbusier's rhetoric. When Le Corbusier claims, in the first of his two lectures in Barcelona on May 1928, that, 'The past and tradition make the sequence of events clear and explain the effects by their causes'[25], he begs the question. A sequence of events is never sufficient in itself to explain cause and effect.

If deductive logic draws conclusions based on general premises, inductive logic attempts to generalize on the basis of 'facts', examples or anecdotes, a procedure necessarily open to contestation. Whenever Le Corbusier talks of 'demonstrating' or 'showing' he is in fact referring to what rhetoricians call 'examples' or 'illustrations' and therefore to the processes of inductive reasoning. If an 'illustration' is the manifestation of an existing principle, the 'example' in rhetoric consists of an observation of the natural world from which it is hoped to extrapolate a general principle. When Le Corbusier appeals to 'the evidence of facts' in the following note he is referring to the inductive logic of 'examples'.

> I will therefore address my lecture to the young men and women who have invited me and endeavour, not with eloquent phrases but by the evidence of facts to show them the magnificent simplicity of architecture in its inestimable richness.[26]

'The evidence of facts' will serve as 'examples' on the basis of which Le Corbusier will construct inductive arguments along the lines of: 'These facts prove that there is a new spirit in architecture'.

In classical rhetoric, inductive rhetoric plays an important role, and Le Corbusier deploys it not only with verbal but also with visual examples and illustrations, using both drawings and transparencies. This is how he commented a drawing showing the difference between Romanesque and Gothic styles:

> In the Romanesque period, the city was composed of simple prisms. The typical house forms were dominated by the horizontal. The purest possible geometry ruled supreme, giving even the landscape a very precise character. After only a century, look how this city and this landscape have been transformed, giving both [city and landscape] a radically different outlook.[27]

Here, Le Corbusier contrasts two pairs of examples – illustrated by the porch of the Romanesque Cathedral of Clermont-Ferrand compared to a Gothic window on the left and a view of the Duomo of Pisa compared with a Gothic townscape on the right – in order to explain the difference between the Romanesque and Gothic styles, as well as the different 'spirit' which animated them. The contrast between

24/*Ibid.*, pp. 106-107.

25/Le Corbusier, lecture in Barcelona, 15 May 1928 (FLC C3(8)89).

26/Le Corbusier, notes for two lectures in Barcelona, 15 and 16 May 1928 (FLC C3(8)102).

27/Le Corbusier, 'L'Esprit nouveau en architecture', *op. cit.*, pp. 30-31.

the sketches brings out the purely formal differences between his examples – horizontal/vertical, pure geometry/complexity – rather than pointing out all the other ways in which they might be distinguished, for example in terms of milieu, construction and social organization.

The image, then, can serve as a rhetorical 'example' in support of inductive reasoning, but can we really talk of a purely visual rhetoric? Roland Barthes thought so:

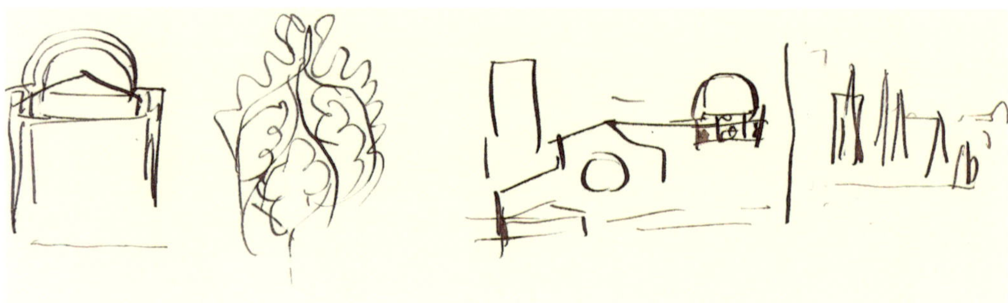

Figure 3
Detail of a page of notes for the lectures of 1924 (FLC C3(8)02).

> It is even probable that there is only a single rhetorical form, common for example to dreams, to literature and to the image. Therefore the rhetoric of the image (that is to say, the classification of connotations) may be specific in so far as it is limited to the physical constraints of vision (different to phonatory constraints, for example) but also general to the extent that its "figures" are always nothing more than the formal relationships of elements.[28]

It is clear, in fact, that juxtaposing contrasting images and accentuating their differences belongs to the tactics of oral rhetoric. But if exaggeration of motifs in a sketch can accentuate formal differences and thus support an argument, visual rhetoric has its limits. From these contrasts, Le Corbusier wanted to draw the conclusion that 'this city and this landscape have been transformed, producing a radically different effect on the eye'. He tried to persuade his audience that the *Zeitgeist* is so strong that the eye sees everything differently in the Gothic period as opposed to the Romanesque one. The abstraction and the complexity of this idea exceed the realm of the visual. Nevertheless, Le Corbusier returns constantly to visual images in his arguments:

> I showed you by the images that I drew on the blackboard that the man who acquires bit by bit a formidable array of skills, discovers, first unconsciously and then more consciously by calculation, the essential principles of his actions; he rediscovers the "standarts": the law of geometry.[29]

28/Roland Barthes 'Rhétorique de l'image', cited by Robrieux in *Eléments de rhétorique et d'argumentation*, p. 27. Robrieux also cites the article by Jacques Durand in which, taking up the challenge laid down by Barthes, he tried to develop a systematic analysis of visual figures: Durand, J. (1970). 'Rhétorique et image publicitaire', *Communications*, no. 15, pp. 70-95.

29/Le Corbusier, 'L'esprit nouveau en architecture', *op. cit.*, p. 29 (FLC C3-8(17-40).

The *ethos*: Le Corbusier's *auctoritas*

After the *logos*, classical rhetoric talks of the *ethos* and the *pathos*. If *pathos* appeals directly to the emotions, the *ethos* has to do with the moral character of the orator, his fame, courage and generosity. For the listener who believes that the orator is a man worthy of being admired and followed, the arguments of the *logos* and *pathos* have already been won. In short, the orator is in need of *auctoritas*. According to Quintilian, the effective orator is a virtuous man who talks well (*vir bonus diciendi peritus*). Translating this precept into the world of architecture, we may say that an effective orator is a good architect who can draw well.

Drawing lends authority to an architect. On his feet, active, creative, the architect with a chalk or crayon in his hand dominates the stage (Fig 4). And during the peroration, when he projects transparencies of his own work, which has already acquired fame through publication, the orator confirms his *auctoritas*.

Le Corbusier was not endowed with a natural *gravitas*. He lacked a loud voice or an imposing presence. Henri Frugès complained of the faintness of his voice when he gave the inaugural speech on 13 June 1926 on the occasion of the visit of the Minister Anatole de Monzie in Pessac. The stenographer had trouble following the architect's words. '[...] you did not speak up and all he could send me were a few scraps which he was able to note down, hoping that you yourself would be able to reconstruct the rest.'[30] His voice and style of delivery, when recorded on tape, do not express a natural *auctoritas*. In front of the microphone he could appear somewhat querulous, with a rising intonation at the end of his sentences, almost as if he expected to be contradicted.

Some people bear witness to an imposing presence, even terrifying, especially towards the end of his life. However, when Le Corbusier, standing in front of an enormous pair of glasses set up by the students on the balcony in Robinson Hall, Harvard, addressed them in 1961, he seemed timid and rather tired.[31] He

Figure 4
Le Corbusier on the stage during a lecture in the 1950s (FLC L4(7)50).

30/Henri Frugès to Le Corbusier 26 June 1926 (FLC H1-20-159).

31/Interview with the French architect Georges Maurios (Paris, 2005), who was present on this occasion.

was nevertheless listened to with respect and reverence. In response to the question about Le Corbusier's 'authority', one of his assistants had no hesitation in replying, 'His authority was his work!'[32] Imposing one's authority on an audience is what Aristotle calls the ethical proof.

By all accounts, in front of a large audience and with a piece of charcoal in his hand, Le Corbusier was sure of himself, deploying joyfully the ingenious turns of his rhetorical arsenal. The daring quality of his arguments and his ability to shock his audience with theatrical coups of rhetoric played an essential role in bolstering his confidence. Form and content are always connected in his lectures, and each time he prepared a lecture, he tried to find a new way of rediscovering for himself this element of surprise and the unexpected.

As his reputation as architect and writer established itself, the authority acquired from the act of drawing in public grew. Many of his later lectures consist of a demonstration of his ideas without any real argumentation. In 1924, this authority was lacking, which explains his anxiety to articulate his arguments from both a historical and logical point of view. Later, in 1929, for example, he had less need to turn to this kind of argument, leaning more extensively on his reputation.

An aspect of the *ethos* consists in understanding the particular nature of each audience in order to be able to reason *ad hominem* (in the selection of the premises, the examples or the language of discourse) and to fit in with the interests, appetites and experience of the audience. This reaching out to the audience is called the *exordium*. Le Corbusier acknowledged this tactic explicitly:

Figure 5a

Le Corbusier giving an *impromptu* talk in the atrium at Robinson Hall, Harvard, in 1961.

Figure 5

Le Corbusier at the Graduate School of Design, Harvard University, 1961 (FLC L4-18-60).

32/Interview with José Oubrerie, 25 September 2004.

> Each city I visit makes a certain impression on me. I detect certain needs. I fix on a certain course of action appropriate to my public, even if I sometimes modify this approach in the course of a lecture. And I improvise, because the public likes to believe that I am creating something for them. Like this, they don't go to sleep.[33]

When he gave lectures abroad, he almost always began with some very positive and perceptive reflections on the people, the vernacular architecture and the landscape, continuing his *exordium* with an analysis of the organization of the city before concluding his lecture with his own urban plan for the city which would resolve all its problems. In Buenos Aires, on 3 October 1929, for example, he abandoned the introduction he had prepared for his first lecture during his transatlantic voyage in order to recount his observations of the city and draw his own conclusions.[34] Instead of introducing his talk with some generalizations and the premises of his arguments, he launched right in like this:

> I have walked all over B[uenos] A[ires], and that's some distance! I have looked, seen and understood. [...] For Buenos Aires is a thing unto itself. There is here a fantastic unity; it's a single block: no crack in its façade, not a fissure in this solid ingot (except in Madame Ocampo's interior). How then can I tell that BA, capital of the new world and animated by a vibrant and insatiable youthfulness of spirit, is a city in error, paradoxically, a city which is neither in the new spirit nor of the old one but quite simply and solely a city of 1870 to 1914 [1929 crossed out], ephemeral, indefensible, untenable, excusable but impossible, impossible like the immense quarters of the city born under the abrupt sign of the industrial expansion of the city at the end of the XIX century, in the most total confusion of ends and means.[35]

The techniques of the *exordium* are evident in the new version: the personal commitment of the orator to discover for himself the Argentinian capital. To refer to Buenos Aires as 'capital of the new world and animated by a vibrant and insatiable youthfulness of spirit' is to hold out the hand of friendship to his audience. And if he goes on immediately to denounce the city 'in error', he will make amends in a fortnight's time in his ninth lecture by proposing a new plan for the city. Note, too, how in the long last sentence his language builds to a crescendo of repetition – a classical rhetorical device – in order to underline the abrupt shift of his discourse, from flattery to violent criticism of the city which has invited him to lecture.

During his eighth lecture in Buenos Aires, Le Corbusier sketched a steel windmill and some of the characteristic forms of Argentinian vernacular architecture (Figs 6 and 7). **There were two points to this. On the one hand he wanted to teach the 'spirit of truthfulness', by praising the simple and honest structures at the back of ordinary houses while criticizing the 'lie' of the pompous façades to the street. But on the other hand he wanted to show his warm understanding of Argentinian vernacular architecture.**

33/Le Corbusier, *Précisions*, *op. cit.*, p. 21.

34/A fourteen page manuscript (FLC C3(07)01-14) and a preparatory outline of four pages, recto and verso (GRI 920083(01) conserve the original structure of the first lecture.

35/Notes for the first lecture in Buenos-Aires, on 3 October 1929 (FLC C3(7)16. Note the slight but important differences between this and the text published in *Précisions*, *op. cit.*, p. 23.

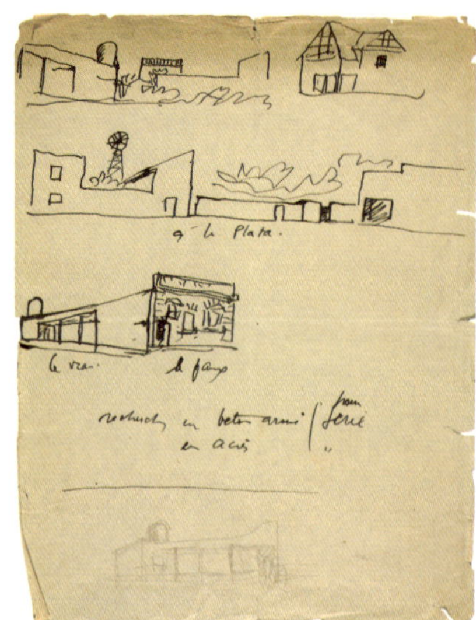

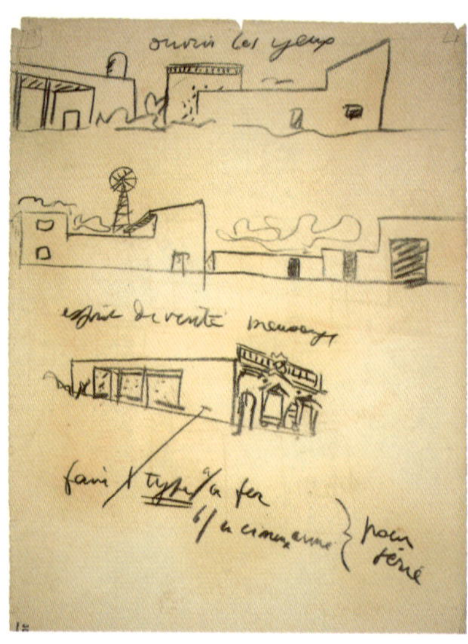

Figure 6
Preliminary sketch for his lecture 'La "Cité mondiale"', Buenos Aires, 17 October 1929 (GRI 920083(11)4).

Figure 7
Sketch made during his lecture 'La "Cité mondiale"', 17 October 1929 (FLC 30295).

Figure 8
Sketch made during his lecture 'Le Plan Voisin de Paris. Buenos Ayres [sic] peut-elle devenir l'une des plus dignes villes du monde?', Buenos Aires, 18 October 1929 (FLC 30303A).

With all this flattery and sympathy for Argentinian culture, we must hope that the Argentinian audience was braced for Le Corbusier's plan for Buenos Aires.

Le Corbusier's project was to resolve all the problems of Buenos Aires with a vast extension to the city on a platform raised over the Rio La Plata on *pilotis*, supporting 12 skyscraper office blocks. A circular aerodrome, further out on the river, a new residential centre along the river front and a new circulation system completed the plan (Fig 8).

In the same way, Le Corbusier offered his audiences in Rio de Janeiro, Antwerp, Stockholm and Paris (again and again) radical plans for the renewal of their cities, always with the same gentle and positive softening up process in the *exordium*.

So, the *exordium*, first part of the *dispositio* of classical rhetoric, is both a means of establishing the *auctoritas* of the orator and a means of making himself loved by the audience. A passionate traveller, Le Corbusier observed with a generous and perceptive eye each country he visited. In a typewritten text he sent the modernist English architect Berthold Lubetkin in September 1935, he dedicates two whole pages to a detailed description of London, taking the trouble to hire an aeroplane from Croydon airport in order better to understand the structure of the city.

> Ten million inhabitants going about their business make the London high street swarming with life, magnificent and intense. The traffic which has to square the circle of huge commuting distances - bus, tube, taxis and motor cars - throws us into a torrent of movement. The buses are splendid; red and covered with beautiful writing, as tall as siege engines, they advance like herds of racing elephants; it's really a spectacle. The London tube stations impress me with their scale, their cleanliness, the comfort offered to the passengers as well as their

le Rio

l'aéroport

la nouvelle cité d'affaires

dock
Les trains
docks

← la Barranca

Reconquista

Florida

le Rio

Valorisation totale

Sud

Nord

resserer la ville

respect for the facilities provided for them. Lining the torrent of cars are the London shops filled with goods, their copper surfaces polished, their marble washed clean and their windows sparkling. You feel the power of merchandise. Finally, mixed up in this violent adventure, the poor pedestrian. What flexibility and what tenacity, what resignation, what optimism! He doesn't revolt; he accepts this new role which his forefathers did not know. All this, as I perceive it and I understand it, is madly amusing, it's like a fairground attraction, with a joyous dynamism. But it's crazy, it's enough to make you weep. Furthermore, it's an economic disaster.[36]

This critique of the great city strangled by its own success was made all the more striking by the generous description of the Londoners and the heroic stoicism. Le Corbusier shows his sensitive understanding in order to drive home the force of his analysis.

Le Corbusier was very aware of the power of keywords and slogans to embed themselves in the minds of his audience and knew how to manipulate his vocabulary to hit the spot with his public, even when his listeners did not agree with his ideas.

The first line of a report he wrote for a committee of the Redressement Français in 1927 is a good example: 'To express a bundle [faisceau] of reasonable ideas [...]'.[37] The word 'faisceau' would have struck a chord with some fascist members of this organization, founded by the electricity magnate Ernest Mercier in 1926 to promote a non-parliamentary technocratic state. On 16 March 1927, in the large hall of the Bourse du Travail he delivered a lecture to an audience of syndicalists entitled: 'Future visions. The Voisin Plan for Paris'.[38]

Henri Froideval of the Comité régional du bâtiment confédéré de la Seine (CRBCS) congratulated Le Corbusier on his brillant exposition of:

[...] the truths which our syndicalist workers' movement has no fear in accepting completely [...] Your idea pleased us because it puts aside petty individualism in favour of a larger idea, that of an awareness of the collective. [...] Your modern city, this standardization of construction, this rationalism of architectural form, we accept all of that.'[39]

This lecture also attracted the attention of the rightwing Faisceau des combattants et des producteurs, whose representative tried to draw Le Corbusier into its circle.[40] He then gave another version of the same lecture, on the occasion of the inauguration of the new hall of the Faisceau, rue d'Aguesseau, on 2 May 1927. It is interesting to note that when the fascist leader Georges Valois[41] described this lecture, he clearly indicated the differences in political ideology which separated Le Corbusier from the Fascist movement in France. The latter tended to favour traditional symbols of French patriotism, such as the image of the Arc de Triomphe which featured on the cover of their journal *Le Nouveau siècle*.[42] But it is at the level of the image that the 'comrades' were won over:

36/Le Corbusier, 'Des idées sont-elles nationales ou humaines?', typescript sent to Berthold Lubetkin, signed and dated September 1935 (FLC A3(2)386, p.2).

37/ Le Corbusier, 'Projet de rapport' (25-page typescript addressed to the 'Section d'Urbanisme' on 19 December 1927 (FLC A3(1)25-49).

38/Announcement 'to all our friends' of a lecture by Le Corbusier on 'Vues d'avenir; le plan Voisin de Paris' (FLC A2(18)19).

39/Henri Froideval to Le Corbusier, 17 March 1927 (FLC C3(5)9).

40/See letter of thanks for the lecture from Paul Binet, writing from 20 rue d'Aguesseau, 19 March 1927 (FLC C3(5)5). The Faisceau, founded by Georges Valois, popularly known as the Blue Shirts, looked to Mussolini's Fascist Italy as a model for an authoritarian corporatist state.

41/Georges Valois was a leading member of the far-right monarchist circle around the journal *Action française*.

42/Valois, G. (1927). 'La nouvelle étape du Fascisme; à la réussite par la pauvreté', *Le Nouveau siècle*, 23 mai 1927 (FLC X1(4)80).

To start with, our comrades experienced a moment of shock at the sight of the projected images. Then, they understood. And they accepted them quite simply with enthusiasm. I repeat, enthusiasm. Before The City of Tomorrow, immense, beautiful, rational, and full of faith, they saw their own ideas materialized.[43]

It is remarkable that Le Corbusier could deliver essentially the same lecture to two groups of different political colour (although there are some links between the anarcho-syndicalist movement and the Fascists in France). But it is likely that he adapted his vocabulary to the key words of the two ideologies. For example, writing to the Redressement Français about the legislation necessary to enable the urban changes he proposed, instead of referring to Louis XIV, Colbert or Baron Haussmann, as he usually did, he called for: 'a strong law, a forceful law [une loi de poigne], a law of public interest [salut public]'.[44] The words 'salut public' referred to the SPQR of republican and imperial Rome[45] and the 'loi de poigne' hinted at the arbitrary power of the dictator.

Le Corbusier practiced 'deliberative' or 'political' rhetoric which, according to Aristotle, appeals to 'exhortation', calling the audience to action or to change its views. He was not content to propose theoretical or purely formal principles, but thought of his lectures as an incitement to make changes. Most of his lectures ended with a plan to transform the home, lifestyles and the city. A fragment in his notes is revealing about his approach:

Your committee took the initiative of calling this evening lecture "Views of the future: l'E[sprit] N[ouveau] in architecture" [...] I have modified the title: "Views of the future: the Voisin Plan for Paris". And I would have preferred to be able to say: "Imminent changes: the centre of Paris must be rebuilt" since I do not like the word "future" or phrases such as "the city of the future", etc. I like to deal with the contemporary. The future is a speculative remedy while, sick as we are, we languish.[46]

This note reflects the state of mind of a man of action rather than an idealist artist or dreamer. He wants to achieve something: the renewal of the centre of Paris. The relationship between lecturing and urban transformation becomes ever closer throughout the 1930s. Furthermore, he was always on the look-out for new architectural or urban commissions arising from his lectures. He was capable of refusing an invitation to lecture if he could not see in it a possible opportunity for a job (however remote). For example, replying to an invitation to address a Swiss group ('Les Heures Alpines'), he referred directly to a scheme of building a museum with Madame Cuttoli, threatening not to reply unless this project was given further consideration.[47]

Looking closely at photographs of Le Corbusier drawing with coloured chalks or charcoal on large sheets of paper during his lectures, it becomes clear that this activity had a very special meaning to him. Drawing is both a private and public act, an act of invention as much as repetition. Although he returned again and again to sketches and diagrams which had already been published in his

43/*Ibid.*

44/Le Corbusier, 'Projet de rapport: Section d'Urbanisme', p. 7 (FLC A3(1)31).

45/Lit.: Senatus Populusque Romanus. The acronym SPQR is found on all municipal works of the Roman Republic.

46/Preparatory notes for the lecture at the Grande Salle du Bourse de Travail, 16 March 1927 (FLC C3(8)105).

47/Invitation from M. Andry-Farcy to Le Corbusier on 26 October 1937 (in which he mentions the project of a museum, in consideration of which he had proposed Le Corbusier's name) (FLC C3(13)62), and Le Corbusier's negative response, on 9 November (FLC C3(13)63).

books and articles and although he invariably sketched out his drawings in advance, the apparently spontaneous gesture of the draughtsman, the choice of colours and the evolution of the drawing constitute a dramatic act of creativity before the eyes of the audience. Le Corbusier used drawings to illustrate his anecdotes, to provide examples of general points in his theory and to represent arguments diagrammatically, often in the form of premise and conclusion, or good versus bad, old versus new and so on.

These drawings go beyond the illustration of his oral exposition; they can constitute arguments in their own right.[48] One of the most effective of the rhetorical techniques is the *demostratio*. It serves to dramatize and make concrete ideas which otherwise might seem abstract. One definition of *demostratio* is: 'making something evident so that the subject grows and manifests itself before the audience'.[49]

Making an idea or a concept concrete by means of an image becomes all the more evocative and real when the image emerges before the viewer's eyes with every stroke of the orator's charcoal. In Buenos Aires he told his audience:

> I am not going to talk to you about poetry and lyricism. I am going to draw things which are specific and reasonable. My diagrams, with their unquestionable truth, will give the mind free rein. These drawings will take us away from traditional practices. More specifically, we are going to understand the state of things today. We will discover that the architecture of today is covered by a rotten layer of yesterday or the day before yesterday. And if you like you can do this: while I draw you will pluck the strings of your lyre, you will give free rein to your lyricism. You

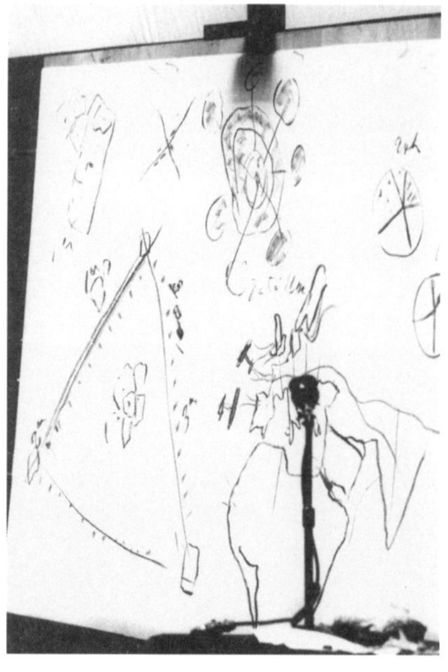

Figures 9 and 10
Le Corbusier drawing his diagrams (based on his book *Les Trois établissements humains*), during his lecture at the Sorbonne, 4 February 1960 (FLC L4(7)91-001).

48/See Chapel, E. (1998). '"Os graficos exprimem..." Da função retórica do desenho' in *Le Corbusier, Rio de Janeiro, 1929-1936*, Rio de Janeiro, Centro de Arquitectura e Urbanismo, pp. 105-109. Chapel identifies four rhetorical functions in Le Corbusier's drawings: comparison or contrast, figurative metaphor, written annotations and diagrams (p. 105).

49/*Rhetorica ad Herennium*, 4.68, quoted by Perelman, C., *The new rhetoric and the humanities*, Reidel, Boston, p. 17.

will create yourselves, for yourselves, the poetic vision of the real today which I will show you.[50]

The sketches produced before the eyes of the audience will be 'true' and 'reasonable', a central and incontrovertible part of the argument. Describing the sequence of his drawings, Le Corbusier concluded: 'In this way the audience will have before their eyes the complete development of the idea.'[51]

Le Corbusier's biographer, Maximilien Gauthier, who no doubt attended several of his subject's lectures, had this to say about his graphical demonstrations:

> On great sheets of white paper rolled out at the back of the stage, his skilful hand, using charcoal and coloured chalks, made concrete the idea which he was simultaneously explaining in words. We are present at a real sprouting [éclosion] of his thought: an extraordinary and very moving spectacle, into which one appears to be implicated in a personal way.[52]

In his preparatory notes for the lecture at the Sorbonne on 4 February 1960, Le Corbusier makes no attempt to comment on his sketches, which are associated in his mind with the ready made explanations in the book he had just published in a new edition of *L'Urbanisme des trois établissements humains* (Fig 10).[53] Following the sequence of his sketches, as he drew them during the lecture, the argument becomes dramatically apparent (Figs 11 and 12).

Starting top left on his paper he draws the 'primitive farm', which becomes transformed by 'the tractor' and other machines during the industrial age into a modern agricultural unit, producing large quantities of food for the cities. Then comes (in the middle at the top) a little sketch in the form of a St Andrew's cross which illustrates the junction between two main roads. A collection of buildings springs up on both sides of the junction where exchange and distribution of every kind of product takes shape. These towns evolve into the great cities which worked acceptably until the industrial revolution strangled them with the railroads and rapid means of transportation. His sketch, top right, shows the modern city bursting its bounds and creating satellite industrial and dormitory towns. These three sketches along the top constitute the premise of his argument and demonstrate the crisis for which he will provide the resolution. Note that his lecture drawing follows very closely the organization and form of the sketch he made beforehand in his notes (Fig 10). This is the point in his explanation at which Le Corbusier was photographed (Fig 11). In the finished drawing (Fig 12), he added, on the right, some pie charts describing the sacrifice of leisure time brought about by daily commuting. He then went on to explain how the 'three establishments' (agricultural factories, linear industrial cities and radioconcentric cities) would resolve the problem posed in his premise: how to organize large numbers of people around the three nodes of agriculture, industry and exchange. On the left, he draws a large triangle linking the 'radioconcentric' cities of exchange with linear cities containing agricultural and industrial production alongside fast road and rail communications, leaving the landscape in between untouched. Finally, he extended the principle of the linear city to the whole of

50/Le Corbusier (1960). *Précisions*, Paris, Editions Vincent, Fréal et Cie, p. 40.

51/*Ibid.*, p. 20.

52/Gauthier, M. (1944). *Le Corbusier ou l'architecture au service de l'homme*, Editions Denoël, Paris, p. 142.

53/Le Corbusier and Norbert Bézard (1945, re-published 1959). *L'Urbanisme des trois établissements humains*, Paris, Editions Denoël.

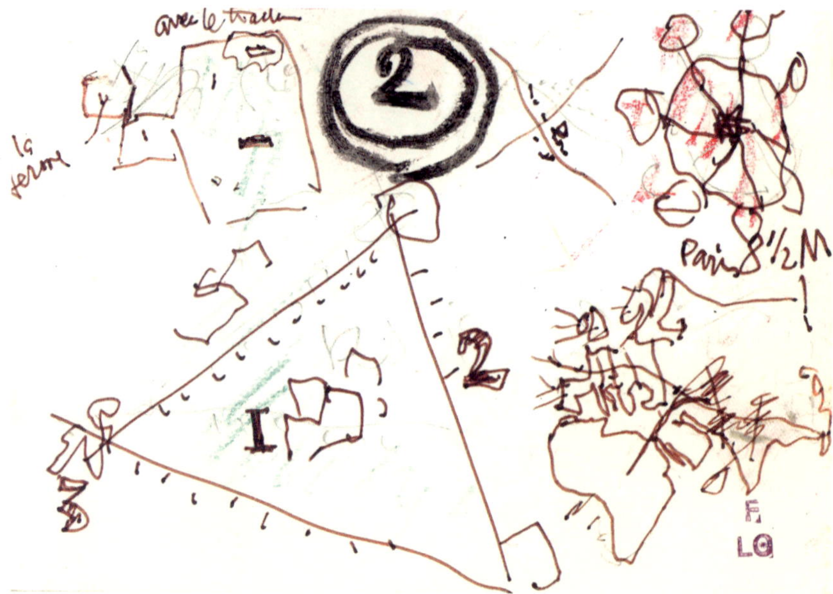

Europe and, by extension, the world, in a sketch bottom right.[54] The drawings work both chronologically, from the past towards the future, but also from cause to effect, as each 'establishment' creates the conditions which determine the next. These are the kinds of reasoning which we identified earlier as that of succession and causality.

Photographs as cause and effect

Photographic images played a necessarily different role in Le Corbusier's argumentation. In his lectures in 1924, as we will see in chapter 2, he used a long sequence of photographs right at the beginning to demonstrate the crisis caused by industrialization and mechanization. Pictures of machines, industrial buildings, ocean liners and aeroplanes, occasionally interspersed with buildings from the past or in historic styles, set the scene. These constitute the premise of the *Zeitgeist* argument: the material world has been radically changed by the machine. The photographs of machines are 'examples' of the principle of mechanization and 'illustrations' of the *Zeitgeist*. Later in his career, he tended to skip this part of the argument. On the other hand, he almost always ended his lectures with projected images of his own work, in drawings, models and photographs of completed works. There is an implied argument linking these images: 'The products of mechanization capture the imagination of the sensitive observer to create a new spirit [*l'esprit nouveau*]. This in turn is manifested [a favourite term of Le Corbusier's] in works of modern architecture [his own].'[55] Evidently, he believed that the impact of his projects, built or unbuilt, was enough to persuade his audience of the rightness of his arguments, while also compensating for the length of his spoken discourse. On a page of notes for a lecture of 7 March 1946, Le Corbusier suggested, 'I offer you some transparencies as proof [underlined sev-

Figure 11

Detail of a page of notes for a lecture at the Sorbonne, 4 February 1960, dated 19 October 1959 (FLC C3(11)89-002).

54/The arguments supporting these drawings can be found in two manuscripts of notes for this lecture (FLC C3(11)89-95), 7 pages, and GRI 920083-9(4), 8 pages.

55/See, for example, the notes for his lecture at Philadelphia on 27 April 1961: "Architecture is the manifestation of a spirit of construction and synthesis" (FLC C3(11)100).

eral times] for you to feast your eyes on'.[56] The possibility of using transparencies to distract and entertain his audience was not lost on Le Corbusier. On a sheet of notes for a lecture in 1927, he wrote the few, cryptic words, 'Lecture: gramophone, play "the wooden trumpet" and show some slides'.[57]

Le Corbusier's argumentation then follows two essential stages: first, establish some 'certainties' about the crisis in the modern world – capable of being understood and accepted by the audience – then proceed to show how the crisis can be resolved. To do so, he illustrates 'examples' – whether in the form of photographs, anecdotes or drawn illustrations – which can be analysed to derive the arguments which will indicate the principles leading to the solutions. These in turn will be demonstrated in 'manifestations' (in rhetorical terms 'illustrations') in the form of sketches and photographs of his own works.

Pathos: Le Corbusier and emotion

Le Corbusier often liked to oppose sentiment and reason in his books and lectures, and yet it is remarkable how often he appeals to emotion in his audience.[58] Looking more closely at his work you quickly realize that he understood feeling and the emotions as fundamental human qualities, capable of being guided by reason but never supplanted by it. For example, in his notes for his lectures in Amsterdam and Rotterdam in January 1932, he writes:

Figure 12

Le Corbusier in front of a projection of the Voisin Plan for Paris (FLC).

56/GRI 850980 folder 1 sheet 4.

57/FLC C3(8)104.

58/Note the juxtaposition of the essays 'Order' and 'Sentiment overflows' (L'*Esprit Nouveau*, 18 and 19 November and December 1923), republished in *Urbanisme*, Editions Vincent, Fréal et Cie, Paris, 1966, pp. 15-38.

3. Je ne prendrai qu'un exemple : un exemple aujourd'hui
Pour illustrer cette FROUSSE qui étreint chacun
La Société des Nations

Et qu'un fait dans s d n
l fait que j'ai connu vécu : la question du Palais

la SDN devait naître et produire
sous quel signe ?
" Demain ? "

Hélas !

Par une spirale foudroyante
elle a chu elle choit
dans dans la mort

MORT (si on a cru
synonyme de sécurité

Nous, les honnêtes les propres (car partout ailleurs,
à chaque occasion depuis 10 ans,
la même scène se reproduit) nous
sommes écrasés par la concussion.

à Genève : Que mensonge
tripatouilles
injustice et
crapulerie

Concours Truqué d'avance

Un lemarquier qui briguait l'académie agissant
avec sécurité,
couvert par . B
Stupéfait de trouver devant
lui, ~~[illegible]~~ l'idée moderne

Reason is static, mathematical. Feeling is passion, unexpected movement, unpredictability. The works of man are a fundamental mixture between these two.[59]

A remarkable example in which Le Corbusier combines *pathos* and precision appears in an extract from his notes for his lectures in Barcelona on 15 and 16 May 1928:

I take great pleasure in presenting this subject in Spain. Spain: the corrida/ the death blow/ just right/ precise/ pure/ economic/ effective or else death. I like architecture to have pathos, be just right. Flamenco, too, has to be just right. And the crowd, tense as at the corrida, cries *olé*![60]

In classical rhetoric, the most common kind of argument using *pathos* is that of pity (*ad misericordiam*), which is often associated with the *ethos* of the orator (his ability to make himself loved). More and more, after 1927, Le Corbusier liked to manipulate the image of the *via crucis* of the prophet and martyr, presenting himself as the victim of atrocious and unjust attacks by those in authority. On his preparatory notes for a lecture in Zurich, before an audience he knew to be generally very sympathetic, Le Corbusier gave vent to his emotions. These pages are torn off in a passionate scrawl, with words frequently underlined in different colours, phrases added and others crossed out (Fig 13) [some key words are picked out to enable the reader to follow the transcription below]:

To illustrate this PANIC [FROUSSE] which grips everyone, I will take just one example - a poignant example - The League of Nations [Société des Nations] and one fact in the SdN, a fact which I know, have lived, the question of the Palace.[61] The SdN was to be born and produced; under what sign? Tomorrow? [demain?] Alas! Through a devastating spiral it fell, it is falling [sketch of spiralling fall] towards death. DEATH [MORT], and we thought it a synonym of security. We, the honest ones, the clean ones [les honnêtes, les propres] (since everywhere elsewhere, every time in the last ten years the same thing happens) we are crushed by the mismanagement of public funds [nous sommes écrasés par la concussion]. In Geneva: what lies, what fiddles, injustice and villainy. A competition judged in advance. Lemaresquier, who was after the Academy[…]; astonished to be confronted by the modern idea.[62]

Figure 13

Notes for a lecture in Zurich, 15 February 1934 (FLC A2(19)10-003).

The language of these notes, and their expressive character, conveys more than a sense of injustice at what happened in Geneva. This is a lament, a direct appeal to the audience's sympathy and pity.

After pity, in the appeal to *pathos* often comes the implication of the shared culpability of the audience. Further down these same notes, Le Corbusier carries the attack to the Swiss nationality of his audience, in terms redolent of Pontius Pilate's betrayal of Christ:

59/FLC C3(8)208, p. 1.

60/FLC C3(8)88.

61/Le Corbusier and Pierre Jeanneret had submitted a competition entry for the new palace for the League of Nations in Geneva and obtained equal first prize with eight other teams. In controversial circumstances, in which the jury member Lemaresquier played a key role, some of these winning architects were given the job, while Le Corbusier was sidelined.

62/Notes for a lecture at Zurich on 13 February 1933 (FLC A2(19)10-24) (transcription Stéphane Potelle).

> Let not Switzerland "wash her hands", saying: the others did this! The head of state himself, representing the country at the League of Nations - overwhelmed by the fearful atmosphere - gave in and abandoned us himself.[63]

Then, in the arsenal of the emotions, comes invective:

> Then, the barricades were raised in every country with orders which were lies, in the name of politics, the spectre of Bolchevism! And by liers: the chambers of commerce threatened, the academies panic-stricken, and some dangerous madmen, liars and mountebanks, of whom you have a prize example in Hugo Von Senger [sic][64] (I will come back to him), Mauclair[65] in France and others whose names I do not know in Germany. No holds barred to achieve the sordid aim: kill off life, protect the egotists and save the status quo and the industrial interests.[66]

In this vein – and it is unfortunately impossible to ascertain whether the lecture itself followed the notes – it seems quite normal to find a conclusion reduced to a purely emotional appeal (Fig 14):

> Today, what is the reply to this question which is asked everywhere? Yes or no? To act? Or to die? Who do you trust? the slanderers? or us, who claim to act on the basis of honesty?

You only have to see his notes to feel the emotion of the speaker. It is evident that this kind of discourse, even if expressed only in the intimacy of his notebook on the train, reveals a therapeutic aspect of the lecture for someone like Le Corbusier. His life was a roller coaster between peaks of fame and harsh setbacks, all of which he felt bitterly. It was only to be expected that he should represent himself occasionally as the tragic hero, and this usually went down well with the right kind of audience.

Le Corbusier believed that architecture depended both on engineering and art. To discuss it, he needed to appeal to logic as well as rhetoric. This was also the point of view of Paul Valéry, who was speculating about Eupalinos, the mythical architect of the temple of Artemis the Huntress according to Plato, in a dialogue between the representative of reason Socrates and the rhetorician Phaedrus.[67] Valéry gives to Socrates the task of praising rhetoric, to the point of saying: 'The real is a discourse, it is above all this song, this colour of voice which we are wrong to treat as details or accidents', only to leave to Phaedrus the role of praising the genius of Eupalinos in terms of reason: 'He gave them [his workmen] only orders and numbers.'[68]

Figure 14
Notes for a lecture in Zurich, 15 February 1934 (A2(19)10-12).

63/*Ibid.*

64/Alexander von Senger was a Swiss Arts and Crafts architect who wrote a highly polemical series of articles against modern architecture and Le Corbusier in particular, published as a series of books in German and French: *Krisis der Architektur*, Rascher, Zurich, 1928; *Le Cheval de Troie du Bolchevisme*, Bienne, 1928; *Die Brandfackel Moskaus*, Zurzach-Schweiz, 1931.

65/Camille Mauclair was the art critic of *Le Figaro* and wrote a number of similar articles published as *La crise du panbettonisme integral; L'Architecture va-t-elle mourir?*, Paris, 1932.

66/*Ibid.*

67/Paul Valéry, *"Eupalinos" and "L'Ame et la danse"*, edition introduced and annotated by Vera J. Daniel, London, Oxford University Press, 1967. Eupalinos is also credited with constructing the first tunnel to have been started at both ends, extending over 1,000 metres.

68/*Ibid.*, pp. 60 and 57.

1 Vous voyez que la question est posée partout.

C'est un fait énorme : une immense agitation

de mon temps Moi de 1900 à 1925 = la question ne se posait nulle part

notre génération a lutté.

aujourd'hui : à cette question posée partout quelle réponse ?

oui ou non ?

agir ou mourir ?

En qui avez-vous foi ? en les calomniateurs ? ou en nous, si j'affirme que agir sur base de l'honnêteté ?

Examinons 1830 1930 = 1 siècle

la nouvelle civilisation éminemment machiniste est née 1830 = 1 siècle gestation

1 fait technique | l'infini des découvertes | le déclenchement des transformations sociales

Dans tumulte on perd pied

appel à la conscience

humanisme l'homme devant nous

Toute notre réforme notre révolution

C'est de ne considérer qu'un HOMME VRAI REEL.

Chapter 2

The origins of the lecture on architecture

Le Corbusier liked to give two lectures, one on architecture and one on urbanism. He rarely had the opportunity, as in Buenos Aires in 1929 or Rio de Janeiro in 1936, to give a series of 10 or 6 lectures. Occasionally, he picked a more specific subject, such as proportion (Milan 1951) or the design of museums (Turin 1961) or India (Sorbonne 1957). One of his first important lectures, in 1923 in Strasbourg, was on urbanism.[1] We will return to this in chapter 3.

The architecture lectures in 1924

Le Corbusier's lectures can be grouped into families, or sequences, during which a set of ideas and examples evolve gradually from one lecture to the next, before being replaced by a new set of themes and interests. Some arguments, however, are common to all his architecture lectures. These were first given full articulation in 1924, when he delivered five versions of what became his staple architecture lecture. He put a great deal of effort into their creation, and in so doing developed the key arguments and rhetorical tactics which he retained, with variations, throughout his career.

This group of lectures is of great interest because we not only have a number of pages of preparatory notes and sketches, but also two stenographic transcripts of his actual delivery. These allow us to understand where he followed his notes and where he extemporized on the basis of key words and sketches and allows us to extrapolate from the notes in other cases, when a transcript does not exist. The transcripts prove that Le Corbusier read or learned by heart whole pages of his preparatory notes, especially at the beginning of his lectures, and did not improvise all of them, as he claimed. On the other hand, it is also clear that he adapted his material to suit each audience, changing the order and adding or subtracting passages of text.

Identifying the existing manuscripts with the lectures Le Corbusier gave in 1924 is not a simple matter. A detailed analysis is given in Appendix 1, p. 189. We know that he gave a lecture in Geneva on 17 February, which he repeated in Lausanne on the next day. According to Le Corbusier's biographer Maximilien Gauthier,

> It was in 1924, in Geneva, in a hall reserved for high society, that he first climbed onto a lecture stage. It was by virtue of his directorship of *L'Esprit Nouveau* magazine. From this moment on, he decided that all his lectures would be improvised. Here, then, as an awkward and perhaps confused beginner, he only managed to astonish a stony faced audience, without achieving either a triumph or a scandal. At the Maison du Peuple in Lausanne, next day, having managed to excite more of a response, he began to warm to his task.[2]

Preceding page

Model of the Villa Niestlé project, Rambouillet, exhibited in the Salon d'Automne in November 1923 (glass lantern slide, FLC).

I associate a ten page stenographic transcript with the Lausanne lecture[3]. These lectures were followed by a prestigious lecture at the Sorbonne, Paris, on 12 June, for which the Swiss performances were effectively a dress rehearsal. This lecture was repeated in Paris on 10 November at the Salle Rapp. It is this last one

1/In his diary (FLC F3(3)6), from 6 January to April 1923, Le Corbusier refers three times to Strasbourg. On folio 4r (ca. 4 February) he noted 'reply Strasbourg Museum'. On folio 9v (after 11 February) he wrote 'Urgent June 1923 reply Strasbourg', and just before 25 March, on folio 35r: 'Pierre, make a plan [...] Diorama for Strasbourg'.

2/Gauthier, M. (1944). *Le Corbusier ou l'architecture au service de l'homme*, Editions Denoël, p. 141. This account is confirmed by a letter to William Ritter of 10 March 1924, where he says that he completely messed up the lecture in Geneva but that it went better in Lausanne. He claimed the reason for giving the lectures was to save *L'Esprit Nouveau* (FLC R3(19)401). The Lausanne lecture is dated by an invitation card and by Le Corbusier's manuscripts. The ten page transcript (FLC C3(6)14-23) mentions the Geneva lecture and devotes several pages to a discussion of the landscape of lake Geneva.

3/See the detailed analysis in Appendix 1, p. 189.

4/'L'esprit nouveau en Architecture', *Le Bulletin de l'Ordre de l'Etoile d'Orient*, 1 March 1924, pp. 24-53 (FLC X1(3)64), and Le Corbusier (1926). *Almanach de l'Architecture Moderne*, Paris, Editions G. Crès et Cie, reprinted Paris, Editions Connivences, pp. 17-54.

5/FLC C3(6)14-23 (see Appendix pp. 200-204).

which is recorded in most detail, in a stenographic transcript which was published, with slight variations, in two places.[4] A second typed manuscript can also be associated with the Lausanne lecture.[5]

Lausanne and the landscape of lake Geneva

Addressing an appreciative audience in Lausanne on 18 February 1924, Le Corbusier makes frequent references to the local landscape. This theme is indicated in a three page manuscript note entitled *'Conférence Lausanne 18 fev[rier] 1924'*.[6] Stanislaus von Moos has noted Le Corbusier's fascination with the North shore of the lake, which he had sketched in 1921-22 in several beautiful watercolours and pastels which have been conserved in an album presented to Raoul La Roche.[7] The handwritten notes include a number of sketches of the steep terraced North shore of lake Geneva, while another sheet of notes relates views of the South shore with the house he was designing for his parents at Corseaux. It seems that the origins of the project to build his parents a small house in the region date from August 1923.[8] In January 1924, Le Corbusier was on the site at Corseaux putting out his first project to tender. Two years later, lecturing in Basel and Zurich, he returned to this theme of the landscape of lake Geneva.[9]

Le Corbusier sketched out the arguments for the 1924 lectures in two sheets of notes[10]. The first one deploys the theories of the *Zeitgeist* in order to show that mechanization had utterly changed not only the material world but also the 'spirit' of intelligent observers. The second page uses sketches to demonstrate the architectural revolution brought about by the new spirit. The word *'pro-*

Figure 1

The Barberine dam (Switzerland), in construction September 1923, illustrated in the 1924 lectures and in *Urbanisme*, 'Nos Moyens', p. 139.

Following double spread

Figure 2

Plan of a lecture, 1924 (FLC C3(6)28).

6/FLC C3(6)24. Three days before this, Le Corbusier had delivered a lecture on 'L'Esprit nouveau' to the Société des Arts, Classe des Beaux-Arts, Athénée, Paris; Ozenfant had offered 'L'art dans la société machiniste' (FLC A2(18)110).

7/Le Corbusier, Stanislaus von Moos et Fondation Le Corbusier (1996). *Album La Roche*, p. 77.

8/See the diary of Le Corbusier's father Georges Jeanneret: '5 August 1923: Edouard proposes to build us a really small "purist" house.' The definitive site, belonging to the viticulturalist Julien Cornu, was found in December 1923 and eventually purchased on 19 May 1924. A first project, published in plan by Baderre in *Paris Journal* on 28 December 1923, was slightly modified in January 1924 (see the plans FLC 9366, 9418 and 9417 for the first project and FLC 9370-3 for the one slightly adapted in January). More changes took place to the design before construction work began in August 1924.

9/See especially folios 73 and 76. These are labeled 'Bâle 1-20', with some pages added as a preface to a lecture at Zurich, dated 24 November 1926.

10/FLC C3(6)24 and C3(6)25.

un ~~état~~ de choses nouveau

la submersion des événements mécaniques
la dissolution d'habitudes séculaires
l'astreinte à des fonctions nouvelles
} état de crise

à quoi bon "tout"

trouble, chaos – doute et négation incroyance.

la loi d'écono…

un état d'esprit nouveau — état de crise

perception des règles

constitution d'un idéal nouveau
une croyance
une ligne de conduite
un état d'esprit nouveau.

exactitude …
l'art et l'i…
le choix et …
terriblement …

un mouvement d'idées nouveau {
des idées affluent. Rencontre d'Oz. Edi…
Incessant rencontre dernier.
Fondation revue EN
le premier éditeur ~~Louis~~ XVII Gauthier
" II " intérêt Chiron
chambre à la rue de Seine
Afflux des étrangers. La Presse unan…
Nouveaux bureaux, organisation. …
Crise. Suppr. capital tous abonnés.
Contre Bruno
le régime des abonnements en capital
Influence à l'étr…

un exemple d'esprit nouveau.
l'architecture.

la cellule. l'agent … de la …

la grande ville. entretien avec jeunes … l'Européen …

suis pas s'exposer pas orateur, amené à occupation de constante introspection, solitaire loin

LG
F

ité Déf.
· fait.

Barberine }
les gratte ciels }
Bindy et moi poète
les inférieurs ne savent pas.

= simple fait d'évolution

l'ordre
des d'Artistes
cavaliers des arts
Citroën enfoncé les lumineux des boulevards. Pérennité Beauté mécanique
la poésie des faits.
la vie intérieure, l'introspection
mépris du ridicule.
libertaire, le libre examen et le choix

les commentaires

condenser
planif.
tableaux par pays
par mois

, les abonnements, un mauvais diffuseur Hasard.
mondial.

liste. Situation en Suisse allemande
un programme rédactionnel.
... de mécaniciens depuis la Karma

rédaction 12 à 90 pages
et clichés : 4
suffirait de 1000 abts

revues Diabrésé
... La Sera la grande ville
oui ou non

chez Mesnil (Humanité petit Bourgeois)

Renseignements de SW Ronéo
Fuges
UP Brno.

verbe de l'avenir

jections' (slide projections) at the foot of this page indicates that Le Corbusier thought the lecture would end there. These two pages, then, are probably a rough sketch for the whole Lausanne lecture, which he later reworked and enlarged. This is confirmed by some overlaps between the manuscript and the stenographic transcript.

A more dense and detailed plan for the arguments of this lecture can be found on a double page sheet (Fig 2).[11] The plan has four main headings: 'Un état de choses nouveau' [New material conditions]; 'un état d'esprit nouveau' [A new spirit]; 'un mouvement d'idées nouveau' [A new movement of ideas], and 'un exemple d'esprit nouveau: l'architecture' [An example of the new spirit: architecture]. Le Corbusier deploys here the difficult reasoning of the *Zeitgeist* which we looked at in chapter 1. The first task is to show that the world is in a 'state of crisis'.

New material conditions:
submersion in the effects of mechanization } state of crisis[12]
the dissolution of the habits of centuries }
obligation to adopt new functions

The material crisis leads to a spiritual one. The repeated use of the word 'new' marks the rupture with the past brought about by industrialization and mechanization. Under the next heading – 'a new spirit' – Le Corbusier demonstrates that there already exist some people (philosophers or poets like himself or his friend Paul Budry) who were capable of understanding the implications of the new material conditions and constructing a new aesthetic accordingly. This dense and concentrated text includes the key words which will be repeated in the lecture, usually illustrated by anecdotes or sketches on the blackboard. For example, the word 'Barberine' refers to his experience of visiting the Barberine dam, high in the Alps to the South East of lake Geneva, which Le Corbusier will describe in detail in the lecture (Fig 1)[13].

	Trouble, chaos. Doubt and rejection of beliefs	What's the use: it's all been done before	Barberine; the skyscrapers (= simple evolutionary facts [in pencil]); Budry and I, the poets; the engineers don't understand; Citroën wipes out the boulevard illuminations
A new state of mind:	Perception of rules	The law of economy, order, bus numbers, the artist's cravat	
	Construction of a new ideal:	exactitude and clarity of judgement	The poetry of facts
	A belief	Art, the ideal, the life of the soul, introspection	
	A strategy	A choice and the scorn of ridicule	
	A new state of mind	Fantastically libertarian, free analysis and a choice[14]	

11/FLC C3(6)28.

12/*Ibid.*

13/Le Corbusier had visited the Barberine dam in construction with Paul Budry in October 1923. On 10 October, Le Corbusier began a letter to his friend: 'Following our emotions at Barberine…' and he went on to ask his help in ordering the photographs they had selected when they were there (FLC E1(9)262).

14/FLC C3(6)28.

All the examples referred to here will turn up in the 1924 lectures. For example, 'Citroën wipes out the boulevard illuminations' can be partly explained by his typewritten card:

> PERPETUITY
> Mechanical religions, ex.[ample]: Citroën's lights kill off all previous admiration for illuminations.[15]

The illumination of the Eiffel Tower, paid for by Citroën as a publicity stunt, was so bright that the lamps on the boulevard paled into insignificance. Every technological advance puts earlier achievements into the shade.

For Le Corbusier, the current crisis consisted in the fact that even those in the know, such as the engineers, were incapable of comprehending the radical upheaval produced by mechanization. This is well expressed in the anecdote of the Barberine dam, recounted in his lectures and in great detail in the pages of *Urbanisme* (the chapter entitled 'Nos moyens'). This is how Le Corbusier tells the story in the Lausanne lecture:

> With an enthusiastic poet, at 2,000 metres [in the Alps], I found an immense mechanism consisting of cables, cranes and steel girders which towered over a chasm which they were filling with concrete and which will become a dam.
> Human power; the force of nature.
> Admiration for the achievement.
> Next day we went looking for the engineers; we told them of our admiration, which they accepted calmly. After some discussion we arrived at this; explaining to them my ideas [to build skyscrapers in inner cities] provoked general mirth and when I protested they exclaimed: 'But you're going to kill off the beauty of the cities by constructing your skyscrapers.'
> These people, capable of creating immense grandeur, were incapable of understanding it.[16]

The crisis, then, consists in the fact that the engineers themselves were incapable of seeing the possible implications of the techniques they were using for architecture and urbanism. In the lecture at the Salle Rapp, Le Corbusier is even more explicit:

> They [the engineers] were totally different to us, precisely because of their mentality. Used to conceiving and executing constructions based on calculation alone they betrayed themselves to us as incapable of imagining, in a different field to theirs, the consequences of their own activity; they remained yesterday's men.[17]

We find the same point made on one of his typed cards, referring to Eugène Freyssinet, who is quoted as saying:

15/FLC C3(6)73.

16/Ten page typescript (FLC C3(6)14-23, see Appendix p. 200). See also Le Corbusier (1966). *Urbanisme*, Paris, Editions Vincent, Fréal et Cie, pp. 138-143.

17/FLC X1(3)64.

> On many fundamental points I think exactly like you, and I believe that your book [*Vers une architecture*] will be extraordinarily useful. On the other hand, some of my other ideas will probably strike you as terribly old-fashioned; for example, I have an absolute horror of Cubist painting and I fail to see how men of good faith can find anything artistic in it.[18]

For Le Corbusier, then, 'the new spirit' included not only an understanding of the new technical possibilities but also the new aesthetic of modern art and the ideas of the avant-garde. It is for this reason that the third part of his lecture plan concentrates on the role of *L'Esprit Nouveau* in the critique and diffusion of the modernist aesthetic. Le Corbusier clearly proposed to go into great detail here, recounting the whole history of the magazine and the key role played by Jean Budry (Paul's brother), who had just re-launched the journal in January 1924. On his plan for the lecture, the high points of this story are noted down:

A new movement of ideas

A rush of new ideas, meeting with Oz[enfant]
Edition des Commentaires [publisher]
The incident of the meeting with Dermée
Founding the review EN [Esprit Nouveau]
The publishing pressures; Louis XV; Gauthier
Move by an interested publisher: Chiron
The room at the rue de Seine
The foreigners join in; the press is unanimous;
the subscriptions; poor distribution by Hazard
New offices, organization, world markets
Crisis; the scheme of raising capital from the subscribers
The Budry contract
The subscription system and capital;
Influence abroad; a list.
Situation in French and German Switzerland
The new editorial programme
Reduction from 120 to 90 pages and pictures. We need 1,000 subscriptions. The new editorial strategy.[19]

Judging by the ten page transcript of the Lausanne lecture, Le Corbusier did not discuss *L'Esprit Nouveau* then, but he did include this theme in his notes for the lecture at the Salle Rapp, and the full transcription of this lecture confirms that he discussed it.[20] The fact that he makes special mention of the 'situation in French and German Switzerland' suggests that he had intended to discuss it in Lausanne. The frequent mention of Paul Budry, who lived in Lausanne and with whom he had visited the Barberine dam in October 1923, confirms that the double page sheet was indeed written before the Geneva and Lausanne lectures.[21]

At last, we arrive at architecture:

18/Card dated 22 November 1923 (FLC C3(6)76), based on a letter from Freyssinet to Le Corbusier on that date (FLC E2(2)425), in which he explains that he had read several issues of *L'Esprit Nouveau* as well as *Vers une architecture* and seen his models in the Salon d'Automne in 1923. *Vers une architecture* was published in October 1923.

19/FLC C3(6)28.

20/The history of *L'Esprit Nouveau* can be found in the preparatory notes for the lecture at the Salle Rapp (FLC C3(8)3) and in the transcript of the lecture, in the *Bulletin de l'Ordre de l'Etoile d'Orient*, pp. 32-33.

21/FLC C3(6)38.

An example of the new spirit: Architecture	The cell	the La Tour [de Peilz] surveyor of roads: precautions taken after Karma	Consequence EN: Ronéo, Frugès, UP Brno [pencil note]
	The great city	discussion with terribly disenchanted young Viennese architect: 'Europe has had it; it's touch and go for the great city.'	Look for Mesnil (?) Humanity, petty bourgeois.[22]

Le Corbusier believed that the new spirit would lead directly to a new architecture. In all his 1924 lectures, he follows this line of argument. From the new technology flows a new spirit which leads in turn to new architectural solutions which he demonstrates on the blackboard. In each lecture, he developed his argument in two case studies – the cell (the dwelling) and the city – the latter usually cut short through lack of time. Phrases like 'the La Tour surveyor of roads' or 'the disenchanted Viennese' recur in his notes for the Lausanne lecture.[23] On one of his typewritten cards, he had already noted: 'The great city: discussion with a disenchanted young Viennese architect: 'Europe has had it' No! Only the West has sufficient reason and a rich enough tradition to express the age. America is too young. We are faced with gigantic programs.'[24] The reference to 'the great city' suggests that this encounter might have taken place during the conference on urbanism in Strasbourg in 1923.[25] We learn more about this in the 'Avertissement [Preface]' of *Urbanisme*:

> Recently, a young Viennese architect - frightfully disenchanted - predicted the imminent death of old Europe; only youthful America can give us hope. "No new architectural programs are being put forward in Europe", he declared. "We have dragged ourselves down the ages on our knees, weighed down, crushed by the heavy burden of successive cultures. The Renaissance, then the Louis, have tired us out. We are too rich, too blasé, we have lost the virginity required to produce architecture." I replied: "The architectural problem for old Europe is the great modern city. It's yes or no; life or slow extinction. One or the other, but if we want it, it will endure. And it is precisely our burden of past cultures which will deliver the pure and mature solution, submitted to the test of reason and an elite sensibility."[26]

At the foot of the page of his lecture plan, Le Corbusier added a short note:

> End with an apology: [I'm] no orator, snatched from a labor of constant and solitary introspection, far from the lawyer's pleadings.[27]

22/FLC C3(6)28.

23/The town of La Tour de Peilz lies on the North shore of lake Geneva, near Corseaux, where Le Corbusier was preparing to build the house for his parents. 'Karma' refers to the Villa Karma, by Adolf Loos, a short distance away on the shore.

24/FLC C3(6)82.

25/See chapter 3.

26/See also FLC C3(6)25 verso, where he adds 'New York = death. Greater Berlin = problem of the garden city. Sauvage, Perret, Tony Garnier. The street = new organ'.

27/FLC C3(6)28.

C3-6-69

Conférence

1 Série projections démontrant — conclusions cantilever

recherche de la fenêtre → d'un mur.

de l'ossature - domino

idem urb. Sauva
Perret
Corbu

p. Genève
Lausanne
l'histoire du paysage
[illegible]

(9)

In fact, this is a perfect example of what rhetoricians call the peroration: he simultaneously charms his audience with his modesty and candour, while positioning himself as a disinterested poet and philosopher, engaged in 'constant and solitary introspection'.

It is unusual to find such detailed and well structured lecture notes among Le Corbusier's papers. Usually, it was enough to list a few key words which would stand for the main part of the lecture. On one sheet of the 1924 lecture notes (Fig 3), he summed up the whole argument of the last part of the lecture in a few words:

> Lectures
> 1 set of lantern slides demonstrating:
> The search for a window - for a wall - conclusion. [sketch of a 'T' shaped cantilevered structure]
> for a domino skeleton
> Idem urb [anism]: Sauvage, Perret, Corbu
> For Geneva, Lausanne, the story of a spoiled landscape[28]

Another attempt to structure the 1924 lectures can be found in a two page draft. (Fig 4), in which he tackles the question of the *Zeitgeist* head on:

> Imagine the world/industry in our grandfather's day - 1850 - it's not long ago! The invention of the typewriter: transformation of commerce, acceleration of competition[29]

And he adds a surprisingly modest sentence:

> Beginning: I'm only going to tell you commonplaces.

Then he proposed to tell the story which he had noted down on one of his typed cards in the autumn of 1923, about Delloire and a project for the Peugeot car company[30]:

> An EN [Esprit Nouveau] fact: Deloire [sic] Peugeot designing a factory. He doesn't know how it will turn out, whether sawtooth roofing, hangar or vaults; it will emerge!

On the card, he was more explicit:

> Delloire Peugeot
> Draw a new factory. The board asked: will it have sawtooth roofing, hangars, truss, hall etc… ?
> Reply: I have no idea. I am studying an organism; I am organizing it; I lay out the successive functions and put them in order; I concentrate it and create some volumes. I will build these volumes when the time comes, according to what your site allows. Only then will I think about what kind of roofing and what kind of walls.
> Here we work from the inside outwards.[31]

Figure 3
Page of notes for the Geneva and Lausanne lectures, February 1924 (FLC C3(6)69).

28/FLC C3(6)69.

29/FLC C3(6)49.

30/In March 1924, Le Corbusier was corresponding with one of the directors of the Peugeot car company, M. Girardet, over a housing project at Audincourt (FLC H1(20), 27 February 1924, I1(05)17, 10 March 1924) as well as about a publicity insert for Peugeot in *L'Esprit Nouveau* (FLC A1(10)142, 3 February 1924).

31/Index card, dated November 1923 (FLC C3(6)74).

SOCIÉTÉ D'ENTREPRISES INDUSTRIELLES ET D'ÉTUDE

SECTION : INDUSTRIES DE L'ALIMENTATION

SOCIÉTÉ ANONYME AU CAPITAL DE 250.000 FRANCS

SIEGE SOCIAL :
PARIS
29 bis, rue d'Astorg
ADR. TÉLÉGR. : JEANARCH-PARIS
TÉLÉPHONE : ELYSÉES 44-27

PARIS

OBJET :

RÉFÉRENCES A RAPPELER S. V. P.

imaginez la société vers 1850. nos grands pères
l'individu
c'est récent

l'invention de la machine à écrire = transformation du commerce et multiplication de la concurrence

debut : Je ne vais vous énoncer que des lieux communs

Fait d'E.N. Delage Peugeot dessinant l'usine. il ne sait comment elle sera. les sheds, en hangars ou voûtes ça résultera.

On the next page, he notes some ideas for a slide sequence: compare a coach building workshop of around 1850 with a Citroën factory; compare Louis XIV's Paris with his project for a Contemporary City for Three Million Inhabitants (1922) and a section of the traditional street with a modern multilevel section including metro and motorway raised on *pilotis*.[32] None of these ideas turns up in the transcriptions of the Lausanne and Salle Rapp lectures. Clearly, we must be cautious about Le Corbusier's lecture notes; he had plenty of ideas which perhaps never

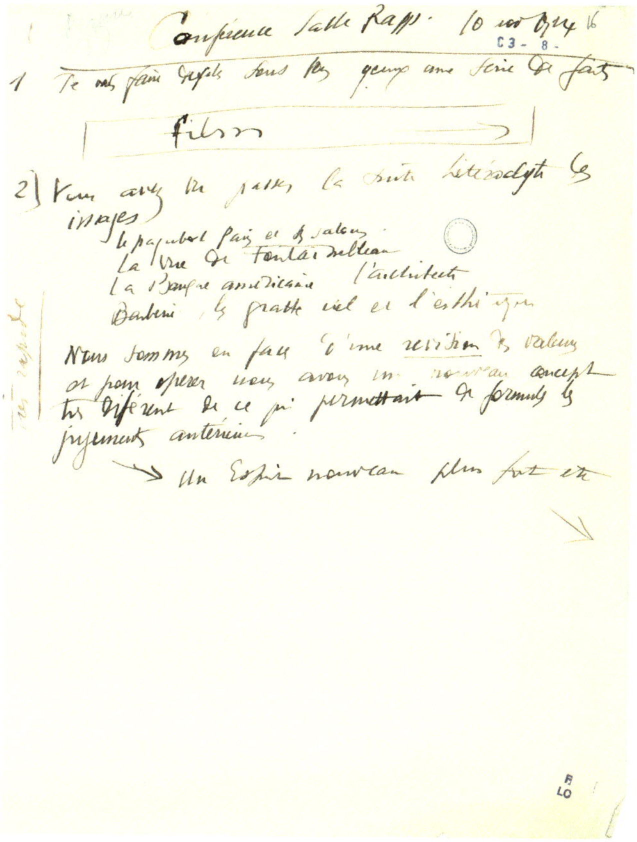

Figure 4

First page of a draft plan for the lectures of 1924 (FLC C3(6)49).

Figure 5

Preparatory note for his lecture at the Salle Rapp, Paris, 10 November 1924 (FLC C3(8)16).

made it into the lectures. In fact, when he prepares his notes for the Salle Rapp lecture, it takes him only half a page to get into his stride (Fig 5).[33]

He states simply: 'I will lay before your eyes a series of facts', in the form of a long sequence of slide projections, which he called 'films'. Then he proposed to comment on this 'heterogeneous sequence of images'. Then, 'very quickly', he summed up the arguments of the *Zeitgeist* and the new spirit, before picking up on the text with which he had begun the Lausanne lecture: 'A new spirit, stronger etc....'. Clearly, he knew this bit by heart. In the end, it took him five pages (in the printed transcription of the lecture in the *Bulletin de l'Ordre de l'Etoile d'Orient*) to describe the images and tell the anecdotes arising from them before he reached the *Zeitgeist* argument. In the end, in the Salle Rapp lecture, he did not use the opening passage of the Lausanne lecture:

32/FLC C3(6)50.

33/FLC C3(8)16.

> A New Spirit, stronger than that of race and stronger than the influence of geographic location, overrides all our customs and traditions and spreads across the whole world with precise and unitary characteristics.[34]

Instead, he picks up the text immediately afterwards. We can compare the sentence of 10 November:

> The precise and unitary characteristics of the new spirit are as universal and human as possible and yet, never has the chasm been so great which separates the old society from the machinist one in which we live.[35]

With the original one of 18 February:

> These characteristics are as universal and human as can be, and yet never was the chasm so great, which separates the old society from our machinist society.[36]

The argument then follows along the same lines up to the point where the Lausanne text begins to discuss the landscape of lake Geneva, which Le Corbusier did not discuss at the Salle Rapp.

The 'films'

At the beginning of his lecture at the Salle Rapp, Le Corbusier announced:

> I will begin by putting before your eyes a series of facts. (A varied series of images is projected on the screen; a hundred images in groups preceded by an 'argument', as in a film)[37]

His tactic was to persuade his audience by manipulating a sequence of 'heterogeneous' photographic images that a 'chasm' divided the contemporary world from the culture of the preceding 400 centuries. The four 'points' became five 'explanations' – typed caption cards serving as chapter headings – which punctuated the hundred images with which he began his 1924 lectures. Le Corbusier called these sequences his 'films'.[38]

During a lecture at Brussels in 1926, Le Corbusier showed an abridged version of his 'films' and explained his use of them in 1924 like this:

> I arranged for the Sorbonne a sequence of slide projections whose purpose was to put the audience into a state of mental shock. Shock derived from a precipitate succession of heterogeneous images – things from the past, from the present, contrasted and juxtaposed, sometimes also in harmony. Unexpected, dramatic relationships which in truth simply represented in visual form the state of the world

34/FLC C3(6)14-23 (see Appendix, p. 200).

35/FLC X1(3)64.

36/FLC C3(6)14.

37/'L'esprit nouveau en Architecture', *op. cit.*, p. 24.

38/Five typed cards (FLC C3(6)33-37) and a manuscript sheet (FLC C3(6)32). We know that he used these in the lectures at the Sorbonne and at the Salle Rapp. At Lausanne, he certainly began with a slide sequence, with or without the five caption cards.

Figure 6

Figure 7

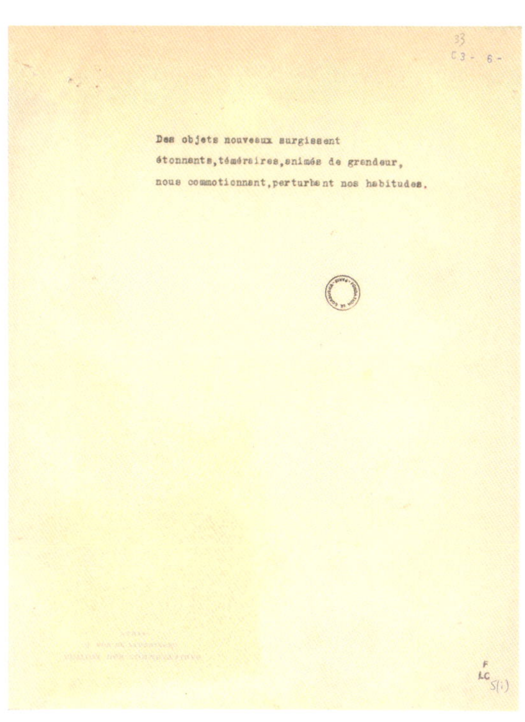

Des objets nouveaux surgissent
étonnants,téméraires,animés de grandeur,
nous commotionnant,perturbant nos habitudes.

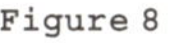

Figure 8

Card 1 (Figure 8):

New objects spring up, astonishing, daring, animated with grandeur, giving us a shock, disturbing our habits.[40]

Figure 9

Figure 6

American factory (*L'Esprit Nouveau*, 2, November 1920, p. 197).

Figure 7

Photo of a Blériot-Spad 33 (1920), pasted onto a sheet of images for the lectures and included as one of the images reprinted with the lecture at the Salle Rapp (FLC C3(6)88).

Figure 8

Caption card 1 for the 'films' (FLC C3(6)33).

Figure 9

Handley-Page bomber (1916-1920) (*L'Esprit Nouveau*, 9, June 1921).

Card 3 (not shown)

Powerful and hitherto unknown means have been revolutionized by a century of science.
We have control of matter.
This century of steel is new, compared to thousands of years of history.
On every continent, a huge development is taking place.
The spirit spreads from people to people and progress precipitates its consequences.[42]

Figure 10

Figure 11

Card 2 (Figure 13):

Precision rules.
Economy directs.
We are led inexorably in a new direction.
Another epoch has begun.
In the pure atmosphere of calculation we find that spirit of clarity which animated the immortal past.
However, our laziness drags on our thoughts and actions: regrets, memories, suspicion, timidity, fear, inertia.[41]

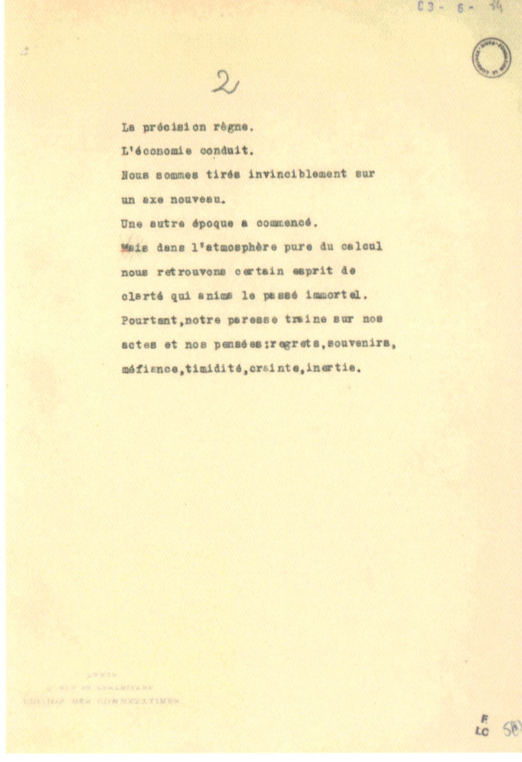

C3- 6- 34

2

La précision règne.
L'économie conduit.
Nous sommes tirés invinciblement sur un axe nouveau.
Une autre époque a commencé.
Mais dans l'atmosphère pure du calcul nous retrouvons certain esprit de clarté qui anime le passé immortel.
Pourtant, notre paresse traine sur nos actes et nos pensées: regrets, souvenirs, méfiance, timidité, crainte, inertie.

Figure 13

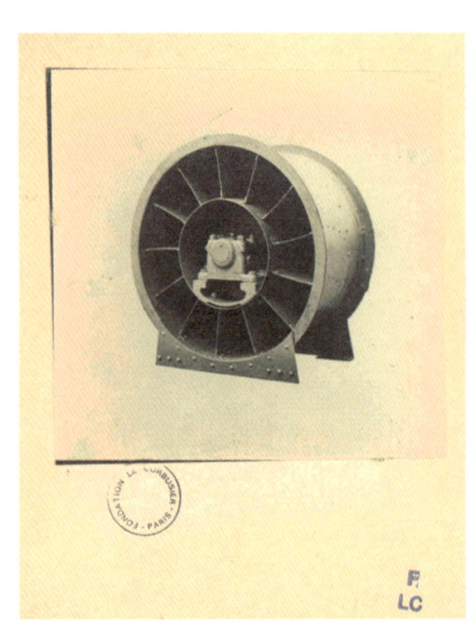

Figure 12

Figure 10

The transporter bridge, Marseilles. Post card in Le Corbusier's collection (FLC L5(6)9).

Figure 11

Propellers (FLC).

Figure 12

Photo of industrial ventilator, pasted onto a sheet as one of a series of images for the lectures (FLC C3(6)92).

Figure 13

Caption card 2 for the 'films' (FLC C3(6)34).

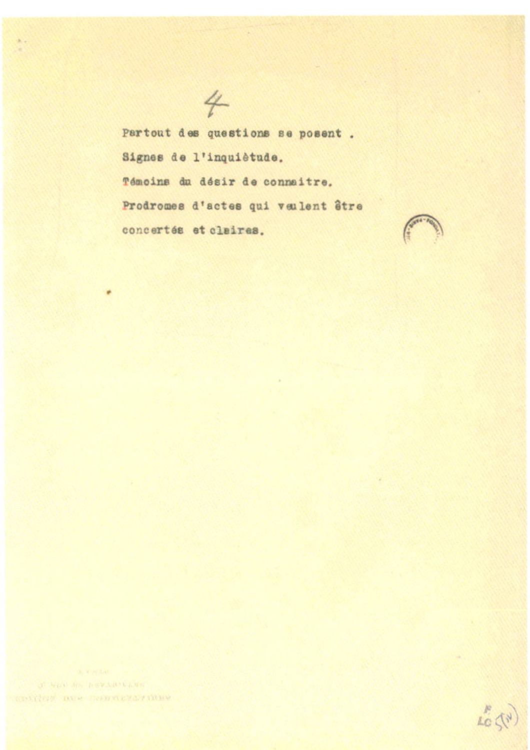
4

Partout des questions se posent .
Signes de l'inquiètude.
Témoins du désir de connaître.
Prodromes d'actes qui veulent être concertés et claires.

Figure 14

Card 4 (Figure 14):

Everywhere, questions are being asked.
Signs of anxiety.
Evidence of a need to understand.
Precursors of actions which should be clear and coordinated.[43]

Figure 15

Figure 16

Figure 14

Caption card 4 for the 'films' (FLC C3(6)36).

Figure 15

G. Sohier, Airship hangar, Issy-Les-Moulineaux. From Le Corbusier's collection of postcards (FLC L5(5)206).

Figure 16

Paris metro in construction.
From Le Corbusier's collection of postcards (FLC L5(6)160).

Figure 17

Caption card 5 for the 'films' (FLC C3(6)37).

Card 5 (Figure 17):

Man is left gasping.
His heart, which is still human, searches for emotion beyond the utilitarian, aspires to disinterested satisfaction.
From these new events is born a violent and radiant poetry.
The heart struggles to associate these brutal facts to the deep-rooted and intimate laws of emotion.[44]

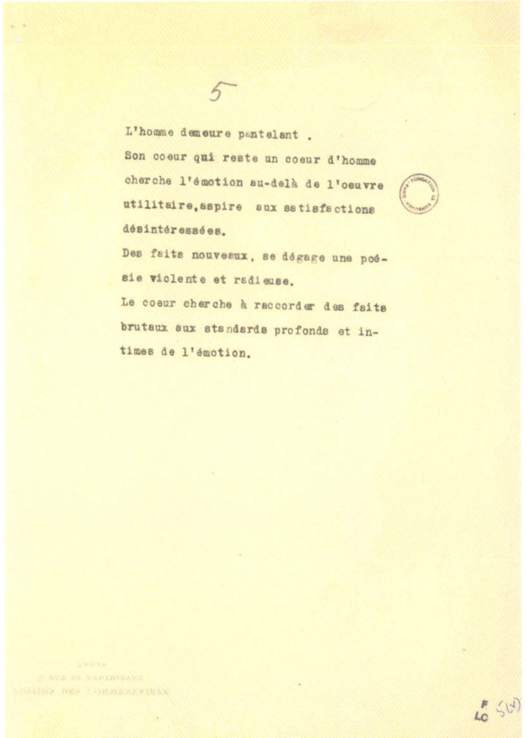
5

L'homme demeure pantelant .
Son coeur qui reste un coeur d'homme cherche l'émotion au-delà de l'oeuvre utilitaire,aspire aux satisfactions désintéressées.
Des faits nouveaux, se dégage une poésie violente et radieuse.
Le coeur cherche à raccorder des faits brutaux aux standards profonds et intimes de l'émotion.

Figure 17

> today. Discordant relationships because we are in a discordant world, cutting ourselves off from tradition, a world giving birth in pain and contortion. But everything confirms that as we leave the age-old harmonies, we are advancing towards a magnificent new future, in which a new order will create new works, a new generation, new surroundings, a new architecture.[39]

As this highly evocative fragment reveals, Le Corbusier's shock tactics, with his 'films', was intended to demonstrate the discordant state of a society in transition between the traditional order and a machinist world. This is a sophisticated manipulation of rhetoric.

The groups of photographic images constituted both the premise of his argument and its proof: they represent the 'facts' (the effects of the machine age), but their juxtaposition also gave them the capacity to provoke an understanding, among his audience, that their 'spirit' (or we might say in this context, 'taste') had been changed by the new events. A few of the images projected as part of the 'films' were reprinted in the *Bulletin* which reproduced in its entirety the lecture at the Salle Rapp (Fig 18).[45] These pictures were clearly selected by Le Corbusier to demonstrate the 'heterogeneous' nature of the illustrations and their shock value, juxtaposing old and new, works of high

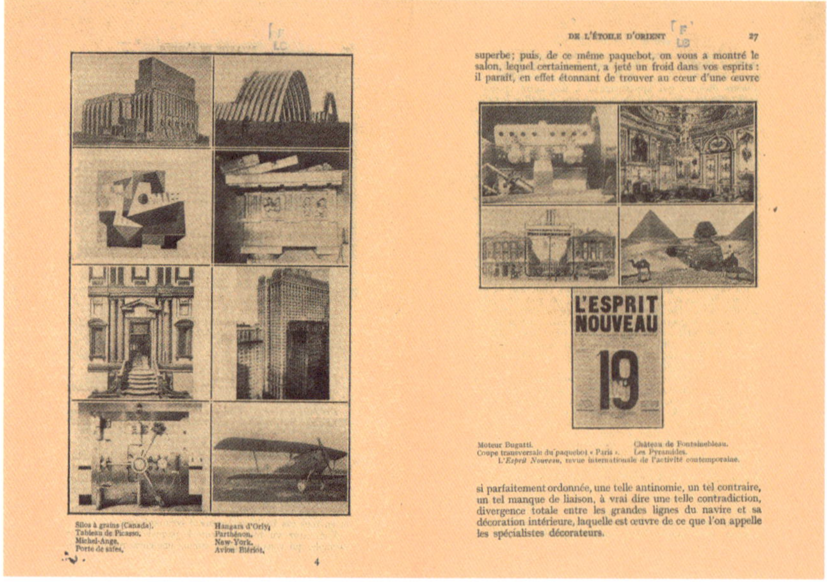

Silos à grains (Canada).
Tableau de Picasso.
Michel-Ange.
Porte de safes.

Hangars d'Orly.
Parthénon.
New-York.
Avion Blériot.

4

DE L'ÉTOILE D'ORIENT 27

superbe; puis, de ce même paquebot, on vous a montré le salon, lequel certainement, a jeté un froid dans vos esprits : il paraît, en effet étonnant de trouver au cœur d'une œuvre

Moteur Bugatti. Château de Fontainebleau.
Coupe transversale du paquebot « Paris ». Les Pyramides.
L'Esprit Nouveau, revue internationale de l'activité contemporaine.

si parfaitement ordonnée, une telle antinomie, un tel contraire, un tel manque de liaison, à vrai dire une telle contradiction, divergence totale entre les grandes lignes du navire et sa décoration intérieure, laquelle est œuvre de ce que l'on appelle les spécialistes décorateurs.

Figure 18
Two pages from the *Bulletin de l'Ordre de l'Etoile d'Orient*, March 1925, showing some of the images projected during the 1924 lectures.

architecture and functional engineering. For those with knowledge of Le Corbusier's ideas, it is clear that both categories of image were, for him, admirable; in both he found the clear, ordered geometric forms he admired.

This is different from the other tactic he often employed, which was to contrast images of 'good' and 'bad' work (Fig 23). This kind of contrast, too, was

39/FLC C3(8)70.

40/FLC C3(6)33.

41/FLC C3(6)34.

42/FLC C3(6)35.

43/FLC C3(6)36.

44/FLC X1(3)64, pp. 24-26.

45/Le Corbusier, 'L'esprit nouveau en Architecture', *op. cit.*

a classic technique of rhetoric which Le Corbusier used to good effect, often producing a violent response from his audience.

The critique of Léandre Vaillant

Le Corbusier selected the sequences of images in his 'films' according to two main principles. We know this because the perceptive and hostile critic Léandre Vaillant, writing under the pseudonym Léandre Vincent, wrote a review of the Sorbonne lecture in the *Paris Journal* on 20 June 1924.[46] Vaillant begins his article like this:

> I went to hear Monsieur Le Corbusier speak at the Sorbonne on architecture and on the "esprit nouveau". His presentation was preceded by a pictorial preamble. He organized his slide projections according to the illustration plan established by the journal L'Esprit Nouveau. This journal presents a tractor opposite a royal carriage, the bridge over the Hudson opposite Notre Dame Cathedral in Paris, and I know not what. The lecturer replaced the juxtaposition by a rapid succession of contradictory images. However, this intermittence seemed as eloquent as the page layout mentioned above. Its effect on the audience, resolutely sympathetic to the lecturer's argument, was visible and immediate.[47]

In the case of the lecture at the Salle Rapp, equally, the slide projection sequence also took place at the outset, apparently without any commentary, and divided into sequences by the five caption cards. Only after the long sequence of pictures did Le Corbusier begin his commentary:

> You have just seen projected onto the screen a heterogeneous sequence of images; this sequence, perhaps shocking for some of you, at any rate striking, constitutes the more or less everyday spectacle of our lives. We are in a situation where we are constantly presented with such troubling innovations, such dramatic contrasts, that we feel harassed and at the least strongly disturbed.

Figure 19
The ocean liner *Paris* (illustrated by Amédée Ozenfant in his critique of the Salon d'Automne (*L'Esprit Nouveau*, 13, December 1921).

46/Léandre Vincent, «Divagations intempestives», *Paris Journal*, 20 June 1924 (FLC C3(6)38), see Appendix, p. 205 for the complete text.

47/*Ibid.*

For example, you saw just now the ocean liner *Paris* which struck you as a remarkable thing, superb **(Fig 19)**. Then, from the same liner, I showed you the salon which certainly sent a chill through you **(Fig 20)**. It seems astonishing to discover at the heart of such a perfectly organized work such an antinomy, such a contrast, so great a lack of relationship, to tell the truth such a contradiction, a total divergence between the great lines of the ship and its interior decoration. The former is the precise product of engineers; the latter is the work of what are called specialist decorators.
Similarly, you will have seen rooms from the Châteaux of Fontainebleau and Compiègne **(Fig 21)** as well as the Colonna Gallery in Rome. These are famous works, brimming with quality of different kinds, which belong to a different era. If you compare them with what constitutes the essence of life today, these works appear shocking and out of place, inducing us to think that we must look elsewhere in our search for examples to learn from. Now, in our schools of art and architecture, the only education we give our young people is that based on the works of yesteryear, so it is easy to understand the confusion they feel and the absolute sense of crisis which forms the context of our struggle.
Next, I showed you the interiors of some American banks **(Fig 22)**. They are so precise, so clean, so functional that we might almost be ready to find them beautiful. The architect responsible for them is certainly a talented man who appears to have been inspired by logic and a great clarity of spirit. Now, in *The Bankers Magazine*, in which these works were published, this same man published an invitation to the readers to come and visit him and, to whet their appetite, could think of nothing better than to publish a picture of his own office. And here, in this photograph, we can see a room furnished with Renaissance tallboys and chests and even, in a corner, a suit of armour, hallebard in hand, a huge Louis XIII table with great turned and sculpted feet, some tapestries… The man capable of furnishing his room like this is the same man who designed the bank interiors, those works of purest logic! There's your contradiction.[48]

Figure 20
Promenade deck of the *Paris* compared with its Art Deco interior (staircase by Edgar Brandt) (from Le Corbusier, *L'Art décoratif d'aujourd'hui*, 1926).

It is clear from this explanation that Le Corbusier's aim with his slide projections, was to point up the contradiction between machine age realism (ocean liner, American banks) and the escapism of architects into the styles of the past (the liner's interior and the architect's office). The juxtaposition of 'good' versus 'bad' had been a leitmotiv of *L'Esprit Nouveau* magazine from its origins (Fig 23).

48/Le Corbusier 'L'esprit nouveau en architecture', *op. cit.*, pp. 26-28.

Figure 21

Tapestry Gallery, Château de Compiègne, from Le Corbusier's collection of postcards (FLC L5(5)142).

For example, the 'decorative' artists Monet and Rodin are unfavorably contrasted with a Cubist painting by Picasso and an African sculpture. On the bottom row, the choice of images suggests that the value of Seurat's work derives from its simplicity and clarity of form, comparable to Antique Greek sculpture. In a similar vein, the noble works of classicism and the Baroque are compared with 'what constitutes the essence of life today'. When Le Corbusier was giving this particular lecture, on 10 November, he had already read Léandre Vaillant's review.

But Vaillant's critique goes further than Le Corbusier himself in explaining the rhetorical techniques of the 'films'. For Vaillant identifies two techniques. The first is antithesis – the kind of binary opposition discussed above – which he identifies as typical of Romanticism. The second involves setting up a sequence of images of a similar kind which is then interrupted by something very different. This is how he described these two techniques:

> After the projection of the first two slides, I was able to classify his system. He doesn't use logic, but a form of stark suggestion. He doesn't prove, he strikes. He advances using regular coupling of antitheses. Antithesis is, like analogy, a philosophical formula used in the search for truth. It is an element of rhetoric: most moving, most effective for dazzling the crowds. Demagogy has no time for syllogism. It thrives in the game of violent contrast. Indeed, antithesis is the essence of the romantic style. A novel by Victor Hugo is always characterized by the development of an antithesis. The more distant the two terms, the more striking the effect. Example: "Beautiful is Ugly".The series of slides used by M. Lecorbusier [sic] to captivate his audience could have the same title as the prologue of "Notre Dame de Paris": "ceci tuera cela" ["this will kill that").
> Then the architect modifies the rhythm, until then binary - image against image - of his slide show; after a series of illustrations of the same order, three or four, ocean liner, aeroplane, engine, it suddenly shows an isolated and

Figure 22

Door of a safe vault (*L'Esprit Nouveau*, 18, November 1923).

Si Claude Monet est déjà périmé, c'est qu'il a méconnu la physique de la plastique. Rodin idem.

MAUVAIS
(Monnet)

MAUVAIS
(Rodin)

BON
(Juan Gris)

BON
(Nègre

Photo Léonce ROSENBERG.

Photo Paul GUILLAUME.

BON
(Seurat)

BON
(Grec

Photo DRUET.

completely different picture: the gallery of the Château of Fontainebleau. This provokes sniggering. Why? Because our understanding of Renaissance architecture and our sense of decoration have withered; they cannot be assimilated by people today? Of course not! This is a nervous reflex to a demonstration of opposites, the result of a psychological calculation that is applicable when needed. Were one to show on screen, after five of six specimens of she-apes borrowed from the Zoo, a figurine by Maillol, or after so many models of sanitary hardware, the Egytian bread-bearer from the Louvre, the surprise would provoke laughter. You allow the audience to associate similar perceptions, shown in a series, you create inertia, then you break the thread and before the mind can free itself to accommodate the unexpected, laughter erupts! Another form of suggestion.[49]

This analysis by Vaillant is very convincing. You only have to imagine the kind of effect Vaillant describes to understand its potential. On a layout in the *Bulletin de l'Ordre de l'Etoile d'Orient* on the right, Le Corbusier juxtaposes a room from Fontainebleau with a Bugatti engine (Fig 18)**. We must assume that in the lecture, these two images were only part of a sequence of works of engineering, of the kind Vaillant describes, interrupted by a picture of Fontainebleau. And, for an example of a similar sequence in *L'Esprit Nouveau* we could cite a double spread where a series of academic designs on the left – labeled 'a badly framed problem' – is interrupted by an image of a Farman Goliath airplane** (Fig 24)**.**[50]

Le Corbusier himself gave a slightly different account of the effect produced by the Fontainebleau sequence, during his lecture at Lausanne:

You saw a set of images in the slide projection earlier: you saw the ocean liner *Paris* and then its drawing room, its dining room, its panelling.
When you were shown the Château of Fontainebleau which is nonetheless a thing of beauty, you expressed the feeling of distance that now separates you from this aesthetic ideal and from the feelings that inspired the people who created this building.
I was in Geneva, in completely different surroundings, showing the same set of slides, which provoked a completely different effect, when the view of Fontainebleau was projected, instead of your laughter, there was the customary admiration at the sight of a beautiful thing.[51]

For Le Corbusier, the reaction to the Château of Fontainebleau – 'distance' or 'traditional admiration' – was a sign of the difference between acceptance or rejection of the new spirit: Lausanne's modernity as against traditionalist Geneva. Was he unaware of the rhetorical effect of these image sequences on his audience ? His articulate discussion of them would indicate otherwise.

Figure 23

Page from *L'Esprit Nouveau* contrasting 'bad' art (Monet, Rodin) with 'good' art (Gris, African sculpture, Seurat, Greek sculpture) (*L'Esprit Nouveau*, 1, October 1920, p. 45)

49/Léandre Vincent, «Divagations intempestives», *Paris Journal*, 20 June 1924 (FLC C3(6)38).

50/*L'Esprit Nouveau*, 9, pp. 986-987.

51/FLC C3(6)17, see Appendix p. 201-202.

Vaillant ploughed on, criticizing the 'hyperbole' of the orator, accusing him of confusing measures of quantity with those of value. Le Corbusier loved to compare the size of an ocean liner with buildings that everyone recognized. He did it in *L'Esprit Nouveau* and evidently also in his Sorbonne lecture (Fig 25)**. Vaillant explained:**

> But here is a picture showing that evidently the length of the ocean liner *France* is greater than the height of the Great Pyramid at Giza and the height of the ship is greater than that of the Arc de Triomphe. Another symptom of the malaise of Romanticism! The pathos of size, the prestige of quantity! For the clear-headed aesthetician, grandeur resides in the rhythm of the relationship between the elements, it is based on a sense of proportion. The diagram of the huge liner confers no grandeur. A 50 cm study by Maillol (as I have already mentioned him) can have grandeur. The slide projection of a New York "*skyscraper*" (*in English in the text*) showing off its forty storeys is merely sensationalism – gone cold though, for having been served up so often. And then, it's good on the screen. Do we really see a skyscraper? No more than a pilot flying over a forest would enjoy its shade. The evocation of mass or figures with multiple zeros, the shock effect of fabulous statistics, here we have other methods handed down from erstwhile romanticism to present-day advertising, the last refuge of imagination gone mad. In rhetoric, this use of the superlative overdrive is called hyperbole.[52]

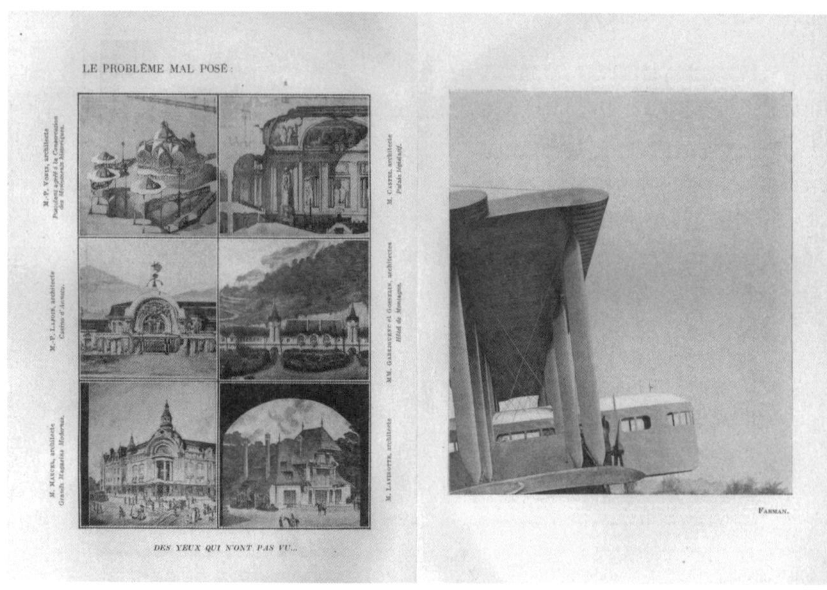

Figure 24
Spread from *L'Esprit Nouveau*, 9, June 1921.

52/Vincent, *op. cit.*

This critique gets to the heart of Le Corbusier's logic. It is clear that the choice and organization of images were not intended only to illustrate the 'facts' of the machine age world. They served to stir the emotions: shock, admiration, derision or respect. On the other hand, they also led to misunderstandings. Le Corbusier did not believe that large scale was a measure of value.

Over and above the precious documentation of what the 'films' consisted of, Vaillant's commentary gives us a unique insight into the impression Le Corbusier made as a speaker. Vaillant goes on:

> Once the slides have been projected, M. Le Corbusier starts to speak. His delivery is spare, flat, with humorous asides carefully deployed. His dogmatism is that of the sermon rather than the ritual of the mass. No decoration on the roof, nor incense on the altar; he is sententious and cold. But the discourse of this builder is so badly constructed!

Figure 25
The ocean liner *Aquitania* of the Cunard Line, juxtaposed with Notre Dame, the Tour St Jacques, the Porte St Denis and the Opéra, in Paris (*L'Esprit Nouveau*, 8, May 1921).

> Is this promoter of impersonal art, of ne varietur mass-produced building, not affected by that human frailty, personal pride? For he overturns the fundamental problems of aesthetics and, with childish self-confidence – this is likeable because natural – emphasizes his own experiments and solutions concerning minor details.[53]

Vaillant's evidence is also valuable because it demonstrates that Le Corbusier did not always explain himself at all clearly. Although he always tried to insist on the importance of the aesthetic dimension and repeatedly argued against functionalism, his continual use of images of machines and industrial buildings and his stress on 'types' led to a certain ambiguity. Vaillant seemed to think that Le Corbusier advocated strict functionalism, and Le Corbusier could not let that ride. Vaillant wrote:

> According to him, the machine is our professor of aesthetics. The house that he wishes to build is no more than a "machine for living". "Beauty is created by the function of efficiency. The maximum result from the minimum of means, form determined imperatively by the materials

53/*Ibid.*

> used", such is the teaching of mechanization. The regular workings of mechanical force have as their corollary the production of geometric shapes. From this arises a doctrine of symmetry, balance and stability. At the basis of a construction built according to the spirit of the machine, one finds a form-type, a tectonic dominant or element which is a prefiguration of the whole and determines all the spatial ratios: the "regulating line". At least this is how I understood the lecturer. If we build our dwellings according to the mechanical and economic imperatives they will "ex ipso" follow primary geometric forms. And, as if by the action of some automatic trigger, beauty will appear.[54]

On 3 July, Le Corbusier replied to his aggressor, citing this passage:

> I said the contrary and I repeat it each time I talk about architecture. I wrote about it, in three chapters of my book *Vers une architecture*: the three main chapters.[55]

And then he cited a string of his slogans stressing the importance of architecture above and beyond functionalism. He added:

> And to make this quite clear, [...] I placed at the very summit [of architecture]: the Parthenon, the vestibule of the Laurentiana Library by Michelangelo, another Parthenon, and my "film" ended with the 100 steps at Versailles and the Sphinx and Pyramids (**Figs 26-27**).[56]

Figure 26

Apse of St Peter's, Rome, included in the final sequence of his 'films' (*L'Esprit Nouveau*, 14, January 1922).

Figure 27

Parthenon, detail (*L'Esprit Nouveau*, 10, July 1921).

54/*Ibid.*

55/Le Corbusier, 'M. Le Corbusier répond', *Paris Journal*, 3 July 1924 (FLC C3(6)38). See the text in the Appendix, p. 207.

56/*Ibid.*

Figure 28

The staircase of the 100 steps, Versailles (FLC).

He also cited his fifth caption card: 'Man is left gasping. [...] His heart searches for emotion beyond the utilitarian work.'

Vaillant had gone on to put into Le Corbusier's mouth the suggestion that the Parthenon could be understood as nothing more than an arrangement of pure and functional forms and thus could be compared with any other form:

> Your washroom, vertical walls, horizontal floor and ceiling, is more beautiful than the Parthenon because it is more pure in form. It is a Parthenon. And it is very good of M. Le Corbusier to mention the Parthenon.
> And this is where the error shows up; without enlightening the blind. Conformity to function is not beauty itself; it is only a premise of beauty. Beauty starts where function has been achieved or superseded. It is the result of a disinterested play of forms; the creative instinct determines its configuration and reduces resistance to matter.[57]

And Le Corbusier responded angrily to this:

> Mr Vincent, do you really take me for an absolute idiot?[58] I have always insisted that the Parthenon is the most overwhelming example of architectural beauty. And if I can talk about it it's because I took the trouble (and joy) to go and see for myself; and for four weeks. I know what it stands for and what it's made of. The end of my book is dedicated to the Parthenon.[59]

What is remarkable about this exchange is that much of the discussion is not about verbal arguments, but about a selection of images, the 'films'. Following on from the 'arguments' in the 'films', Le Corbusier deployed his more formal explanation of the *Zeitgeist* theory.

> An *Esprit Nouveau* [new spirit] that is more powerful than race and stronger than the influence of geographical

57/Vincent, *op. cit.*

58/ Le Corbusier, 'M. Vincent, me prenez-vous décidemment pour un noc fini?' 'Noc' is Parisian *verlan*, i.e. backwards slang.

59/Le Corbusier, *op. cit.*

conditions is passing over all our customs and traditions and is spreading all over the world with clearly defined and unifying characteristics.
These characteristics are [more] universal and human than ever, although the gulf separating the old society from the mechanized society has also never been so wide.
One century (this last century) contrasts with the 400 previous centuries. The machine founded on calculations [derived from the laws of nature, has established, in opposition to the possible wanderings of the mind] ensures the coherent system of the laws of physics; the machine imposes its consequences upon our [existence and forcing] our spirit towards purity [modifies the framework of our lives. The gap is a huge and growing one] between two generations.
We should stop in front of this chasm and think carefully before seeking a way through the confusion of a difficult and widespread crisis.
Revolutions are not only carried out with guns and bloodshed, one can see many examples in history of complete transformations, one can witness the complete destruction of a spirit and the accession of another spirit and another culture; for example, in our country in the XIth century we saw the disappearance of the Mediterranean spirit, driven out by the spirit of the North, we can see the consequences of this accession and, in the order of things that interest us, complete modification of the forms that shaped our surroundings.
Not only have everyday [architectural] forms been transformed by this spirit, but the consequences have been far-reaching and have affected even everyday objects; the landscape itself has changed.
The follow-on of centuries of work by what we call culture was necessary to rediscover elements of Mediterranean culture, towards which we are once again directing our attention.[60]

The role of drawing

Figure 29
Le Corbusier, second page of notes for the Lausanne lecture on 18 February 1924 (FLC C3(6)29).

Part of this argument is reproduced in note form on the second of the pages of preparatory notes (Fig 29).[61] This page is interesting in showing the transition from verbal argument to visual demonstration. The little sketches represent demonstrations which Le Corbusier would draw on the blackboard. The first row illustrates the 'annihilation of a Mediterranean spirit, driven out by a new spirit from the North'. We can recognize a Gothic window, on the left, contrasted with the Romanesque portal of the Cathedral of Clermont-Ferrand. Le Corbusier worked up these arguments in an article with a virtually identical title in April 1924.[62] In the article, Le Corbusier described the consequences of the arrival of Gothic as

60/Stenographic typescript of the lecture at Lausanne, 18 February 1924 (FLC C3(6)14-23). Gaps in this typescript have been completed from the manuscript notes (FLC C3(6) 24) between square parentheses (see Appendix, pp. 200 and 198-199).

61/FLC C3(6)29.

62/*L'Esprit Nouveau*, 22, April 1924. The portal of Clermont-Ferrand Cathedral featured as the header illustration.

S2

C3- 6-
29

Les revolutions ne se font pas par à coups de fusil et dans le sang versé

On a assisté à diverses reprises dans l'histoire à l'anéantissement de l'esprit et d'une culture et à l'avènement d'un autre esprit et d'une autre culture

Par ex : l'Esprit du Nord contre Méditerranée XI siècle.

Conséquence : système des formes (choses villes paysages) ont changé

Il faudra des siècles de travail pour retrouver les lumières de la culture méditerranéen

S3

Mantelets

1 la forme fondamentale

2 le paysage urbain

LC

Nous sommes comme les touristes dans un paquebot

F
LC

B) vers le pur, de l'esprit contre la pratique Fonctionnaliste

il y a un effort de l'intelligence pour atteindre malgré les difficultés, un stade antérieur

Bramante
M-Ange
Palladio

'immense'. For centuries, he says, 'Latin clarity and Hellenic purity' disappeared under the tortuous and complicated forms of Gothic. Only now are the 'clarity of intelligence' and the 'joys of sunlight' being rediscovered. The new spirit is one of the orthogonal. His Lausanne audience would have certainly understood this in terms of tensions between French and German Switzerland.

On the right, a Gothic cityscape in silhouette is set against a view of the Romanesque Duomo and Baptistery of Pisa. Two little supplementary sketches are very revealing. Above the Gothic cityscape, a sketch compares a house with a pointed roof and two fir trees, suggesting that the 'Northern' spirit was in part a product of the landscape. On the right, Pisa is associated with a Provencal *mas* (farmhouse) with its almost flat roof and sunny climate. Le Corbusier believed that farmhouses of this kind in the region of his native La Chaux-de-Fonds were built by refugees from the South of France, thus allowing him to see, in the contrast between roof profiles, a struggle with both racial and topographic roots.

He captions these sketches: 'We are like coal-trimmers in an ocean liner'; in other words, we don't see what's going on. According to Le Corbusier, only the prophets and the poets can read the signs of the transformation of the world and the arrival of the new spirit.

Below, he sketches a sequence of roof profiles, from pointed Gothic, via Renaissance (with the pitched roof hidden behind a parapet), to the flat roof dictated by the use of a reinforced concrete structure. This choreographic sequence of sketches creates its own, purely visual, argument, as if progressively flattening itself according to some inner dynamic.

> It is, precisely, the object of this evening's talk to demonstrate that progress – the consequence of science – leads us directly to this constructional system.
> The reinforced concrete slab responds automatically, and without technical problems, to an orthogonal mentality [*état d'esprit*] which has always been an objective over the centuries as culture has evolved in our country.[63]

Sometimes, on the other hand, the sketches served as indexical signs or mnemonics to verbal arguments, rather than as visual arguments in themselves. In his notes and sketches, Le Corbusier referred to ideas already well rehearsed in the pages of *L'Esprit Nouveau* (the articles written between 1920-22 which were republished as *Vers une architecture* in October 1923). On one sheet, he assembled all the arguments for the rest of his lecture (Fig 30).[64] Starting top right: the history of the window, the development of the wall, his claims for the universal laws of physiology, the Platonic solids, the comparison of the traditional house with its paralyzed plan compared to the modern reinforced concrete section with its 'free plan'. All you need is familiarity with the text of *Vers une architecture* to fill out this program with over an hour of demonstrations. Windows and walls, like roof profiles, change automatically in response to new constructional techniques. Like a Darwinian natural selection, the new materials and constructional techniques dramatically alter architectural forms. An intriguing note – 'here a picture of Innovation' gives us pause. The 'Innovation' suitcase, with its hanging space and built-in drawers, often featured in Le Corbusier's lectures and in the pages of *L'Esprit Nouveau*.[65] For Le Corbusier, the 'Innovation' suitcase was an

63/FLC C3(6)16.

64/FLC C3(8)25 (top half of page, see Figure 36 for the lower half of this sheet).

65/See Stanislaus von Moos (1987). *L'Esprit Nouveau. Le Corbusier et l'industrie 1920-1925*, p. 270-271. In September 1923, Le Corbusier was negotiating with the Innovation company to create a set of advertisements (as well as 3,000 copies of a publicity brochure) for *L'Esprit Nouveau*. These advertisements contained slogans such as 'Furniture makes the home' (FLC A1(17)35 and 26).

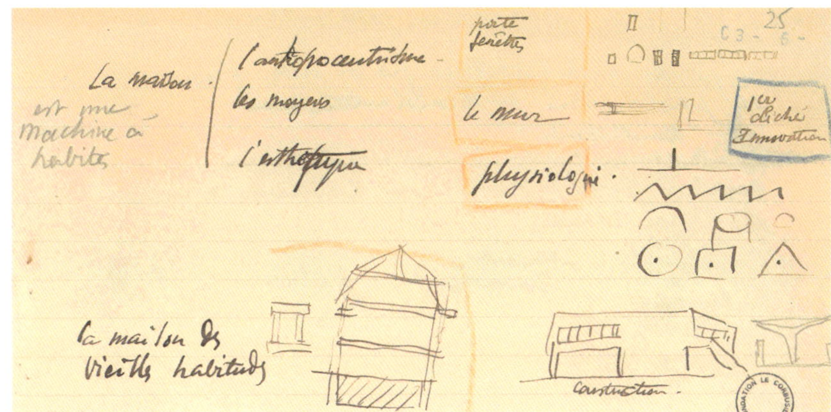

Figure 30
Third page of notes for the Lausanne lecture on 18 February 1924 (FLC C3(6)25 top half).

architectural metaphor: geometrically pure on the outside but rich and complex on the interior. In a letter to Madame Meyer, on 24 February 1926, Le Corbusier explained: 'Now, we have devised an architectural poem rather like an 'Innovation suitcase'. Open the case, the casket, and inside is a box of surprises.'[66]

The word 'physiology' refers to the theory of empathy which Le Corbusier and Ozenfant placed at the center of the theory of the Purism art movement. According to this theory, lines and shapes (indicated in the sketch by a series of wavy and zigzag lines) have a direct effect on the emotions. This is how Le Corbusier elaborated this part of the lecture at the Salle Rapp:

> This aesthetic needs some fundamental principles if it is to gain currency. What could these be?
> A useful point of departure is the physiology of sensations. This physiology of sensations is our sensory reaction in response to a given optic phenomenon. My eyes transmit to my senses the spectacle before them. Confronted by these various lines, which I am drawing on the blackboard, different sensations are generated. The difference between a broken or continuous line is enough to stimulate the heartbeat, in response to the shocking or soothing effect produced by the forms.
> Now, if we look into the effects on our sensibility of these physiological sensations, we begin to make distinctions: this broken line is unpleasant; this continuous line is pleasing; this jumble of lines disturbs us; this rhythmic composition calms us. You quickly realize that a choice has to be made, some preferences, and that you inevitably find yourself in the position of every artist, who has to select lines and forms which satisfy our senses.[67]

According to 'the lesson of Rome', the geometry of the Phileban solids has a universal aesthetic effect: the fundamental principles of beauty do not change across the centuries, despite the vagaries of fashion and taste. But this universal principle is modified by contingent culture and the impact of modernity. Le Corbusier

66/FLC H3(1)17.

67/Le Corbusier 'L'esprit nouveau en architecture', *op. cit.*, p. 44.

demonstrates this, at the foot of the page, by contrasting 'the old-fashioned house' with a Corbusean design. This turns out to be the 'Type A' concrete house designed for Henri Frugès in December 1923.[68]

Le Corbusier usually deployed images as part of an argument of inductive logic: observations of nature or architectural history are cited as evidence in support of an argument. Thus, addressing his Swiss audience in Lausanne, Le Corbusier developed his argument on the physiology of sensations by drawing on the cultural tension between French (Mediterranean) and German (Nordic) cultural sensibilities. Amazingly, he does this, not by comparing Gothic and Romanesque (or Classical) buildings, but by contrasting the profiles of different mountain ranges facing the Swiss on the South shore of lake Geneva (Fig 31)**. This is how the stenographer transcribed his words:**

> Here is a country, a beautiful country.
> The site[69] has even become famous, houses such as these are built there:
> a country where the late summer has a very romantic feel to it.[70]

As can be seen from the sketch (Fig 31)**, the jagged profile of the landscape which he draws on the left is that of the picturesque 'Dents du Midi' (southern teeth) on the South East corner of lake Geneva.[71] He went on to associate this picturesque profile with 'a previous generation' (under the sway of the Romantic movement promoted by the English and the Germanic Swiss). The North East shore, from Montreux to Vevey, had been developed in the nineteenth century as a tourist site by the English, French and Germans. Gustave Courbet lived for a while in the town of La Tour de Peilz, where he designed a fountain called 'Liberty'. Gustave Eiffel came here for a while after 1887.[72] Le Corbusier's lecture notes continue:**

> Next to this first mountain [the "Dents du Midi"] there are some other mountains with quite a different silhouette.

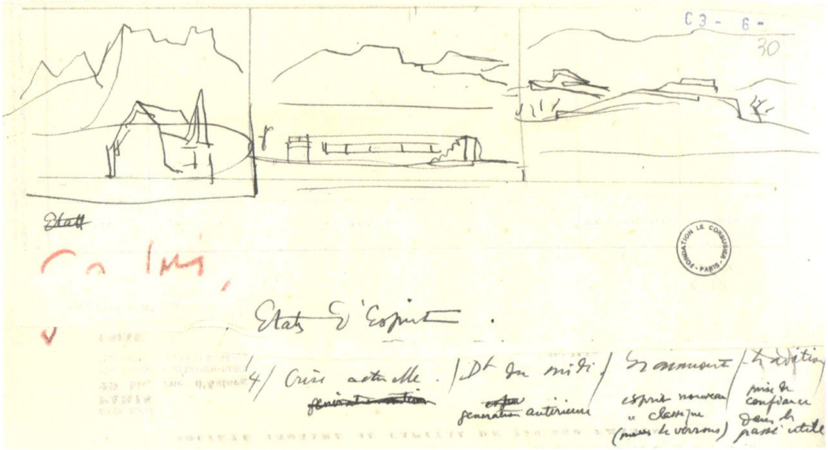

Figure 31
Le Corbusier's preparatory sketches on the theme of 'states of mind', comparing three views of lake Geneva: the mountain range known as the Dents du Midi, the Gramont (with the design for the little house for his parents in the foreground) and the landscape around Rivaz, February 1924 (FLC C3(6)30).

68/Le Corbusier designed this for three houses at Lège, near Bordeaux, and reused the plan for his housing scheme for the Peugeot automobile company at Audincourt. The only house of this kind actually constructed was the 'prototype house' built in the yard of the Tonkin factory belonging to Henri Frugès, the so-called 'Tonkin house'. See Tim Benton, 'Pessac and Lège revisited: standards dimensions and failures', *Massilia* (Barcelona), 2, 2004, pp. 64-99. The houses built at Lège in 1924-25 werde designed by Henri Frugès himself.

69/He may have been thinking of Jean-Jacques Rousseau who spent some time at Clarens and who praised the spirit of liberty in the Swiss cantons on the North shore of lake Geneva. Victor Hugo also lived here for a while, as well as Gustave Courbet.

70/FLC C3(6)16.

71/This distinctive profile appears in many of the sketches of lake Geneva by Le Corbusier. Morgens Krustrup has suggested that

> There is also a new generation which is bored by that mountain [the "Dents du Midi"]. But just next to it is a mountain range [the Gramont] with a superb profile which calls to mind some fundamentals: the calming configuration of the horizon. And it is in front of this mountain that I am building a house just now, which looks like this.[73]

In this middle sketch, Le Corbusier drew the smooth profile of the Gramont mountain, and he captioned this sketch 'the new spirit, a classical [spirit] (as we'll see)'. Facing it, he drew the elevation of the house 'Le Lac' which he was designing for his parents at this time at Corseaux (Fig 33).

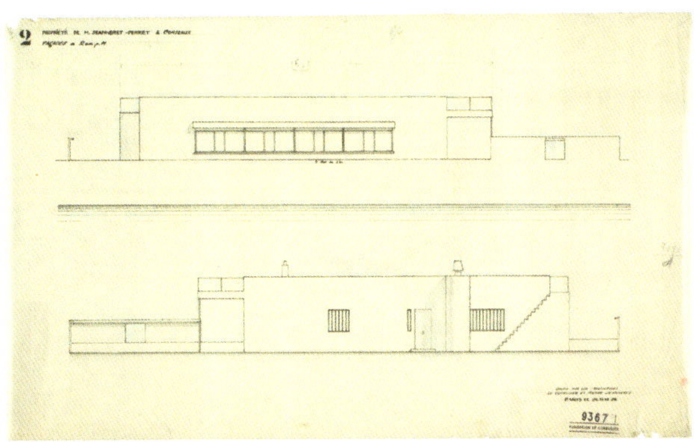

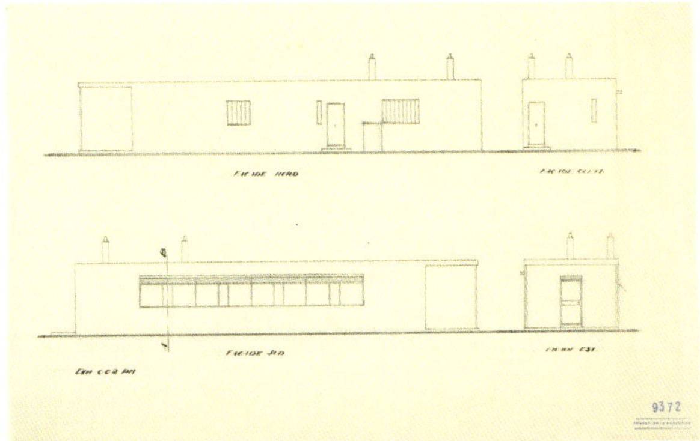

Figure 32
North and South elevations of 'Le Lac', 25 May 1924 (FLC 9367).

Figure 33
North and South elevations of the little house for his parents 'Le Lac' on the North shore of lake Geneva, January 1924 (FLC 9372).

This sketch, in which he combined aspects of the North and South elevations, shows the design in a form similar to the contract drawings of 25 May 1924.[74] Characteristic of this project was the external staircase giving access to the roof on the North West corner (Fig 32). **It is distinctly different to the drawings prepared in January for the first set of contract tenders, in which this external staircase does not appear** (Fig 33).[75] **But the sketch shares with this earlier project the low profile, the roof terrace lacking the low parapet of the later project. It is consistent therefore to consider this little sketch as belonging to an intermediary phase between January and May.**

The sketch on the right (Fig 31) **shows the steep slopes of Rivaz, with its precipitous vineyards. Here he noted: 'Tradition: the confidence derived from past utility.' It is clear that Le Corbusier admired the terraces built by the monks in the Middle Ages. On another sketch he wrote: 'Man and landscape; man makes the landscape; the landscape of lake Geneva, all made by hand, at Rivaz'.[76] He was fascinated by the blending of natural and man-made forms. Among the papers for the Lausanne lecture is another sketch of the spectacular Rivaz landscape where, once again, Le Corbusier tried to analyze the relationship between natural forms and artificial construction** (Fig 34 and Fig 35).[77] **Below this sketch he rehearses once again the historicist argument of the *Zeitgeist* using the example of the window to trace the evolution from the vertical to the horizontal window.**

For Le Corbusier, the *Zeitgeist* could be tested as much by a particular appreciation of landscape as the consequences of a system of construction. By

the Dents du Midi inspired the motif of the Open Hand (conversation with the author, 25 September 2004, Paris).

72/See *Album La Roche*, op. cit., pp. 67-69 and Gubler, J. (1977). 'Les Identités d'une région', *Werk-Archithese*, vol. 6, p. 3-8.

73/FLC C3(6)17.

74/The numbered set of 25 May 1924 was prepared for the second set of tenders (FLC 9365, 9367, 9368, 9369, 9374, 9385, etc.

75/The drawings for the first project, published in December 1923, include FLC 9366, 9418 and 9417. The first set of contract drawings, produced at the end of December or the first week of January, include FLC 9370, 9371, 9372, 9399, 9414, 9415, 9373, 9363, 9359.

76/FLC C3(6)25.

77/Some of these sketches were based on the watercolours Le Corbusier made of this landscape for Raoul La Roche in 1921-22 (Le Corbusier, von Moos. *Album La Roche*).

C3 - 6 - 26
FONDATION LE CORBUSIER PARIS
le mur – projectio
FLC

contrast with the Romantic view of nature as sublime and terrifying, which he identified with the Dents du Midi, Le Corbusier saw in the profile of the Gramont a spirit both classical and modern. In this extraordinary passage of his lecture, Le Corbusier reveals landscape not only as a source of inspiration for architecture but in some sense its very content.[78] Returning now to the second page of his preparatory notes, the argument about landscape is developed in the lower half of the page (Fig 36).

Figure 35
The Rivaz landscape. The large house above the stone terraces was built after Le Corbusier's sketch (Photo Tim Benton 2005).

Figure 34
Le Corbusier, sketch for the Lausanne lecture, 18 February 1924, illustrating the countryside around Rivaz, on the North shore of lake Geneva, 1924 (FLC C3(6)26).

In a sketch on the left he gives graphic expression to the idea of a 'common harmonic measure – mountains, houses, physiology'. The jagged mountain profile corresponds to the pointed Gothic roofs dear to the Romantic imagination. On the right he sketches the calm mass of the Gramont above the lake and writes 'Orthogonality'. It becomes clear how, in Le Corbusier's mind, there was a relationship between these different natural profiles and the successive styles of architecture (Romanesque, Gothic, Renaissance).

Lower down he noted and underlined 'This site is a theatre – Karma; one must find the style of the theatrical box, that is to say of the house.' The Villa Karma, on this shoreline a few kilometres from Corseaux at Clarens, near Montreux, was partly designed and built by Adolf Loos between 1903 and 1906. It was Loos who wrote of the villa in the countryside being like a box at the opera. He meant by this that the box might well be small, but the view spectacular. The mysterious phrase 'the road surveyor at La Tour [de Peilz]', which appears several times in these notes, must refer to some conversation about the changing nature of the North shore of lake Geneva and the effect on it of new villas. On one of his pages of notes he wrote, 'The road surveyor of La Tour, precautionary measure after Karma'.[79] These comments can be compared to the article 'Architecture', in which Adolf Loos had condemned the villa created by an architect for ruining the natural landscape.[80] Perhaps Le Corbusier was reflecting on the fact that Loos's own Villa Karma was seen by some as ruining the landscape, prompting the establishment of 'precautionary measures' to protect the shoreline of lake Geneva. On one of his typed cards, Le Corbusier had earlier noted: 'The road surveyor at La Tour. The landscape ruined. The landscape created. Alexandre Cingria.'[81] Alexandre Cingria-Vaneyre was at the head of a movement to celebrate the Mediterranean culture within French Switzerland. On the recommendation of his

78/Le Corbusier developed this idea in his lecture 'Architecture en tout. Urbanisme en tout.', on 8 October 1929 in Buenos Aires (see Précisions, op. cit., p. 77-78).

79/FLC C3(6)28.

80/Adolf Loos, 'Architektur', first published as 'Über Architektur', *Der Sturm*, Berlin, 15 December 1910, reprinted in Adolf Opel (ed.) (1995). *Adolf Loos: Über Architektur. Ausgewählte Schriften*, Prachner, Vienna, pp. 75-86. Le Corbusier knew this article well.

81/FLC C3(6)84.

friend William Ritter, Le Corbusier had bought his copy of Cingria's book *Entretiens à la Villa du Rouet* in Geneva in October 1910 and read it avidly while working in the Berlin suburb of Neu-Babelsberg in the office of Peter Behrens.[82] Le Corbusier mirrored Cingria's arguments closely in his notes for the Lausanne lecture. 'Geneva must be Greco-Latin' had proclaimed Cingria (in the voice of one of his characters, Constance) and he had launched an attack against Northern Romanticism for having perverted the true Mediterranean spirit of classicism.

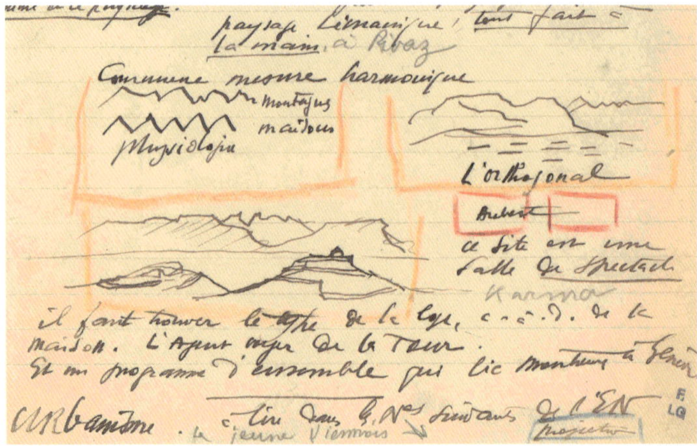

Figure 36
Lower half of the third page of preparatory notes for the lecture at Lausanne, 18 February 1924 (FLC C3(6)25 below).

On 23 November 1910, Le Corbusier had written out his conclusions on Cingria's work:

> […] absolutely agree with the brilliant spirit in general terms […]; this book has been a beneficial aid to my orientation. It provokes closer examination, the conclusions are reasonable, clear, luminous; for me, he loosens the German noose.[83]

Cingria had described the Jura countryside in classical terms, to be compared with Greece and the country around Istanbul, and had concluded that architecture should take its cue, in the direction of classicism, from the countryside. Behind Cingria's thinking lay the racial theories of the Comte de Gobineau, who believed that to each race belonged a particular landscape and a specific architectural style. But Cingria goes beyond race in his reasoning.[84] Cingria's character Gaudens explains why the people of French Switzerland 'had a latin character': 'I put it to you now that this isn't because we speak French in the Western cantons, but that the nature of the land and its climate determined which races came to live there and remain Latin.'[85] His conclusion was that, 'it is the regularity of the landscape which gives it the character you do not wish to define.'[86]

On the phrase 'the young Viennese', in pencil at the foot of his page of notes (Fig 36), we can glean some further information in a note of an exchange of views:

> Discussion with disenchanted young Viennese architect […] "Europe has had it". Not at all! The West alone is

82/Cingria-Vaneyre, A. (1908). *Entretiens de la Villa du Rouet*, see Turner, P. V. (1987). *La formation de Le Corbusier: idealisme et mouvement moderne*, Paris, Macula, pp. 91 and 214.

83/*Ibid*, p. 383.

84/Comte de Gobineau (1853). *Essai sur l'inegalité des races humaines*, Paris.

85/Cingria-Vaneyre. *Entretiens à la Villa du Rouet*, p. 89.

86/Ibid., p. 90.

> reasonable and rich enough in its traditions to be able to express the spirit of the age. America is too young. We have vast projects before us.[87]

After delivering his lecture in Lausanne and Geneva, Le Corbusier sums up for himself which direction the lecture should go in future:

> Lecture. The Lausanne plan was a good one. But do not forget the question of landscape architecture. Demand a large blackboard (slate). Furthermore: carry out by example a complete demonstration of the Besnus house on the blackboard. Plans, windows, etc., façades and regulating lines. Urban leaflets. Finish with urbanism slides, do not go into too much detail, but calmly and comfortably deliver the substance and make the link to the question of the dwelling. Specify "the fervour" (Paul Budry) of precise plans, exact prisms, of a worked out solution. Make an analysis of the Parthenon (details of mouldings); go to the Beaux-Arts Library (Giraudon) for the profiles.[88]

On 23 October 1923, after their visit to the Barberine dam, Le Corbusier had reflected on a criticism which his friend Paul Budry had made of him:

> Your purist asceticism leads you to reject the totally fulfilling life of the Baroque. You lose the sensuality of the Baroque. Reply: I took myself off to see the Parthenon and the apses of St Peter's, two purely Baroque events. The Baroque is the study of volumes and proportions rather than utilitarian problems.[89]

In the margin he added, 'Budry's fervour for the pure prisms of Corbu' and went on:

> If I search for purity of forms it is to get at the heart of the problem. It is not asceticism but a passion for the sensuality of forms in harmony. I prefer the Venus of Milo to a Hottentot fetish.[90]

It is interesting to see how Le Corbusier argues with someone even more ascetic than himself; he is coming out squarely in favour of the sensuality of form. Later, Paul Budry defended his friend against the virulent attacks of Alexander von Senger.[91] While criticizing von Senger for his inattention to the poetry and the formal richness of Le Corbusier's work, Budry also takes Le Corbusier to task for '[...] welding together poetry and technology. Architecture and construction and finally the mind and the machine [...] The machine, a phenomenon of our era, conspires to give us a taste for pure forms, rapid and economical. To argue from this that the age tends to 'machinalise' [sic '*machinaliser*'] the spirit is the opposite of the truth. It liberates us, rather, by freeing us from mechanical activities.'[92] This is a good example of the kind of difficulty which arises from the *Zeitgeist*

87/FLC C3(6)82.

88/FLC C3(6)27.

89/FLC C3(6)42.

90/*Ibid*.

91/P. Budry (10 April 1930). 'De l'Architecture considérée comme un des Beaux Arts'. This is about Alexander von Senger (1928). *Le Cheval de Troie du bolchevisme*.

92/*Ibid*, p. 1. And in a note he adds, 'As much as I applaud Le Corbusier when he calls for a break with the past and innovation, I hesitate when he seems to seriously think that things really work out like that'.

argument. It was not enough to persuade his audience that the machine had profoundly modified the world; the next step, that architecture should be transformed in a similar way, did not necessarily follow, as Budry pointed out. A reasonable response might be to say that if the machine had taken the drudgery out of manual tasks, more time would be left for spiritual things. Le Corbusier went on to demonstrate the principle of structural rationalism with a series of historical examples. This persuaded him that structural forms in architecture were determined by their historical context. All that remained to be proven was that 'the laws of beauty' were independent of 'the styles' of architecture and were based instead on fundamental laws of order and geometry. Pure and simple forms responded perfectly well to the machinist world. His peroration at the Salle Rapp, for which he was rewarded with strong applause, concluded like this:

> We will eventually achieve new forms of urban planning. Whether for Paris, London, Berlin, Moscow or Rome, these capitals must be totally transformed within their own confines, however much that will cost, however radical an upheaval it will cause. And here again, I repeat, the only possible guide will be the spirit of geometry.[93]

Figure 37
Le Corbusier's glass transparencies (FLC, photo Tim Benton).

The slide projection finale

Le Corbusier finished with a series of slides of his own work, essentially models and drawings in plan and perspective, always with an apology for showing his own work.

On a double page (Fig 40), he laid out some thumbnail sketches of images of his own projects.[94] These refer almost certainly to the sequence of glass lantern slides to project at the end of his lectures in 1924. Among the pictograms we can pick out a perspective of the Citrohan 1 houses (1920), a photo of the model of Citrohan 2 (1922), plans of the Immeubles-Villas apartment block (1922), the model of the Niestlé villa for Rambouillet (October 1923), the model of the La

Figure 38
Lantern slide of the model of the Niestlé villa, proposed for the forest of Rambouillet and exhibited at the Salon d'Automne, November 1923 (FLC).

93/Le Corbusier, 'L'esprit nouveau en architecture', *op. cit.*, p. 50.

94/FLC C3(6)56.

Roche house (October 1923), a perspective of the Besnus house (1922-23) and the Type A house for Lège (December 1923) and the Contemporary City for Three Million Inhabitants, with a plan showing it adapted to Paris (bottom right). Some of these glass plates still survive (Fig 38) and (Fig 39).

In 1924, transparencies played two quite distinct roles, at the beginning and end of his lectures. At the beginning, as we have seen, the transparencies presented images of the real world transformed by industrialization provoking the changes leading to the new spirit, displayed as a 'heterogeneous sequence of images' and without commentary. They thus helped establish the premise of the argument. At the end of the lectures, the images of Le Corbusier's own work demonstrated the effect of the new spirit on the work of the architect. They constitute the climax of the peroration, demanding applause from the audience.

Figure 39

Lantern slide of the Contemporary City for Three Million Inhabitants, 1922 (FLC).

By 1924, very few of Le Corbusier's buildings in his Purist manner had been completed, and so he was obliged to show mostly models and drawings in plan and perspective. Apart from a few sheets such as the one we have looked at (Fig 40), we have little precise information about which transparencies he projected at the end of his lectures. As his built oeuvre swelled, the visual peroration became increasingly impressive, to the point, in the early 1930s, when he was able to include films of his buildings, including those of Pierre Chenal.

Le Corbusier deployed the full range of classical rhetorical techniques in his lectures. Despite a style of delivery often criticized as rather dry and sometimes unconvincing, he learned how to create a form of oratory – both visual and verbal – which was highly effective. This efficacy depended above all on the selection and combination of images, on his 'demonstrations' drawn on the blackboard, on his effective use of memorable slogans (often exaggerated to make a point) and on the way he used personal anecdotes to engage the sympathy of the audience. Even his enemies were touched by his personality. The 1924 lectures provided him with a methodology, a confidence and an arsenal of weapons (anecdotes, examples, arguments, images) which he used again and again in his later lectures.

Following double spread

Figure 40

Page of sketches indicating lantern slides to be included in his lecture (FLC C3(6)56).

La cellule

la série

portes et fenêtres
le mur comme
pas de fondations.

prix.

esthétique

cliché Innovation

1 page Corbu

1 page Co

FONDATION LE CORBUSIER - PARIS

soleil d'été
les sports
la maternelle
ombre d'été
une autre famille
une famille
soleil
la montagne
d'hiver

Chapter 3

The origins and development of the lecture on urbanism

The first lecture for which we have a text, delivered at Strasbourg in 1923, was not about architecture but about urbanism. It was the exhibition of the drawings, models and diorama of the Contemporary City for Three Million Inhabitants in November 1922 which first caught the attention of the popular press and led to Le Corbusier being invited to give important public lectures. This was the first time that the national and international press had paid attention to his work. Furthermore, the lecture at Strasbourg was a new departure in his thinking. Whereas Le Corbusier had published his articles on architecture in *L'Esprit Nouveau* magazine before his lectures in 1924, all but one of the articles on urbanism were published between November 1923 and January 1925 and therefore followed his first lecture, in Strasbourg, in 1923.[1] Le Corbusier's lectures on urbanism became his battle cry; they gained him unprecedented notoriety, and the lecture format allowed him to express himself more forcefully and freely than in print.

'The centre of great cities', Strasbourg, 1923

The lecture in Strasbourg was part of a very important international conference, organized by the French Society of Urbanists (SFU) and bringing together well-known French and European town planners.[2] Ebenezer Howard and Raymond Unwin, founders of the garden city movement in England, were there, although they did not deliver papers. Henri Prost (who gave a talk on planning the coastal region of the Côte d'Azur in the Var) and Marshall Lyautey were among those representing France and its colonies. Léon Jaussely, Louis Bonnier, Augustin Rey and Henri Sellier and many other acknowledged experts on urbanism and housing were in the audience. The detailed agenda was divided into four sections: 1. Legislation, 2. City plans, 3. Urban hygiene and 4. Housing. Le Corbusier's lecture was in section 2. He probably owed his invitation to his participation, between 1922 and 1923, in the technical committee of a group known as The Renaissance of Cities, of which the President of the SFU was also a member.[3]

A typescript exists at the Getty Research Institute (GRI) in Los Angeles, marked up with significant corrections and additions (Fig 1).[4] These manuscript corrections were incorporated in a text included in the article 'La Grande Ville' in *L'Esprit Nouveau* and then in Le Corbusier's book *Urbanisme*, as well as in the official publication of the conference (see Appendix, pp. 192-197).[5] If the typescript was indeed a text used for a lecture, these corrections might indicate how Le Corbusier perceived the difference between spoken and printed communication.

There are no other preparatory notes for this lecture, and there is no certain way of knowing whether this text corresponds to Le Corbusier's lecture as delivered or whether it was written up afterwards for publication. I will suggest, however, that there is internal evidence in the text to indicate its use as a lecture. For example, the kind of corrections made on this typescript do not conform to Le Corbusier's usual practice in editing a text for publication. They incorporate much more extensive additions and cuts than usual. I believe that the typescript for this, his first lecture to a large audience, represents the text that he read out at the conference, and the manuscript corrections were inserted to turn this into a printable version for the Conference Proceedings.

Previous page
Le Corbusier in front of a drawing explaining his Unité d'Habitation de grandeur conforme, probably in the drawing office at the rue de Sèvres.

Figure 1
First page of the typescript of preliminary notes for the lecture in Strasbourg in 1923 (GRI 920083-2/1).

1/In the 'Avertissement [Preface]' of *Urbanisme*, Le Corbusier suggests that he wrote much of the book in the summer of 1924, *Urbanisme*, p. ii.

2/Most of the delegates were French, with some Belgian, Dutch, British, Czech and Italians, but no Germans. Several French government ministers and the mayors of several French and Belgian towns were present, along with technical experts of all sorts.

3/La Renaissance des Cités was founded in 1916 by the women Tarrade-Page and Adar-Mitrecey and awarded charity status in 1922. Its aim was to assist in the reconstruction of the areas devastated by the war. Le Corbusier contributed to the technical committee, chaired by Louis Bonnier, alongside A. Dervaux, Georges B. Ford (New York architect who was the town planner of Reims), Jaussely, Letrosne and Lafollye (also a friend of Le Corbusier). Anon. (1935) *La Renaissance des Cités 1916-1935*. Paris, pp. 51-52. Le Corbusier is also listed among the 'propaganda lecturers' (Ibid., p. 113). His contribution to this group is documented in his diary (Saturday, 10 February 1923: '5 pm Renaissance City on the dot' (FLC F-3-3-6, p. 9, recto); third week of March, 1923: 'Go to Renaissance City to look for plans' (Ibid., p. 31 recto)). An article by 'G.M.' in *Le Petit Journal* (25 February 1923) tells of a lecture by Le Corbusier

LE CENTRE DES GRANDES VILLES

Les municipalités et les édiles des grandes villes s'occupent aujourd'hui du problème de grande banlieue et cherchent à chasser au dehors les populations qui se sont précipitées dans la capitale avec la force d'une invasion ; ces recherches sont louables ; elles sont incomplètes ; elles laissent de côté le problème capital qui est celui du centre des grandes villes . On soigne les muscles de l'athlète , mais on ne veut pas savoir que son coeur malade , archi-malade et que sa vie est en danger . Le problème du centre des grandes villes se pose avec la plus profonde nécessité .

Il est bon de préciser ce que représente le phénomène de la grande ville. La grande ville n'est pas que 4 ou 7.000.000 d'individus qui se sont réunis par hasard en un endroit déterminé ; la grande ville est un organe quasi biologique de l'organisation du pays , de l'organisation nationale, et de l'organisation internationale . c'est le coeur ,centre agissant du système cardiaque ;c'est le cerveau centre dirigeant du système nerveux

Toute l'activité du pays, et toute l'activité internationale naissent de la grande ville . La grande ville c'est le lieu de contact des élements agissant du monde , ce contact doit être immédiat ,main contre main, car les décisions sont la conséquence d'un débat au rythme précipité et toutes décisions entrainent les agissements du pays et des pays entre eux . Le télégraphe , le chemin de fer, l'avion ont activé la rapidité des contacts internationaux . La marche des idées se tient dans l' étroit espace du centre des grandes villes ; c'est ce centre qui est à proprement parler, la cellule vitale du pays .

Or, les centres des grandes villes sont actuellement des outils de travail presque inutilisables ; le contact nécessaire ne s'établit

The lecture seems to have been partly based on the text accompanying the exhibit at the Salon d'Automne in 1922 on the Contemporary City for Three Million Inhabitants. This was organized as a series of statements.[6]

> The big city is a recent event dating from the 1950s.
> The growth of big cities has exceeded all expectations.
> Modern industrial life and modern commercial life are new phenomena. [...]
> The new phenomenon of the big city arose from the existing structures of cities.
> The disproportion is such that it provokes an intense crisis.
> THIS CRISIS IS IN ITS BEGINNING STAGES. It can cause revolutions.
> Cities that do not adapt quickly to the new conditions of modern life will be suffocated: they will perish; other more adaptable cities will replace them.
> The persistence of the city's old structures paralyzes their growth.
> Industrial and commercial life will be eradicated by these old-fashioned cities.
> The conservative system of big cities prevents the development of transportation, congests the cities, chokes activity, kills progress, discourages initiatives.
> The decay of old cities and the intensity of the modern workload is giving people stress and disease. Modern life calls for the recovery of wasted energy. Hygiene and moral wellbeing depend on the layout of cities. Without hygiene or moral wellbeing, the family cannot survive. A country that allows the institution of the family to collapse perishes.
> Today's cities cannot respond to the changes of modern life. They must be transformed.
> To transform cities, it is necessary to find the fundamental principles of modern urbanism.
> Big cities govern the life of the country.
> If the big city suffocates, the country stagnates.[7]

These declarations constitute the premise of an argument: great cities are sick and dysfunctional, and their inhabitants too are sick. The forces of modernization, and hence of economic growth, will be strangled in the old cities. The remedy, it seems, was rather drastic. If the great city is to survive, it must first be destroyed.

It seems that another text for the 1922 exhibition, which has not survived, completed the argument thus announced. Emile Henriot cited, in the pages of *Paris-Midi* (5 November 1922), the four apparently contradictory preconditions of the contemporary city: decongestion of the city centre, increasing its density, developing public transport and multiplying green spaces.[8] The lecture in Strasbourg was built around these four principles.

at the house of Mme Tarrade-Page, at 23 rue Ballu, chaired by M. Peuch, President of the Municipal Council, under the title 'The urbanism of the great city' (FLC X1(3)23). According to *Les Géomètres experts*, he gave this again on 4 March 1923 (FLC X1(3)33).

4/Getty Research Institute, Santa Monica, Los Angeles (GRI) 920083-2 (1) entitled 'The centre of the great cities'.

5/See *L'Esprit Nouveau*, 23, May 1924, and *Urbanisme*, op. cit., pp. 88-95, where the text is identified as part of a lecture in Strasbourg, and also the Conference Proceedings: *Où en est l'urbanisme en France et à l'étranger?*, op. cit., pp. 247-257. See also a flyer for this publication (FLC A2(18)125).

6/Le Corbusier certainly included plans and sketches from his exhibit of the Contemporary City for Three Million Inhabitants in his lecture. At the beginning of March 1923, he noted in his diary (FLC F-3-3-6, p. 18 recto): 'Lecture photo diorama', and again on p. 35 recto: 'Pierre, make a plan of the diorama for Strasbourg'.

7/FLC 29710.

8/ FLC X1(02)47.

Attentive to his audience, Le Corbusier targets his enemies with precision. He begins his Strasbourg lecture by criticizing town planners' belief in the garden cities as a solution to urban and suburban problems. Needless to say, most of the conference delegates, from Ebenezer Howard to Henri Sellier, were passionate believers in garden cities. For Le Corbusier, moving people into the suburbs or into garden cities amounted to a treatment of the symptoms, not the cause of the malady:

> We are taking care of the athlete's muscles; but we don't want to know that his heart is seriously ill and that his life is in danger. *It is absolutely essential that we consider the problem of city centres)* [my italics].[9]

The typescript in the GRI attacks the garden cities head-on. Le Corbusier moderated some of the more outspoken phrases in the GRI text for the printed version. For example, he softened the italicized phrase in the passage above by a more reasoned argument:

> Although it may be a good thing to encourage the population entrenched in the faubourgs to move outside, we must remember that every day, at the same time, the crowds who enjoy better housing in the garden cities will have to travel to the city centre. Improving housing by creating garden cities still leaves the city centre problem intact.[10]

Compared with the first sentence, above, Le Corbusier had proclaimed in his lecture: 'The city councils [...] try to chase out the people who have swarmed into the city centre.'

He then launches into an analysis of the modern city, contrasting the tenfold rises in population during the nineteenth century and the evolution of means of rapid transportation with the fixed structure of city centres. These arguments, which he later worked up in the articles published in *Urbanisme*, were accompanied by diagrammatic plans of city centres, the exponential demographic growth, the strangulation of circulation in medieval street patterns, all this made worse by the arrival of the railheads which disgorged the masses from the suburbs and beyond.[11] These diagrams recur in all Le Corbusier's lectures on urbanism.

What was to be done? Contemporary urbanists such as Henri Sellier argued for the displacement of the business and administrative centre to the periphery of the city. Le Corbusier added a manuscript passage (for publication) in which he rejects this idea.

> In relation to the wheel (railways, periphery, suburbs, distant suburbs, main roads, subways, tramways, administrative and commercial centres, industrial and residential areas), the centre never moved. It stayed in the same place. It must stay where it is. What is more, it represents a huge asset, and in wishing to move it, an important part of the wealth of the nation would be eliminated by decree. To say: "It is simple, let us create

9/GRI 920083-02 (1).

10/Ibid.

11/Le Corbusier, *Urbanisme*, op. cit., pp. 89-92.

> the new centre of Paris in Saint-Germain-en-Laye" is to talk nonsense, or to promise the moon. It is "a gambit" used endlessly by the supporters of stagnation to gain a little time. The centre must be modified where it is. It crumbles and reconstructs itself over the centuries, just as a man changes his skin every seven years and a tree produces new leaves every year. We must confront the city centre, and transform it, which is the simplest solution and, more simply, the only solution.[12]

His solution has the dramatic but flawed logic with which he continued to astonish his audiences throughout his life and which he never completely renounced. He picks up the four principles, first announced on the stand of the Contemporary City exhibit in November 1922:

> So we are led to define the basic notions of modern city planning using four stark, concise proposals that provide precise responses to the dangers in question.
> The conclusion is the following:
> 1. Unblock the congestion in city centres in order to respond to the demands of traffic.
> 2. Increase the density of city centres in order to ensure the connections demanded by business.
> 3. Increase traffic flow, that is to say to entirely modify the present conception of the street which is ineffectual faced with the phenomenon of modern means of transport, subways or automobiles, tramways, aeroplanes.
> 4. Increase planted surfaces, which are the only means to ensure sufficient good health for the inhabitants of the city and the tranquillity necessary for attentive work that the rhythm of business demands of each person.
> These four points appear to be irreconcilable. On the contrary; the technical means of the times furnish the harmonious solution and the question then becomes fascinating and we can appreciate the imminence of a new cycle of grandeur and majesty.[13]

Formulated like this, the argument seems quite plausible. Simply as a solution to circulation and the healthy management of high population densities, the association of high density offices and dwellings with green spaces has its merits. But of course Le Corbusier ignored the psychological and practical problems resulting from this kind of drastic change, with its destruction of the traditional urban fabric. For the printed version, Le Corbusier qualified the dramatic 'on the contrary' to read:

12/Ibid. (see p. 193).

13/Ibid. (see p. 193).

It is useful to recognize their exactness, to measure their urgency. Then, with the problem expressed in this way, city planning can provide answers. And it can provide answers, contrary to appearances.

Modern techniques will allow the urbanist to achieve the miracle of increasing density while relieving congestion and incorporating green parks, by the use of the skyscraper and a hierarchy of motorways and public transport. Of course, the existing city fabric will have to come down, but the spirit of the capital, the heart and brain of the nation, will remain in place and become healthy once again.

The lecture concludes (pp. 9-10 of the typewritten text) with the application of these principles – already formulated at the exhibition of the Contemporary City in 1922 – to the special case of Paris. These pages are deleted from the printed text in *Urbanisme*, because Le Corbusier devotes Chapter 15 to the centre of Paris and the Voisin Plan. Francesco Passanti drew attention to the fact that it was at Strasbourg that Le Corbusier spoke extensively for the first time about what would become the Voisin Plan for Paris. He also noted that the architect published a sketch of the plan of Paris with the legend: '1922. First draft of the development plan for the centre of Paris (Salon d'Automne).'[14] Passanti also extracts a plan for a skyscraper city from a page from a diary dating from 1922.[15] This almost indecipherable sketch represents a square composed of cross-shaped towers with an extension of towers towards the left.

On the verso of the typewritten lecture notes preserved at the GRI, Le Corbusier drew sketches of plans, which can be identified with the application of the Contemporary City plan to Paris and compared with illustrations in *Urbanisme* and the colloquium report published by the French Society of Urbanists: *Où en est l'urbanisme [...]*?[16] One of these sketches can be matched with the diary sketch from 1922.[17] It is possible that Le Corbusier had already applied the plan of the Contemporary City to Paris at the time of the lecture to the Renaissance of Cities group on 25 February 1923, since 'G. M.' mentions the Tuileries in his account of the lecture.[18]

Le Corbusier's plan for Paris covered a quadrangle located between the Gare de l'Est and the Gare Saint-Lazare. Leaving out the area bordering the Seine, 'the magnificent Paris of the past, from the Place des Vosges up to the Etoile' (including the Tour Saint-Jacques and the Louvre), it included the business district of the Stock Exchange and banks but also 'the maquis bequeathed by the 17th and 18th and 19th centuries... These districts have no artistic value. On the other hand they suffocate the life that tried to emerge.' The largest part affected by his project had already been designated as 'Unsanitary Block #1' (inhabited by more than 12,000 people). Le Corbusier would have replaced it with a business district and a large new East-West avenue providing access to it.

In *Urbanisme*, Le Corbusier reproduced an article by the journalist Gustave Téry, 'To avoid congestion', first published on 27 October 1923:

14/Passanti, F., 'Le Corbusier et le gratte-ciel: aux origines du Plan Voisin', in Cohen, J-L. and H. Damisch (eds). *Américanisme et modernité...*, 1993, pp. 171-189, p. 185 and note 38. (also Passanti, F., 'The skyscrapers of the Ville Contemporaine', *Assemblage* 4: 52-65, p. 62 and note 38.)

15/Passanti, F., 'The skyscrapers of the Ville Contemporaine', op. cit., p. 62 and fig. 13.

16/*Urbanisme*, p. 265 and *Où en est l'urbanisme en France et à l'étranger*, p. 255.

17/In *Urbanisme*, Le Corbusier declares that this sketch would have been shown at the Salon d'Automne of 1922 along with his plans for the Contemporary City. Passanti also notes two references to the plan of Paris in articles commenting on the stand of 1922 (*L'Humanité*, 11 November 1922, p. 5, and *L'Architecture* 35, no. 23, 10 December 1922, pp. 361ff.). One can also observe that on the painting of the Voisin Plan of 1925 there is a label with the years 1922 and 1923.

18/G.M., 'La cité de demain d'après un urbaniste', *Le Petit Journal*, 25 February 1923,: 'Ils [les gratte-ciel] ont au moins 250m de large, et c'est comme si chaque fenêtre donnait sur les Tuileries' (FLC X1(3)23). The lecture is also cited in *Le petit Parisien*, 25 February 1923 (FLC X1(3)26).

> Now, take a pencil and a map of Paris: draw a line from the Concorde to Châtelet, another from Châtelet to the Gare de l'Est, a third from the Gare de l'Est to Saint-Augustin, a fourth from Saint-Augustin to the Place de la Concorde. You thus obtain a quadrangle which contains the whole problem [...] [19]

Téry's solution consisted in banning all automobile traffic within this quadrangle. This rectangle corresponds with that of Le Corbusier's plan. Was Téry aware of this plan, or was the discussion of urbanism in Paris so well disseminated that a journalist like Téry could target without hesitation the Right Bank as the central cause of Paris's problems?

In this part of the typewritten text, most likely given at Strasbourg yet replaced for publication, Le Corbusier pushed his classification analysis further, all the way to a bold hierarchy of the urban population itself:

> Those at the tip of the pyramid have their base [correction: place] at the centre of the cities, they are the leaders; then come the more modest participants and then those who have not found the paradise they were seeking and who remain uprooted, drifters, poor impoverished refugees in the misery of the poor quarters and who make up a whole disturbing section of the population of the cities. There are also those we can call city dwellers, that is to say those who have a taste for life in the city; for its diverse resources, its bustle and for those whose destiny is to express the fundamentals of human thought, who also need to be in direct contact with the huge spiritual potential embodied by the city.
> Let's classify:
> 1. Those in business, the leaders and their assistants whose schedule demands a defined presence in a precise location: the centre.
> 2. The housing for city dwellers around and close to the city centres. The centre for business and housing for the city dwellers constitutes [sic] in fact the city centre.
> 3. The floating population must be classified as being beyond the slums in the garden cities, far away from the centre: garden cities that would accommodate all the people of middling condition and who in the normal way plan to bring up a family. The garden cities are intended as entirely new elements, where rational development is possible. Here the question of suburban transport arises and it is a huge responsibility that rests with the Railway Companies and subway managers.
> It is no longer a question of recognizing that a few of the privileged or fanatical suburbanites can assume the heroic role of garden city resident (I say heroic because through negligence the Railway Companies have imposed a state of

Figure 2
Sketch by Le Corbusier of a business district on the Left Bank of Paris (GRI 920083-2, p. 9 of the typescript, verso).

19/Gustave Téry, 'Pour éviter la congestion', in Le Corbusier, op. cit., p. 122. The clipping is dated 27 October 1923.

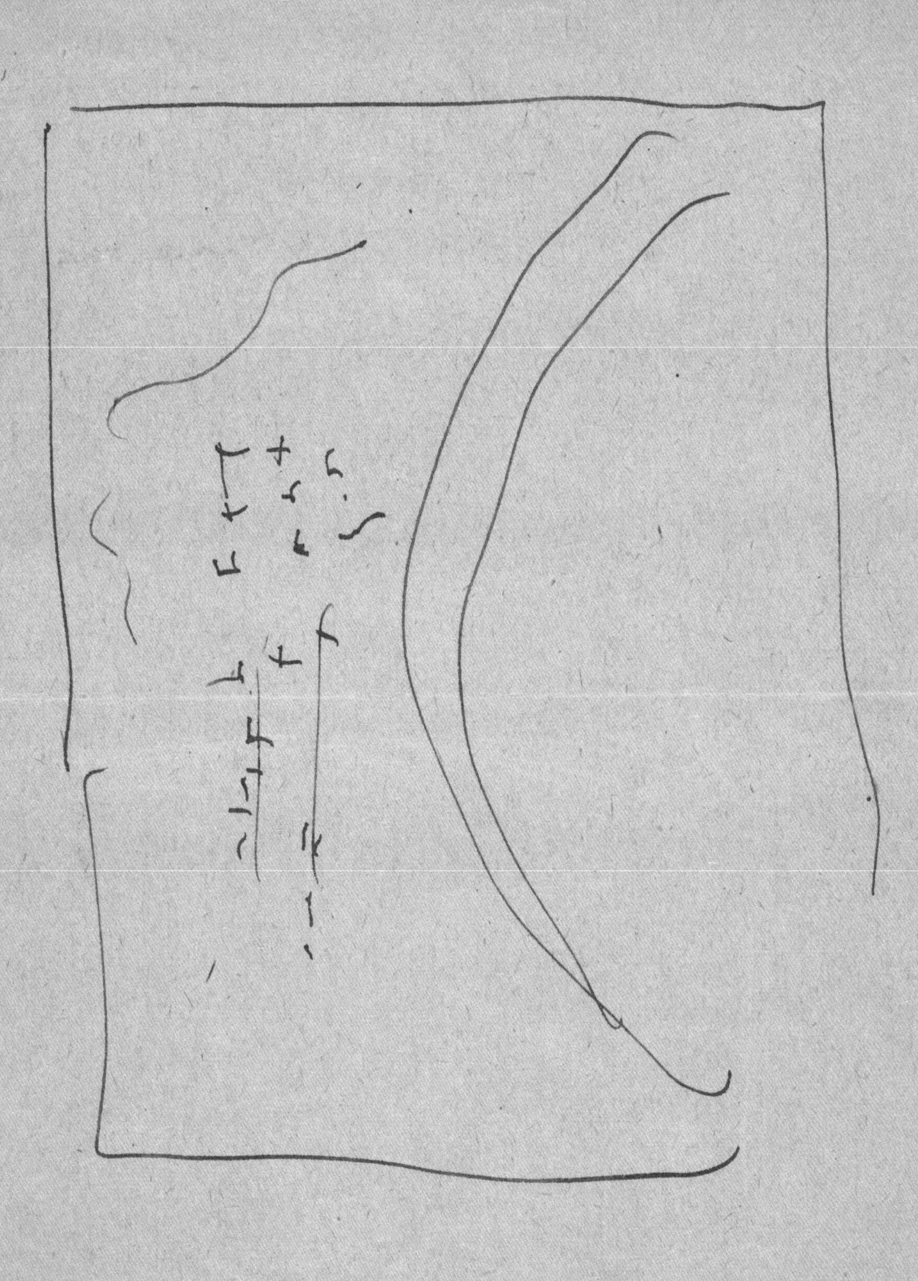

affairs that is simply grotesque). If the centre of a capital city attracts 500,000 to 800,000 individuals attending to business every day, if the rest of the city centre accommodates roughly 1,000,000 city dwellers, the garden cities must accommodate the two other millions to make up a city of 3,000,000 inhabitants, one can see that necessarily a railway question arises.[20]

In the published version, his analysis is more conciliatory and reasonable:

It is useful to be aware of the different types of inhabitants of a city. As the seat of power (in the widest sense of the word: leaders in business, industry, finance, politics, masters in science, teaching, thought, spokesmen for the human soul, artists, poets, musicians, etc., etc.), the city focuses all ambitions, drapes itself in a glittering mirage of fairyland; the crowds pour in. The city centre is the seat of the powerful, the leaders, and their assistants down to the most humble, whose presence is necessary at set times in the city centre, but whose destiny tends to be limited to the organization of family life. Families are poorly housed in the city. Garden cities provide better conditions for their cohesion. Lastly, there is industry, with its factories, which, for various reasons, are concentrated in large numbers around the centre. With the factories will be the large numbers of workers satisfied with their social status as residents of the garden cities.
Let's classify them. Three sorts of population: the resident city dwellers; the working population who spend half their time in the centre and half in the garden cities; and the labouring masses who divide their time between factories in the suburbs and the garden cities.
To tell the truth, this classification is already a city planning programme. Putting it objectively into practice is to start to reshape the cities. Because, following their spectacularly rapid growth, they are now in a terrible state of chaos: everything is confused. This city planning programme could, for example, be defined as follows, for a city of 3,000,000 inhabitants; in the centre and for daytime work only, 500,000 to 800,000 people; at night the centre is deserted. The city residential area absorbs some, the garden cities the rest. Let's say then half a million city dwellers (in the inner ring) and two and a half millions in the garden cities.
This clarification, only in principle, unconfirmed as far as figures are concerned, calls for measures to create order, sets the guidelines of modern city planning, determines the proportions of the city (centre), of the

20/GRI 920083-02(1), p. 4 (see p. 194).

residential areas, poses the problem of communications and transport, provides the basis for a programme of urban sanitation, determines the method of division of land into plots, the alignment of streets, their layout, fixes the density and consequently the construction methods for the centre, for the residential areas and for the garden cities.[21]

This ruthless classification of the classes would feature less commonly in later lectures. Perhaps someone had criticized him after the lecture and he decided later to tone this down. Nevertheless, this classification of the social classes subtends all his urbanistic thinking until the design of the Radiant City in the early 1930s.

Le Corbusier also felt he had to strengthen his arguments about the use of skyscrapers in the city centres. In the typescript he had simply stated:

The centre of the city is reserved for business. The density there has to be ten times higher than it is at present in Paris, the thoroughfares must be 100 metres wide instead of the 7, 9, 11 or 15 metres inherited from the previous centuries: building areas could be 5%, planted areas 95%, density about 2000 instead of the average 350 for Paris; in that case the centre of cities must be laid out with widely-spaced skyscrapers. It should not be in the form of pointed towers. These skyscrapers are no longer towers (in the fashion of the Venice Campanile) as in New York, but huge buildings rising to 60 floors with no courtyards and achieving, with their cross-shaped ground plan, the suppression of courtyards and a considerable extension of façades facing the light as well as maximum stability.[22]

In the rewritten version for publication, he sought to set his ideas into context and defend against the argument that life in a skyscraper was inhuman:

The question of skyscrapers is a preoccupation in Europe. In Holland, in England, in Germany, in France, in Italy, the first theoretical attempts have been made. The skyscraper cannot be isolated from the study of the street and of horizontal and vertical transport.

The centre of the town would then be permanently purged of family life. In the present state of things, it would seem that skyscrapers cannot accommodate family life. Their internal organization demands a complex system of circulation and organization, the cost of which can only be met by businesses; the way in which the means of circulation are organized, like stations in the air, cannot be suitable for family life.

21/*Urbanisme*, op. cit., p. 93.

22/GRI 920083-02(1) (see p. 195).

> Urban residential quarters could be developed from the same rational transformations. Main streets would criss-cross them at intervals of 400 metres from axis to axis. Contrary to age-old usage, buildings would not be grouped in rectangular blocks overlooking the street, with internal subdivisions into numerous courtyards. A system of land division [presented in *L'Esprit Nouveau*, 4, 1921] eliminating the courtyard would leave intervals of 200 to 400 or 600 metres between houses that could form parks bigger than the Tuileries Gardens. The town would become one huge park: 15% buildings, 85% planted areas, density equivalent to that of our congested Paris of today, main streets 50 metres wide only transecting every 400 metres (automobile traffic demands the elimination of two thirds of the existing streets); sports fields and pleasure gardens adjoining housing, elimination of courtyards, radical transformation of the aspect of the town, architectural contributions of prime importance. Etc., etc.[23]

In his book *La Ville radieuse*, published in 1935 but largely consisting of articles published in the previous five years, Le Corbusier gets rid of the suburb altogether. The main housing provision would have been in long slabs zigzagging through open parkland. It is clear that, in this short paper, Le Corbusier does not have space to develop his whole cultural argument. The problem is stated in functional terms and the resolution found in technical and rationalist solutions. The brutality of the argument (Le Corbusier's own word) must be in part explained by the *succès de scandale* of the Contemporary City stand and Le Corbusier's wish to make a mark by distancing himself radically from his professional colleagues.

This was the period of his break with Auguste Perret and his attempt to establish an avant-garde stance opposed to that of the modern 'masters'.[24] He takes care to attack the forerunners of modernism, one after another: 'Let us thus try to criticize the three systems recently proposed by eminent urbanists.' Without naming them, he targeted Tony Garnier, Henri Sauvage and Auguste Perret (all absent at the conference). In 1917, Tony Garnier had published *La Cité industrielle*, a collection of plans and perspectives with factories, a passenger terminal, hospitals and little concrete homes with flat roofs. Le Corbusier characterized *La Cité industrielle* as 'unambitious' ['de petite envergure']; he criticizes the dwellings – 'an estate of family homes' – as unacceptable for the heart of a city.[25] Henri Sauvage proposed a systems of terraced apartments, of which the Parisian prototype had been constructed on rue Vavin (1912) and which he recommended as a large-scale solution. For Le Corbusier, these terraced houses, even though ingenious from the point of view of lighting, did not solve the problems of the roads and, thus, of the traffic.[26] In addition, the absence of parks adversely affected the hygiene of the city. With regard to the skyscrapers proposed by Auguste Perret in 1920, to be erected over the ring of fortifications around Paris or along a twelve-kilometre avenue, Le Corbusier thought they were unsuitable for either offices (because of the distance that separated one from the other) or for residences: 'It appears that familial life would not find any advantage within them.'[27] In 1923, Le

23/*Urbanisme*, op. cit., pp. 94-95.

24/See Fanelli, G. and R. Gargiani (1990). *Perret e Le Corbusier confronti*, Rome, Laterza; and Dumont, M.-J. (ed.) (2002), *Le Corbusier: lettres à ses maîtres, 1. Lettres à Auguste Perret*, Paris, Linteau

25/Garnier, T. (1917). *Une Cité industrielle. Etude pour la construction des villes*. Paris, Editions Vincent, Fréal et Cie.

26/Henri Sauvage and his partner Charles Sarazin had patented their terraced construction system in 1912 and had constructed a small prototype at 26 rue Vavin (1912-1913), before undertaking a bigger project on the rue des Amiraux (1913-1927). Le Corbusier included a sketch of the rue Vavin block on one of his drawings for the Dom-Ino system, in 1915 (FLC 19135). Sauvage published an article illustrating his proposal for terraced streets (Henri Sauvage (10 October 1922). 'Les Tendances de l'architecture moderne', *L'Amour de l'art*, p. 333-334.). See also Loyer, F.

Corbusier had no intention of installing residences in his skyscrapers. With regards to Perret, he concludes: 'The skyscraper has the capacity to decongest circulation, so it must decongest the city centre; there is no point decongesting the suburbs, which are not congested in the first place.'[28]

The Voisin Plan; The urbanism of a big city (Metropolis), Brussels 1926

Encouraged by the success of his exhibition of the Contemporary City for Three Million Inhabitants and of his subsequent lectures on the subject, Le Corbusier launched another attack during the summer of 1925 at the time of the Exposition Internationale des Arts Décoratifs et Industriels Modernes in Paris. There, he unveiled two components of the architectural and urbanistic revolution: a full-size dwelling model – the Pavillon de l'Esprit Nouveau – and the plans and dioramas of the Contemporary City and the Voisin Plan for Paris. All the lectures on urbanism that follow will be accompanied by slides of the imposing diorama of the City for Three Million Inhabitants and the Voisin Plan for Paris, as well as the slides of the model and drawings that accompanied it (see chapter 2, Figs 39 and 40).

When Le Corbusier was asked to give a lecture, he often chose to split it over two days, thus separating the topics of architecture and urbanism. Thus in Brussels, on 4 and 5 May 1926, he gave two lectures: 'The Voisin Plan for Paris – Urbanization of a Great City' and 'Architecture – Furniture – Works of Art'.

Writing to his mother, he notes that his first lecture had an impressive audience, including presidents of professional groups and senators.

Figure 3
Announcement of the lectures on 4 and 5 May 1926 in Brussels (FLC A2(18)111).

and H. Guéné (1987). *Henri Sauvage: Les Immeubles à gradins*, Liège, Mardaga.

27/GRI 920083-2, p. 8 (see p. 195). Perret's proposal of 'tower houses' separated by 250-m-wide streets was published for the first time in an interview in *L'Intransigeant*, 25 November 1920. In *L'Illustration* of 12 August 1922, his student Jacques Lambert published a perspective of an avenue of towers in Perret's style, driving from Paris to Saint-Germain-en-Laye. The text by Jean Labadié accompanying this perspective associates the towers with the military zone occupied by the ring of fortifications still encircling Paris. See also Passanti, F., 'The skyscrapers of the Ville Contemporaine', op. cit.

28/This part of the text, criticizing Tony Garnier, Henri Sauvage and Auguste Perret, was diplomatically cut out of the extract published in *Urbanisme*.

> I was distracted, distant, but a great success, which astonished me: at least the audience appeared to be impressed. Improvised. Ibid tonight at Palais du Peuple. Another audience on architecture, furniture, works of art. I swam like a fish in the sea, at ease, brilliant, even.[29]

A banquet for forty people followed. Six speeches sang his praises: 'I assure you that Corbu is a gentleman in Belgium. I am telling you immodest things to reassure you.'[30] Le Corbusier had just lost his father (January 1926) and he regularly wrote to his mother to support her. 'When the slides were projected, there was a gasp at the appearance of the small Léman house. I saw little papa. Poor papa! These large-scale slide projections were impressive.' The Belgian architects then kept him up drinking until five in the morning and woke him up early next day to visit Brussels in a Voisin car. The following day, Friday, he went to Antwerp to see his client, Guiette, and returned at 10 p.m. to Paris, having another lecture to give on Saturday.

This glimpse of Le Corbusier's itinerary allows us to better understand the difficulties he had in preparing his lectures. If there were notes for the urbanism lecture in Brussels, he did not have time to make any for the lecture on architecture, a topic about which he claims he 'swam like a fish in water.'

Le Corbusier planned his urbanism lecture on one sheet of paper (Fig 4).[31] It is interesting to note that on this page, which summarizes some other notes, he indicates three points for the projection of lantern slides. He identifies the first with the title 'Voisin Plan (new age)'. This first set of slides played a double role: on the one hand it paid homage to the sponsor of the Voisin Plan, the industrialist Gabriel Voisin, but it also was an expression of the *Zeitgeist*, of the new spirit of the age. On page 1 of his notes, he explains the origin of this association. He proposes a 'syllogism' according to which automobiles, having killed the great city, were responsible for saving it.[32] This was thus how he thought of the automobile and, 'in particular of the automobile and mass publicity'. He thought of André Citroën (or the Peugeot brothers) as the new 'Haussmann' or a new 'Colbert'. It is thanks to his friend Mongermon, manager of Voisin automobiles, that he could find financial support from the industrialist and he called it, 'the Voisin Plan for Paris; I liked that better than the Le Corbusier Plan.'[33]

Then he developed his urbanistic argument. The obstacle is what he calls 'the road surveyor', which is to say the system of controls and land values that makes radical modification of the city difficult: 'The road surveyor applies formulas; [he applies] rules; sanctioning of use. The present general disruption necessitates other activities than the road surveyor. Rather, the era stimulates the sudden surge of out-siders [sic], which is to say people that are concerned with other things, who, at each step, overcome obstacles.'[34] He lists the interests of these outsiders: 'practical, hygienic, social, economic, aesthetic [...] This solution is off the beaten track [...]' He goes on to speak of Taylorism and then explains his personal journey, from decorative arts to architecture and urbanism.

Figure 4
Outline for the Brussels lecture on urbanism, 1926 (see transcription, p. 210).

He then proposes a second series of projections. As proof of the indivisible nature of architecture and urbanism – but, even more, to show his *ethos*, his ability to design modernist houses – he showed already built villas (the Besnus villas, the Ozenfant studio, the La Roche villa) and the models of the Citrohan house, the Ribot house and the villa for Daniel Niestlé in Rambouillet (see chapter 2, Fig 38).

29/Letter from Le Corbusier to his mother, 6 May 1926 (FLC R1(06)122).

30/Ibid.

31/FLC C3(8)46. There is also a page of notes entitled 'École d'architecture Trelac printemps 1926', where he proposed to start with general ideas, followed by a series of projections, 'about which I will express my opinion later' (FLC C3(8)41). It is likely that this page served as the introduction for the lecture on architecture on 5 May 1926. For transcriptions of these notes (FLC C3(8)46-65) see pp. 210-219.

32/Discussed in chapter 1, p. 26 (FLC C3(8)48).

33/*Ibid.*

34/FLC C3(8)49. See also the discussion of the surveyor in chapter 2, p. 85.

16

C3- 8-

(page 1)

P avions voisin. (temps nouveaux)

P villas Corbu et PJ[ne] rassurer le coeur (Terrasse Maison [?] Prostem[?] ou arrête le progrès vous êtes les milieux corporatifs et on vous instruit en erreur.)

(pas Pessac à la fin)

[illegible] [illegible] ton villa[?]

+ 1 vue de Gratte ciel Hardelot

Le plan voisin.

lettre de Mr Ledoux «si votre idée était bonne...»

j'apporte une solution technique / financière.

Sellier disait: mais ns. n'avons pas d'argent.

si je fais en tête ces conférences sur Plan Voisin c'est pour révéler la mine de diamant

«si cette idée était bonne d'autres l'auraient trouvée depuis longtemps» Ledoux

page 2
3
3bis
4-
5
6

page 6. 7. 8. 9 9bis. 9ter 9quater. 10

P Dessins[?] (la totalité) puis conclusion 11 et Pessac P

E
LC

To justify the projection of his villas during the lecture on urbanism, he explains: 'the harmonious and licit cell is the key to all urbanism. I have just come from Frankfurt: problems of planning, of houses, of industry [...]'[35] He then excuses himself for showing his own urbanism plans, 'a labour that might apear a bit dry, at least at first sight (since in reality it's fascinating)'.[36] Without a doubt, he understood that the problems of urbanism were more difficult to communicate than those of architecture.[37]

He also felt obliged to respond to the critics who found his urbanism plans abstract, cold and inhuman. 'On the other hand, you may think that I am leaving the human being out of the picture, with his heart and his need for wellbeing, that I am making him enter into some dreadful mechanical device, a Prussian barracks, a prison for convicts. I now defend myself energetically. Man, the individual, is the key of these experiments and I think of him at every moment. And, to prove my point, here are a few images of houses made in the same spirit.'[38] Obviously, he thought that his villas were sufficiently appreciated to communicate the humanity of his spirit and, as a consequence, of his urbanism projects. His reasons for lecturing on urbanism and architecture together become clearer. Urbanism presented the hard-line logic (the *logos*) of the necessary future disruption of the city. Architecture allowed Le Corbusier to win the support of the public (*pathos*) with the beauty of his projects.

The juxtaposition of cold reason with a burning passion becomes the trope of his lectures on urbanism. Addressing the women of his audience at a lecture at the Louvre on 28 February 1930, he announced:

> A personal confession: [I have] a strong love of art, passion for the beautiful, a thirst for harmony. And yet, this thirst for harmony has made me appear to be a revolutionary. No! I am a thinker and a builder. I analyze; I study laboriously. And then the idea emerges, fed by a passion for functional, sculptural, organic beauty. Please believe me.[39]

After the projections, he repeats the argument already used at his lecture in Strasbourg. It consists of the lesson of Henry Ford:

> To make a new plan - a plan - you must know how to live. We do not know how to live. We live badly, falsely. This cannot go on. Everything must be thought through anew. An urbanistic proof: we work all day like convicts [or] manual labourers. Everyone is overworked: employees and bosses. The ingenious [Henry] Ford proposed five days of work and two days of consumption [and] destruction. To create jobs you must interrupt work, you must destroy. This is a pretty insight. We have to revise our ideas. The interruption of work at midday is a disaster for the great city. It's typical. The quality of work suffers. The day, for men and women, is torture. The home cannot legitimately survive because we do not have time to look after it.[40]

35/FLC C3(8)50. The city of Frankfurt, under its energetic city architect Ernst May, was building modernist housing estates along the valley of the Nidda river and attracting international attention with its review *Das neue Frankfurt*. He repeats this lecture later in Zurich.

36/FLC C3(8)51.

37/In his notes for a lecture at the Labour Exchange on 16 March 1927 he warns: 'I risk being very lengthy, since I am improvising. Please clearly show your boredom [...] If you are growing impatient, let me know with eloquent signs' (FLC C3(8)105).

38/Ibid.

39/FLC C3(8)115.

40/FLC C3(8)52.

From this, Le Corbusier deduces the theory of the 24-hour solar rhythm, which should be reorganized into three eight hour segments (work, leisure, sleep) to bring urban life into the natural rhythms of the human body.

First of all, he confirms his authority as rhetorician on the basis of reason and of his faith and optimism:

> Reasoning is analysis.
> Invention is synthesis.
> Optimism = divine strength.
> I am always talking about it because it drives us on.
> A collective optimism for the times. My faith.[41]

He continues by tracing the evolution of his ideas (again the *ethos* of the orator) to arrive at his epiphany: 'One day the truth was revealed, fruit of my studies of 1910: it was the donkey which laid out the plan of modern cities! And we are paying for it today.'[42]

He continues by revisiting the arguments of the Strasbourg lecture on the traffic problems in big cities and sketches a matrix consisting of bands of essential functions – work, leisure, sleep – in one direction, and the classification of categories of the population in the other. Resolving the relation between these functions and these groups of people would be the challenge of urbanism. It is there that he takes up his chalk and draws the whole evolution of the city, from the Roman camp to the fortified towns (Aigues-Mortes, Monpazier), from the urbanism of the French kings to Haussmann, finishing with his Voisin Plan for Paris. The sketches that explain the evolution of the historic town, the advent of the railway stations, the strangulation of the city by traffic and, finally, the solution, are the same that he used throughout his life.[43]

After explaining how to solve the problem of traffic in city centres, Le Corbusier tackles the financial question. He refers to the critiques that Henri Sellier addressed to him in Strasbourg in 1923: 'Mr. Sellier will not find the millions he needs from charity or philanthropy, but in the product of a judicious widespread operation including high finance and technology.'[44] Le Corbusier's argument is that which was criticized by Jules Ferry, the author of the *Comptes fantastiques du baron Haussmann*[45]. Urban renewal would be paid for by speculative investment arising from the increased value of city plots. The enormous cost of the destruction and reconstruction of the Right Bank in Paris would not be a loss but an investment, producing unprecedented wealth. The rebuilt city would thus become a 'diamond mine.'[46] He vigorously underlined in green: 'make them understand this!!!' (Fig 6) The efficiency produced by better traffic circulation, the attraction of the site and the concentration of the business district would add so much value that the buildings would finance themselves. 'We need to provoke an immense re-evaluation of the city; the positive solution [that of Le Corbusier] is as rich as the present impasse is poor.'[47] To sustain his argument, he appealed for an economist to come forward and cost his Voisin Plan.[48]

The Voisin Plan would have destroyed a large part of the Right Bank in Paris. Anticipating critiques on this point, Le Corbusier notes (Fig 6):

Following pages

Figure 5 and 6

Pages of preparatory notes for the lecture in Brussels, 1926 (FLC C3(8)57 and 59, see transcription pp. 215 and 216).

41/FLC C3(8)53.

42/Ibid.

43/FLC C3(8)56.

44/FLC C3(8)61.

45/Ferry, J. (1868). *Les Comptes fantastiques d'Haussmann*. Paris, Armand Le Chevalier

46/FLC C3(8)59.

47/FLC C3(8)60.

48/Le Corbusier already made this appeal in *Urbanisme*, p. 277.

L'ESPRIT NOUVEAU
REVUE INTERNATIONALE ILLUSTRÉE DE L'ACTIVITÉ CONTEMPORAINE
29, RUE D'ASTORG PARIS (8e)

8 - 57

Urb—

8

Densité doit rester au Centre
donc modifier la coupe.

actuel

bon

construire en hauteur au centre des villes

Elargir énormément les rues du centre.

donc détruire le centre.

Horreur? bâtir une CITÉ.

L'histoire n'a jamais fait autre chose

3 millions

Résidences = vie urbaine spéciale
hotels, écoles, chancelleries
parlements, théâtres
etc

la rue corridor

corridor.

quand il y a. Thos Cook agit

rompre par redents
on gagne superficie. On monte en hauteur

attention développer.
a/ appartement
b/ palais
parlement
etc
système Cook
cas Banque Zurich

ATTENTION ! IMPORTANT

Plan Voisin. Je vais vous expliquer la ~~chose capitale~~ du plan Voisin :

Si mesure d'ensemble = Diamant

Si usages actuels = dépenses folles totalisées

Faire comprendre ça !!!

dépenses folles

la mine

Destruction !!? (l'histoire n'a jamais fait autre chose : Le centre demeure à travers les siècles et ne se déplace pas. De Lutèce à Haussmann

Lutèce.
Henri 4.
Louis XIV
XVe
Haussmann.

pas de place à l'Édi. (la Cité)

en 1830 il y a encore : Louvre plein de maisons.
Campagne à Montmartre.

Tout se transforme rapidement mais 10 années sont l'oubli pour nous. —

> Destruction!!? History has never done anything else. The [city] centre has remained down the centuries and has not moved. [He then surveys the history of Paris] From Lutetia [the ancient name of Paris] to [Baron] Haussmann [...] No embankments lining the Seine[...] In 1830 there is a crisis: the Louvre is still full of houses, there is countryside at Montmartre. Everything was transformed rapidly but we have forgotten those ten years.[49]

It was important to show that the proposed destruction of the Voisin Plan was not without precedent. At the Louvre on 28 February 1930 he maintained:

> The Kings (make no mistake about it) were big demolishers. Observe the plan of Lutetia, of the Romans, of the Gauls, of the Middle Ages. They demolished and acted. They had the confidence in their times and faith in their reason. But today it's the age of the machine. It is intense and magnificent[...] We must act like the Kings, with faith, intelligence and love of beauty.[50]

Le Corbusier not only takes the position as an artist/philosopher but also as a king.

In conclusion, he returned to the argument which he had criticized in Strasbourg, according to which the business centre should be built outside the city and the population dispersed in the suburbs:

> This, Mr Sellier, is the reason why this hypnotic Greater Paris outside the walls is only a chimera, a nice little dream of cottages and children's games. It is true we wish for little houses like cottages with pigeon-lofts.[51]

Before projecting the images of the Voisin Plan, he reiterates the arguments constituting the chapters 'L'Ordre' and 'Le Sentiment déborde' in *Urbanisme*. He then explains the origins of the Voisin Plan:

> So having gone to the heart of the analysis and been aware of the organism of a 1922 city / formulating itself / in fact one had to conclude / s[o] to s[peak] talk to people of today of things of today.
> So: Paris.[52]

49/FLC C3(8)59.

50/FLC C3(8)117.

51/FLC C3(8)61.

52/FLC C3(8)62.

This is how he commented the slides:

> Aesthetics: mechanized life, geometry, love (I will talk about this tomorrow),
> Speed, necessity for horizons.
> Modern attitudes: space and order
> New factor, } seen from the sky
> soon } human achievement, geometric.[53]

In the appendix, he adds a page announcing the topic of the next day's lecture, on architecture:

> You may perhaps have been persuaded by the harmonious and reasonable mechanism of the idea. But in your heart, faced with this exact mechanism you may have thought fearfully of yourself and you will have said to yourself: "Very beautiful, but I don't want to be part of it."
> I would like to reassure you. The lecture tomorrow has architecture as its subject. And not the architecture of palaces because there is no urgency for that at present, but of the house, the dwelling. Tomorrow I will be able to show you a similar development of the idea along a path of reason. But you will see that people are never abandoned to become slaves to material or spiritual cerebral mechanics. Mechanics are to serve the people, order is for the benefit of people and brings them freedom. Freedom reconquered is the object of my research. Today we are in a full state of slavery in dead surroundings that stifle us.[54]

There is a page of notes for a conclusion, with a page number – '11' – in pencil (Fig 7). This sheet of paper is undoubtedly the conclusion of the lecture 'l'architecture, mobilier, œuvre d'art,' given on 5 May.[55] The projections were of the Pavillon de l'Esprit Nouveau and the group of houses at Pessac, near Bordeaux, that Le Corbusier had designed for the industrialist Henri Frugès. These houses were almost finished and would be visited by the Minister Anatole de Monzie on 23-24 May. The ten other pages of notes for this lecture (if they really did exist) are lost. We can imagine that the first part of the lecture followed the regular format, explaining the origins of the modern house, the theory of the *fenêtre en longueur*, of *pilotis* and the open plan. It would have been interesting to know his reasoning for *le mobilier* (the furniture; promised in his title), because there are no existing notes on furniture before the lecture 'L'aventure du mobilier', given in Buenos Aires in October 1929. This page of conclusion tells of the tribulations of the Pavillon de l'Esprit Nouveau at the Exposition Internationale des Arts Décoratifs et Industriels Modernes in Paris (1925), with the projection of the pavilion and the Voisin Plan.[56] He recalls the obstacles confronted by the architects Magne and Bonnier to prevent the construction and the opening of the pavilion. Le Corbusier then shows slides of the terrace of the La Roche house, with its lilacs in bloom, a challenge for those who pretended that terrace-gardens did not conform to French culture. He does not lose the opportunity to critique Auguste Perret for his sky-

53/FLC C3(8)58.

54/FLC C3(8)63.

55/FLC C3(8)65. Another possibility would be the lecture he gave in Zurich on 24 November 1926 (and the one in Basel shortly thereafter).

56/See *Almanach de l'architecture moderne*, 1926, for 'l'histoire brève de nos tribulations [the short history of our tribulations]' (pp. 198-199).

65

11

Conclusion :

Comment arriver à une telle solution ?

De qui prendre les avis ?

~~L'avenir~~ La confusion règne, provenant soit de divergences, soit d'ignorance, soit de malicieux antagonisme.

Ainsi [illegible]

~~tout le programme était celui de l'EN~~ pavillon de l'EN Silence de Mr [illegible]

P 2 [illegible] art Pavillon

Plus que cela invite en garde contre les tendances anti français la terrasse c'est honteux elle arrête le progrès, vous êtes métier corporatif en vous ment pas passion et ignorance

P ~~terrasse~~ Auteuil

Voici Mr Bonnier dans 1 comité : ~~l'eau~~ l'eau ne montera pas, les réservoirs de Paris

Supposons 1 comité de financiers, banquiers

Aug Perret gratte ciel périphérie jardins au centre

Aug. Perret, en passant, mais en terminant sa conférence : béton armé pas p. maisons ; c'est une opinion

Aux grands praticiens : Blériot guerre 1908

et le béton armé petites maisons :

Avec acier on peut construire pont de Brooklyn mais pas de automobile.

" " " " les voies de chemin de fer, mais pas la loco.

" la loco, mais pas le chronomètre du mécanicien, etc.

Voici Pessac et ~~[illegible]~~ fenêtres, portes, escalier.

industrialisation. équipes.

prix de revient

confort

diversité

esthétique

bonheur moderne.

Paris attend de l'Époque

P Comment l' [illegible] pas un lon[illegible]

P pessac

scraper project on the periphery of the city (not in the centre) and for his 'opinion' on the inappropriateness of concrete for little houses. Le Corbusier shows the absurdity of this argument in taking the use of steel as an example. If steel had been good enough for the Brooklyn Bridge, would it not be used for automobiles? This *reductio ad absurdum* is not very convincing. Perret, who used concrete for the Pierre Gaut and Chana Orloff studios, undoubtedly implied that reinforced concrete wasn't economical enough for small construction projects. He was certainly correct and Le Corbusier was, moreover, completely aware of the standardization problems, notably for the 51 houses in Pessac.[57] After he showed the slides of Pessac, he finished with the Voisin Plan. The audience being different than the night before, he could repeat the arguments of his first lecture.

Evolution of the lecture on urbanism

When Le Corbusier gave his lecture on the Voisin plan at the Labour Exchange in Paris on 16 March 1927, he cited Brussels, Prague and Zurich as places where he had already brought up the history and theory of the Voisin Plan. There were surely others. Starting with his trip to South America, in October and November 1929, he started adapting the principles of the Voisin Plan to the topographies of the cities in which he was located. His notes for the ninth lecture in Buenos Aires (18 October 1929), entitled 'le plan Voisin de Paris et le plan Buenos-Aires' started in a surprising way:

> By a clairvoyant and passionate vision and by an icy reason, can Buenos Ayres [sic] become one of the most dignified cities in the world?[58]

After a long digression on French politics, Le Corbusier takes up the argument again:

> I ask the Jockey Club to endow Buenos Ayres with a doctrine of urbanism which is not regulatory (which is to say correcting the existent) but a guiding plan (which is to say something to put in front of the country, in front of the parliament, in front of the country's president, in front of the populace).[59]

Figure 7

Page of preparatory notes, probably for the conclusion of the lecture 'Architecture, furniture, works of art', delivered on 5 May 1926, at Brussels (FLC C3(8)65).

Le Corbusier then joins his words with a gesture, drawing a 'guiding plan' for Buenos Aires, which he '[puts] in front of the populace.' He would do the same in Rio de Janeiro, Antwerp, Algiers, Stockholm and Rome. It is by the bias of these lectures that, starting in 1929, Le Corbusier radically modifies his approach to urbanism. Over the course of his lectures, the celebration of the Voisin Plan, the rigid checkerboard, takes more subtle forms, adapted to the terrain.

In the notes for the lecture on urbanism in Algiers in March 1931 we find precious indications of the first ideas for the Obus Plan for Algiers (Fig 8). Yet for the most part, the lecture notes, prepared in advanced during the trip, do not show evidence of the plans conceived for the cities that he was visiting, because

57/See Benton, T., 'Pessac and Lège revisited: standards, dimensions and failures', *Massilia*, 3, 2004, pp. 64-99.

58/FLC C3(7)71.

59/FLC C3(7)77. For a discussion of this lecture and its published version in *Précisions*, op. cit., see p. 168.

it was only once arrived, and perhaps during the lecture itself, that Le Corbusier realized his sketches. In the case of the lecture in Stockholm (January 1933), the notes show no indication of the plan for Stockholm, yet it is likely that he would have drafted one during the lecture.[60] Two years later, the notes for the lecture to the women of Algiers (6 March 1933) are full of sketches for the urbanism of Algiers.[61] In the case of the lecture in Antwerp, Le Corbusier commented on his urbanization project for the Left Bank, at the time that the project had been dismissed by the jury of the international competition (Fig 9).

'Take the staff of the pilgrim' and lead the crusade for his ideas in the cities of the world progressively becomes the main objective of Le Corbusier. He thus sets aside arguments about architecture to concentrate on urbanism. After

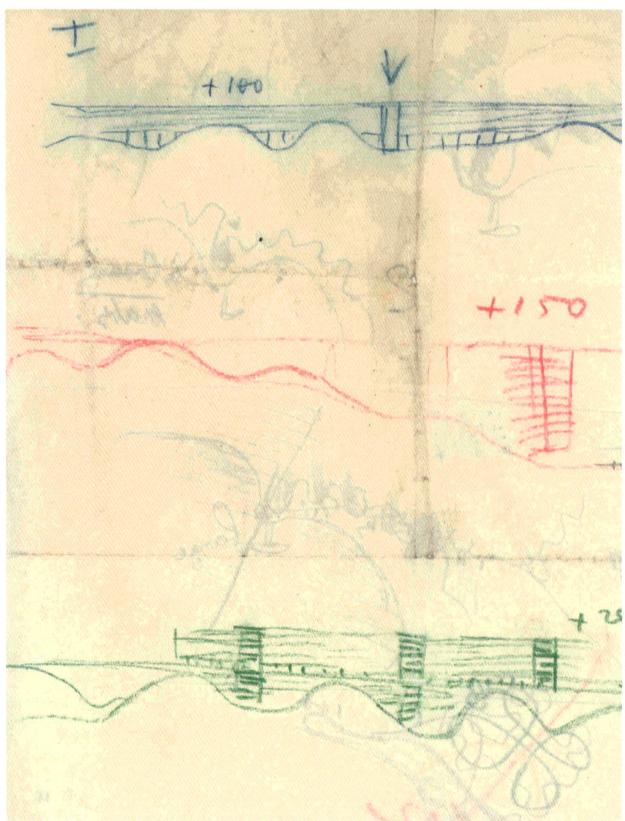

Figure 8
Page of notes for the lecture in Algiers (1 March 1931), showing the first ideas for the Obus Plan (FLC C3(6)215-1).

1930, he enjoyed proclaiming that the architectural revolution had already been achieved and that it now helped to solve the problems of dwellings and urbanism in the big city. During the 1930s, the urbanistic question was that of *La Ville radieuse*. After the war, the *Quatre routes* and the *Trois établissements humains* defined its discourse. These lectures were thus paced in two ways: first, a long introduction, often autobiographical, then a visual demonstration from *Trois établissements humains*.

60/FLC B1(20)99-107.

61/FLC B2(11)31-48.

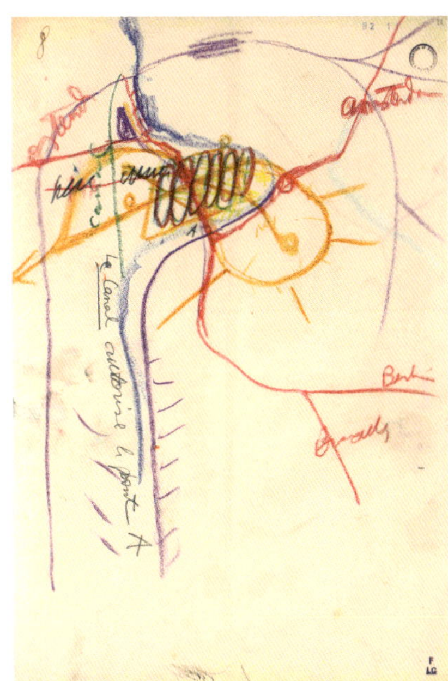

Figure 9

Sketch of the development plan for the Left Bank of Antwerp, in the preparatory notes for the lecture of 19 October 1933 (B2(11)15-008).

Architecture and urbanism, Brussels 1958

The lecture in Brussels on 26 June 1958, recorded on tape, is one interesting example of his later lectures on urbanism.[62] The notes, the recording and the transcription have been preserved (Appendix p. 220-243). The speech, which was meant to be broadcast on the radio, was in the end not transmitted, supposedly because of technical difficulties. Le Corbusier received a transcription of his lecture on 30 September, yet instead of amending in this transcription, he wrote an entirely new version on 31 March 1959, at the time of his sojourn in India.[63]

We might be shocked by the decision to refuse the radio broadcast of the speech. The sound quality is indeed perfectly acceptable, as was apparent at the time of its re-broadcast on France-Culture on 3 March 1995. The radical nature of the content and a rather informal presentation are probably the reasons for the original censure.

Listening to the recording, it seems evident that, if Le Corbusier had prepared a preliminary text, he quickly abandoned it. We also understand why he completely rewrote the text. The event had started badly. Despite the professional care of the personnel of Radiodiffusion Française, an amplification problem disrupted the speech.

62/For the preparatory notes: FLC F2(19)133, 7 May 1958; C3(10)88 and C3(10)125-132 (June 1958). Transcription by hand with corrections (by Le Corbusier) of a transcription of the recording send by Simone Menin's secretary on 30 September 1958 (see FLC C3(10)113): U3(8)307-323 (manuscript 31/3/1959) and U3(8)324-345 (type-written version by Le Corbusier's secretary, 31 March 1959). The recording is preserved at the Archives Radio INA: DLR 19950303.

63/FLC U3(8)307.

> Le Corbusier: What I am going to explain in this lecture may be considered as subversive by some people. A sort of opening... can everyone hear me?
> Some listeners: No.
> Le Corbusier: No? Well, what can be done? Are there any electricians in the audience? [laughter] No, but you see, I'm speaking loudly, I'm speaking normally; I can't speak any louder. And if the electricity is not working, I'm very sorry. Tell me if that is better? Yes... yes...
> Listeners: Yes.
> Le Corbusier: Right, I have to stand here and I am going to draw over there, it won't be easy.[64]

The reaction of the professionals from Radiodiffusion Française hearing themselves be called 'electricians' is not known. Jan Doat, the sound engineer, explained that the recording had been 'catastrophic':

> And yet, you would like to recall, master, that you had, on several occasions, changed the place of the microphones. I add that the violent shock of the stand of the microphone on the ground, during its displacements, broke the membrane of one of these devices.[65]

The displacements of the microphones are indeed very audible on the recording. For these technical reasons, Jan Doat refused to send a transcription of the tape, '[...] not conforming to professional standards,' or broadcast it on the radio, as with other lectures by scientists, industrialists and artists who had been chosen to represent France in Brussels. The sound engineer adds that it would be impossible for listeners to follow a talk illustrated with visuals. 'It is a great disappointment for us not to have been able to broadcast over the airwaves, as we had done for all the other lectures, a magnificent speech from an illustrious man.'

Once the amplification was fixed, Le Corbusier, it seems, read a page of his text. His pronunciation is rather monotonous and without rhetorical effects, which clearly distinguishes the first minutes of his talk from what followed. Once he begins to start drawing, everything changes. The talk goes from analytical to demonstrative. Le Corbusier introduces the descriptions of great rivers seen from the air – the 'loi du méandre [law of the meander]' – already put forward during his lectures in South America in October 1929 (Fig 10).**[66]**

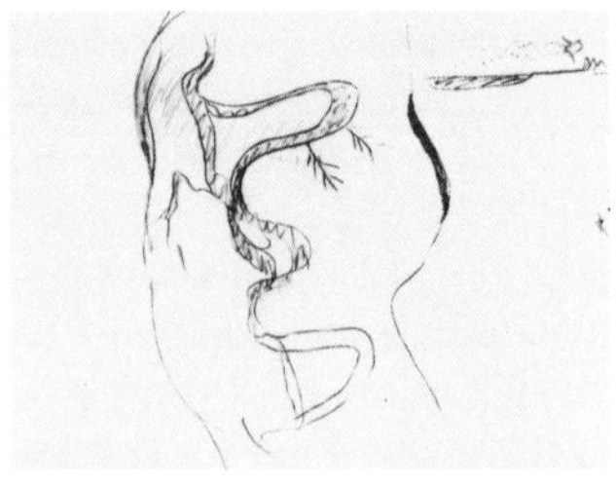

Figure 10
Sketch illustrating the law of the meander, drawn during the lecture of 26 June 1958 in Brussels.

> A time of crisis is when only two conclusions are available to us, two extremes, two poles of any problem. It is good, it is necessary to be familiar with the two banks of the river. But the stream, the river of life, the flow of life run between these two banks, sometimes closer to one, sometimes to the other, sometimes drawn "towards", sometimes pushed away "by". At every instant, the situation is different, but through grouping, adhesion or solidarity a current is formed that goes sometimes to the left, sometimes to the right. The task of each day is the necessity of moving

64/Recording INA DLR 19950303 FCR 18; original number 430D583, see pp. 235-243. (author's transcription).

65/Jan Doat (Radiodiffusion Française, Brussels) to Le Corbusier, 28 July 1958 (FLC C3(10)109).

66/Le Corbusier (1930). *Précisions*, op. cit., p. 142. The origins of this evocative metaphor in 1929 are discussed on pp. 162-163.

> forward, getting through [...]
> A bird's eye view over the estuaries of the great rivers of Asia or America - North or South - is an invitation to meditation. In the end, as you will see, everything flows to the sea, but how and in what state?[67]

It is interesting to note that the expression 'vol d'oiseau', used in the lecture, is substituted with 'vol d'avion' in the version written for publication (see Appendix, p. 218). The airplane has played multiple roles, that of the point of view but also that of the vector of modernity, that which will transform the destiny of Bogotá. The description of the river is profoundly metaphorical:

> I'm drawing the bank of something, and another bank; it's the bed of a river seen from an aeroplane. The riverbed, during the rainy season, is there and fills with water. There's no question about it, both banks are occupied. At mid-season, in the between-seasons, the water follows certain strange, unexpected paths, it's seeking its way. Here it's meandering, making islets, making bends and [...] I am going to do this again [...] I do this if necessary, sometimes to the left, sometimes to the right. [sound of the pencil on the paper] First of all here you will see the essential thing of the permafrost strata attacked by erosion. Here, on the contrary, on the opposite side we have sands that have slowly built up as alluvial deposits, haven't we? [he moves away from the microphone] and you will see, when the rains start to fall, you will see places where there are sorts of violent currents in the... in the... er... rocks that are being eroded, natural rocks, and others making complicated courses.[68]

The water system evidently corresponds to the urbanistic problems which confront the modernist prophet. Between left and right, there is a reasonable, sensible solution, but there is also a perilous alternative, digging its way into the rocks in a violent way.

> This is the story of an atmospheric cycle. It can be shown with this diagram. You have the sea (with or without an accent) [Le Corbusier is referring here to the identical pronunciation of mer = sea and mère = mother, translator's note], the plain, the mountains, and you have a necessary equilibrium charged with relativity, charged with counterweight, which means that here you have water evaporating in droplets [sound of the pencil tapping on the paper to make dots] which create clouds, which create storms, which make winds, lightning, and the water that flows down from the mountains and comes down again to the sea.[69]

67/INA DLR 19950303, see p. 235.

68/Ibid.

69/Ibid.

The connection between 'mer [sea]' and 'mère [mother]' is striking but not unexpected from a man who venerated his almost 100-year-old mother. Reading aloud, Le Corbusier creates the drama of the rain water system, corresponding to the sounds of the daily struggle he knew. This parable of the cosmic waters descending towards the *mer/mère* must be read on several levels. Le Corbusier concretizes his examples for the listener. Instead of simply writing: 'Every day of life creates for us the necessity of searching for and finding a solution [...]' he describes:

> But it is this cycle and the way it is expressed here that shows you the range of difficulties, the range of possible solutions. The opportunity presented by a day as it passes and time as it passes. Here you have [...] the first of the month, there it will be the first of the second month [...] the third month, and every day of your life you will be under the obligation, you will find it necessary[...] to seek and to find a solution.[70]

What did the secular audience of Brussels understand by this elaborate description? Le Corbusier insisted that 'creating something' by drawing in colour on large sheets of paper provided an artistic performance that allowed him to articulate complex and extremely ambiguous ideas, in front of a sympathetic audience. These four minutes of introduction served to establish three points, in the lecture's rhetoric:

1. The *ethos* of the great master: great voyager and savant of the world
2. The *ethos* of the prophet/philosopher: river searching for the sea while others did nothing but meander
3. Premise of the argument: urbanism is not a thing of form or style but belongs to the cosmic, to the elementary.

The drawing allowed Le Corbusier to introduce the elements of his argument as integral parts of a concrete narrative. When he drew 'le bourg [the town]', 'la ville [the city]', he avoided the problems of classification and the explanatory details. The historical chain of events it literally 'shown'. On the other hand, language allows the orator to use effects of exaggeration:

Repetition:

> I say this and I maintain what I say, what clips the wings and shackles the progress of solutions is base interest, immediate gain, submitting to the interest for money that deprives research of its possibility for momentum which is a thing, the thing one should expect.[71]

Drama:

> During those times, technology was developing, and in these towns the residential question could be solved by the creation of vertical communes - with no political element of course - the commune created around the hearth, around the family, around the 24-hour solar cycle of daily life, of

70/Ibid. (see p. 235).

71/Ibid. (see p. 236).

everything, of whoever and whatever the ideas of anybody, it's there … the 24-hour solar cycle which is the fundamental key to the life of all beings on earth must be respected and the malformation of the tentacular city has no respect for the solar cycle or for its status in the countryside. The solar cycle can regain its equilibrium in the creation of units each housing 2,000 individuals, if you wish. I am going to make you shudder, but it doesn't matter, these 2,000 individuals are, can go in and out through one single entrance, and as they go in and out, and having elevators available to distribute the inhabitants to the inside streets at the various levels, and being 50 metres high in order to provide lodgings that are all in natural surroundings, in the countryside, in the hills, on the plain, in the meadows, on the lawns, mountains wherever you like.[72]

The French pavilion at the Exposition Universelle in Brussels was an engineering masterpiece, designed by the architect Guillaume Gillet, together with the engineers René Sarger and Jean Prouvé.[73] The structure was composed of an enormous inclined triangle, made with steel beams applied to a single anchoring point, with a counterweight formed by a 65-metre-tall beam creating a tower. The roof was created by two large hyperbolic parabaloids, covering 102-metre width, with a network of prestressed cables and a light membrane made of sheet metal. Compared to the little Philips pavilion designed by Le Corbusier with Yannis Xenakis, the French pavilion was very imposing.[74] From the point of view of engineering, Le Corbusier had been surpassed and we understand why he preferred talking in public about urbanism rather than architecture, where his originality was more formal than scientific in nature. In preliminary notes for this lecture, Le Corbusier spoke of the glorious tradition of French engineering from Eiffel and De Baudot up until his own works (Palais des Nations, Palais des Soviets). 'Today the industry takes hold of the building. Yet the problem is, what to build?'[75]

On a page of notes dated 18 April 1958, Le Corbusier indicates the day of the lecture (5-7 pm, 26 June) and drafts a few notes.[76] He indicates that he had 'telephoned on 24/4/58 to ask Mme Menin [the administrator for the general council for the French pavilion at l'Exposition Universelle in Brussels] for a helicopter and hotel for June 26.' A week before the conference, he sends a message to the architect of the pavilion, Guillaume Gillet, indicating the desiderata of the lecturer, as if Gillet were nothing but an administrator.[77] The sheets of paper he required had to measure 1.5 m tall by 2 m wide, be nailed at 4-5 cm intervals in such a way that they could be easily detached. He also stipulated that the drawings had to be conserved, pinned and entrusted to the general commissioner. One other important indication: a single glass of water, at the beginning of the session, would suffice.

A handwritten text of eight pages introduced the subject with a prologue of three pages (four typewritten pages), where he mentions the sight of rivers from above in an airplane, which Le Corbusier analyzes as a 'meditation' of the decisions to be made in urbanism 'between the two shores' of the practical constraints.[78] One of the five sketches made during the lecture (and published with

Following pages

Figures 11 and 12

Preparatory notes and sketches for the lecture of 26 June 1958 in Brussels (FLC C3(10)129 and 130).

72/Ibid. (see p. 238).

73/Picon, A. (ed.) (1997). *L'Art de l'ingénieur*, Paris, Centre Georges-Pompidou, Editions du moniteur, pp. 98-100.

74/Le Corbusier and N.V. Philips' gloeilampen-fabrieken Eindhoven Netherlands. (1958). *Le poème électronique, Le Corbusier. Pavillon Philips pour l'Exposition universelle de Bruxelles*, Paris, Editions de Minuit; Michels, K., 'Le Corbusier: poème électronique: die Synthese der Künste im Philips Pavillon, Weltausstellung, Brüssel 1958', *Idea: Jahrbuch der Hamburger Kunsthalle*, 4, pp. [147]-163.

75/FLC F2(19)133.

76/FLC C3(10)88.

77/Le Corbusier to Guillaume Gillet, 18 June 1958 (FLC C3(10)97).

78/FLC C3(10)126 (see p. 221).

79/This book (Brussels, E. u. e. i. d. (1959). *Entretiens et conférences donnés à l'Auditorium du Pavillon de France d'avril à octobre 1958*. Dijon, Commissariat Général de la section française) contains the full text of the lecture (pp. 125-134) including four of the five drawings done by Le Corbusier during the lecture. A manuscript (U3(08)324) from 31 March 1959 is annotated: 'Text reconstructed according to a tape recording of the lecture given by L-C, made

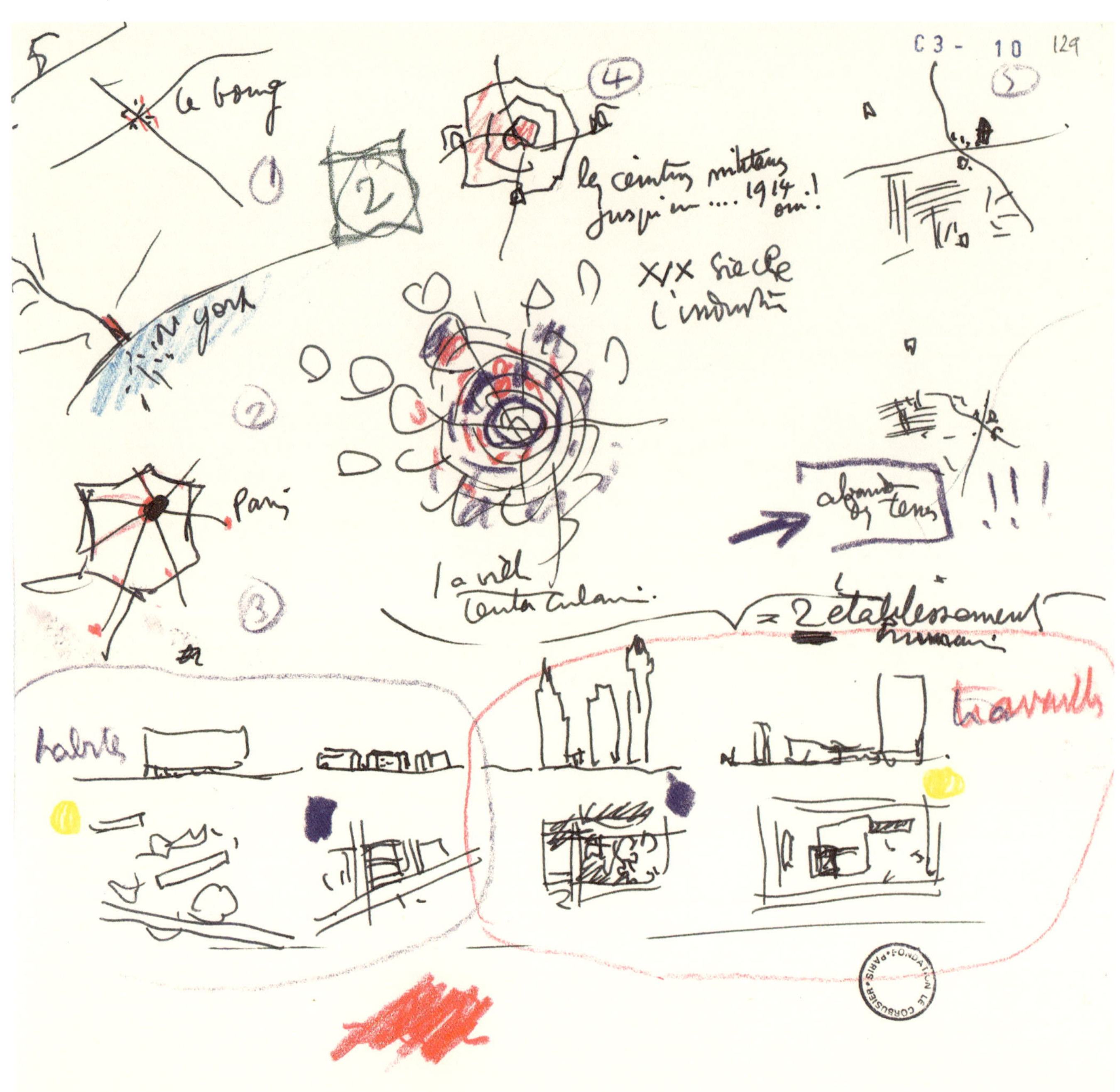
C3 - 10
129
le bourg
1
2
4
les ceintures militaires
jusqu'en 1914
oui !
5
N york
XIX siècle
l'industrie
2
Paris
3
la ville
tentaculaire
au grand
des temps
!!!
= 2 établissements
humains
habitat
travaille
FONDATION LE CORBUSIER PARIS

6/ le machinisme
les "unités de grandeur conforme"

C3-10 130

les 3 établissements

1/ l'unité d'exploitation agricole de grandeur conforme
2/ la cité linéaire industrielle
3/ la ville radio concentrique des échanges : a/ marchandises b/ idées c/ gouvernement/

3

1

2

3

école théâtre

N°3

unités d'habitation grandeur conforme avec services communs
= le prolétarien
les 24 heures solaires

cité industrielle linéaire
dénoue impasse
ville tentaculaire

= la nouvelle unité : industrielle

N° 2

4

tentaculaire

matin Banlieue Paris

classement et contacts →

1 2 3

= occupation du territoire par les travaux de la civilisation machiniste

the account of the lectures and discussions[79]) illustrated this argument (Fig 10). Le Corbusier developed his prologue by using the example of Bogotá, a city for which he undertook urbanism projects with José Lluís Sert. Bogotá allowed him to use, for the third time, the image of the airplane. This time, the airplane appeared as a liberating agent allowing men to arrive from the four corners of the globe to modernize the city, while, during four centuries, Bogotá 'remained asleep' because of its geographic position. From Bogotá, Le Corbusier continued on to Paris and described the creation of the ASCORAL team, where the ideas of *Trois établissements humains de la civilisation machiniste* were developed.

Up until this point, Le Corbusier's handwritten notes precisely delineated the argument as well as the key words and examples for his upcoming speech. Arrived at the explanation of the *Trois établissements* (p. 223), the notes give way to sketches (Fig 13), anticipating those made during the lecture.

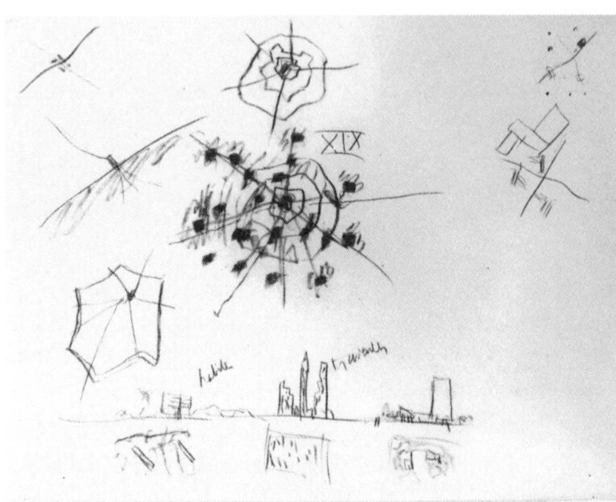

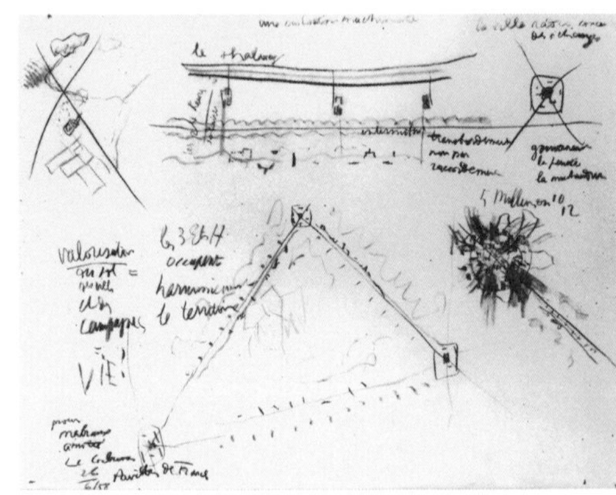

Figures 13 and 14
Sketch of the *Trois établissements humains* done during the lecture of 26 June 1958 in Brussels (FLC B88) p. 128 or FLC L4(7)106-001).

Le Corbusier noted with precision at once his visual demonstration and his commentary. The recorded text allows us to follow the way in which he explains his sketches.[80]

After having transcribed and corrected the recorded text, Le Corbusier asked his secretary Jeanne to send the typewritten text to Jean Petit, suggesting that he create a pocket booklet 'that would serve as publicity and introduction to the book *Les Trois établissements humains,* in preparation in the series "La Recherche Patiente".'[81] In fact, this sketch (Fig 14) would be included, as a negative, facing page 11 of the book *L'Urbanisme des trois établissements humains*, written by Jean Petit for les Editions de Minuit in 1959.[82]

The lecture in Bruxelles was not a big success for Le Corbusier. Even if his text was finally included in the book *Entretiens et conférences*, with 63 others, the objective, which was to reach the general public, was far from achieved. The other contributions were, for the most part, timely lectures on the scientific and artistic achievements of France. No other architect was included. Jean Cassou had lectured on the Ecole de Paris (6 June), Pierre Balmain on fashion (3 June), and Jean Cocteau had delivered his elegant reflections on the position of France in cultural terms (20 September). Each had made the effort to combine refined yet accessible language with a clear and interesting narrative. In this context, Le Corbusier seemed stuck in his own mythology, doctrinaire and rigid.

23 (or 27) June 1958 […]'. It contains the substantial corrections and additions that will be integrated in the typewritten version (FLC U3(08)307) as well as in the version printed in the book.

80/Compare pp. 224-226 with the transcript of the lecture (pp. 237-243). On one of the sketches created during the lecture, he wrote a dedication to André Malraux. His intention was that the minister would receive the five drawings as a gift, undoubtedly to exhibit them in an office. Yet the office of the minister sent back the drawings to the architect, after having loaned them to a Belgian journal for publication. A long correspondence traces the circumstances of this exchange.

81/FLC U3(08)347.

82/Le Corbusier, N. Bézard, et al. (1959). *L'Urbanisme des trois établissements humains*. Paris, Minuit.

The lecture of 26 June 1958 is not an example of profound originality in Corbusian thought. Many other lectures deal with the same ideas and had already been published since 1945.[83] Yet these show the great simplification of the rhetoric of Le Corbusier near the end of his life. It sufficed for him to offer a relatively short introduction, adapted for the audience and often rooted in his personal experiences, and then launch into a formulaic explanation of theory (generally *Les Trois établissements*). These lectures on urbanism were always prepared in a very minimal way. For many of them, there is no preparatory text. Only the sketches indicate the content.

Two lectures at Columbia University, April 1961

A series of prestigious lectures was organized in 1961 at Columbia University, on the initiative of the new dean of the School of Architecture. The idea was to ask the four 'masters' of modern architecture – Frank Lloyd Wright, Walter Gropius, Mies van der Rohe and Le Corbusier – to offer their opinions on modern architecture to the students and professors. Le Corbusier spoke twice, for the general assembly of the faculty – where he received a gold medal for architecture – and for a conversation with the students.[84] These talks, which were recorded, were quite short. Two texts in English, loosely translated by Charles Rieger and Richard Arndt, present a summary of the two lectures. The recording allows us to realize the listening difficulty experienced by the American audience and the problems of transcription. Le Corbusier spoke in French, assisted by a translator. Yet, quickly and impatiently, he started interfering in the translation. The task of the translator became impossible and Le Corbusier finished by talking partly in English.

For the lecture given to the general assembly, his speech was formal and modest. After a prologue of only six lines, Le Corbusier launched directly into the theory of the *Trois établissements*, illustrating his reasoning with a sketch. He presented this theory of the *Trois établissements* as the fruit of forty or fifty years of struggle.'

He started his sketch (Fig 15) in the upper left, explaining the two historic human establishments (that of agriculture, with its cattle and horses, and the radioconcentric model, of exchange). On the right, he showed how the 'sprawling city' had been destroyed by industrialization. The following line represented the third establishment, which still remained to be constructed: the linear city with centres 200km apart. Finally, at the bottom, he showed the triangular system of linear cities, stretching in all direction and leaving the countryside open. He finished his drawing with a human gesture of gratitude – 'my only political act' – a sketch of an open hand – 'open to give and open to receive' – that he offered to the professors of Columbia in thanks for the risk they took in inviting him.

The following drawing (Fig 16) shows the international development of a network of linear cities, with Columbia University represented in the shape of a temple on the New York coast. In choosing orange as the colour for the plan, Le Corbusier remarked, 'that it is impossible to signify things that colours are incapable of invoking.' He proclaimed that the international network was a fraternal conjuncture and proposed the association of engineers and architects, in an ideogram in red and blue (with joined hands). He used red for the engineers, symbol-

Following double spread

Figure 15

First drawing done during the lecture given in front of the general assembly at Columbia University in New York on 28 April 1961. This drawing, like the three others done at the lectures at Columbia, measures approximately 1.5 m by 2 m (Avery Library Drawings Collection).

83/For example, the lecture for the André Philips committee, 'L'urbanisme ordonnateur social par excellence [Socially organizing urbanism par excellence]' (FLC C3(17)28-35) dates from 14 February 1945 and concludes with the exposition of the principles of the *Trois établissements*. See also Bézard and Le Corbusier (1945). *Les Trois établissements humains*. Paris, Editions Denoël.

84/Publication of the lecture, pp. 164-167 and 168-171. This brochure and the tape recording are located in the audiovisual archives of the Butler Library, Columbia University.

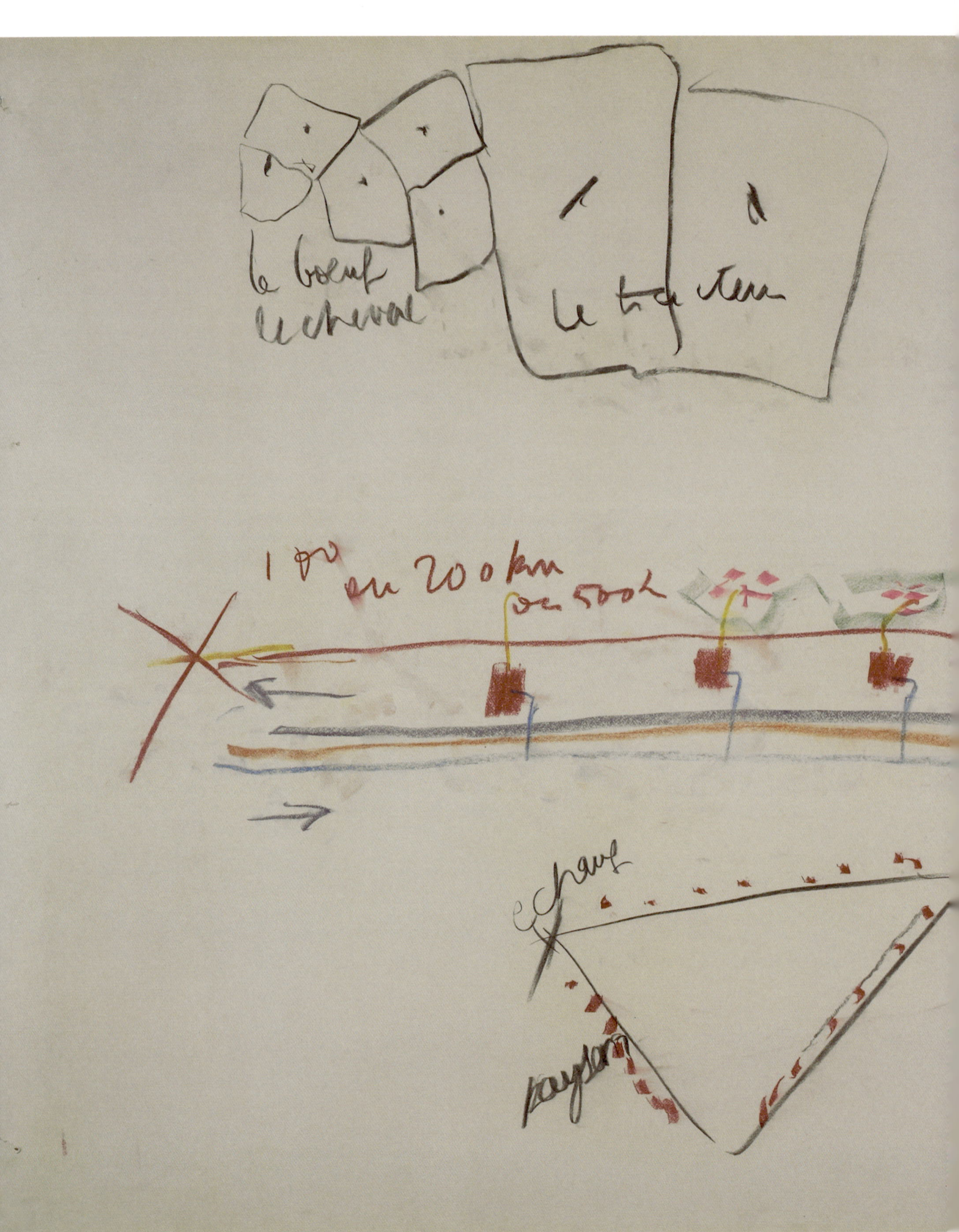
le boeuf
le cheval
le tracteur
ou 200km

la ville radio concentrique des échanges

ville tentaculaire

marchandises
idées
etc

"la main ouverte

pour recevoir
et
pour donner

izing action and force, and blue for the intellectual work of architects. To conclude he signed his sketch: 'L-C reconnaissant [L-C grateful].'

This lecture was reduced to its simplest and most functional level yet allowed Le Corbusier to express his humanity. The other lecture, presented to the students, was lighter. The tone of his speech was a lot more relaxed than that of his speech to the professors. In very little time, he managed to speak about housing, the *Trois établissements* and the plan for Paris. After a muted compliment on the models made by the students, he declared that his subjects would be more modest and proceeded to comment on the Unité d'Habitation in Nantes meant for 2,000 people (which garnered approving applause). In describing this Unité (Fig 18, top left), he insisted on the innovation of the bridging crossing the lake, which had become the principal access point, a challenge of regulations as Le Corbusier stressed.

Then, he continued by drawing the history of the *Trois établissements* with the help of synchronized sketches, in particular, indicating the 800,000 suburbanites ('disaster') of the sprawling city. This detail shows the interest that Le Corbusier expressed to the suburban forms of American cities, even if he here showed the example of Paris.

On the second drawing (Fig 17), Le Corbusier drafted a view of Paris in the future, with the four skyscrapers of the business centre and the new East-West roadway, which he proposed in the Voisin Plan and continued to show in his plans for Paris. In the English transcription, the lecture stops abruptly, with the sketch and this message of hope.

With this vision of Paris, the series of lectures on urbanism returns to its origins in Strasbourg in 1923. Saving Paris thanks to radical surgery was always the greatest and most desperately impractical goal in the Corbusian pantheon. This topic, omnipresent in his lectures, inevitably provoked a violent reaction confirming, every time, Le Corbusier's status as an avant-garde prophet.

Figure 16

Second drawing for the convocation lecture, Columbia University (Avery Library)

Figure 17

Second drawing made during the lecture for the students of Columbia University in New York on 28 April 1961 (Avery Library).

Following double spread

Figure 18

First drawing made for the lecture for the students, 28 April 1961 (Avery Library).

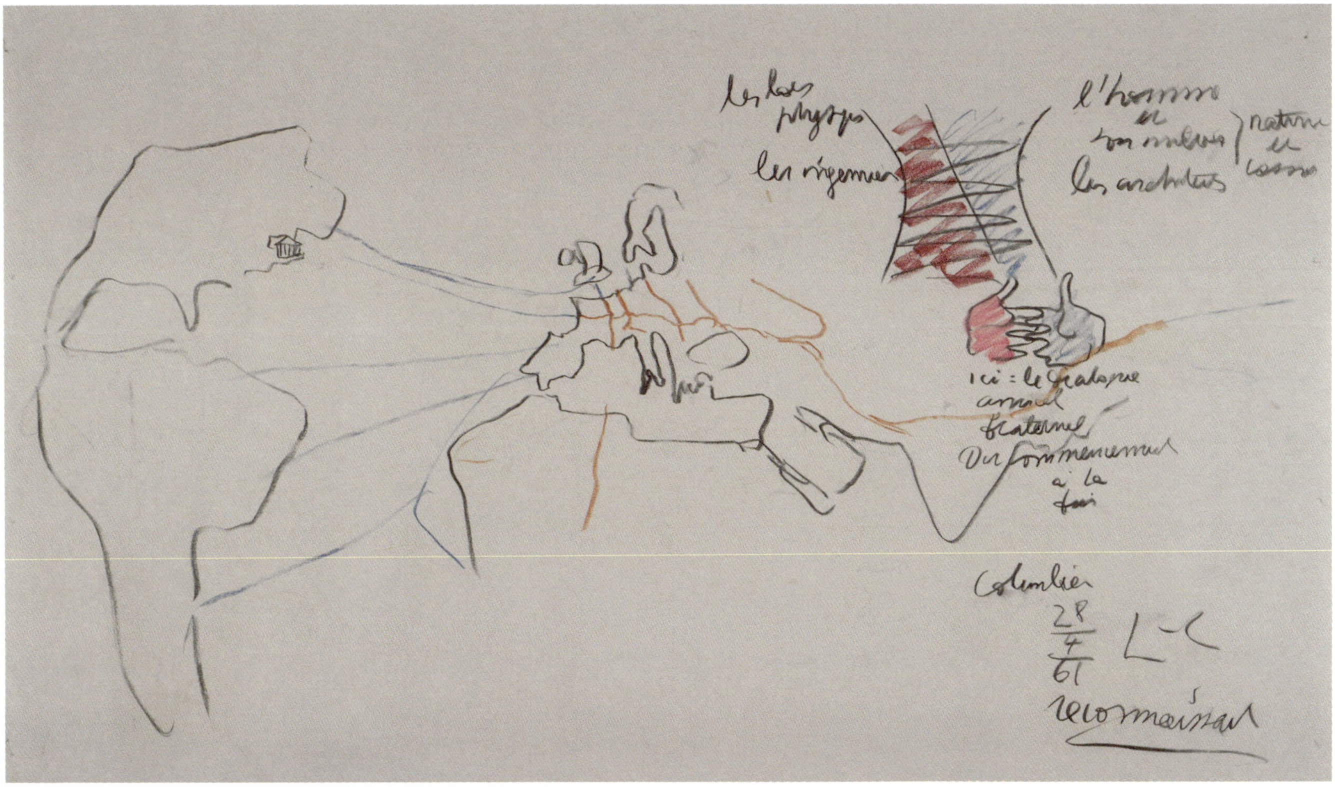

les lois physiques

les ingénieurs

l'homme et son milieu

les architectes

nature et homme

ici : le dialogue amical fraternel Du commencement à la fin

Colombie 28/4/61 L-C

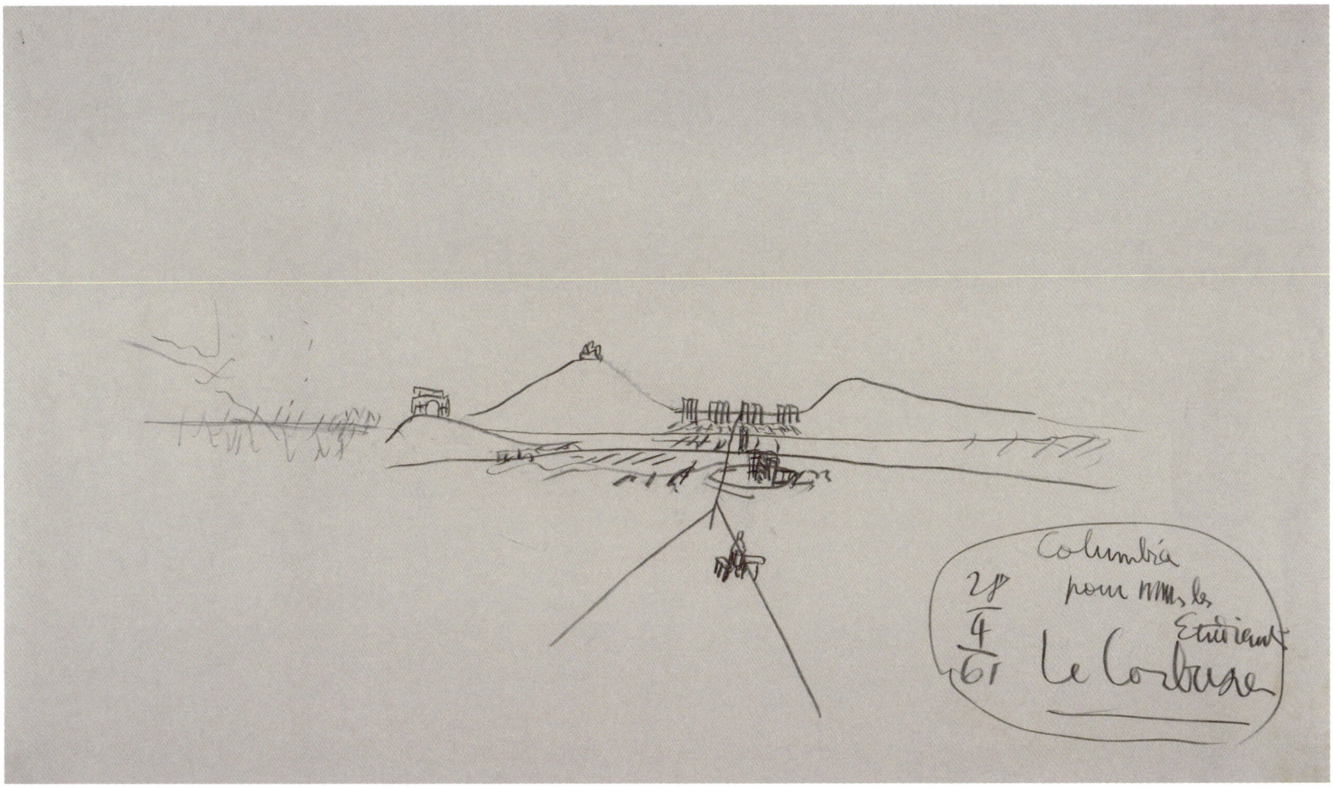

reconnaissant

Colombia 28/4/61 pour mes amis les Étudiants Le Corbusier

joies essentielles

2000 habitants

6

ville radio concentrique

d'échanges:
marchandises
idée

tracteur

1

1

28

4

6

colombia

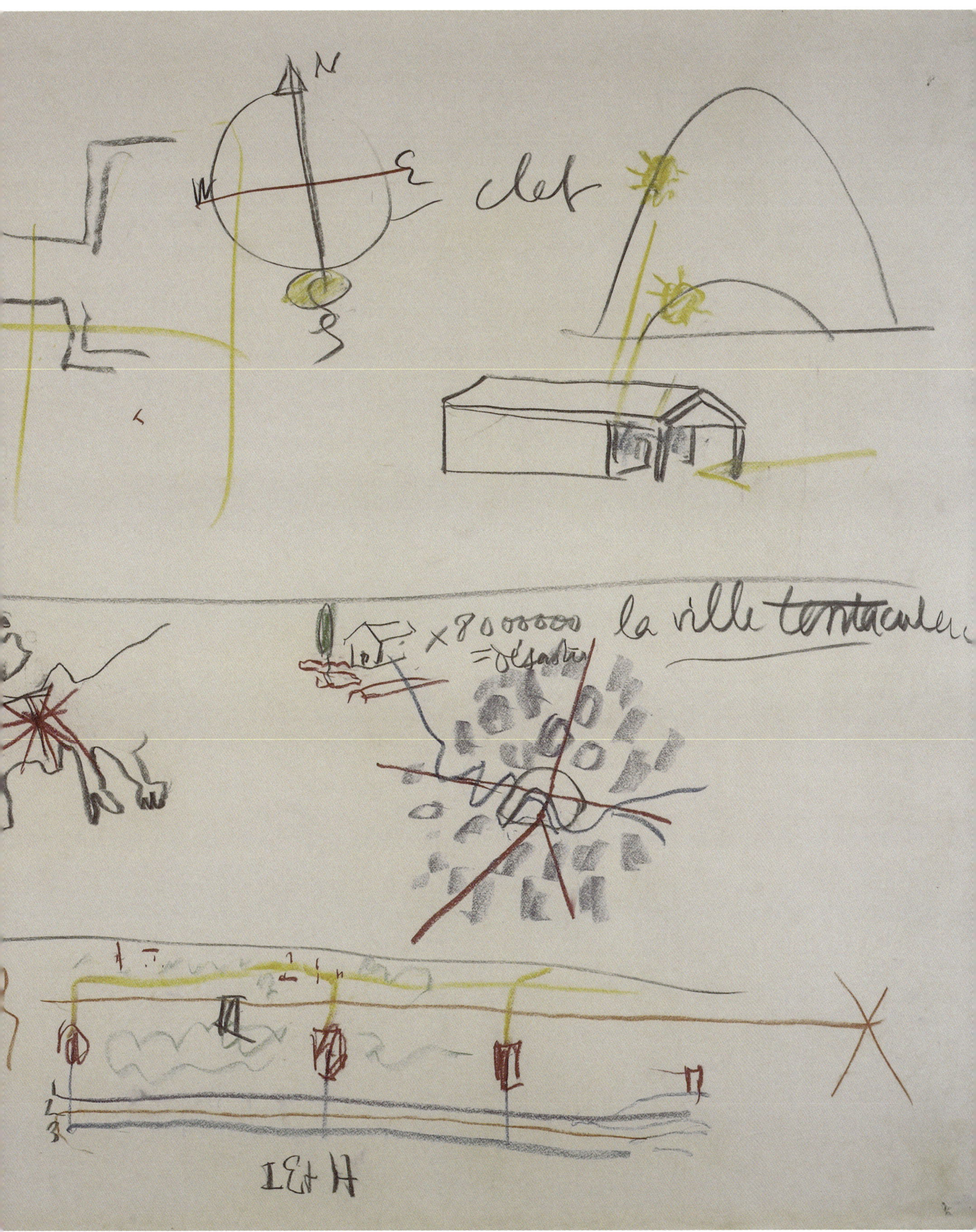
N
W
E
S
clef
× 8000000
= désastre
la ville

le navire

le palais

le paquebot

SDN

le gratte ciel

la colline artificielle

Chapter 4

The ten lectures in Buenos Aires

In Buenos Aires, between 3 and 19 October 1929, Le Corbusier gave ten lectures that would be published the following year under the title *Précisions sur un état présent de l'architecture et de l'urbanisme* (*Precisions on the present state of architecture and city planning*) (Fig 1).[1] Then, between the end of November and December, he revisited these topics in four lectures given in São Paulo and Rio de Janeiro. This set of talks constitutes the culmination of the architectural revolution of the 1920s, yet it is also the best example of Le Corbusier's strategy as a rhetorician. In *Précisions*, the lectures are preceded by an 'Avertissement [Preface]' and by a 'Prologue américain [American Prologue]', and followed by three texts entitled (in an almost journalistic fashion): 'Corollaire brésilien [Brazilian Corollary]' (lecture at Rio de Janeiro on 8 December 1929), 'Température parisienne [The Temperature of Paris]' and 'Atmosphère moscovite [The Atmosphere of Moscow]'. Le Corbusier wrote these additions while onboard the ocean liner *Lutétia*, at the time of his return trip to Europe, a transatlantic voyage lasting 12 days, from 10 to 22 December 1929. Comfortably installed in a first-class cabin, he had himself photographed with the large sketches he had made during his lectures (Fig 2).

The ten texts reproduced in *Précisions* are faithful transcriptions of the lectures given by Le Corbusier, except for a few alterations; certain passages were suppressed; others enhanced by the addition of previously published texts. The book is illustrated with 64 images, of which 56 are reproductions of the sketches drawn during the lectures.[2] These large, splendid sketches, which measure approximately one metre by 70 centimetres, were done with charcoal and coloured chalk.

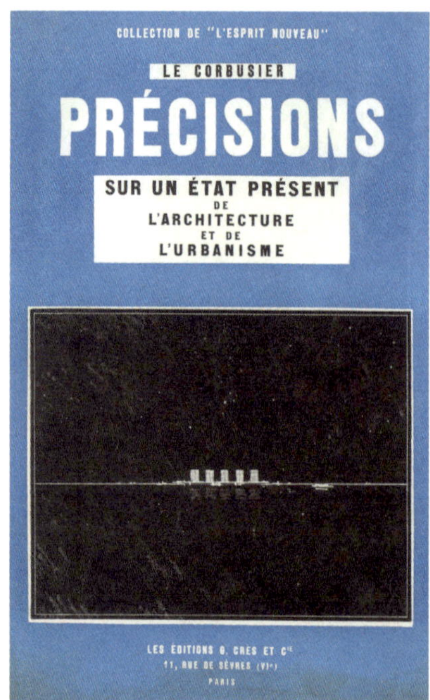

Preceding page
Drawing made during the lecture 'Les Techniques sont l'assiette même du lyrisme', in Buenos Aires, on 5 October 1929.

Figure 1
Proof of book cover for *Précisions*.

1/Le Corbusier, *Précisions*, op. cit. References to the English edition of the book, Le Corbusier, *Precisions on the present state of architecture and city planning*, Cambridge, MA, MIT Press, 1991, will appear as Precisions, op. cit. For the circumstances surrounding his trip and his sojourn in South America, see Fernando Pérez Oyarzun, 'Le Corbusier in South America: reiventing the South American city', in Benton, T., P. Carl, et al. (2003). *Le Corbusier & the architecture of reinvention*, London, AA Publications, pp. 14-153.

2/Seventy-seven large sketches done during the lectures of October to December 1929 are preserved at the Fondation Le Corbusier. Fifty-six of the illustrations in *Précisions* are identical to these sketches, of which two feature two drawings on the same page. Eighteen sketches are doubles, addressing the same subject in a slightly different form. These are discussed on p. 187. Three sketches (FLC 30297B, 33525A and 33526B) are different from the illustrations in *Précisions*, not chosen at

Figure 2

Le Corbusier aboard the *Lutétia*, between 10 and 22 December 1929, upon his return from South America. It is during this trip that he fine-tuned the manuscript for *Précisions*.

***Précisions* is a brilliant synthesis of Le Corbusier's ideas on architecture and urbanism, a fact which he himself would later confirm: 'All my theory – my introspection and my retrospection on the phenomenon of Architecture and Urbanism – comes from these improvised and drawn lectures.'[3] The South American lectures constitute the apogee of the teaching and rhetorical techniques of Le Corbusier in his first period as a lecturer.[4] They are the conclusion of a five-year campaign over the course of which he tried to impose his point of view on what modern architecture and urbanism should become. In *Précisions*, he writes:**

> I think that these ten lectures in Buenos Aires will be, for me, the last on the subject: "The architectural revolution fomented by modern technology". The world – Buenos Aires, São Paulo, Rio, New York, Paris, the U.S.S.R. – is drawn toward the realization of urgent tasks, is trembling on the verge of "great works". *The Hour of Great Works*: such is, it seems to me, the theme now offered to our reflections.[5]

the time of the book's editing.

3/Extract from the soundtrack, *L'Aventure Le Corbusier*, Fondation Le Corbusier, 1951.

4/Pérez Oyarzún, F. (1991). *Le Corbusier y Sudamerica: viajes y proyectos*, Santiago, Ediciones Arq, pp. 35; and Tsiomis, Y. and Centro de Arquitetura e Urbanismo do Rio de Janeiro. (1998). *Le Corbusier: Rio de Janeiro 1929, 1936*. Rio de Janeiro, Centro de Arquitetura e Urbanismo do Rio de Janeiro; Prefeitura da Cidade do Rio de Janeiro.

5/*Precisions*, op. cit., p. 269.

The organization of the Buenos Aires lectures and preparatory notes

The ten Buenos Aires lectures are very extensively documented.[6] On 28 July 1929, Le Corbusier had already prepared a list of ten lectures (Fig 3).[7] The order of the lectures on this sheet of paper corresponds to a set of handwritten notes, written clearly and confidently, that prepare the argument for each of the lectures.[8] Each page of notes has, at the upper left, the number of the lecture according to this list. However, this order was not followed, either in the lectures themselves or in the layout of *Précisions*. Furthermore, the content of the lectures was altered, reflecting Le Corbusier's experience of visiting Buenos Aires, so there is every indication that these notes were written before arriving in Buenos Aires, probably aboard the ocean liner *Massilia*.[9] There are from ten to 18 numbered pages for each lecture. I will call these manuscripts the 'lecture notes', because Le Corbusier often cited whole passages from these in his lectures.

The table below allows for the comparison of the number given to each lecture in the preparatory notes (first column), the reorganization of the sequence after 11 October (second column), then the date, numbered order and the location of the lectures as they were actually given.

Number on the 'lecture notes'	Renumbering around October 11 [10]	Date of the lecture	Chronological sequence	Location of the lecture	Lecture AA =Amigos del Arte FS = Faculty of Pure, Applied and Natural Sciences AC = Amigos de la Ciudad	Order in *Précisions*
1	1	October 3	**1**	AA	To free oneself entirely from academic thinking	1st
2	2	October 5	**2**	AA	Technology is at the very heart of poetry	2nd
3	3	October 8	**3**	FS	Architecture in everything, urbanism in everything	3rd
4	4	October 10	**4**	FS	A housing cell to a human scale	4th
6	5	October 11	**5**	AA	The plan of the modern house	6th
5	6	October 13	**6**	AC	A man = a housing cell ; some cells = the city	7th
8	8	October 15	**7**	FS	A house – a palace	8th
10	10	October 17	**8**	FS	The world city and some perhaps untimely considerations	10th
9	9	October 18	**9**	AA	The Voisin Plan for Paris: Can Buenos Aires become one of the great cities of the world?	9th
7	7	October 19	**10**	AA	The furniture adventure	5th

6/In November in São Paulo and in December in Rio de Janeiro, Le Corbusier delivered two lectures (at each location), of which the one from Rio of 8 December is reproduced as 'Corollaire brésilien [Brazilian Corollary]' (*Precisions*, op. cit., pp. 233-245).

7/FLC C3(7)108.

8/Most of these notes are found at the Fondation Le Corbusier (boxes C3(6) and C3(7)). Others are at the Getty Research Institute (GRI) and the Canadian Centre for Architecture in Montreal (CCA). In certain cases, the notes from one lecture are shared between the collections of the Getty and the Fondation Le Corbusier. There are also proofs of *Précisions* (FLC B2(9)1-264, with a few corrections and additions) as well as typewritten pages (FLC B2(9)291-473 et 651-663) which constitute the typescript of the work.

9/On one page of preparatory notes, a clipping of an ocean liner is accompanied by the annotation 'Massilia' (FLC B2(9)666).

Figure 3

List of lectures for Buenos Aires, written 28 July 1929 (FLC C3(7)108).

Figure 4

Invitation from la Facultad de Ciencias Exactas, Fisicas y Naturales de la Universidad de Buenos Aires on 2 October 1929, annotated by Le Corbusier on 11 October (GRI 920083-01(2)3).

Following double spread

Figure 5

Outline, drafted on the *Massilia*, indicating the titles of the lectures, the subjects to be addressed and the drawings and transparencies (on the right) (GRI 920083-01(2)3).

The numbers that we will use here are those (indicated in the table in bold) corresponding to the order of the lectures as they were given. The rightmost column shows the order in which the lectures were printed in *Précisions*. A preparatory outline for all ten lectures on a double sheet of paper is organized in three columns, with the titles on the left, formulas and arguments in the centre and an iconographic list on the right (Fig 5).[11]

Certain of the topics indicated were abandoned when he came to give the lectures or were moved from one lecture to another, yet, generally, this outline represents the central themes as well as the sketches to be created.[12] Studying this outline, the evolution of Corbusian thought is relatively clear. The first lecture is devoted to the argument of the *Zeitgeist* (the world disrupted by mechanization requires a new kind of architecture). The second lecture is a demonstration of the consequences of the *Zeitgeist* in the architectural domain: reinforced concrete and the aesthetic effects that result from its use. In the third lecture, Le Corbusier elaborates his own aesthetic. The fourth lecture starts to build the link between the problems of architecture and those of urbanism, by addressing low rental housing. At this point, the lectures start to diverge, between this outline, the preparatory notes and the planned order. To understand these divergences, one must appreciate the different audiences to which he was speaking. At the end of the first lecture, he established a distinction between the 'general public' and the 'professionals', between the Amigos del Arte (Friends of Art) and the Faculty of Pure, Applied and Natural Sciences.

The four lectures for the Faculty of Pure, Applied and Natural Sciences on the one hand and the five for the Friends of Art (plus one for the Amigos de la

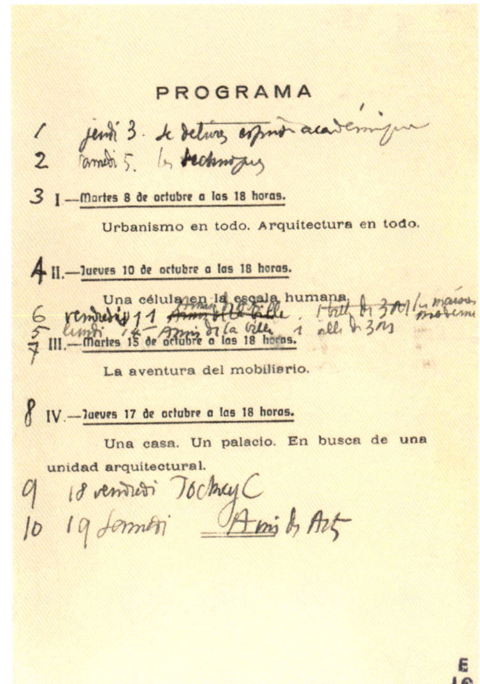
PROGRAMA

I.—Martes 8 de octubre a las 18 horas.

Urbanismo en todo. Arquitectura en todo.

II.—Jueves 10 de octubre a las 18 horas.

Una célula en la escala humana.

III.—Martes 15 de octubre a las 18 horas.

La aventura del mobiliario.

IV.—Jueves 17 de octubre a las 18 horas.

Una casa. Un palacio. En busca de una unidad arquitectural.

10/Based on an annotated invitation from the Faculty of Pure, Natural and Applied Sciences (FLC C3(7)116 and another list amended after the fifth lecture (FLC C3(7)38), see below.

11/GRI 920083-01(2)3. This page is entitled 'Ten lectures in Buenos Ayres, Sept. 1929, Massilia.'

12/For example, for 'Le Plan de la maison moderne' he indicates 'schéma à la main paquebot' [sketch of an ocean liner], but this sketch and the analysis that accompanies it will appear finally in 'Une cellule à l'échelle humaine'.

10 conférences à Buenos Ayres sept 1929 "Massilia"

1 Se libérer de tout esprit académique

2 Les techniques sont l'assiette même du lyrisme: elles ouvrent le cycle de l'architecture moderne

3 Urbanisme en tout, architecture en ~~tout~~ — le constructeur { ingénieur + poète } circulation

4 Une cellule à l'échelle humaine { standardisation, industrialisation, taylorisation }

5 Un homme – une cellule. Des cellules – la ville — + ville contemporaine de 3 Millions

6 Le plan de la maison moderne — classement

7 l'aventure du mobilier — casiers, meubles, objets utiles, siège à penser
+ digression sur la machine

8 Une maison – un Palais

9 Le Plan Voisin de Paris — une vision de Buenos Ayres

10 La Cité mondiale

pas harmonie ne fonctionne pas
... fonctionne pas, ...

lyrisme = création individuelle
son esprit ... épique

projection - composition tracé régul...

croquis Bibliothèque nat.
UM
UP

croquis Bib Nat
Pessac
UM
N.P

rétrospective maisons ... mentalité

...s par la technique, nous permettent une totale invention
calculs de l'économique nous donnent de toutes la solution

Domino

Loucheur
+ comparaisons main

pavillon EN

...main machiniste, nouveau, remet tout en cause

immeubles villas
alvéoles
cités fermées
redent

pavillon EN

circulation

schémas à la main paquebot

croquis

meyer

savoye

...er pour servir
...nous se faire en lui, en pensant

schéma rapide

La Roche
Cluny ...
EN

maison plan
Loucheur
Savoye

...l'académisme, l'avènement de l'Esprit Nouveau

paquebot ... N

Seule l décision d'Etat, une loi,
une opération fermée permet d'urbaniser
Car urbaniser c'est ... de l'argent
ce n'est pas ... dépenser
l'opération fermée seule gagne de l'argent

plan voisin
+ redent
+ alvéoles

... le but permanent porte à servir l'entité
l'organisation du monde.

cité mondiale
Mundaneum

Ciudad [Friends of the City] at the Jockey Club) on the other hand, constitute two independent series that Le Corbusier distinguished one from the other, while at the same time keeping a sense of continuity across the ten lectures.

On 11 October, after five lectures had been delivered, Le Corbusier modified the order of the last five (Fig 4).[13] **'The furniture adventure', scheduled for 15 October before the Faculty of Pure, Applied and Natural Sciences, would not be delivered until the end of the series, and then to the Amigos del Arte. He would finish his lectures at the Faculty of Pure, Applied and Natural Sciences with 'A house – a palace' and 'The world city'. When he came to deliver this last lecture, he began:**

> Ladies and Gentlemen, this lecture will be lop-sided. The subject: "The world city" was intended for the general public rather than for the professionals seated in this amphitheatre - architects, engineers, architecture students.[14]

The reason for replacing 'The furniture adventure' by 'The world city' remains uncertain. Another reason for the reorganization could have been a hesitation on the content of some of the talks. This would perhaps explain why 'The plan of the modern house' – a well prepared topic from other lectures and from previous notes[15] – was placed before 'A man = a housing cell; some cells = the city'. For this last, Le Corbusier had trouble specifying the content and radically revised his notes.[16]

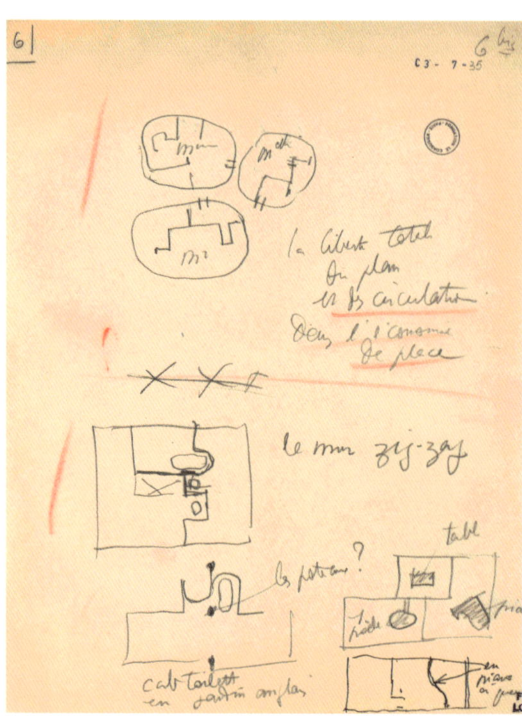

Figure 6
Notes for the fifth lecture 'The Plan of the Modern House', sheet 6bis (FLC C3(7)35).

13/GRI 920083-01(2)3. The official invitation from the Facultad de Ciencias Exactas, Fisicas y Naturales de la Universidad de Buenos Aires (Faculty of Pure, Natural and Applied Sciences) dated 2 October 1929, p. 3, announced 'L'aventure du mobilier' for October 15 and 'Une maison - un palais' for 17 October (FLC C3(7)116). Annotating the invitation, Le Corbusier adds the lecture of 18 October given in front of the Amigos de la Ciudad (at the Jockey Club) and inverts the order of the fifth and sixth lectures. On another list (FLC C3(7)38), a line is drawn after the fifth lecture, indicating a date around 11 October, and the seventh lecture is indicated as 'mobilier', the eighth as 'PdN' (Palais des Nations or League of Nations Headquarters, which must be the same as 'Une Maison un Palais' which deals with this competition), followed by the ninth lecture 'Centre de Paris' (the Voisin Plan) and finally the tenth lecture 'Cité mondiale = organisations'.

14/*Précisions*, op. cit., p. 215 (author's translation). Because of the change of audience for this lecture, Le Corbusier shortened the text to four pages and addressed another subject: 'If I were to teach architecture'. See also note 48.

15/The preparatory notes for this lecture are found at the Getty Research Institute (GRI 920083-1(1) 1-7 [sheets number 1, 3, 6, 7, 8]) and

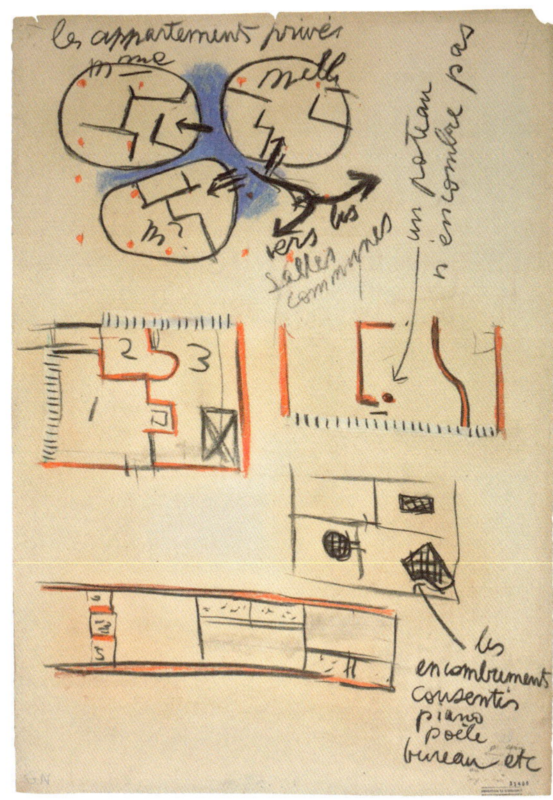

Figure 7

Sketch made during the fifth lecture 'The plan of the modern house' (FLC 33496).

The lecture notes

In certain cases, as we will see, the preparatory notes are followed point by point in the lecture. Some elements – key words and whole phrases – are often textually cited, and some of the preparatory sketches are almost identical to those drawings made during the lectures (Figs 6 and 7).[17] Sometimes, however, the notes are almost completely abandoned. For example, the first notes for the third lecture, 'Urbanisation en tout, architecture en tout' (Urbanism in everything, architecture in everything), have almost nothing to do with the speech delivered on 8 October 1929.[18] Similarly, Le Corbusier did not write extensive notes for the lecture 'The Voisin Plan for Paris' while aboard the *Massilia*, probably because the topic was familiar to him.[19] Once arrived in Buenos Aires, Le Corbusier wrote more notes on paper with the Hotel Majestic letterhead. On one of these pages, he drafts the outline for the lecture on the Voisin Plan. He planned to start with 'a word about the history of the plan for Paris', then address a list of four topics:

1. First of all surgery-medicine
2. Adding value. Making millions with modern technology
3. But who or what gives life to modern technology? Answer: Community Involvement
4. Authority? The State? No, the deep-rooted force of great altruistic convictions.[20]

at the Fondation Le Corbusier (FLC C3(7)32-36 [sheets number 2, 4, 5, 6 bis, 9 and 10]).

16/FLC C3(7)39-46. The 18 pages of notes that he prepared for this lecture were put aside or adapted for the fifth and ninth lectures.

17/FLC C3(7)35 and FLC 33496.

18/Six pages of preparatory notes for the third lecture are preserved at GRI (920083-11(2)1-4 and 920083-11(6)2).

19/Only four pages of preparatory notes can be associated with this lecture as well as five pages constituting the continuation of the notes from the fifth lecture (GRI 920083-1(1)8, 920083-1(3)3, 920083-11(3)1, 920083-11(7), for most of the sketches and GRI 920083-1(1)8-12). There are also notes for the sixth lecture that addresses the same topics.

20/FLC C3(7)113. Point 1 is mentioned in *Précisions*, op. cit., p. 172 and illustrated in a sketch FLC 33490, printed on p. 172 of *Précisions*. Point 2 appears in *Précisions*, op. cit., pp. 178-9; point 3 on p. 188, and point 4 on p. 192.

This page is probably the only framework used for the lecture. A large part of this was devoted to the complex history of projects for the city of Paris and his ideas for Buenos Aires, yet the framework built around the four points above remained at the foundation of everything.

Other notes inform us about the work done by Le Corbusier at the time of his return voyage, aboard the *Lutétia*, with regards to the finalization of *Précisions*. Provided with a shorthand text, Le Corbusier made a few changes. For example, the lecture on the Voisin Plan was expanded by three-and-a-half pages, taken from an article published in *L'Intransigeant* on 20 May 1929.[21] There are also typewritten texts, with a few handwritten corrections – a preliminary draft of *Précisions* prepared in Paris after his return – as well as a set of proofs showing a few corrections and additions.[22]

The lectures

To understand the context of the ten lectures in Buenos Aires, one must recall that Le Corbusier was, at the time, attacked on all sides, from the progressives to the conservatives. If the critiques of the rightwing partisans – Alexander von Senger or Camille Mauclair – were expected or accepted, those of the functionalists – friends of the struggle, such as his Czech friend Karel Teige – affected him greatly.[23] As a consequence, wanting to convince his audience that he was not a functionalist but someone enamoured with beauty and seeking nobility in architecture, it is here, in Buenos Aires, that Le Corbusier elaborated his personal aesthetic.

Lectures intended for the 'general public'

Neither the chronological order of the lectures, nor the order in which they appeared in *Précisions*, nor the originally conceived order can perfectly explain Le Corbusier's reasoning. To attempt this, it seemed more judicious to divide the group in two: those meant for an amateur public, that is the audiences associated with the Friends of Art and the Friends of the City, and those more specifically dedicated to the professional public, that is the students and professors of the Faculty of Pure, Applied and Natural Sciences. We can suppose that certain enthusiasts followed the entire series, and Le Corbusier occasionally referred to lectures in the 'other' sequence.

First lecture: 'To free oneself entirely from academic thinking' (Amigos del Arte)

A page of notes unveils his strategy for the first lecture. Starting with a preamble, as in a book, seemed risky: 'As in a [...] book, the readers only get as far as the preamble and close the book; so with an audience.'[24] In Le Corbusier's mind, the first lecture should resemble the indicator board in the hall of a building with the names and floors of the businesses. The ten lectures thus represented a ten-sto-

21/*Precisions*, op. cit., pp. 196-200. The notes for this article also include an extended description of Buenos Aires, not included in the text of *Précisions* (GRI 920083(8)). The bold text on p. 192 was added at the last moment on the proofs (FLC B2(9)190). Another important addition appears on pp. 194-5 (from 'And when the triumphal highway will be built [...]' to '[...] it would also go to Saint-Germain en Laye' (FLC B2(9)199).

22/FLC B2(9)292-473 and 651-663 (typescript); FLC B2(9)5-256 (proofs).

23/From the right, the main attacks came from the Swiss architect Alexander von Senger (see von Senger, A. (1928). *Krisis der Architektur* and *Le Cheval de Troie du bolchevisme*) and from the French critic Camille Mauclair from whom the reactionary articles appeared in *Le Figaro* from 1928 to 1932, notably in Mauclair, C. (1930). *La Farce de l'art vivant II: Les Métèques contre l'art français*, and (1933) *La Crise du panbettonisme intégral. L'Architecture va-t-elle mourir?*. From the left, the main accusations came from the Czech poet, artist and architect Karel Teige, a friend of Le Corbusier; see Baird, G. 'Documents: Karel Teiges Mundaneum and Le Corbusier's in Defense of Architecture, 1933' in *Oppositions*, no 4, October 1974, pp. 79-108.

24/FLC C3(7)115.

rey building – modern and, of course, made with reinforced concrete – each floor being independent (the open plan), 'but the *pilotis* will pass through.' This lovely metaphor conveys the conceit of a structure of ideas running through a series of free variations on a theme. The Buenos Aires lectures have a theoretical spine, concerning how the new methods must be exploited aesthetically in the service of society. Both sets of lectures (general and professional) progress, in principle, from the domestic to the urban scale.

There exists a first rough draft of four pages, written before the preparatory notes, in which Le Corbusier tries to organize his argument for the first lecture (Fig 8).[25]

Without preamble, in the upper left, he poses the usual argument of the *Zeitgeist*: '1 World full [of] disruption. [...] communication; interpretation; sudden intense mobility...'.[26] This phrase is reused almost word for word on the third page of preparatory notes (Fig 9).[27]

The schematic format of these notes is characteristic of the evolution of Corbusian thought. He proceeds from the simple to the more complex. In this rough draft, he thus starts his analysis:

A world [of] complete upheaval A new event – mechanization – disrupts everything	Communication Interpenetration Sudden, intense mobility	in the family [in] the city	
	Brutal, rapid rupture	of traditional customs, of habits of thought. Everything is false; rings hollow; ~~we must adjust~~ moral and social concepts	Sociology Economics Politics, obviously[28]

The third page of preparatory notes textually transcribes this first preliminary draft, with a few additions. For example, in front of the enumeration of the three categories – sociological, economic, political – he adds: 'the 3 key fields of urbanism have come into play' (Fig 9).[29]

For the lecture itself, this structural framework was developed at length, yet the key words are emphasised in italics in *Précisions*:

> Mechanization has disrupted everything:
> *communications*: in the past, men organized their enterprises to the scale of their legs: time had a different duration. The notion of the earth was grand, limitless. The human flora (I mean by this the spiritual flowering produced by the creative mind) was diversified, multiple; customs, habits, modes of action and thought, clothing were ordered by innumerable small administrative centres like the little clouds of morning, and which expressed the primary shape of aggregation, of

Following double spread

Figure 8

First page of notes for the first lecture (GRI 920083-1(2)14).

25/GRI 920083-1(2) pp. 1r to 2v (4 pages).

26/GRI 920083-1(2) p. 1r.

27/FLC C3(7)3.

28/GRI 920083-1 (2) p. 1.

29/FLC C3(7)3.

I monde pleine perturbation. l'évén. neuf : le machinisme bouleverse tout

Qui est le perturbateur ? l'ingénieur. Son œuvre ne [illegible]

Qui est le visionnaire, le lecteur, le prophète ? ? le poète. Qu'est ce que le [illegible]

l'aspect du temps présent ? la brutalité des chiffres, du [illegible]

un Tour vrai, une déchéance

Oui, tout est là le nouveau pour qui ne [illegible]

il est étiré, déchiré, di[illegible]

" " " la plus prodigieuse épopée. [illegible]

ô poète, inutile de te pencher sur [illegible]

vies, de renaissance, d'actes passé[illegible]

époque vivante des cathédrales "

Tournant le dos aux machines

Pourquoi évoquer les machines. Parce que le présent [illegible]

la machine moderne est encore engagée dans [illegible]

Il y a les janissaires. les [illegible],

Ils sont à tous les robinets, comme l'[illegible]

l'académisme

Qu'est-ce que l'académisme ?

[illegible]cation
[illegible]
[illegible] subsiste [illegible]

dans la famille,
la ville
les usages [illegible]
les habitudes de penser
tout est faux
ne donne plus
~~il faut [illegible]~~
concepts moraux
sociaux

sociologique
économique
politique [illegible]

nouvelle morale
" éthique
" esthétique.

Rien ne subsiste, il faut se l'avouer.
Essayez de voir ce qui reste.
Tous les rapports sont brisés
Une seule constante dans cette débacle:
l'homme avec ses passions
son cœur
sa raison.

et en cette affaire d'art ; ses dimensions.

[illegible] ; elle est la [illegible] analyse.

[illegible]? celui qui en face des éléments sait les voir, les lire, percevoir les rapports, démêler des rapports, désigner des rapports, clamer des rapports. Désigner la vérité nouvelle.

[illegible], de la [illegible] de [illegible] du corps des pays (serait-il mortel) un désespoir?

[illegible] pas. mais subsiste, pour qui reste les pieds posés sur [illegible].
[illegible] Tout pour lui n'est pas mort
[illegible] les rencontres [illegible], les découvertes inouïes, les rencontres sensationnelles
gracieuses [illegible] d'autrefois. Le monde entier [illegible] de
Il suffit de voir, de lire d'apprécier. "Une grande

[illegible] encore [illegible]

[illegible] ~~[illegible]~~ [illegible] le nez.
[illegible] les ~~[illegible]~~ actions [illegible]
[illegible]non
[illegible] ~~[illegible]~~ pas longs
[illegible] calme [illegible], et l'estomac à la gorge

1)

C3 - 7-3 3

les communication
l'interpénétration
l'anéantissement des cultures régionales { les villes internationales
1 mobilité subite, intense | dans la famille (calme paysan) / dans la ville (dont les maisons ont perdu leur fonction originale)

une rupture brutale rapide { des usages séculaires / les habitudes de penser / tout est faussé, nous ne sommes plus / à réajuster / concepts moraux et sociaux

les 3 grandes bases de l'urbanisme sont entrées dans le jeu { sociologique / économique / politique bien entendu } car { nouvelles usages / et éthique / et esthétique / et quelle mode d'autorité?

Tous les rapports anciens sont brisés, essayons seulement un instant d'imaginer les pensées, l'existence, les concepts de nos grands pères

Une seule constante demeure, dans cette débâcle

administration: one manages what one sees, what one can attain, what one can control [...]
Interpenetration: one day Stevenson invented the locomotive. People laughed. And as business people – the first captains of industry who were to become the new conquistadores – took it seriously and demanded concessions, Monsieur Thiers, the statesman who was leading France, intervened immediately in Parliament, begging members to tend to other more serious matters: "Never will a *chemin de fer* [lit. iron way, later the accepted term for railway, translator's note] [...] be able to connect two cities [...]"![30]

Le Corbusier developed the basic structure by illustrating it with examples, with anecdotes adapted for his audience and spiced with humour. Regarding the 'interpenetration', he takes emigration to the New World as an example:

Hordes of migrants crossing the seas, new national entities suddenly appearing, formed by a melting pot of all the races and all the peoples: the USA or your country. A single generation suffices to create this lightning alchemy.[31]

And, for the 'destruction of regional cultures', Le Corbusier takes an example from the cinema:

Here, in your cinemas, you hear the voice of the North-American sea, the crash of the waves against the rocks; you hear the crowds shouting at a boxing match on the other side of the world.[32]

By using the classic rhetorical trope of the example, Le Corbusier succeeds in transforming somewhat dry and abstract topics into a persuasive message by using mental images, sensations and experiences shared by the audience.

At other times, he reads his prepared notes word for word:

A brutal, rapid rupture:
of ancient habits
of thought processes
Everything is wrong
no longer sounds right
to be readjusted:
moral concepts
social concepts
What I affirm here is already implied in what I have just told you.[33]

Figure 9
Third page of preliminary notes for the first lecture (FLC C3(7)3).

30/*Precisions*, op. cit., p. 26.

31/*Ibid.*

32/*Ibid*, p. 27.

33/*Ibid*, p. 29.

To conclude this part of his speech, Le Corbusier restates the formula already indicated:

> The age of mechanization has disrupted everything
> communications
> interpenetration
> destruction of regional cultures
> sudden mobility
> brutal rupture of ancient habits
> ways of thinking
> The three great bases of city planning have entered the stage
> the sociological
> the economic
> the political
> We are adopting new habits
> we aspire to a new ethic
> we are seeking a new aesthetic
> And, for all this, what mode of authority?[34]

If we compare these few lines with the third page of his preparatory notes (Fig 9) **it seems evident that Le Corbusier had this page in front of him during his lecture. The self-proclaimed improvised character of his lectures, often asserted by the architect, needs to be reassessed. He worked around a well-defined structure, occasionally referring to the precise text of his notes and frequently embroidering with examples, demonstrations and anecdotes.**

The argument is the familiar one: the world has been shattered by the engineer. Only the poet can resolve the situation because he is blessed with imagination and an eye for the new situation, not seeing it as a 'black hole, decline, or despair'[35] but as 'the most prodigious epic, of unknown heroisms'. Following his notes closely, Le Corbusier continued:[36]

> Oh poet, it is useless to labour over graceful minuets: the whole world is bursting with life, with rebirth, with positive actions. You need only see, read, appreciate; "A great epoch has just begun".[37]

He continues by attacking the Academy that, according to him, encourages people to accept the folly of modern life without asking 'why' and without 'inserting your "me" into each question.'[38] This passage presents a rare moment of divergence between the preparatory notes and the lecture itself. In his notes, Le Corbusier describes the attitude of the Academy and then compares it to his own personal attitude:

> It is constraint and this constraint is instigated by the academies. It is acting in accordance with one's habits and not according to oneself.
> Not according to oneself. Then what? Well, it is the renouncement of happiness itself, for happiness comes

34/*Ibid*, p. 31.

35/FLC C3(7)4-5; *Precisions*, op. cit., p. 31.

36/For example, the pages of notes FLC C3(7)5-6, 8-11 more or less corresponding to pp. 31 to 35 in *Precisions*, with only a few divergences around page 7 of the notes (*Precisions*, op. cit., p. 33).

37/FLC C3(7)5, GRI 920083-1(2) p. 1r and *Précisions*, p. 32 (author's translation).

38/FLC C3(7)6 and *Precisions*, op. cit., p. 32.

solely from oneself, from one's own strength, one's own impulsion, one's individual creative power.
Judging for oneself. Appreciating by one's own judgement; in fact, creating one's own idea. This is, at each step one takes in life, the certitude of the effort made towards what is right, and that alone can bring happiness. Do you really believe, after reflection, that this happiness can come from millions of dollars, of pounds, or of pesos, if one has not awakened within oneself the creative spirit to use them?
I am utterly convinced by personal experience. Having left school at the age of 13, I suffered terrible and unremitting anxiety. Always facing me the question: How? Why?[39]

This is one of the most powerful expressions of the solitary and prophetic mission to which Le Corbusier was committed. This passage, not repeated in *Précisions*, was either suppressed at the time of the lecture or, more probably, cut from the book and replaced with a more 'reasonable' and less personal sentence:

In a life devoid of tranquillity, in a life of constant worries, I have tasted the powerful joy of "how" and of "why".[40]

If the poet is blessed with a vision and intelligence to understand the new state of things, the engineer, while perfectly competent in the mechanical world, is incapable of appreciating his own work. Le Corbusier qualified the engineer as 'simply appalled by the children he creates', because the uncluttered structures he builds are the result of nothing more than a calculation aiming at the economy of materials. 'If sufficient funds become available, look how he assassinates his own work!'[41]

The argument of this first lecture is central to Corbusian thought and we find it at the beginning of all the lectures on architecture in the 1920s.

Another process intervenes in the preparation of the lectures. After the *inventio* – the organization of the arguments – Le Corbusier often adjusts his delivery to better manipulate his *dispositio*. After a short introduction and before the argument we have been looking at, he added a three page text written after his arrival in Buenos Aires.[42]

The text is a description and analysis of the city.

Have walked the length and breadth of B[uenos] A[ires] and that's some distance. I have looked, seen and understood [...][43]

By showing his interest in the city which is his host, Le Corbusier deploys a classic *exordium* – making himself appreciated by the audience – while making his critical and radical point of view known with regards to the urbanistic solutions proposed for Buenos Aires. It is interesting to note that a passage from these notes was suppressed from *Précisions* or was omitted in his delivery:

39/FLC C3(7)7-8.

40/*Précisions*, op. cit., p. 34 (author's translation).

41/FLC C3(7)10 and *Précisions*, op. cit., p. 35 (author's translation).

42/*Precisions*, op. cit., pp. 23-4.

43/FLC C3(7)16. Compare with *Precisions*, op. cit., p. 23. See quote on *ibid.*, p. 16.

> I have 1 [one] way to establish my discourse: it is to invoke the old colonial architectural traditions. But putting my foot right in it, is there an echo of them here? The austere but so human whitewash; the wisdom of forms so eloquent in their efficiency and their nobility? If you will allow me to plant my feet on this past, with its wisdom, then what I say will have a solid foundation, otherwise it will float adrift. But [my] discourse will also gather strength from another living phenomenon: national identity [...]. You are defending something that is not quite here yet but which will arrive.[44]

This remarkable empathy for Argentina is reflected again later in the notes:

> I invoke the Argentinean soul, to arouse the poet who will express, in the overall planning of the country, the grandeur that is available, the grandeur that is possible in a new country, that has the good fortune not to be stifled by the past.[45]

This invocation does not appear in *Précisions*. Was it ignored in the lecture or, more probably, was it suppressed from the book, intended for a French audience?

By this double dislocation, the central argument which came at the beginning of the lecture notes – the impact of revolution brought about by mechanization – does not appear until the third page of the text printed in *Précisions*. By narrating his discoveries in Buenos Aires, Le Corbusier thus accomplishes another *desideratum* of rhetoric: illustration. Providing concrete and vivid examples, appealing to the experience of the listeners, allows them to more fully engage with the speech.

In *Précisions*, the first lecture ends abruptly, while the preparatory notes continue for four pages with a description of the remaining nine lectures. Le Corbusier almost certainly cut this in the book to avoid repetition. In the preparatory notes, there is another *exordium*, also omitted in the book, in which he presents himself as a tightrope walker:

> You will see me treading the tightrope of reason, recklessly defying gravity, trying, with the lofty intention that inspired this research, to arrive at an architecture of the era. These efforts, which go back 20 years and which profit from magnificent contributions from the sciences and from the research of our predecessors, have led to certainties.[46]

He continued by assuring his audience that the international movement in favour of modern architecture would produce 'dazzling works of efficiency illuminated by beauty'.[47] Then, as encouragement, he added that the following lectures would be punctuated with sketches and slide projections. Perhaps he was aware that long speeches in French might be tough going for his Argentinean audiences:

44/FLC C3(7)17. This passage continues: 'However here, at the start of the estuary of the Rio de La Plata, there are a few stable points [...]'; the text is used again in the printed version (see *Precisions*, op. cit., p. 24).

45/FLC C3(7)18.

46/FLC C3(7)12.

47/FLC C3(7)13.

> I will draw a lot […], [I will be] very active. 400 [slide] projections will materialize the diagrams of the drawings. These drawings, first of all for the General Public; then [for the] professionals. Here are some quick images, more explanatory than words.[48]

The last sentence indicates that he projected slides at the end instead of finishing with a spoken conclusion. There is unfortunately no way of knowing which slides he showed but it is very probable that they displayed his own buildings and projects.

Second lecture: 'Technology is at the very heart of poetry' (Amigos del Arte)

The title for this lecture, in French, 'Les techniques sont l'assiette meme du lyrisme' (lit.: techniques are the very dish of lyricism) does not translate easily into English. The preparatory notes for the second lecture start like this:

> [I] have asked you to free yourselves of any academic attitudes. [I] talked to you [about the] reticent engineer. Now [we] are going to use the available constructive forces. The means of the era, the essential route towards the well-being of reason. And [we] shall see in indisputable facts the development of the great

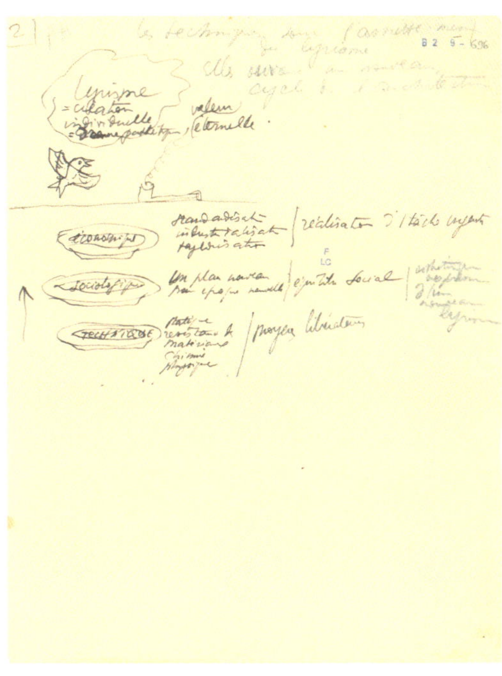

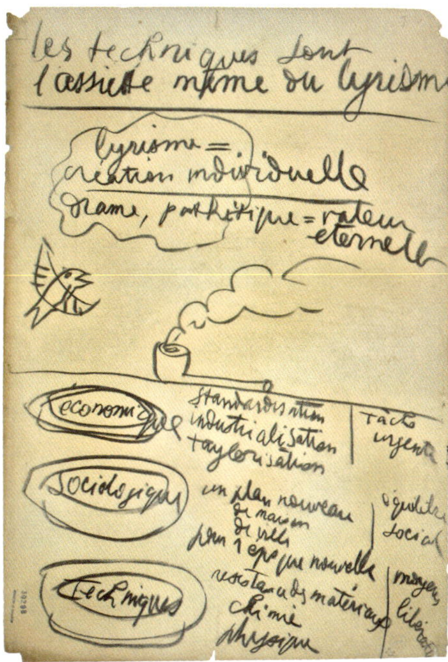

Figure 10
Preparatory drawing for the first sketch of the second lecture (FLC B2(9)696).

Figure 11
First sketch of the second lecture (FLC 30298).

48/FLC C3(7)15, see also note 14.

architectural revolution that has nothing in common with the past in its forms. But from its eternal spirit [I] address the general public. For [the] professionals I offer an analysis of the great contemporary events and a base from which to work.[49]

Abandoning this somewhat pompous introduction, Le Corbusier launched straight into a graphic demonstration of his ontology – his theory of the relationship between technology and the spiritual world of creation.

He started by drawing a horizontal line to separate the material world from the spiritual world (Fig 11).[50] He had already explained what he meant by 'economic,' 'sociological' and 'technical' in his first lecture. He now compared these concepts to the three courses of a meal, essential nourishment for the modern architect in his relationship with the world. In the preparatory drawing (Fig 10)[51], an arrow, on the left, indicates the sequence of the drawings: from the 'technical' to the 'sociological' to the 'economic'. We also clearly see how closely Le Corbusier reproduced his preparatory drawings in the finished sketches. Having eaten his dinner, the architect digests, smoking a pipe when, all of a sudden, like a bird that breaks into song, inspiration arrives. It is difficult to imagine a more perfect example of the classic *demostratio* ('bringing things to life in such a way that the subject manifests itself and develops in plain sight'). With a few strokes of his charcoal, the architect materialized a complex metaphysical idea.

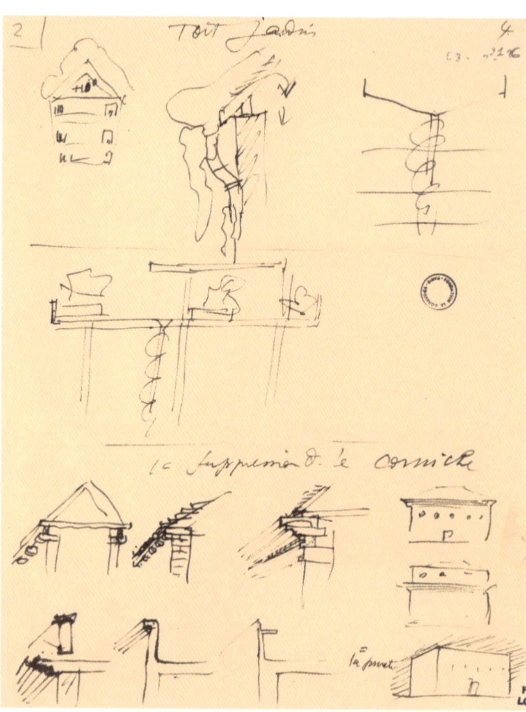

Figure 12
Preparatory sketch for the second lecture showing the advantages of the flat roof and the suppression of the cornice (FLC C3(7)21).

49/FLC C3(7)20. The notes for the second lecture are divided between the Fondation Le Corbusier and the Getty Research Institute. The page C3(7)22, numbered '8', being the list of slides, supposes that there were seven pages of notes for this lecture. C3(7)20, without a number, is the first. GRI 92083-11(5)2 and 3 are numbered '2' and '3', and contain outlines for the sketches FLC 32089 (*Precisions*, op. cit., opposite p. 42), FLC 33517 (*Précisions*, p. 47) and FLC 33502 (*Precisions*, op. cit., p. 53) and another page GRI 920083-11(5)1, that prepares the sketch FLC 33503 (*Precisions*, op. cit., p. 57). FLC C3(7)21 is numbered '4'.

50/FLC 30298.

51/FLC B2(9)696.

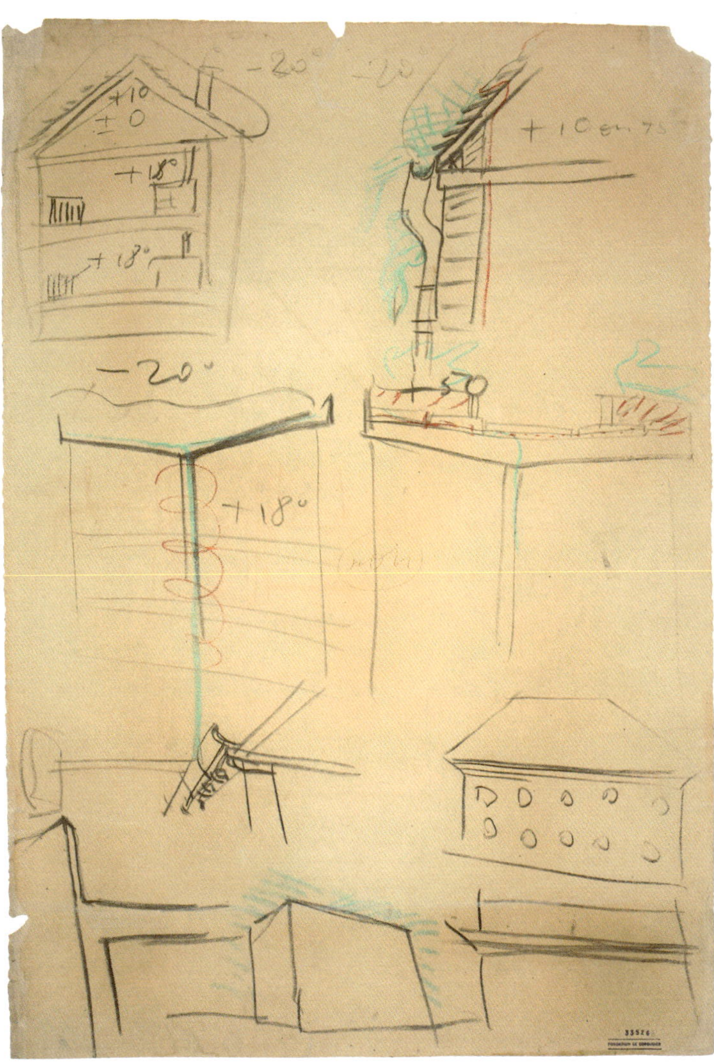

Figure 13

Sketch explaining the advantages of the flat roof, drawn during the second lecture (FLC 33526B).

The second demonstration published in *Précisions*, a section of a traditional house compared to that of a house on stilts, does not exist as such in the notes and must have been improvised.[52] On the other hand, on the fourth page of the preparatory notes for the second lecture, a sketch demonstrates one of the arguments in favour of the flat roof: the effects of snow in cold countries (Fig 12).[53] **The traditional roof poses water seepage problems around the gutters:**

> The [pitched] roof? I'm not including one. The study (and the practice) of constructions with central heating *in countries with deep snow*, has shown me that the water from melting snow should be evacuated *inside the house, in the warm* (I will explain).[54]

52/*Precisions*, op. cit., facing p. 38. The original sketch is lost and the drawing does not appear in the proofs (FLC B2(9)43). The argument and an abbreviated version of the sketch appear on p. 2 of his notes (GRI 920083-11(5)2, see Figure 12).

53/FLC C3(7)21.

54/*Précisions*, op. cit., p. 41.

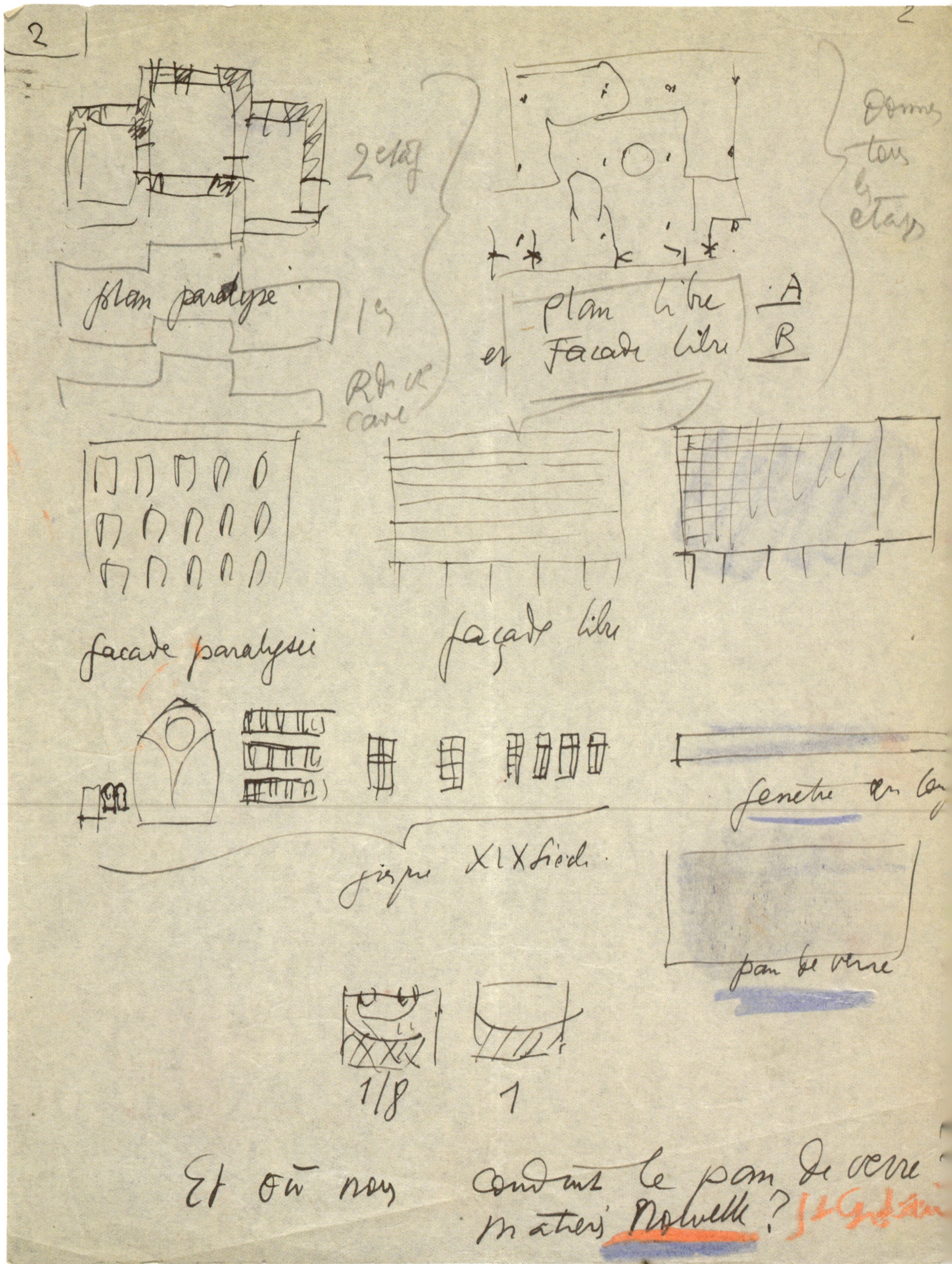
2
2
2e étag
1er
RdC
cave
plan paralysé
Donne tous les étages
plan libre
et façade libre
A
B
façade paralysée
façade libre
fenêtre en long
jusqu'au XIXe siècle
pan de verre
1/8
1
Et où nous conduit le pan de verre ?
matériaux nouveaux ?

In fact, Le Corbusier had learned this from bitter experience. The La Scala cinema he had partially designed in La Chaux-de-Fonds (1916-17) had suffered precisely this problem, with water infiltrating the walls as a result of icicles in the gutters. There is, in fact, a sketch, not used in the book, which was produced during the lecture (Fig 13).[55]

On this sketch, as on the one made during the preparation for the lecture (Fig 12), there is also an illustration of the suppression of the cornice. We can suppose that Le Corbusier omitted this argument from *Précisions* because it was a bit weak and outdated for French readers. Page 2 of his notes brings together a series of diagrams that unite several ideas around the theme of the window (Fig 14).[56]

Le Corbusier lays out his diagrams in support of his usual lessons, the 'paralyzed plan' versus the 'open plan', 'the history of the window', his two preferred solutions (the ribbon window and the glass wall) and the proof of the value of the ribbon window based on photographic exposure sheets. At the end of his notes, Le Corbusier proposes an important series of slide projections, divided into six groups (Fig 15).[57]

This list of projections follows the arguments of the conference, separated into six groups: (1) the sources of engineering at the heart of the new architecture (from the pyramids to the ocean liner), (2) the application of new freedoms in the architecture of his own villas (Villas Cook, La Roche and Stein and the Weissenhof houses), (3) the application to urbanism (culminating in the Voisin Plan), (4) eco-

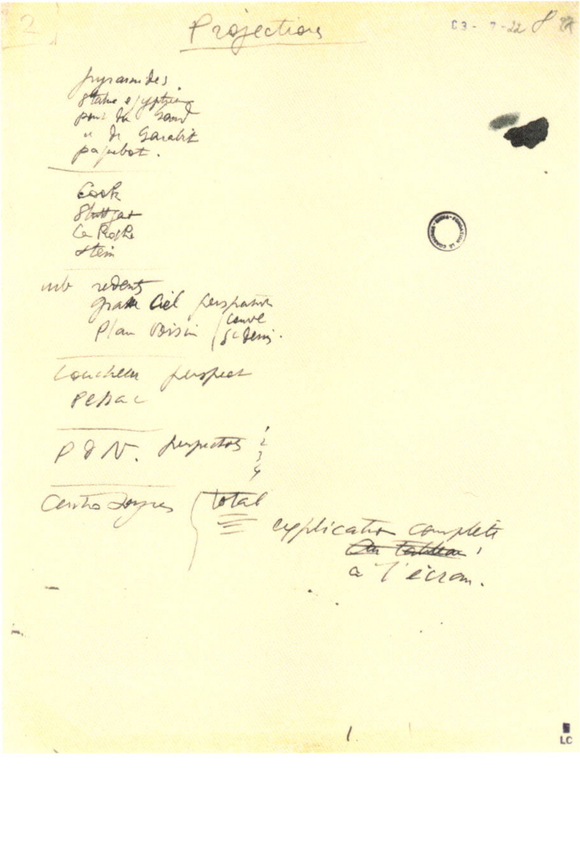

Figure 14

Page of preparatory notes for the second lecture 'Technology is at the very heart of poetry' (FLC 920083-11(5)2).

Figure 15

List of slide projections planned for the second lecture (FLC C3(7)22).

55/FLC 33526B.

56/GRI 920083-11(5)2.

57/FLC C3(7)22.

nomic housing projects (Maisons Loucheur and Pessac), (5) the League of Nations project and (6) the Centrosoyus building in Moscow ('complete and full explanation on the screen'). Once again, the slides acted as 'proofs' – at once of the reality of the mechanized world but also of the impact of the architectural solutions proposed by the master.

Fifth lecture: 'The plan of the modern house' (Amigos del Arte)

In his fifth lecture, Le Corbusier applied the technical and aesthetic lessons from the first lectures to the problem of the dwelling. The lecture was structured around a series of processes – dimensioning, circulation, composition and so on. He began by summarizing the two lectures he had previously delivered to this audience, confirming the fact that he kept this series separate in his mind from the four delivered to the Faculty of Pure, Applied and Natural Sciences.[58] The first

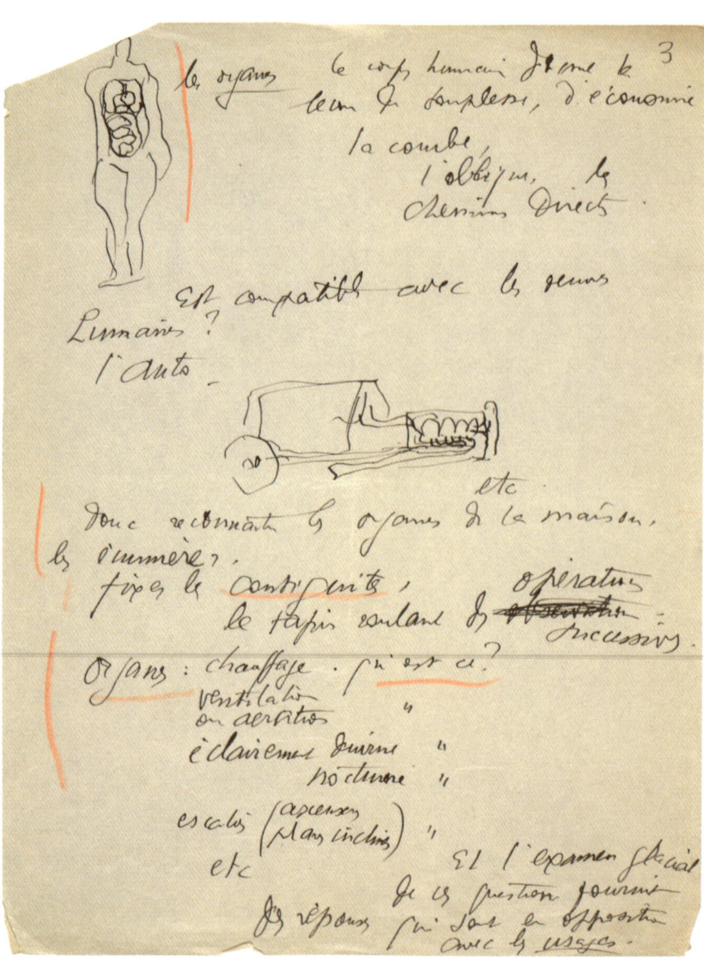
3
les organes le corps humain donne la leçon de souplesse, d'économie
la courbe,
l'oblique, le
chemin direct.
Est compatible avec les sens
humains?
l'auto.
etc.
Donc reconnaître les organes de la maison,
les lumières,
fixer les contrepoints,
le tapis roulant des opérations successives.
Organes: chauffage. qu'est ce?
ventilation ou aération "
éclairement diurne "
nocturne "
escaliers (ascenseurs plans inclinés) "
etc
Et l'examen spécial de ces questions fournit des réponses qui sont en opposition avec les usages.

Figure 16
Third page of notes for the lecture 'The plan of the modern house' (GRI 920083-1(1)3).

58/GRI 920083-1(1)1.

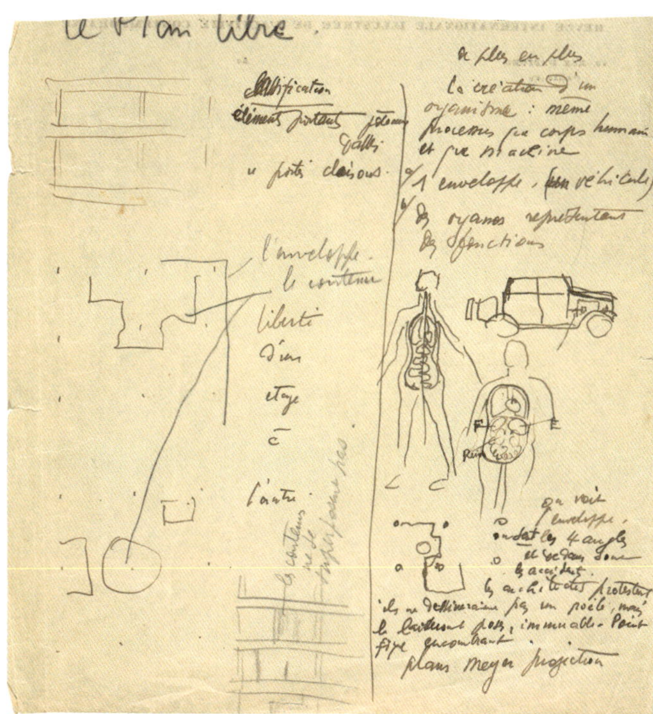

Figure 17

Preparatory drawing for the fifth lecture, exploring the image of human and mechanical organs as a metaphor of organic design (GRI 920083-11(1)1v).

page of notes, recapitulating the lessons of the second lecture, returns to the idea of the liberation of the spirit by technology and the importance of attaining poetry.[59] He contrasts the layout of the traditional house juxtaposed with that of a modern house, entitled 'freedom'. This topic is indicated in a peremptory fashion on the first page of the printed lecture and on the two very rough drawings in the upper right of the first sketch of the lecture.[60] Then, on the second, fourth and fifth page of notes, he addresses the argument of classification (classification, dimensioning and circulation).[61] In this sequence of notes there is a drawing of a body that has been sectioned to show the internal organs and a section of a car (Fig 16).[62] He annotates this drawing as follows:

> The organs. The human body provides a lesson in flexibility, economy: the curve, the oblique, the direct routes.
> Is [it] compatible with human works?
> The automobile [sketch] etc.
> So recognize the organs of the house; number them, fix the contiguities, the conveyor belt of successive operations.[63]

We have seen that the diagram of the body already appeared on the outline (plan) introducing the ten lectures (Fig 5).[64] We find it again on another page of notes (Fig 17).[65]

59/GRI 920083(1)1.

60/*Precisions*, op. cit., p. 123.

61/FLC C3(7)32-34. This is faithfully reproduced in *Precisions*, op. cit., pp. 124-128.

62/GRI 920083-1(1)3.

63/GRI 920083-1(1)3. He follows on with the questioning of the elements of the house: 'Heating: what is it?' etc., that can also be found on p. 126 of *Precisions*.

64/GRI 920083-1(2)3.

65/GRI 920083-11(1)1v.

More and more, the creation of an organism: same process in the human body and the machine.

a) 1 envelope (vehicle)

b) organs representing functions

One sees the envelope, one feels the 4 angles [= walls] and inside are the accidents. Architects protest; they would not design a stove, but let it be installed, immutable.

A cumbersome fixed point.

Meyer Plans projection.[66]

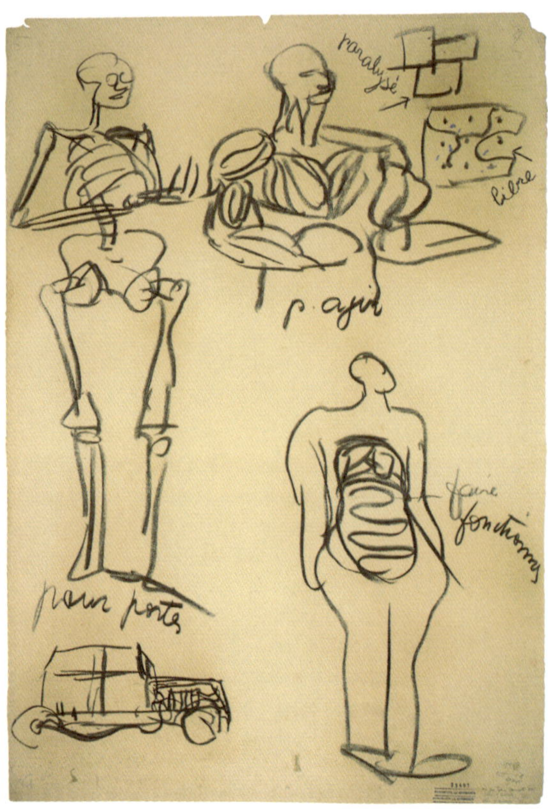

Figure 18
'A bit of preliminary biology': the three Vitruvian elements of architecture, for 'The plan of the modern house' (FLC 33497).

How should these statements be interpreted? The '4 angles' of the exterior, compared to the 'accidents' of the interior, linked to the mention of the Meyer Villa, are very revealing. In the annotations written on the letter-drawing sent to Mrs. Meyer in October 1925, Le Corbusier had already formulated this idea: 'We have insisted that the viscera should be on the inside, classified, tucked away and that only a limpid mass appear on the outside [...].'[67] The idea of the viscera – the complex, shapeless and biomorphic elements of the house hidden inside the prismatic form – is central to Le Corbusier's concept of domestic architecture. Yet this idea took a whole other form in the charcoal drawing demonstration during the lecture (Fig 18).[68]

66/GRI 920083-11(1)1v.

67/FLC 31525.

68/FLC 33497.

A little preliminary biology:
this skeleton *to carry*
this muscular filling *for action*
these viscera *for circulation and utility*
A little automobile construction
a chassis
bodywork
a motor with its organs for supply and exhaust?[69]

It is impossible to deny the obvious connection with the Vitruvian formula *firmitas, utilitas et venustas* (solidity, utility, beauty). Le Corbusier implied that the morphological idea has evolved, from an opposition between geometric exterior and biological interior, towards a unity of the parts and a reaffirmation of the universal truths of architecture as exemplified by Vitruvius. In addition, the male skeleton symbolizing *firmitas* – clearly a self-portrait – contrasts in a stereotyped way with the very feminine *utilitas*. On the other hand, completely unexpected is the representation of *venustas* (generally symbolized by the feminine Venus), which takes the form of a muscular athlete's torso, 'to take action'. This demonstration set the tone of the lecture as, on the one hand, very basic and, on the other hand, highly artistic.

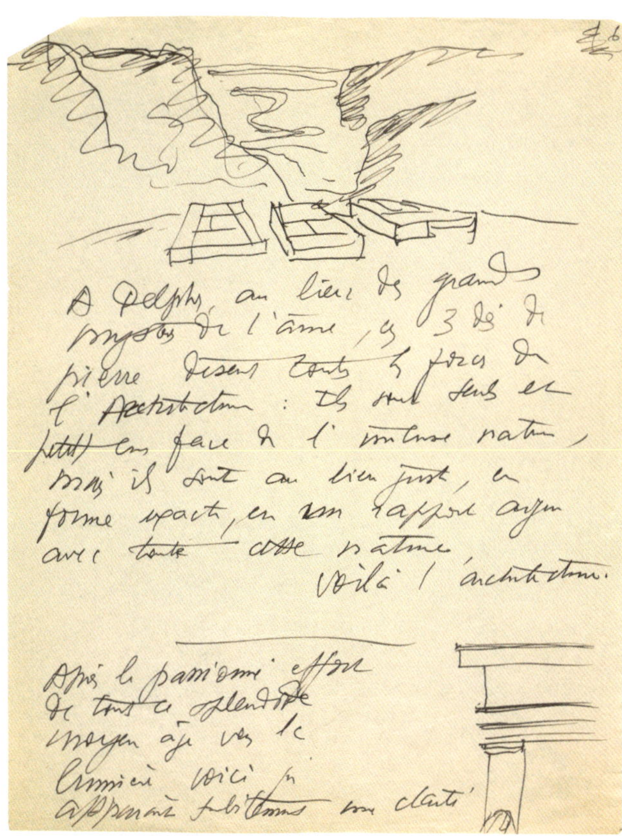
A Delphes, au lieu des grands ... de l'âme, ces 3 dés de pierre disent toutes les forces de l'Architecture : Ils sont seuls et petits en face de l'immense nature, mais ils sont au lieu juste, en forme exacte, en son rapport aigu avec cette nature.
Voilà l'architecture.

Figure 19
Page of preparatory notes for the fifth lecture (GRI 920083-11(6)2).

69/*Précisions*, op.cit., pp. 123-124 (author's translation).

Figure 20

Sketch for the lecture 'The plan of the modern house', showing the Green Mosque of Bursa and the Villa Savoye (FLC 33493).

At times, Le Corbusier used slides showing drawings. On one page of preparatory notes, he reuses a drawing that he had made at Delphi in 1911.[70] This sketch is accompanied by a significant comment:

> At Delphi, instead of the mysteries of the soul, these 3 blocks of stone announce the whole strength of Architecture: they are alone and small, facing the intensity of nature, but they are in the right place, their form precise, in poignant relationship with all this nature.
> That's architecture.[71]

A glass lantern slide of this sketch exists, and it is likely that Le Corbusier projected it – instead of redrawing the motif – perhaps with other photos of Greek architecture, to reinforce the idea that architecture reaches its ends thanks to simple forms.

70/GRI 920083-11(6)2.

71/GRI 920083-1(1)4.

As in the case of the first lecture, Le Corbusier faithfully followed his preparatory notes in this part of the lecture.[72] For example, on page 6bis of his notes (the 'bis' indicates that this was an addition) , he makes a sketch (Fig 6)[73] which he labels: 'The complete freedom of the plan and of the circulation in the economy of place.' The sketch was closely followed in the drawing he made during the lecture (Fig 7).[74]

With the fourth topic, Composition, Le Corbusier addresses Architecture with a capital A. On page 7 of his notes, he sketches the Green Mosque of Bursa (near Istanbul), which he visited in 1911, to demonstrate a lesson on the composition of spaces and the effects of light, an analysis that was similarly developed in *Précisions* (Fig 20).[75]

Figure 21

View of the entrance hall of the Villa La Roche, entrance on the right, under the footbridge (Photo Tim Benton).

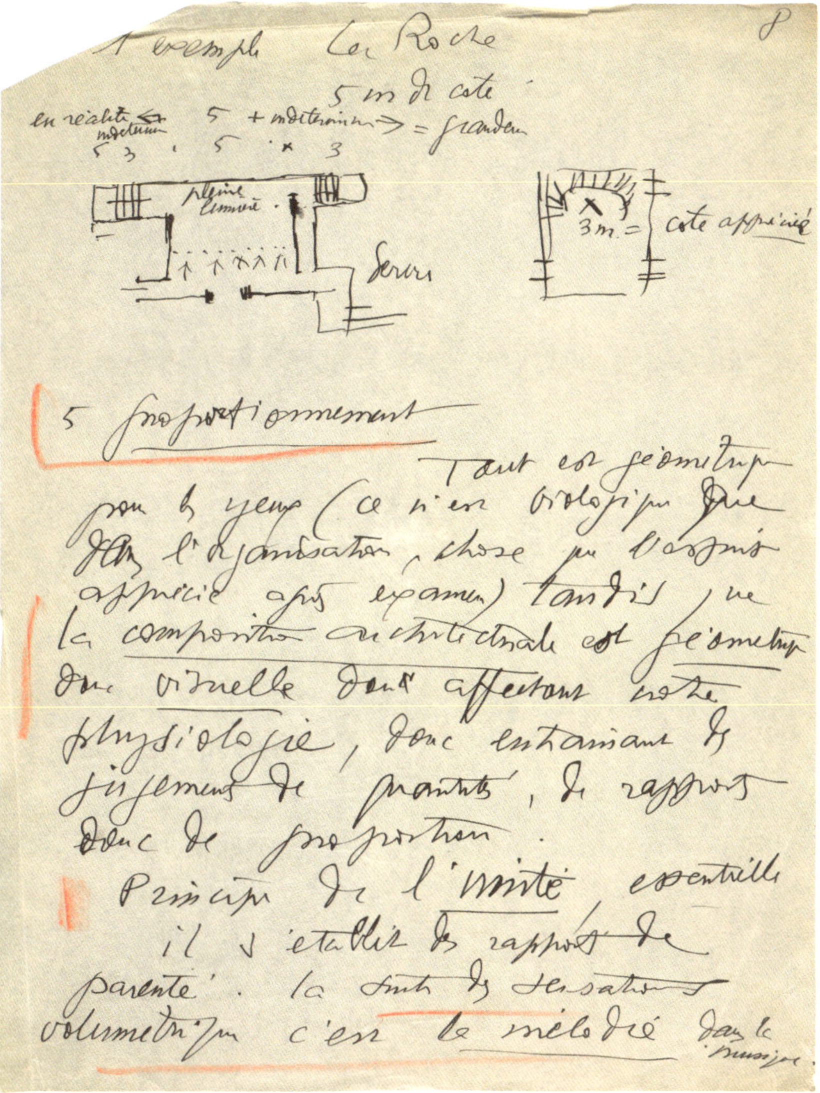

1 exemple La Roche 8

5 m de côté

en réalité <= 5 + méditerranéen => = grandeur

5 3 . 5 x 3

pleine lumière

Serres

3m. = côté apprécié

5 proportionnement

Tout est géométrique pour les yeux (ce n'est biologique que dans l'organisation, chose que l'esprit apprécie après examen) tandis que la composition architecturale est géométrique donc visuelle dont affectant notre physiologie, donc entraînant des jugements de quantités, de rapports donc de proportion.

Principe de l'unité essentielle il s'établit des rapports de parenté. la suite des sensations volumétriques c'est la mélodie dans la musique.

Figure 22

The entrance hall of the Villa La Roche as an example of *Composition*. Page 8 of the preparatory notes for the fifth lecture (GRI 920083-1(1)7).

72/The manuscript pages have to be read in this order:
FLC C3(7)32 (p. 2)
GRI 920083-1(1)3 (p. 3)
FLC C3(7)34-5 (pp. 4 and 5)
GRI 920083-1(1)5 (p. 6)
FLC C3(7)35 (p. 6bis)
GRI 920083-1(1)6-7 (pp. 7-8)
FLC C3(7)36-37 (pp. 9-10).

73/FLC C3(7)34.

74/FLC 33496.

75/FLC 33493. On the sheet of preparatory notes (GRI 920083-1(1)6), the section is captioned 'On respire ces volumes successifs' [This succession of spaces is satisfying] and there is no sketch of the Villa Savoye as on the drawing made during the lecture (Figure 18). In *Precisions*, op. cit., p. 133, Le Corbusier reproduced only the top half of FLC 33493 here (displacing the bird's eye view of the Villa Savoye to p. 138).

His description takes the form of a cartoon or a film treatment, working from left to right in section: 'I draw a man. I have him enter the building; he discovers first this size and shape of space, then that and, above all, the influx of light from the window or from the glass wall.'[76] On this page, Le Corbusier also sketched the Villa Savoye in cavalier perspective. In *Précisions*, he placed this bird's eye view of the villa later, with the other sketches of the house. Its presence here, associated with the Green Mosque, might illustrate this sentence, reproduced in the introduction of the villa in the second edition of *L'Œuvre complète*: 'Arab architecture has precious lessons to teach: it is appreciated *on foot*.'[77]

Then Le Corbusier arrived, on page 8 of his notes, at another example of composition, the entrance hall of the Villa La Roche (Fig 22).[78] These notes are accompanied by a small sketch, very valuable for an understanding of the architectural strategy adopted in this innovative example of modern architecture. Instead of placing the staircase on the wall facing the entrance – the traditional solution (indicated on the right with a cross) – Le Corbusier drew two flights of steps, one on the right, the other on the left, liberating the wall facing the entrance and making it the stunning receptor for the light streaming in through the window above the entrance (Fig 21).

On the following page, he quotes Erik Satie – 'Melody, is the idea; harmony is the method, the tool, the presentation of the idea' – and continues by declaring: 'The simple in architecture is not poverty, it is concentrated, a product charged with energy. We had to search for the simple, having started with the complex.'[79] This last passage is not reproduced in *Précisions* – perhaps because this idea is expressed in other parts of the book – yet it properly introduces the analysis of the four plans that follow. Page 10 groups the plans of four of his houses (La Roche-Jeanneret, Stein-de Monzie, Baizeau and Savoye), four types of composition leading to simplicity and transcending complexity.[80]

Sixth lecture:
'A man = a housing cell; some cells = the city'
(Amigos de la Ciudad)

This lecture was addressed to the Asociación de los Amigos de la Ciudad (Friends of the City) and, like the five lectures to the Amigos del Arte, formed part of the series of 'public' lectures focusing, appropriately enough, on the city.[81] His aim was to demonstrate that the city must be considered in a radically different way: 'The urbanism that is practiced today is primarily aesthetic, a matter of embellishment, of gardening. It's "playing with sandcastles" while the house is up in flames.'[82] Instead of starting with the arguments he had prepared in his notes, he apparently launched into his talk as follows: 'The moment has come to reveal the "law of the meander".'[83]

A mystery surrounds this. Le Corbusier does not seem to have 'discovered' the law of the meander until his flight to Asunción ten days after the delivery of this lecture. Furthermore, the preliminary notes which sketch it out were made on paper with the letterhead of the Hotel Terminus, São Paulo, in Brazil, where he gave two lectures in December (Fig 23).[84] It is possible that this sketch, and the metaphor of the law of the meander itself, were first delivered in Brazil in December, and then collaged into this lecture at a later stage. At any rate, the lec-

76/*Précisions*, op. cit., p. 132 (author's translation).

77/Le Corbusier and Pierre Jeanneret (1964). *Œuvre complète*, volumes 1929-1934, 1935, Les Editions d'architecture, Zurich (7th edition), p. 24.

78/GRI 920083-1(1)7.

79/FLC C3(7)36. The Satie quotation is repeated in *Precisions*, op. cit., p. 133.

80/FLC 33492 and *Precisions*, op. cit., p. 135.

81/The preparatory notes are preserved at the Getty Research Institue and at the Fondation Le Corbusier; in the following order: FLC C3(7)39-42 (pp. 1-4), FLC C3(7)43 (p. 11), GRI 920083-1(1)8-11 (pp. 12-16, 17, 18, -), FLC B2(9)680 (Number 13bis).

82/*Precisions*, op. cit., p. 143.

83/*Precisions*, op. cit., p. 141.

84/FLC B2(9)670 Above, Le Corbusier writes: 'Here is no despairing city like Paris, Berlin. Or [no] streets without hope like in B[uenos] A[ires]", and, below: 'There is no doctrine of urbanism; no aesthetic but equipment." Approximately ten days after the lecture, Le Corbusier draws in his sketchbook (Sketchbook B4, sheet 249) an aerial view analyzing meanders, apparently at the time of his return from Asunción, after 24 October.

ture drawing survives (Fig 24).[85] To explain the law of the meander, Le Corbusier drafted a sort of comic strip, from left to right, of natural evolution. The river (yet also, as he explains, the idea) runs naturally straight to the sea but, after encountering an obstacle, is deflected to one side, then returns and, progressively, creates ever bigger meanders, which are increasingly inefficient. Then the loops touch each other and the river straightens (becoming rational again). 'Thus the pure idea has emerged, the solution has appeared. A new phase begins. Life will once again be good and normal [...] but only for a short time. [...] Thus the idea follows the law of the meander. The moments of the "*simple*" are the resolution of critical and acute crises of complexity.'[86] This demonstration is typically Corbusian: it is an observation made metaphysical in order to reach an aesthetic and ethical conclusion.

Among the notes for this lecture, we find an example of the attention Le Corbusier paid to the dynamic evolution of his visual arguments. Showing the development of a series of sketches in front of the eyes of the audience is undoubtedly more dynamic than projecting slides.

A series of diagrams (Fig 25)[87] will be partly reused in one of the sketches done during the lecture (Fig 26).[88] The arrows allow us to understand the sense of the narrative. On the drawing completed at the time of the lecture, the top sketch shows a city assaulted by railroad tracks and the arrival of automobiles and trucks, looking much like a fortress under siege. On the red plan that followed, Le Corbusier drew the density of traffic, concentrated in the downtown core, and, in the next diagram, the present state of the network of roads, wide in the outskirts and narrow in the city centre. The crisis that results is symbolized by a black tornado in the business district (bottom right). The remedy is drafted in blue under the line: avenues that grow wider as they approach the city centre, producing equilibrium. The blue (representing tranquillity) replacing the red (rage and frustration) is typical of Le Corbusier's colour symbolism.

Figure 23

Page of notes on paper with Hotel Terminus letterhead, with the law of the meander (FLC B2(9)670).

Figure 24

First sketch for the lecture 'A man = a housing cell; some cells = the city': the law of the meander (FLC 30294B).

Following spread

Figure 25

Page of notes made in preparation for sixth lecture, 'A man = a housing cell ; some cells = the city' (GRI 920083-1(3)1).

Figure 26

Sketch illustrating sixth lecture, a variant of the sketch illustrated in *Précisions* (FLC 30294A).

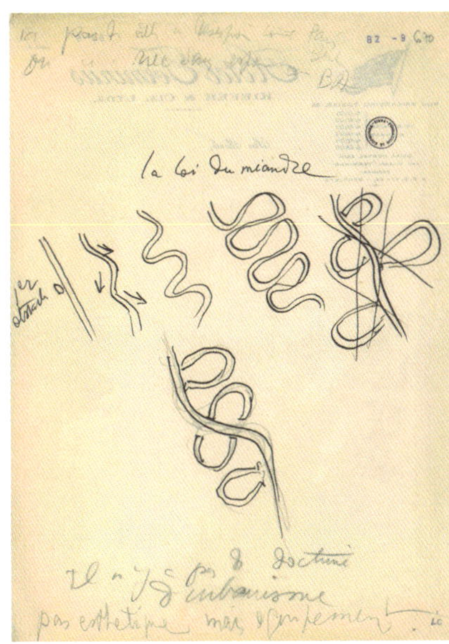

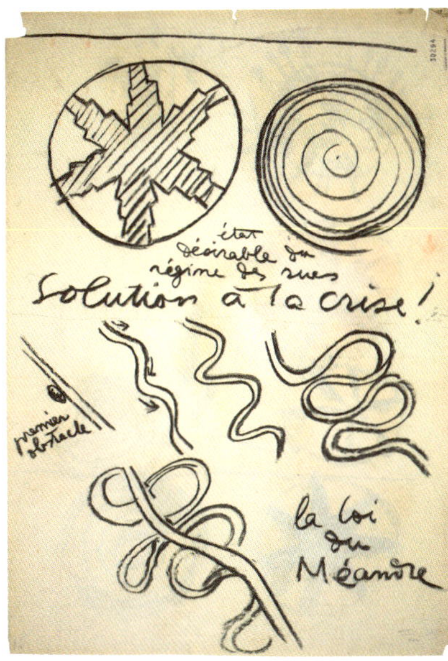

85/FLC 30294B. As we saw (pp. 118-120), Le Corbusier continued to use the metaphor of the law of the meander for twenty years, giving it increasingly complex meanings.

86/*Précisions*, op. cit., p. 143 (author's translation).

87/GRI 920083-1(3)1 and see *Precisions*, op. cit., pp. 147-8.

88/FLC 30294A. This is a variant of the one reproduced in *Précisions*, p. 148 (FLC 33500A). One of these was probably used in one of the four Brazilian lectures.

"L'age du chemin de fer"
Le Souvenir de Thiers

1850
les gares

1920

Louis XIV

Napoléon

VITESSE

1850

1900

Cheval

Auto

1920 Auto et Avion
telephone T.S.F

= Schema

or c'est le contraire
de ce qui existe

il faudrait

voici
l'état des rues

ou

résultat

circulation

Etat
actuel
(croissance

5) Résumé :

les éléments plastiques

" " poétiques

de l'Urb moderne

d'abord en plan

les espaces diversifiés

puis en coupe

les rues en l'air Rio important

autostrade. 3 rues superposées

la nati

la nature : les parcs base de l'Urb

éléments à l'échelle humaine

les arbres.

Certain elements of the notes for this lecture would be revisited in the ninth lecture on the Voisin Plan for Paris, delivered to the Amigos del Arte. One page of the notes, prefiguring the illustration of the Radiant City, with which he finished his lecture, indicates a very strong relationship between this lecture and the ninth lecture and prefigures the new plan for Buenos Aires (Fig 27).[89] At the centre of the page, the elevation of the new city demonstrates the central idea of the new plan for Buenos Aires. Le Corbusier noted, in purple crayon: 'Streets in the air, 3 superimposed levels; Rio [Plata] important.'[90] In the elevation of the street, on the left, is drawn the idea of the airport on the Rio Plata. This project will be drafted in a detailed manner in the ninth lecture (see chapter 1, Fig 9).

Ninth lecture: 'The Voisin Plan of Paris: Can Buenos Aires become one of the great cities of the world?' (Amigos del Arte)

The formula: 'We must kill the corridor-street' – a topic already evoked in the notes for the sixth lecture – opens this ninth lecture (Fig 28).[91]

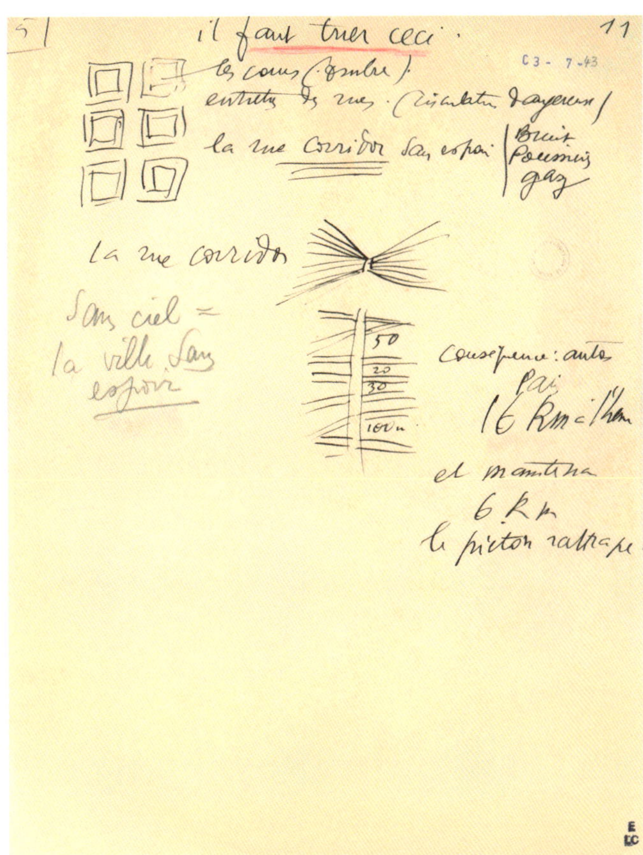

Figure 27

Page of notes for sixth lecture (page 3bis) (FLC B2(9)680).

Figure 28

Page of notes on the rue-corridor for sixth lecture, reused for ninth lecture about the Voisin Plan (FLC C3(7)43).

89/FLC B2(9)680, see also *Precisions*, op. cit., p. 156.

90/GRI 920083-1(3)3 is another page of notes with similar sketches.

91/FLC C3(7)43 and FLC 30300B (identical to *Precisions*, op. cit., p. 171) and 30299B (variation).

Le Corbusier then abandoned a large part of his notes for this lecture in order to evoke the well-known topics of his usual lecture on urbanism and the Voisin Plan of Paris.[92] Lecture 9 is an example of the greatest divergence between what was said in Buenos Aires and what was published in *Précisions*. In view of the fact that most of the Amigos del Arte had not heard the sixth lecture, given to the Amigos de la Ciudad, Le Corbusier felt obliged to repeat the main urbanistic arguments for this new public, as he did in the sixth lecture. It is likely that in the editing of *Précisions*, he masked these repetitions by adding new, more specific material for his Parisian public. For example, to illustrate how a simple act of will by the authorities – a decree – could solve an urbanistic deadlock in Paris, he was obliged to add a small pen sketch to illustrate this 'document' (Fig 29).[93] The probable explanation is that this passage of text and its illustration were added for the book – and the Parisian readers – and that he did not include it in the lecture in Buenos-Aires.

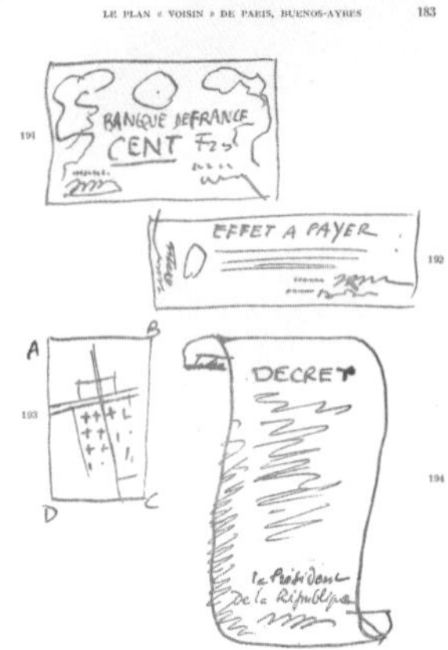

Figure 29

Pen illustration of the decree of the State which will found the new city, made especially for publication (*Précisions*, p.183).

Figure 30

Page 134 of the proofs of *Précisions* (p.139 of the finished book) (FLC B2(9)141).

Following double spread

Figure 31

Pen and watercolour drawing of the Radiant City made specifically for *Précisions* (p.156) (FLC B2(9)686).

There are other examples of illustrations added at the last moment for the publication in *Précisions*.[94] These drawings date from his return to France, just before publication: they are not even in the proofs of the book.[95] A nice example is the ink drawing of the layout of a colony of Villa Savoye houses (Fig 30)[96], juxtaposed with a photograph of part of the lecture drawing with the Green Mosque (see Fig 20). Another nice example of a drawing made especially for the publication is the perspective of the Ville Radieuse, reproduced on page 157 of *Précisions* (Fig 31).[97]

The second part of the ninth lecture, reproduced in *Précisions*, contains many pieces of text added at the time of the editing of the book, stressing the opposition to his ideas.[98] It is only after 37 pages of printed text that we return to the narrative of the lecture, as prepared in the notes, with the plan of Buenos Aires.

Tenth lecture: 'The furniture adventure' (Amigos del Arte)

In treating the topic of furniture, the tenth lecture, delivered to the Amigos del Arte the day after the lecture on the Voisin Plan, reverses the progression from domestic to urban. The preparatory notes for this lecture are numerous and well preserved.[99] Le Corbusier faithfully followed the first six pages of his notes, reading them almost word for word, then gave himself more liberty when it came to commenting on his sketches. Once again, he uses a metaphorical demonstration – this time a verbal one – as an introduction. On page 8bis of his notes and on another sheet of paper, he evokes the reform in fashion performed by modern woman (Fig 32).[100]

Undoubtedly stimulated by the arrival of the very modern Charlotte Perriand in the studio in fall 1927, Le Corbusier inserted this page after the analysis of old and new furniture.[101]:

> Already a huge reform has removed thick layers of
> academicism: this is the reform of female dress.
> it's a fact
> hair cut short

92/Already delivered in Brussels in 1926 (see chapter 3), and to the Labour Exchange in Paris on 16 March 1927.

93/*Precisions*, op. cit., p. 185.

94/See *Précisions*, op. cit., pp. 110, 156 (Fig 31), 183 (Fig 29), 194 and the drawing in the lower half of page 139 (Fig 30).

95/See for example B2(9)185, where there is a blank space for p. 183.

96/FLC B2(9)141.

97/FLC B2(9)686.

98/Passages of the text, such as the one that starts with 'Et lorsque sera construite la Route Triomphale [...] [And once the Via Triumphalis was built...]' were added by hand in the proofs (FLC B2(9)199.

99/The Fondation Le Corbusier preserved 16 pages of notes, numbered 1-8, 8bis, 10, 10bis, 11-15, a list of slides, and an added page (C3(7)90-107). A page preserved at the Canadian Centre for Architecture (DR 1985: 623) is numbered '9' and completes the series. Another sheet, FLC B2(9)671 shows a very approximate version of FLC 33514 (*Precisions*, op. cit., p. 117). All the sketches done in charcoal illustrated in *Précisions* are preserved (FLC 33522, 33523, 33514, 33495 and 33498). The illustration on p. 110 (prepared by the sketches on p. 8 of the notes [FLC C3(7)97]) was

141

133

soleil
F
LC

FONDATION LE CORBUSIER · PARIS ·

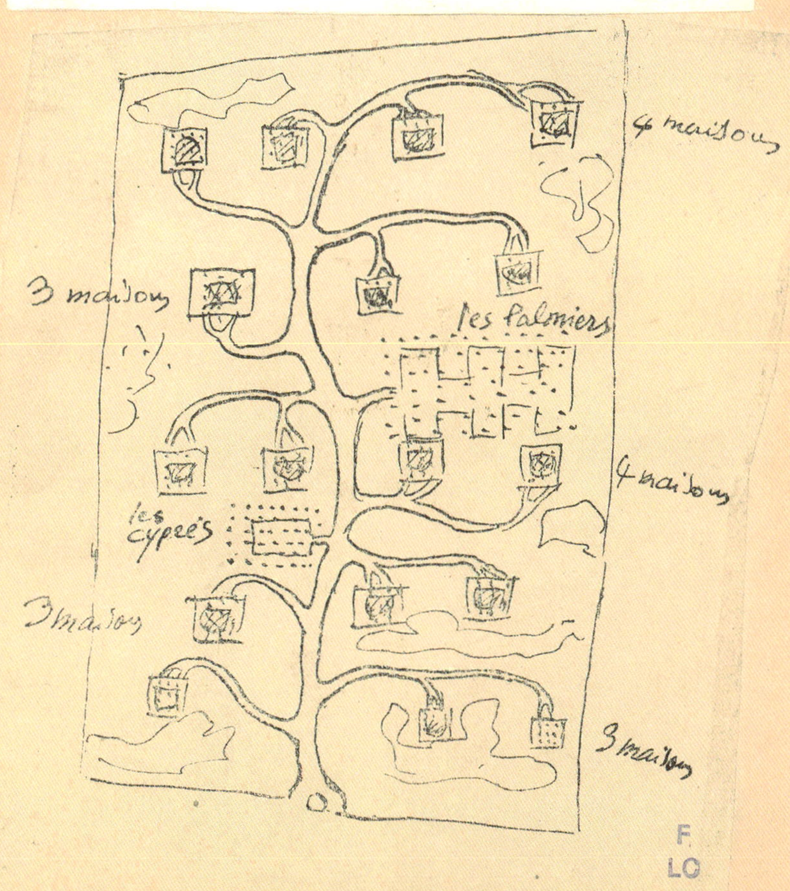
4 maisons
3 maisons
les Palmiers
4 maisons
les cyprès
3 maisons
3 maisons
F
LC

134

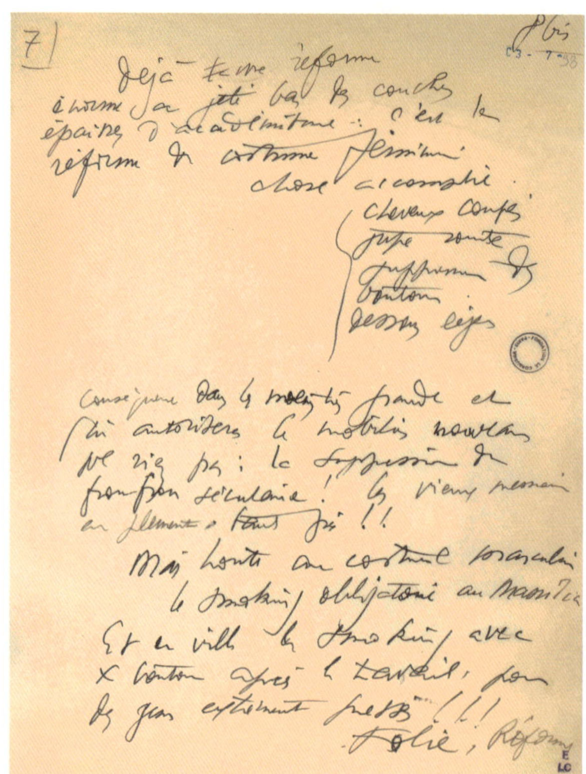

Figure 32
Page of notes for 'The furniture adventure': the reform of female dress (FLC C3(7)98).

> skirt shortened
> removal of buttons
> light underwear
> very important impact on lifestyle, which authorizes the new furniture. Do not laugh: the removal of old-fashioned frilliness! The old gentlemen are weeping! Too bad!!
> But shame on the male suit […].[102]

On the following page, he noted, 'Women's clothes weigh 125 grammes; look at us with our 8 kilos!'.[103]

> Man: The height of his elegance, his "suit", means resembling the generals of the Grand Army, Nap[oleon]'s generals. His working clothes are a contradiction in terms. 1 [One] is in a hurry: count the buttons [to do up]. In the evening one dresses; twice more: the buttons! A modern man works. The modern man works with paper, with papers. The age of steel is giving way to the age of paper. And yet the style of correct dress is to be precise, close-fitting: a sheet of machine paper in a pocket distorts the line! And yet we need wallets, papers of all sorts. One has to choose between working and being elegant.[104]

made especially for the book in ink. It replaces the information contained in the 'red diagram.' (Figure 31)

100/FLC C3(7)98.

101/FLC C3(7)97, also reproduced in *Précisions*, op. cit., p. 106.

102/FLC C3(7)98.

103/FLC C3(7)107.

104/*Ibid*.

The style of these notes is that used to address a new subject. Le Corbusier decided to move the metaphor of fashion and the feminine revolution towards the beginning of his lecture, just after this challenging sentence:

> Have you ever, one day, in your living room, examined the things surrounding you and asked yourself *what is their meaning*? In fact, generally, you are faced with the *most staggering nonsense*.[105]

It is interesting that, in the version delivered for the Amigos del Arte, Le Corbusier toned down this topic by changing the 'vous [you]' into 'nous [us]'. The example of feminine fashion was very strategic: it allowed Le Corbusier to make functionalism seductive while putting conventional morals on trial.

The list of slide projections for 'The furniture adventure' starts with the indication 'red diagram'. It is rare to find such a precise indication. In this exceptional case, it is evident that he is referring to a particular slide that illustrates some diagrams indicated in his notes.[106]

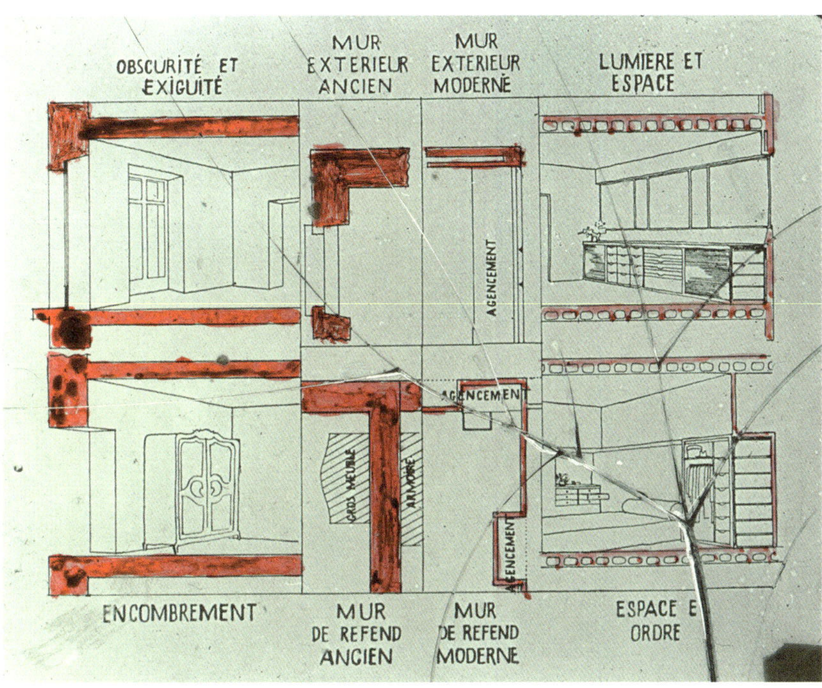

Figure 33
Glass lantern slide illustrating 'The furniture adventure' (FLC slide collection).

105/FLC C3(7)90.

106/FLC C3(7)97 and 100. This slide (in the FLC archive) revisits the diagrams that Le Corbusier had sketched in the form of advertising for the Innovation suitcase company in *L'Esprit Nouveau*.

The 'Professional' Lectures

Third lecture:
'Architecture in everything, urbanism in everything'
(Faculty of Pure, Applied and National Sciences)

In the first lecture delivered for the Faculty of Pure, Applied and Natural Sciences, Le Corbusier addresses primarily the architectural students. This tactic allowed him to captivate the attention of the students while embarrassing their professors: 'Alas, would you take it against me, in the Faculty, for perhaps deeply disturbing a few young people?'[107]

A radical sketch attacking the Academy and their styles of architecture followed, which Le Corbusier prefigured in his notes (Fig 34).[108] By enthusiastically crossing out pediments and colonnades, Le Corbusier declared: 'This is not architecture; these are styles.' What could be more captivating for young people who had spent their first years drawing the orders and learning the rules of classical architecture? This St Andrews cross reminds us of the one that Willy Baumeister had drawn on the poster of the exhibition of the Deutscher Werkbund at the Weissenhof Siedlung in Stuttgart in 1927.

Figure 34
Page of notes for third lecture (FLC C3(7)27).

107/*Précisions*, op. cit., p. 69.

108/FLC C3(7)27 and *Précisons*, op. cit., facing p. 70.

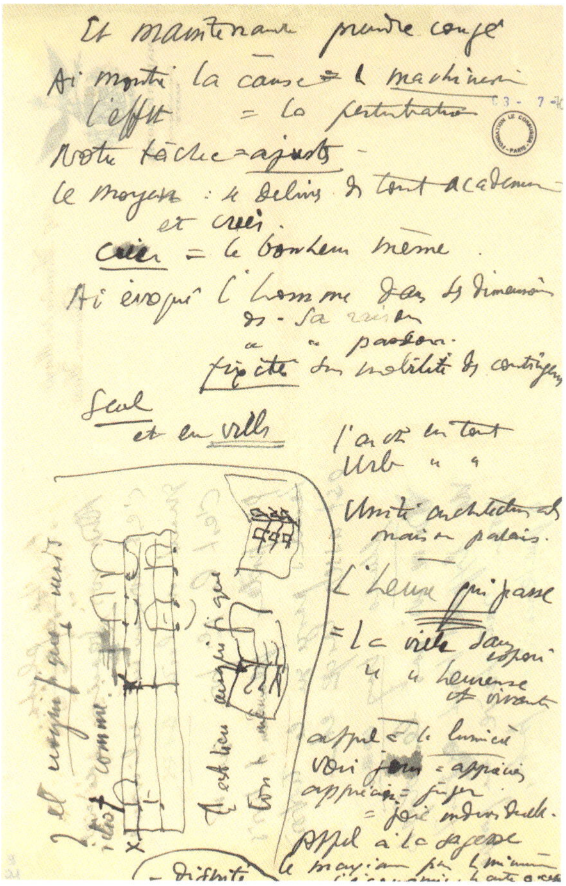

Figure 35

Page of notes for the third lecture (FLC C3(7)70).

In the upper left of his first page of notes, he wrote: 'I showed [that] technology [is] the basis [lit. dish] of lyricism. But to what do we apply lyricism in architecture? What is architecture?' This is a case where he seems to assume knowledge of the second lecture in the other series.

Then: 'I would like to know who decreed [that] Greek art [is] eternal? I know [the] Acropolis.' Le Corbusier often played with his deep knowledge of Greek architecture. This page of notes is inserted amongst other numbered ones, which were ignored for this lecture.[109] There follows three pages of notes, in which he defines both architecture and urbanism in terms of circulation and organic biology on the one hand and formal, aesthetic values on the other, before inspiring the students: 'Art, product of the reason-passion equation, is for me the site of human happiness.'[110] He also makes a claim for the power of the mind to create in isolation, in the presence of nature and reason, concluding, 'Your gauchos are heroes and philosophers'.[111] It is possible that he included some of this material in the lecture but left it out in *Précisions*, either because it was too personal or too closely associated with Argentina. One unidentified page of notes captures the mood of this lecture (Fig 35):

109/FLC C3(7)23-26, 29 and 30 (numbered pp. 1-4, 8 and 9). A very short list of projections exists (FLC C3(7)19), with notes on the verso. Other notes, FLC C3(7)27-8 and 31 and GRI 920083-1(4)1-2, 920083-11(2)1-5 and 920083-11(6)2, are not numbered and represent different moments in the evolution of the argument.

110/*Precisions*, op. cit., p. 68 and FLC C3(7)25.

111/FLC C3(7)24.

To create = happiness itself. [I] have invoked man in the dimensions of his reason, [of his] passion. Fixity without mobility of contingencies. Alone and in town.
Arch[itecture] in everything
City [planning] in everything
Architectural unity – [a] house [a] palace
The hour that passes = the city without hope
[the city] happy and alive
Call for light. To see clearly = to appreciate;
to appreciate = to judge; = individual joy.
Call for wisdom: the maximum for the minimum;
economy […] = dignity[112]

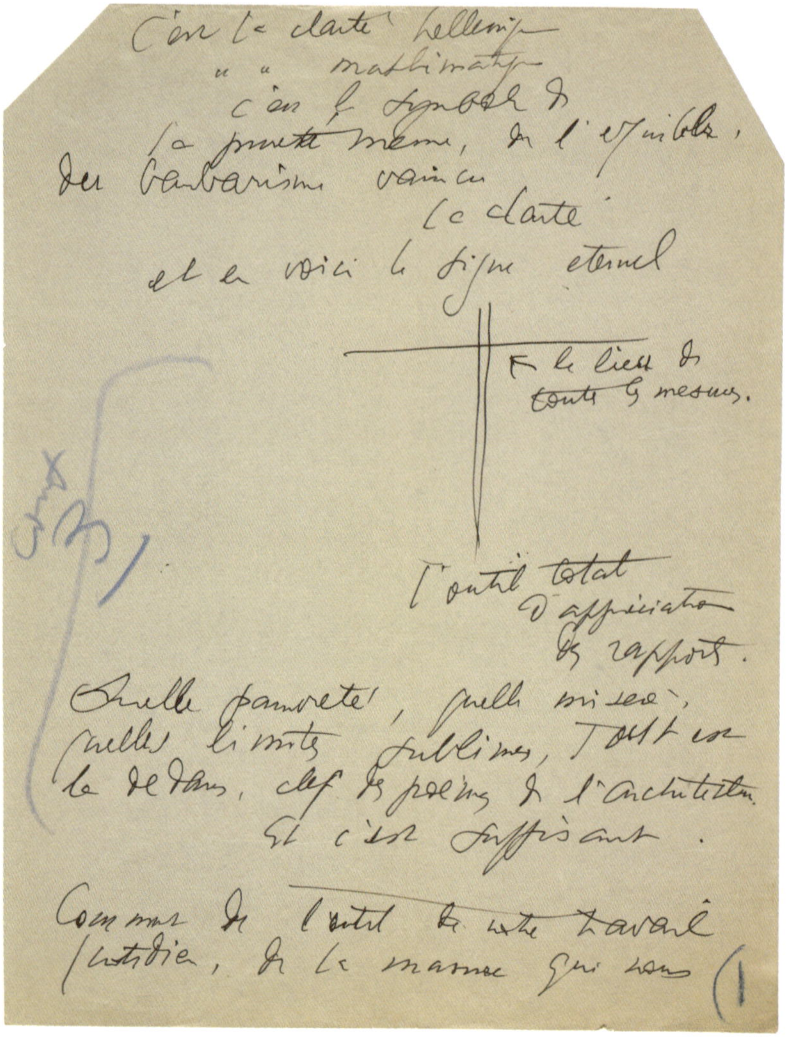

Figure 36

Page of notes for third lecture 'Architecture in everything, urbanism in everything' (GRI 920083-1(4)1).

112/FLC C3(7)70.

To illustrate this declaration of aesthetic belief, Le Corbusier drafts a line of music: 'It's magnificent, yet idiotic like this: [a stave with random notes on it]; It is quite magnificent all the same.' The musical stave has only four lines instead of five and the notes make no musical sense. It is only an image suggesting that 'the simple is not poverty', in a form associated with the pure emotion of music. Le Corbusier, son and brother of musicians, often referred to music as the arbitrator of emotions.

The main goal of this lecture was to show the full dedication to beauty, union of pure geometry and of untamed nature. The topic of 'Hellenic clarity' served as a model:

> It is Hellenic clarity. [It is] mathematical [clarity]. It is the symbol of purity itself, of balance, of barbarity conquered: clarity, and here is the eternal sign [right angle], the place of all measurements – the complete tool for the appreciation of ratios. What poverty, what misery, what sublime limits. Everything is there, key to architectural poetry. And it is sufficient.[113]

What followed was the development of an architectural theory based on the union of reason and passion, nature and geometry and the laws of perception, in a reduced form at its most simple and fundamental. It is one of the strongest of Le Corbusier's personal aesthetic convictions. The argument is summarized on a page of notes where the entire history of architecture is concentrated in a sequence of diagrams aiming at pure form and the formula: 'the simple is not poverty."[114] In an unused page of notes, the architect expressed himself in a surprising manner: :

> 2 human attitudes: man acts to live: industry; trade:
> Man (some men) have the function of meditating. Nature is an intense place of meditation. Why? This is our law; we are born in nature. [We are] attuned to [nature].
> By reason of balance, our actions dictated by a conscious will, through unconscious determinism concur with the great laws of nature. Thus harmony.
> Man alone, the shepherd with his flock, can live in almost exclusive meditation: facing nature and its events. And our surveyor brain, measures and appreciates, judges, concludes: it can conclude the most noble thoughts. Your gauchos are heroes and philosophers.[115]

For the lecture, Le Corbusier abandoned these notes and contented himself with a few sketches and comments to build his argument. 'Architecture in everything, urbanism in everything' is one of the best examples of his method of visual demonstration: the choice of drawings to be made and the principles which emanate from them determined the form of the talk. Le Corbusier was proud of the final product, not hesitating to send a copy of the text to two friends: Michel Seuphor, of the Cercle et Carré group, and Philippe Lamour, from Redressement Français.[116]

113/GRI 920083-1(4)1.

114/This drawing (sketch), on a sheet of paper with the letterhead of the office at rue de Sèvres, is found on the verso of a perspective of one of the guest rooms of the Citrohan-type house at the Weissenhof Exhibition, Stuttgart, 1927 (see Roth, A. [1927]. *Zwei Wohnhäuser von Le Corbusier [pseud.] und Pierre Jeanneret*, Stuttgart, F. Wedekind & Co., p. 29). Revisited in the sketch FLC 33528 (*Précisions*, p. 81).

115/FLC C3(7)24.

116/See FLC B2(9)367 ('remise à Seuphor, Cercle et Carré' 13/5/1930) and B2(9)366 ('pages 75-77 remis à Philippe Lamour p. Grand Route').

Fourth lecture: 'A housing cell to a human scale' (Faculty of Pure, Applied and Natural Sciences)

For the fourth lecture, 'A housing cell to a human scale', delivered to the Faculty of Pure, Applied and Natural Sciences two days after the preceding talk, all that remains is a list of images to be projected – 'Dom-ino, Loucheur, Pessac, Pavillon E[sprit] N[ouveau], Secrétariat P[alais] d[es] N[ations], Pyramide Mundaneum' – yet it is sufficient to realize that the first part of the given lecture was very different from what he had planned.[117] In the lecture, such as it was printed in *Précisions*, Le Corbusier started by analyzing two exemplary models of dwelling, the ocean liner (pp. 87-90) and the Val d'Ema Charterhouse (pp. 91 and 97). Only after these demonstrations does he address the explanation of the Domino projects, the Apartment-Villas and the Loucheur houses (pp. 92-101). Le Corbusier prepared his audience for the lessons of modern architecture by evoking 'proofs' drawn from the architecture of the Renaissance as well as from the modern mechanized world. He understood that his housing 'cells' could shock and alienate his public. What better to convince them than to show that the cells of Carthusian monks offered an idyllic and calm lifestyle in the countryside or that the luxurious life aboard a transatlantic ocean liner could be organized around a 10-square-metre cabin?

Seventh lecture: 'A house – a palace' (Faculty of Pure, Applied and Natural Sciences)

This lecture, already delivered several times in Europe (Zurich, Madrid, Barcelona), was also published in the book of the same name.[118] The iconography – photographs and drawings – with which Le Corbusier illustrated his arguments in *Une maison – un palais* is of capital importance in understanding his strategy in the lectures of 1927-29. The analysis of this lecture in Zurich and its variations will not be addressed here but suffice it to say that it existed, as a model, for understanding the summary character of the text published in *Précisions*: barely five pages. It is probable that Le Corbusier suppressed certain elements in the book that he considered too similar to his earlier book, *Une maison – un palais*.

The preparatory notes for the seventh lecture in Buenos Aires are divided, like the lecture in Zurich, into a 'thesis' followed by an 'explanation' (the analysis of the project for the League of Nations Palace).[119] After a few pages in which he closely follows his preparatory notes, the text in *Précisions* becomes a much abridged account of his speech, using the past tense – 'I drew the hut of the savage [...] I then drew and explained everything' – to avoid repeating arguments already published.[120] Given the degree of precision of the sketches, it appears that a large part of the lecture had been devoted to the analysis of the project of the League of Nations. A series of drawings done on paper with the letterhead of the Compagnie de Navigation Sud-Atlantique – numbered from 'a' to 'd' – completed on board the *Massilia*, forecasts the sketches done during the lecture.[121]

117/This page, numbered '12', indicates that several pages are lost (FLC C3(7)109).

118/See the complete notes for this lecture given to the Lesezirkel Hottingen in Zurich (9 November 1927), FLC B3(4)504-541. See Le Corbusier (1928). *Une maison – un palais. A la recherche d'une unité architecturale*. Paris, Editions G. Crès et Cie, and the thesis of Poole, C. A. (1997). *From private to public: Le Corbusier and the House-Palace 1926-1928*. School of Architecture. London, University of Westminster.

119/FLC C3(7)48-55 (Numbers 1-4, 9-12) and GRI 920083-1(4)3 (Number 5). The pages 920083-11(6)1-2 reproduce images shared with the third lecture.

120/*Précisions*, op. cit., p. 159 (author's translation).

121/See two sketches in the archive of the Canadian Centre for Architecture: CCA DR: 1985:619 et DR: 1985:620.

Eighth lecture: 'The world city and some perhaps untimely considerations' (Faculty of Pure, Applied and Natural Sciences)

'Ladies and gentlemen, this lecture will be lop-sided." Thus began the lecture entitled 'The world city'. In fact, we have already noted, Le Corbusier was scheduled to present this lecture in front of the Friends of Art and not in front of the 'professionals' of the Faculty. He had, nevertheless, prepared 13 pages of notes in which he had elaborated his analysis of the Mundaneum project as well as a series of digressions on the principle of the organization and evolution of what he called the 'idea'.

Figure 37
Sketch illustrating the Mundaneum project for the eighth lecture (FLC 33513A).

> You know what the idea is: a long incubation and all of a sudden a flash of light. The idea is the wave. Once the idea is brought forth, no more obstacles, nor mountains, nor seas
> nor cages of iron or glass
> nor Institutes nor academy
> the idea strikes wherever there is a receiver.[122]

It is with this idealist tone that Le Corbusier begins his peroration:

> We are moving with great strides towards a pure and grandiose materialization of a new world. A new era has been born. The era of mechanization […] This era is organizing a new cycle of civilization […] Architecture is this thing that magnifies all ideas, because architecture is an undeniable event that arises at a particular moment from the creative force of the mind […][123]

There is a single drawing of Mundaneum (Fig 37), with a variant, yet its precision, as well as the amount of detail on it, indicate that the analysis lasted several minutes.[124]

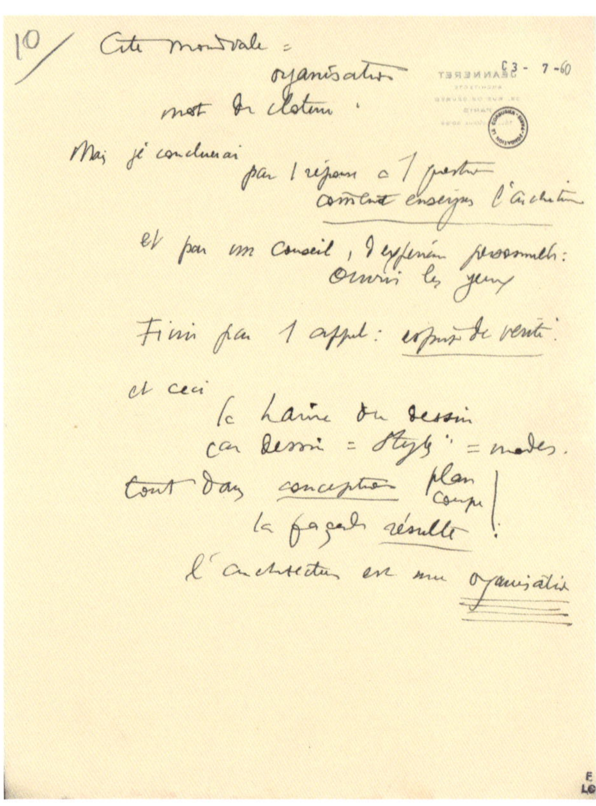

10/ Cité mondiale =
organisation
mot de clôture.

C3 - 7-60

Mais je conclurai par 1 réponse à 1 question
comment enseigner l'architecture

et par un conseil, d'expérience personnelle:
Ouvrir les yeux

Finir par 1 appel: esprit de vérité.

et ceci
la haine du dessin
car dessin = style = modes.
tout dans conception plan
coupe
la façade résulte!
l'architecture est une organisation

Figure 38
Page of notes for the eighth lecture 'The world city', planning the teaching of architecture (FLC C3(7)60).

122/P. 8 of the notes (FLC C3(7)66), see also *Précisions*, op. cit., p. 218.

123/Pp. 9-11, passim (FLC C3(7)67-69). See *Précisions*, op. cit., p. 219 (author's translation).

124/FLC 33513A. The variant FLC 33509B shows the word 'non [no]' in the handwriting of Le Corbusier, indicating that it was rejected for *Précisions*.

Then Le Corbusier switched to a completely different topic (Fig 38)**. In the text of *Précisons*, he announces: 'Let us now face the impromptu subject of this farewell lecture: *If I were to teach you architecture?*'[125] In fact, the last page of notes for this lecture indicates that this change was not 'impromptu':**

> World city = organization. Closing words.
> But I will conclude with a reply to a question: how to teach architecture.
> And with a piece of advice, a personal opinion: open your eyes.
> Finish with a call: spirit of truth
> and this: a hatred of drawing, because drawing = styles = fashions.
> Everything is in the conception: plan/cross-section.
> The façade is the result.
> Architecture is an organization[126]

After a small digression about Buenos Aires, he banished the 'orders', while appealing for respect for the masterpieces of architecture from antiquity and the Renaissance. Then, he addressed the young students: 'How do you make a window? [...] You do not know what the *orders* are. Nor the "style of 1925" [Art Deco].' He then described some design exercises, by reusing a few demonstrations from his first lecture ('Architecture in everything, urbanism in everything').

To illustrate the topics 'opening your eyes' and 'spirit of truth', indicated in his outline, he drew vernacular buildings observed in Buenos Aires and in La Plata (see chapter 1, Figs 8 and 9)**.[127] And he commented, as he drew:**

> You are thinking, "Right, now he is creating a modern village!" Not at all, I am drawing the houses of Buenos-Aires. There are a good fifty thousand like this. They were built – they are built every day – by Italian builders.[128]

According to Le Corbusier, this vernacular architecture should be the basis of modern architecture in Argentina. He recounts the long walk he took along the streets of La Plata with Gonzales Garraño, from which these examples were taken.

> Ah! You burst out laughing because I am drawing a metal windmill, the sort that turns all over Argentina next to the houses. You think I am going to discredit this windmill because it is neither Doric, nor Ionic, nor Corinthian, nor Tuscan, but simply metalwork? I say this to you: When you are doing a project for a house, first of all draw in the steel windmill. And your house, attached to the windmill, which is an honest thing, will be good![129]

On 24 October, at the time of his visit to Asunción, the capital of Paraguay, Le Corbusier had drawn figures and houses.[130] Among these drawings, one scene of two women, a house and a windmill in the background, resembles the sketch

125/*Precisions*, op. cit., p. 219.

126/FLC C3(7)60.

127/FLC 30295, *Precisions*, op. cit., p. 229.

128/*Précisions*, op. cit., p. 228 (author's translation).

129/*Précisions*, op. cit., pp. 228-9 (author's translation).

130/Sketchbook B4, pp. 246-248. Numbers 246 and 248 are dated 24 October 1929.

made during the lecture. This lesson on vernacular architecture is not complete, however, without a rueful criticism of the Italian builders:

> But in front, on the street, where one puts one's house number and name, where one says: "this is my house", the Italian builder has called on Mr Vignola and his orders. What a horror! The pretty little South American cake-shop.[131]

On the preparatory drawing he writes 'fake' for the façade of this house and 'genuine' for the back. On the sketch done during the lecture, the same judgement is more elegantly formulated by the association of the terms 'spirit of truth' and 'untruth'.

The signs of Le Corbusier's evolution of thought of around 1929, his increasingly enthusiastic openness to the vernacular, his sensibility to human psychology, his research increasingly motivated by the beautiful, the spiritual, the expressive, are evident in these lectures. But among the radical changes which took place in South America, none are more extraordinary than the evolution of Le Corbusier's thought with regards to urbanism.

Lectures in São Paulo and Rio de Janeiro

Two months after the lectures in Buenos Aires, Le Corbusier delivered another four lectures, in São Paulo and Rio de Janeiro.

Very little information has survived from these four lectures. Only the speech delivered to the Association of Architects in Rio on 8 December 1929 is reproduced in *Précisions*, in the Chapter 'Corollaire brésilien ... qui est aussi Uruguayen. [Brazilian Corollary ... which is also Uruguayan]." This text is a mix of rhapsodic observations about Rio and fragments of the lectures already given in Buenos Aires. One must suppose that the two lectures given in São Paulo were similar to those at Rio, adapting the topics of the ten lectures to the landscape and plans proposed for Rio and São Paulo.

Le Corbusier started this lecture by revisiting his plan for Buenos Aires – 'You have seen the diagram for the creation of a business district in Buenos Aires' – then mentioned his ideas for Montevideo and São Paulo.[132] Yet the most surprising plan is that proposed for Rio (Fig 39).[133]

131/*Précisions*, op. cit., p. 230 (author's translation).

132/*Precisions*, op. cit., p. 237 and 239. The sketch FLC 30301 shows his plan for Montevideo (above) and for São Paulo (below).

133/FLC 32091, *Précisions*, op. cit., facing p. 242. See also the preparatory drawings FLC B2(9)679 and 681.

The same sketch, drafted in his preparatory notes, demonstrates Le Corbusier's enthusiasm for Rio, even indicating the location of his hotel, the Gloria (Fig 40).[134] He annotated his preliminary sketch with 'Top' and 'Bottom', to indicate its orientation.

On another page of preparatory notes, Le Corbusier wrote the peroration for this series of lectures:

Figure 39

Sketch for the lecture in Rio on 8 December 1929 (FLC 32091).

Figure 40

Sketch for the plan for Rio, in the notes for the lecture in Rio on 8 December 1929 (FLC B2(9)679).

Following double spread

Figure 41

Lecture drawing for 'A man = a housing cell […]', similar to the one reproduced on page 148 of *Précisions* (FLC 33500B).

Figure 42

The drawing reproduced on page 148 of *Précisions* (FLC 30297A).

134/FLC B2(9)679.

57

l'âge du cheval 1850

l'âge du chemin de fer

vitesse

avion
télégraphe
TSF
Téléphone

régime des rues

ou

l'âge du cheval : jusqu'à 1850

l'âge du chemin de fer

TSF

avion

Télégraphe

paquebots

chemin de fer

Préhistoire

Égyptiens

Romains

Invasions

Charlemagne

Louis XIV

Napoléon

la vitesse 18|50

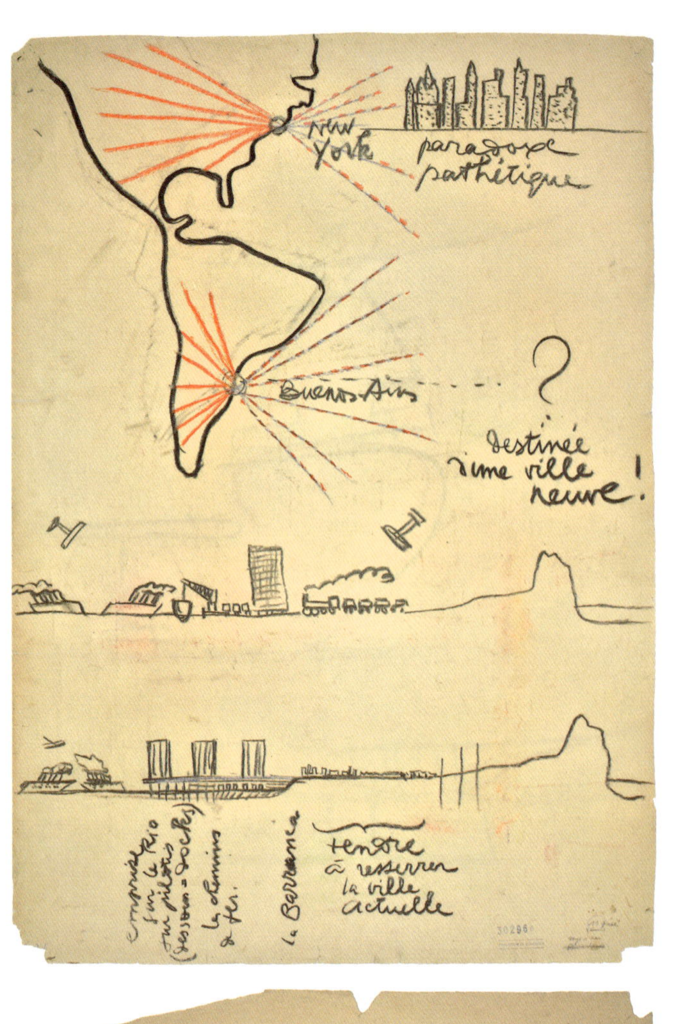
New York
paradoxe pathétique
Buenos-Aires
?
destinée d'une ville neuve!
tendre à resserrer la ville actuelle

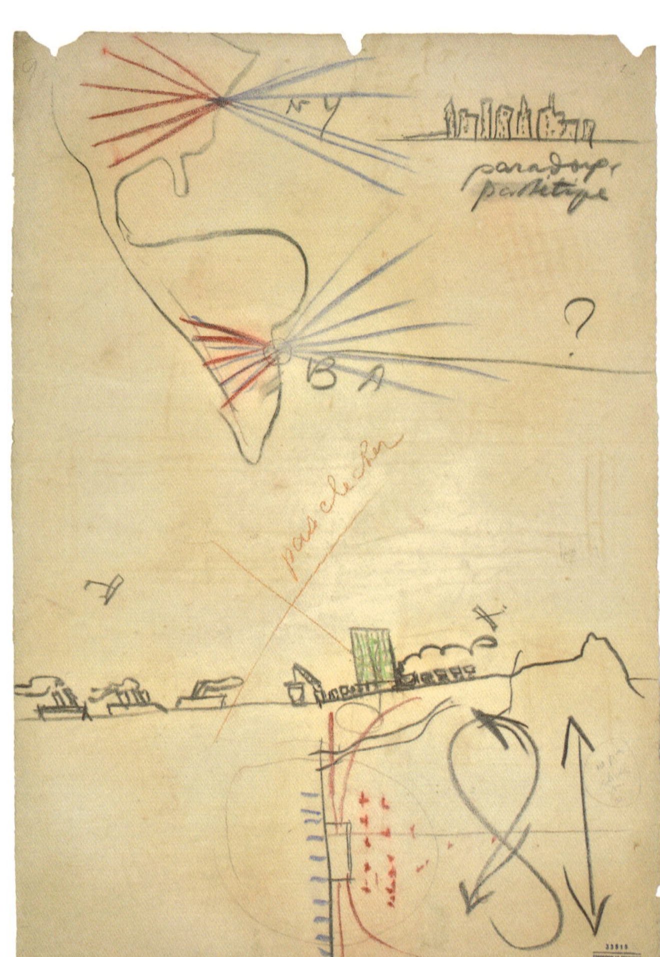
N Y
paradoxe pathétique
?
B A

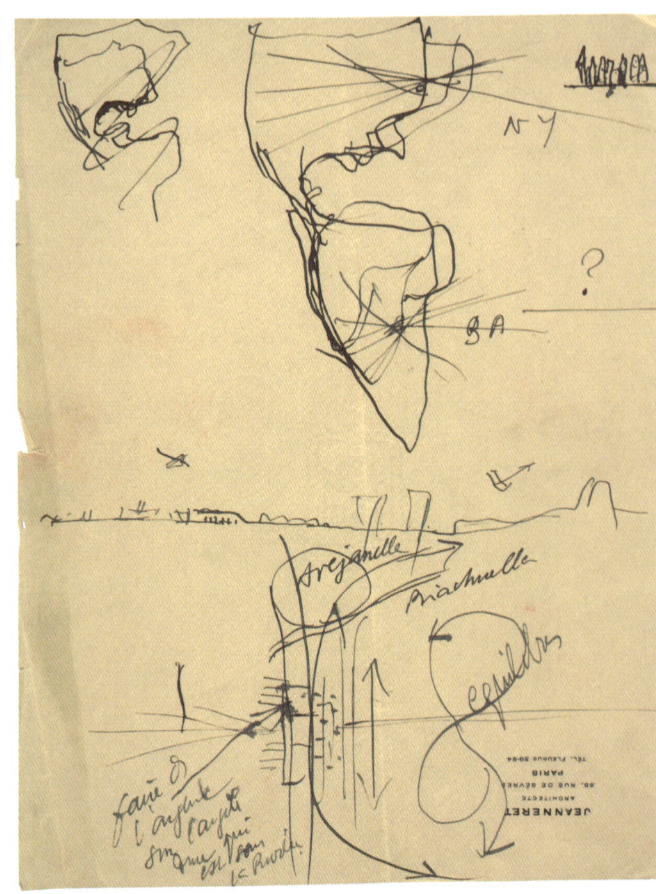
N Y
?
B A

Conclusion
From private enterprise towards great integrated projects.
Towards a new scale of grandeur.
POETRY.[135]

The first architectural revolution – developing an expressive and poetic language using the elements provided by the machinist age – had been successfully achieved. In Rio, Le Corbusier discovered a form of language, equally expressive and free, to solve the big problems of urbanism. This lesson would find its next application in the Obus Plan for Algiers.

An indication that the Brazilian lectures repeated an important part of the content of the ten Argentinian lectures is the fact that there are doubles for eighteen of the lecture sketches. Le Corbusier chose the best variants for publication. For example, there are two versions of a sketch for the sixth lecture.

The comparison of these two pages of drawings (Figs 41 and 42)[136] **reveals differences of layout but a great similarity in argumentation. Clearly, the first sketch, having been damaged, had to be set aside in favour of the second.**

Sometimes, there are several variants of the same subject. If we look at the two sketches illustrating the plan for Buenos Aires (Fig 43 and chapter 1, Fig 8)**, we can associate two variants with them** (Figs 44 and 45) **in which the elements are differently organized.[137] These can be compared with the sketch in the preparatory notes** (Fig 46).[138]

It is probable that the first two were used to illustrate the ninth lecture in Buenos Aires, while the second two were used, one in São Paulo and the other in Rio de Janeiro.

It therefore seems that Le Corbusier had picked out some of the subjects addressed in Buenos Aires to repeat in the lectures at São Paulo and Rio de Janeiro.

It is interesting to observe that the most original sketches for the ten lectures in Buenos Aires – the metaphorical examples such as 'Technology is at the very heart of poetry' (Fig 11)**, 'A bit of preliminary biology'** (Fig 18) **or even the comparison of the Green Mosque of Bursa with the Villa Savoye** (Fig 20) **– do not exist in multiple copies, suggesting that they were not used in Brazil. In the space of only one or two lectures, he could not develop his arguments as forcefully as he could in the ten lectures in Buenos Aires. The ten Argentinian lectures allowed him to explore new ways of expressing himself, such as the exceptional visual metaphors we have analyzed. The Argentinian cycle therefore represents the most brilliant conclusion to Le Corbusier's lectures of the 1920s.**

Figure 43
Sketch showing the new plan for Buenos Aires (FLC 30296B).

Figure 44
Variant of sketch 30296B, showing the new plan for Buenos Aires (FLC 33515B).

Figure 45
Variant for sketch 30303A, showing the new plan for Buenos Aires (FLC 30302).

Figure 46
Preparatory drawing for the ninth lecture (FLC 920083-11(3)).

135/FLC B2(9)681.

136/FLC 33500B and 30297A and see *Precisions*, op. cit., p. 147.

137/FLC 30296B, 33296B and 30303A.

138/GRI 920083-11(3).

aunicipalités et les édiles des grandes villes s'oc
i du problème des grandes banlieues et cherchent à ~~e~~
les populations qui se sont précipitées dans ~~le~~ ca
rce d'une invasion ; ces ~~recherches~~ sont louables ;~~e~~
plètés ; ~~elles~~ laissent de côté le problème ~~capital~~
entre des grandes villes . On soigne les muscles d
mais on ne veut pas ~~savoir~~ que son coeur malade ,~~et~~
que sa vie est en danger . ~~Le problème du centre de~~
~~se pose~~ avec la pl~~us profonde né~~cessité .
bon de ~~préciser~~ ce ~~que~~ représente le phénomène de l
la grande ville n'est pas que 4 ou 7.000.000 d'indi
~~t~~ réunis par hasard en un endroit déterminé ; ~~le~~
~~un organe quasi~~ biologi~~que~~ ~~de l'organisation~~ du pay
tion nationale, ~~et de~~ l'organisation internationale
centre agissant du système cardiaque ;c'est le cerv
igeant du système nerveux
l'activité des pays, ~~et toute l'activité~~ internation
grande ville . La grande ville c'est le lieu de co
gissant du monde , ce contact doit être immédiat ,~~m~~
car les décisions sont la conséquence d'un débat a
et ~~toutes décisions~~ entrainent les agissements du

Appendices

Identification of the manuscripts for the lectures of 1924

Le Corbusier gave a lecture at Lausanne on 18 February 1924, another the day before at Geneva and perhaps a third, just before this, at Zurich. It was probably his friend, the poet Paul Budry, who lived in Lausanne, who invited Le Corbusier to give this lecture. In December 1923, Le Corbusier noted in his diary: 'write Paul Budry for date of lecture', and two pages below, 'Write [me] P. Bud[ry] for lectures'.[1] The invitation card for a lecture to be held at the Maison du Peuple, Lausanne, by 'Mssrs Ozenfant et Jeanneret directors of *L'Esprit Nouveau'* indicated the time as 'Monday 18 February at 20.30', without indication of the year.[2] Now, the only year in which 18 February falls on a Monday, between 1920 and 1925 (the five years of *L'Esprit Nouveau*) is 1924. The subject was 'Life and art in the machinist age' and the event was sponsored by the Swiss Arts and Crafts association *L'Œuvre*. The autograph manuscript entitled 'Conférence Lausanne 18 fév 1924' confirms this date.[3] On 15 February 1924, Le Corbusier and Ozenfant had given two lectures ('Art in the machinist age' and 'L'Esprit nouveau') to the Société des Arts, Classe des Beaux-Arts at the Athénée in Paris.[4] There are no notes attributable to the lectures in Paris or Geneva.[5]

On 12 June 1924 Le Corbusier delivered an important lecture at the Sorbonne (University of Paris), which, according to him, he repeated on 10 November at the auditorium of the Salle Rapp in Paris. A complete transcription of this lecture establishes a fixed point in this chronology. This text exists in the form of galley proofs[6] and two printed versions: *Le Bulletin de l'Ordre de l'Etoile d'Orient*, Spring 1924, entitled "L'Esprit nouveau en architecture" and in one of Le Corbusier's books, *Almanach de l'architecture moderne*, Paris, 1925. It is clear that this text was captured stenographically during the delivery of the lecture at the Salle Rapp. There are some minor differences between these two published versions: five pictures, illustrating page 27 of the *Bulletin*, do not feature in the *Almanach*. Le Corbusier took advantage, in fact, of the interval between the 1924 lectures and the publication of the *Almanach* (April 1926) to bring some of these illustrations up to date, adding a series of photographs of the La Roche-Jeanneret house, which had just been completed in 1925. These published texts refer specifically to the lecture given at the Salle Rapp on 10 November 1924, and there is also internal evidence which distinguishes this from the Sorbonne lecture in June or the Swiss lectures in February. For example, Le Corbusier refers to recently planting gardens in the autumn.

Ten typed pages of a lecture with a slightly different emphasis are more problematic, being neither identified nor dated.[7] I identify this with the lecture at Lausanne and am certain that it is a partial stenographic transcription of the lecture. Might the ten page transcription be a record of the Sorbonne lecture rather than Lausanne? Three reasons argue against this possibility. On 20 June Le Corbusier replied to a journalist from *L'Habitation moderne* who wanted the text of the lecture: 'Unfortunately, I cannot help you, since this lecture was not written but extemporized.'[8] Secondly, Le Corbusier refers in the ten page typescript to a lecture he had just delivered in Geneva and this, coupled with the detailed analysis of the landscape around Lausanne, points to Lausanne as the site. And thirdly, there is a detailed description of the Sorbonne lecture by Léandre Vaillant (discussed in chapter 2), from which it emerges clearly that there are significant differences between the Sorbonne and the Lausanne lectures.

The ten page typescript is the source for a third typed document, this time three pages long, which is a digest of it and includes some corrections of mistakes in it.[9] It must therefore follow the ten page document. Mysteriously labelled 'Lecture Corbusier Sorbonne 1924; Programme for Prague; Bulletin Allendy', it may have been intended as a digest of the Lausanne lecture, intended to provide advance notice for the lecture at the Sorbonne or for a planned lecture in Prague. The heading given to the three page typescript, mentioning the Sorbonne and Prague can be readily explained. Le Corbusier had been thinking about the prestigious Sorbonne lecture since the New Year.[10] His friend Robert Allendy had invited him in January to contribute to a series of lectures for 'our study group for the examination of new ideas' at the Sorbonne.[11] Perhaps Allendy had asked him for a synopsis in order to publicize the Sorbonne lecture, or perhaps he was already thinking of the publication in the *Bulletin de l'Ordre de l'Etoile d'Orient*, with which Allendy also had close contacts. As far as Prague is concerned, Le Corbusier had been invited to give a lecture there to take place in May, probably in association with his and Ozenfant's painting exhibition.[12] Writing to his parents on 17 March 1924, Le Corbusier was thinking of visiting Prague and Brno at the beginning of April, but this has already fallen through by 2 April, when he announced his intention to visit Prague on 5 May. But this trip, too, did not take place, since the Architects' Club of Prague wrote on 5 May excusing themselves for postponing his invitation, on the grounds that his text had arrived too late.[13] My hypothesis, therefore, is that the three page typed text was a synopsis for the Prague lecture, intended either for publication or to allow for a Czech translation to be prepared in advance.

To complete the documentation for this group of lectures, there is a collection of 13 small index cards, on which Le Corbusier typed brief notes on particular topics.[14] They can be dated to late 1923 and refer to anecdotes and themes used in the 1924 lectures.[15] For example, on one card he noted, 'Disquiet, ex[ample]: Barberine', which refers to his visit to the Barberine dam in the valley of the Finhaut, near MontBlanc, which he recounts in his Lausanne lecture.[16] Another reference, the mysterious 'La Tour [de Peilz] road surveyor' is repeatedly mentioned in the notes for these lectures.[17]

There are some other pages of notes which may be associated with the 1924 lectures, but Le Corbusier reordered them and reused them several times in different lectures, which makes them hard to decipher.[18] A sequence of sheets, some of them cut up and collaged, were renumbered in red crayon: 'S1', 'S2' and so on, up to '7' (see chapter 2, Fig 29). I read these as notes originally made for the Lausanne lecture, which Le Corbusier proposed to reuse for the Sorbonne lecture.[19] It is notable that the sheets marked up in this way do not refer to the landscape around Lausanne. There is another sequence of numbers (encircled) which groups together some of the same sheets but adds some others. This indicates that the encircled number sequence was for another lecture. The order of this sequence follows closely the order of the lecture at the Salle Rapp on 10 November.[20] This is confirmed by the sheet C3(8)2 (number '2' in the encircled pencil sequence, which replaces the sheet C3(6)19 in the 'Sorbonne' sequence), which refers to planting gardens in the autumn.[21] Le Corbusier's little house for his parents at Corseaux was in construction by August 1924. The horticulturalist Richard Schyrr is corresponding with Le Corbusier about the choice of plants (a catalpa and a paulownia) on 20 October 1924.[22]

1/FLC F3(3)8 pp. 31 and 33.

2/FLC A2(18)115.

3/FLC C3(6)24.

4/FLC A2(18)110.

5/See FLC C3(6)17 for mention of the lecture at Geneva and the mention on another sheet (FLC C3(6)69): 'For Geneva, Lausanne, the history of the spoiled landscape' (see chapter 2 to explain this reference).

6/FLC C3(8)17-40.

7/FLC C3(06)4-13. This typescript is full of gaps and mistakes and is interrupted at the tenth page. Another version of the same has a few manuscript corrections (FLC C3(06)14-23).

8/FLC C3(6) 235.

9/FLC C3(8)10-12 (with corrections), C3(8)13-15 (corrected version).

10/The invitation to give the lecture at the Sorbonne, sent by Robert Allendy, dates from 19 January 1924 (FLC E1(1)91). Allendy, author of books on psychoanalysis, was organizing the series of lectures at the Sorbonne to which Le Corbusier contributed.

11/FLC E1(1)91. Darius Milhaud, Nicolas Beaudoin et Pitoeff were also listed as lecturers in the series. This letter, as so often occurred with correspondence in January, is wrongly given the date of the previous year.

12/Le Corbusier and Ozenfant had an exhibition of paintings at the Léonce Rosenberg Gallery on 28 February 1924 and this exhibition then went on to Prague, where Ozenfant and Le Corbusier had already published a long article in the journal *Jívot* in 1923.

13/FLC C3(8)308 and E1(16)354.

14/FLC C3(06)72-85. The cards are given codes (on the left: 'I6', 'I2' etc. and on the right: 'Z', 'D', etc.) whose meaning is not apparent. This suggests to me that Le Corbusier imagined a vast and encyclopaedic system of notes to support his lectures, which he soon abandoned.

15/One typed card is dated 15 September 1923 and recalls 'an interview with Selder, director of *The Dial*'. Another card (FLC C3(6)76) is dated 22 November 1923 where he quotes a comment by Eugène Freyssinet on *Vers une architecture*. In his diary for the period between December 1923 and January 1924, Le Corbusier notes 'Lecture; write Freyssinet and Girardet…' (FLC F3(3)8, p. 28). An article on the airship hangars designed by Freyssinet at Orly was published in *L'Architecture* in 1923 (René Le Bœufle and Paul Guadet, "Les Hangars à dirigeables de Villeneuve-Orly") and Le Corbusier illustrated them in his articles. Girardet was one of the directors of the car company Peugeot, to whom Le Corbusier sent his housing project for Lège (13 December 1923) and for whom he designed a housing estate for Peugeot workers at Audincourt (27 February 1924, FLC H1(20)179) based on the Lège houses.

16/FLC C3(6)73. The Barberine dam, constructed between 1919 and 1925, is situated on Emosson lake, near the Finhaut valley to the South East of Lake Geneva. The dam was replaced by the much bigger Emosson dam (1969-75) which now drowns the old dam under 45 metres of water. Le Corbusier devotes to it large sections of his lectures at Lausanne (FLC C3(6)4-13) and the Salle Rapp (FLC C3(8)17-40) as well as several pages in the chapter 'Nos Moyens' in *Urbanisme* (pp. 138-143).

17/'The La Tour road surveyor. The landscape ruined; a landscape created. Alexandre Cingria.' (FLC C3(6)84). Le Corbusier was very impressed by *Les entretiens de la Villa du Rouet. Essais dialogués sur les Arts Plastiques en Suisse-Romande*, by Alexandre Cingria de Vaneyre when he read it in 1910, on the recommendation of William Ritter. Cingria argued for a French Switzerland turning to the Mediterranean and an acceptance of the classical ideals rather than the medievalist tradition of the *Heimatkunst* in the North.

18/There are at least three different sequences of numbers on these sheets.

19/The sequence 'Sorbonne' consists of: 'S1' FLC C3(8)1, 'S2' and 'S3' C3(6)29 , 'S4' C3(6)31, 'S5' C3(8)8 and '7' C3(8)7.

20/The encircled number sequence (Salle Rapp lecture) consists of: '2' FLC C3(8)1, '3' C3(8)2, '4' C3(8)3, '5' C3(8)4, '7' C3(8)5, '8' C3(8)6 and '9' C3(8)7. Unnumbered, but logically taking their place between the '5' and '7' are the sheets C3(8)9 and C3(8)8.

21/'Now we are in the autumn; the time to plant gardens; I have just planted two of them.' *Bulletin de l'Ordre de l'Etoile d'Orient*, 1925, p. 31.

22/FLC H1(5)125.

Lecture at Strasbourg, 1923

Typescript with handwritten corrections by Le Corbusier.[23]

The handwritten corrections and additions are printed in cursive script. Strikethrough text was erased on the typescript.

At present city councils and local officials are concerned with the problem of the suburbs and are seeking to *attract* **~~chase out~~ the populations that have swarmed into the capital ~~city~~** *cities* **with the force of invading hordes; their ~~quest~~** *efforts* **are praiseworthy; they are incomplete; they leave aside the ~~main~~** *root of the* **problem which is what to do about city centres. We are taking care of the athlete's muscles; but we don't want to ~~know~~** *perceive* **that his heart is ill ~~seriously ill~~ and that his life is in danger. ~~It is absolutely essential that we consider the problem of city centres.~~** *Although it may be a good thing to encourage the population entrenched in the faubourgs to move outside, we must remember that every day, at the same time, the crowds who enjoy better housing in the garden cities will have to travel to the city centre. Improving housing by creating garden cities still leaves the city centre problem intact.*

It is useful to ~~be clear about what is meant by~~ *have a clear idea of* **the phenomenon of the city. A city is not only 4 or ~~7~~ 5 000 000 individuals who have gathered ~~themselves~~ together by chance in a certain place. ~~The city is a quasi-biological organ in the organization of a country, of~~** *there is a reason behind the city. In the biology of the country, it is the principal organ; on it depends* **national organization, and** *national organizations make* **international organization. The city is the heart, the active core of the cardiac system; it is the brain, the power base of the nervous system.**

~~All~~ *And* **the activity of the country***ies*, **and ~~all the activity~~ international** *events* **are born in and** *emanate from* **the city.** *Economics, sociology, politics all have their centre in the city, and every modification arising from this particular place has an effect on individuals faraway in the provinces.* **The city is the point of contact for active elements of the world. This contact must be immediate, hands on; ~~for~~ the decisions** *that emanate from it* **are** *the effect* **~~the consequence~~ of a debate with an impatient beat and they ~~all the decisions~~ provoke the activities of the country and of the countries with each other. The telegraph, the railway, the aeroplane have** *in less than 50 years accelerated* **~~activated~~ the speed of international contacts** *at such a rate that work patterns have been revolutionized.* **The march of ideas** *operates* **~~is contained~~ in the confined space of the city centre;** *these centres are,* **~~it is this centre which is~~ clearly, the vital cells of the** *world* **~~country~~.**

But at the moment city centres are almost inexploitable tools; the necessary connections can be established only with *precarious exactness* **~~uncomfortable speed~~ through the network of encumbered streets. More than this, [space]** *a real fatigue is born* **~~of the collisions~~** *of the congestion,* **a ~~malaise born of the confinement of~~** *dangerous handicap threatens* **these business premises with their stuffy corridors and gloomy offices.**

One may conclude ~~that firstly,~~ *first of all, that* **prejudicial** *exhaustion* **tiredness wears rapidly** *affects, even beyond their working conditions,* **those who need to keep alert and maintain great clarity ~~rapidness~~ in their thought processes.**

~~Secondly~~ *Then* **that the country that has well-organized city centres** *has every chance of acquiring* **~~will probably have~~ superiority over the others,** *the superiority* **of an industrial entrepreneur ~~who~~ possess[~~es~~]ing good machine tools. The national economy ~~may~~** *will* **suffer the positive or negative effects.**

One *should* **~~must~~ then pay ~~all ones~~** *particular* **attention ~~to the case of~~ the malady of the cities;** *this is absolutely essential.* **~~From the viewpoint of city planning, the~~** *The map of present-day* **cities shows that** *following* **their ~~crushing development~~** *modest origins* **(early small towns)** *and the extraordinary development that has been made in a century,* **the centre ~~of cities is~~** *remains* **in the form of ~~little~~ short narrow streets; only the periphery has larger arterial roads.**

~~But the centre of cities is the place where~~ *It is towards the city centre that* **a huge amount of traffic congregates; ~~and~~ the periphery** *is relatively comfortable,* **as it accomodates only family life ~~proceeds from sufficient arterial roads~~.**

23/GRI 920083-2(1). See chapter 3, Fig 1 and pp. 94-104 for a detailed discussion.

If one overlays, on the graf*ph* of the streets of a city, the graf*ph* of the traffic, one is aware that there is a formal opposition ~~between these two states of affairs~~. Graf*ph* of the streets: early state of affairs; grafph of the traffic: present-day state of affairs. There is a crisis (unneccessary to labour the point, we suffer the *disastrous* effects ~~today~~ in all cities). But we should look at the temperature chart of the crisis and *admit* ~~persuade ourselves~~ that it shows a dramatic rise; *we are heading for deadlock.*

~~Also~~ Figures ~~show~~ *prove* that the city is a recent event, dating from fifty ~~50~~ years ago *and that the growth of agglomerations* ~~it~~ has exceeded all the forecasts. From 1800 to 1910, in ~~100~~ *a hundred* years, Paris has grown from 600 000 to 3 000 000 inhabitants; London from ~~6~~ *8* 00 000 to 7 000 000; Berlin from 180 000 to 3 500 000; New York from 60 000 to 4 500 000. But these cities are built over their early constructions, on their early traces dating from before the spectacular rise shown on the population and traffic charts (see, on the grafph, ~~the~~ rise in traffic from 1885 to 1905, movement of persons, movement of merchandise). *The unrest is such that anxiety is a growing problem. The term city planning only appeared a few years ago, proof of germination of ideas.*

Following a very human inclination, the first efforts sought the line of least resistance: the suburbs. There is also a more profound cause; we need to study anew the basic notions of a form of housing that can answer the needs of a style of family life that has been completely transformed by mechanization.; the garden suburb house allows us to isolate the problem and experiment. On the other hand, by the law of economy of effort, because of the cruelty of the only possible remedies, and faced with the horrifying spectacle of city centres, we turn our backs on the difficulty and listen to clever people loudly proclaiming: "The centre must be transported elsewhere, a new town must be built, a new centre, faraway, beyond the suburbs, where it will be comfortable, no constraints, no pre-existing state of affairs. A fallacious argument. A centre is contingent, it only exists in relation to the things that surround it, and it is fixed from afar by innumerable converging lines of all sorts that cannot be changed; moving the hub of the wheel means moving the whole wheel. Concerning the city, it means moving an entity whose radius is 20 or 30 kilometres, which is clearly impossible. The hub of the wheel has to be fixed. In Paris the hub has oscillated for a thousand years from left to right and from right to left, between Notre-Dame and the Place des Vosges, the Place des Vosges and Les Invalides, Les Invalides and the Gare de l'Est, the Gare de l'Est and Saint-Augustin. In relation to the wheel (railways, periphery, suburbs, distant suburbs, main roads, subways, tramways, administrative and commercial centres, industrial and residential areas), the centre never moved. It stayed in the same place. It must stay where it is. What is more, it represents a huge asset, and in wishing to move it, an important part of the wealth of the nation would be eliminated by decree. To say:" It is simple, let us create the new centre of Paris in Saint-Germain-en-Laye " is to talk nonsense, or to promise the moon. It is "a gambit" used endlessly by the supporters of stagnation to gain a little time. The centre must be modified where it is. It crumbles and reconstructs itself over the centuries, just as a man changes his skin every seven years and a tree produces new leaves every year. We must confront the city centre, and transform it, which is the simplest solution and, more simply, the only solution.

So we are led to define the basic notions of modern city planning using four stark, concise proposals that provide precise responses to the dangers in question.

The conclusion is the following:

1. Unblock the congestion in city centres ~~for speed~~ *in order to respond to the demands* of traffic.

2. Increase the density of city centres in order to ~~ensure~~ *create* the connections demanded by business.

3. Increase traffic flow, that is to say to entirely modify the present conception of the street which is ineffectual faced with the new phenomenon ~~which is new~~ of modern means of transport, subways or automobiles, tramways, aeroplanes.

4. Increase planted surfaces, ~~which are~~ the only means to ensure sufficient good health ~~for the inhabitants of the city~~ and the tranquillity necessary for attentive work *demanded by the* ~~that the~~ new rhythm ~~of business demands of each person~~ *of business.*

These four points appear ~~to be~~ irreconcilable. ~~On the contrary;~~ *It is useful to recognize their exactness, to measure their urgency. Then, with the problem expressed in this way, city planning can provide answers. And it can provide answers, contrary to appear-*

ances. **The technical and** *organizational* **means** ~~**available in our**~~ **of the times** ~~**furnish**~~ *offer* **the harmonious solution and the question then becomes fascinating and we can appreciate the imminence of a new cycle of grandeur and majesty. In the course of a period of development, architecture marks the culmination; it is a result that provides the mind with a system. City planning is the medium for architecture. A new form of architecture, expressed and no longer irresolute, is imminent. We are waiting for city planning to be its release mechanism.**

It is useful to be aware of the different types of inhabitants of a city. As the seat of power (in the widest sense of the word: leaders in business, industry, finance, politics, masters in science, teaching, thought, spokesmen for the human soul, artists, poets, musicians, etc., etc.), the city focuses all ambitions, drapes itself in a glittering mirage of fairyland; the crowds pour in. The city centre is the seat of the powerful, the leaders, and their assistants down to the most humble, whose presence is necessary at set times in the city centre, but whose destiny tends to be limited to the organization of family life. Families are poorly housed in the city. Garden cities provide better conditions for their cohesion. Lastly, industry, with its factories, which, for various reasons, are concentrated in large numbers around the centre. With the factories will be, the large numbers of workers satisfied with their social status as residents of the garden cities.

Let's classify them. Three sorts of population: the resident city dwellers; the working population who spend half their time in the centre and half in the garden cities; and the labouring masses who divide their time between factories in the suburbs and the garden cities.

To tell the truth, this classification is already a city planning programme. Putting it objectively into practice, is to start to reshape the cities. Because, following their spectacularly rapid growth, they are now in a terrible state of chaos: everything is confused. This city planning programme could, for example, be defined as follows, for a city of 3 000 000 inhabitants; in the centre and for daytime work only, 500 000 to 800 000 people; at night the centre is deserted. The city residential area absorbs some, the garden cities the rest. Let's say then half a million city dwellers (in the inner ring) and two and a half millions in the garden cities.

This clarification, only in principle, unconfirmed as far as figures are concerned, calls for measures to create order, sets the guidelines of modern city planning, determines the proportions of the city (centre), of the residential areas, poses the problem of communications and transport, provides the basis for a programme of urban sanitation, determines the method of division of land into plots, the alignment of streets, their layout, fixes the density and consequently the construction methods for the centre, for the residential areas and for the garden cities.

~~**The history of towns shows us their development with blocks built between the streets; first and foremost this tends towards the straight line, only possible solution for traffic, and extension of the distance between the streets.**~~

~~**The study of fast traffic shows that it is necessary to reduce the number of crossroads to a minimum, which corresponds anyway to the regular [space filled in by hand] increase of the network of streets over the centuries (see diagram XIVth, XVIIIth and XIXth centuries): traffic demands a far more extensive module in the network of streets and we should accept that the lines of the network should be at a distance of about 400 or 500 metres from each other.**~~

~~**To summarize, we should eliminate 2/3 of the streets in existing towns to solve the problem of fast traffic.**~~

~~**Another phenomenon to be studied it is that of classifying the population of cities.**~~

~~**For many reasons, from all the countries and all the provinces crowds throng to the capital. Their ambitions are varied, their activity crumbles on the slippery flanks of the pyramid of power.**~~

~~**Those at the tip of the pyramid have their base [correction: place] at the centre of the cities, they are the leaders; then come the more modest participants and then those who have not found the paradise they were seeking and who remain uprooted, drifters, poor impoverished refugees in the misery of the poor quarters and who make up a whole disturbing section of the population of the cities. There are also those we can call city dwellers, that is to say those who have a taste for life in the city; for its diverse resources, its bustle and for those whose destiny is to express the fundamentals of human thought, who also need to be in direct contact with the huge spiritual potential embodied by the city.**~~

~~**Let's classify:**~~

~~**1. Those in business, the leaders and their assistants whose schedule demands a defined presence in a precise location: the centre.**~~

~~**2. The housing for city dwellers around and close to the city centres. The centre for business and housing for the city dwellers constitutes [sic] in fact the city centre.**~~

~~**3. The floating population must be classified as being beyond the slums in the garden cities, far away from the centre: garden cities that would accommodate all the people of middling condition and who in the normal way plan to bring up a family. The garden cities are intended as entirely new elements, where rational development is possible. Here the question of suburban transport arises and it is a huge responsibility that rests with the Railway Companies and subway managers.**~~

~~**It is no longer a question of recognizing that a few of the privileged or fanatical suburbanites can assume the heroic role of garden city resident (I say heroic because through negligence the Railway Companies have imposed a state of affairs that is simply grotesque). If the centre of a capital city attracts 500 to 800 000 individuals attending to business every day, if the rest of the city centre accommodates roughly 1 000 000 city dwellers, the garden cities must accommodate the two other milions [sic] to make up a city of 3 000 000 inhabitants, one can see that necessarily a railway question arises.**~~

~~**The centre of the city is reserved for business. The density there has to be ten times higher than it is at present in Paris, the thoroughfares must be 100 metres wide instead of the 7, 9, 11 or 15 metres inherited from the previous centuries: building areas could be 5%, planted areas 95%, density about 2000 instead of the average 350 for Paris; in that case the centre of cities must be laid out with widely-spaced skyscapers.**~~ *The skyscraper, a powerful tool for decongestion, has been built to an unfortunate design in New York; it should not be in the form of tall and narrow towers.* ~~**These skyscrapers are no longer towers (in the fashion of the Venice Campanile) as in New York, but huge buildings rising to 60 floors with no courtyards and achieving, with their cross-shaped ground plan, the suppression of courtyards and a considerable extension of facades facing the light as well as maximum stability.**~~ *Including the skyscraper in modern city planning will allow for wide open spaces.*

~~**For example, these skyscrapers could be 400 metres from axis to axis, be 200 metres in width, leaving 200 metres empty between their extremities. They could each accommodate between 40 000 and 60 000 employees (with an average surface area of 10 metres per employee). In reality they form a district or a quarter of the town covering a few thousand square metres instead of 160 000 metres of low, spread-out buildings.**~~

~~**The subway stations are right under each skyscraper; the main streets can vary from 50 to 120 metres wide and be provided with autodromes, i.e. 40-metre-wide bridges raised to a height of 6 to 8 metres and carrying fast automobile traffic with no crossroads.**~~

~~**The planted surfaces then cover 95% of the centre of cities. So the four fundamentals listed above can be easily established.**~~

The question of skyscrapers is a preoccupation in Europe. In Holland, in England, in Germany, in France, in Italy, the first theoretical attempts have been made. The skyscraper cannot be isolated from the study of the street and of horizontal and vertical transport.

The centre of the town would then be permanently purged of family life. In the present state of things, it would seem that skyscrapers cannot accommodate family life. Their interior organization demands a complex system of circulation and organization, the cost of which can only be met by businesses; the way in which the means of circulation are organized, like stations in the air, cannot be suitable for family life.

Urban residential quarters could be developed from the same rational transformations. Main streets would criss-cross them at intervals of 400 metres from axis to axis. Contrary to age-old usage, buildings would not be grouped in rectangular blocks overlooking the street, with internal subdivisions into numerous courtyards. A system of land division (presented in L'Esprit Nouveau, no. 4, 1921) eliminating the courtyard would leave intervals of 200 to 400 or 600 metres between houses that could form parks bigger than the Tuileries Gardens. The town would become one huge park: 15% buildings, 85% planted areas, density equivalent to that of our congested Paris of today, main streets 50 metres wide only transecting every 400 metres (automobile traffic demands the elimination of two thirds of the existing streets); sports fields and pleasure gardens adjoining housing, elimination of courtyards, radical transformation of the aspect of the town, architectural contributions of prime importance. Etc., etc.

Studied through the filter of reason and animated by a suitable lyricism, city planning can provide solutions that are as intensely practical as they are highly architectural. They arise from a purely theoretical analysis of the problem; they revolutionize our habits. But have our lives not already been revolutionized in the past few years? Man reflects theoretically, acquiring theoretical certitudes. Using theory, he formulates a line of conduct; and on the strength of his basic principles, apprehends typical cases of daily life.

~~Concerning residential quarters, the same interval of 400 metres between streets could be recommended and the division of blocks of buildings, previously in quadrilaterals that separate streets and areas into numerous courtyards, would be replaced by a system of plots with indents accommodating 12-storey buildings overlooking wide streets, with no courtyards, on gardens 200 to 400 metres wide. Density: about 400 inhabitants per hectare whereas the average density for Paris is 360.~~

~~The study shows that skyscrapers, at least in the present situation, cannot be considered suitable for accommodating families. Their interior organization, demanding such a particular system of circulation, can only be suitable for business: the running costs are as responsible for this as the practical details themselves.~~

~~These proposals are the result of the purely theoretical analysis of the problem; they revolutionize our present habits. But for several years now has life in the cities not become so unbearable that the time would now seem right for suggesting some remedies? Man thinks theoretically, he acquires theoretical certitudes. With theory he formulates a line of conduct, he fixes fundamental principles. He can envisage typical cases in daily life.~~

~~But in city planning we seem to be terribly afraid to give the problem a thorough examination and come to conclusions that seem so far removed from the possiblity of accomplishment.~~

~~So let us apply ourselves to the critique of three systems proposed recently by eminent city planners.~~

~~a) One has studied an industrial city (small in size it is true).[24] The municipal buildings are in the centre, tidily arranged, but nearby there is a housing estate of family houses (one family per house) right next to the centre of the town; this is a very ingenious estate because it puts forward a new solution for urban ownership ? but classification appears to be insufficient; one cannot put family dwellings in the centre of a town.~~

~~b) An ingenious architect[25] proposes to build towns with houses in tiers; houses in tiers give more width to the streets and allow light into the appartments, and consequently allow for as many storeys as desired without ever blocking the light. But the street itself is never affected, it remains in its original state; so the problem of traffic is never considered.~~

~~Another point is that the town in tiers is covered with buildings that are spread out, around normal streets; no planted areas are introduced in the town. The question of public health is not considered.~~

~~c) It has been suggested that a ring of skyscrapers be built on the fortifications around Paris; a wreath around the town.[26] The idea is poetic. But business is not conducted on the periphery of towns and especially not along an extended boulevard; so, these skyscrapers would be reserved for family life and it appears that family life would not find them suitable. The skyscraper has the potential to relieve congestion, must relieve the congestion in city centres; it doesn't need to relieve congestion on the periphery of towns, which is not congested.~~

Let us examine Paris: Let us try to make a survey of the sick Paris of today. All the life of Paris is clearly in the quarters stretching from the Gare de l'Est to the Gare St Lazare; Place de la République to Etoile; the left bank remains calm, residential. By the Seine, the magnificent Paris of the past, from the Place des Vosges to Etoile.

Between the Gare de l'Est and the Gare St Lazare, there is the hinterland left over from the XVIIth and XVIIIth and XIXth centuries: streets that are 7, 9 and 11 metres wide with a few boulevards that clearly show the need for main thoroughfares and a few of Haussmann's incisions which//on their side//prove that a/such/a surgical// operation//s were//was able to be made in a century when mechanization//powerful modern equipment, technical and financial// was hardly born.

24/Le Corbusier is referring to Tony Garnier's *Cité industrielle, 1917.*

25/This is Henri Sauvage, whose terraced apartment block, rue Vavin (1910-11) was admired by Le Corbusier and who made a number of ambitious projects using set-back terraces.

26/Auguste Perret, whose project to build skyscrapers in the outskirts of Paris (either around the line of the walls or along a great western avenue) had been published in 1922, was to publish a wounding attack on Le Corbusier in December 1923.

These quarters have no artistic value. They do however stifle the life that flows into them. The houses are old and have cracks, they are gradually being demolished, but they are gradually replaced with new buildings in the same places; there are no rules of conduct to manage this gradual reconstruction of the city centre. In the last ten years the automobile has become a working tool and and since the war the automobile has made the centre of Paris a regular nightmare.

Is it beyond the means of our era to transform the centre of Paris? Where the previous centuries have modelled the face of Paris, is our era incapable of adding a new feature that could be worthy of our century?

~~**New equipment is such that it represents a revolution with regard to the one hundred previous centuries.**~~

Are we not on the eve of a grand period of architecture? The scale of the modern illness of the cities corresponds to an equivalent scale of constructive procedures, organizational methods, financial power. Following Haussmann's works, is Paris, a city which has been constantly transformed over the centuries, resigned to falling asleep for ever? Our archeologists, our museum curators are beginning to bore us. There are still creative forces at work in the world; there is even a wonderful creative strength throughout the world, entirely novel in its scope, in all the domains of technology and organization. Why would architecture be dead? Modern equipment is such that it represents a revolution compared to the previous one hundred centuries; the war seems to have proved this. Ocean liners are bigger than skyscrapers, and they float on the water!

The only street in Paris where traffic can circulate is the Champs Elysées; and it ends in a cul-de-sac: the Place de la Concorde. To go beyond that point would mean demolishing the Louvre, the City Hall, etc... Unthinkable. However, by drawing a new thoroughfare parallel with the Champs Elysées passing in front of the Opera to join East to West, it would be possible to return health and vitality to the stifled city.

Skyscrapers could be built between Gare de l'Est and Gare St Lazare. They would absorb the whole population that is at present crammed into a height of 6 storeys, allowing vast open spaces in the centre of Paris, where the most dense traffic ~~**would rush**~~ *could move* **more easily, where greenery** *mingling with gigantic buildings* **would create a city of startling dimensions. This is a problem for the years to come.**

The financial means ensue directly from this situation: by multiplying the density of these quarters by ten, buying power is also multiplied to the same extent; consequently modes of expropriation are simple. Haussmann restored the Emperor's finances by replacing 6 storey slums by 6 storey mansions; the Paris of today could count on a brilliant financial situation by replacing the 6 storey slums with magnificent 60 storey skyscrapers.

The economy of the city, its finances, its public health and its beauty would acquire a splendour worthy of our ~~**era**~~ *time.*

From a practical point of view, ~~**it would not be difficult**~~ *the enterprise is not problematic.* **As skyscrapers occupy 5% of the surface, work could start without having to move the inhabitants. Once the skyscrapers are built, the population would move and the slum districts would be demolished.**

An ultimate obstacle remains: the Administration! The administration manages the inextricable details imposed by the present situation with care and attention, so it would at last be relieved and calmed when confronted with a clear and logical problem where all the consequences ensue harmoniously one from the other and automatically resolve the difficulties. The present administrator is a martyr: daily life with constant pin-pricks. Let's remove him from this melancholic and illogical situation and give him the opportunity to become an efficient tool.

This only needs a series of directives, we only need to create a general vision. All human enterprise proceeds in the same way: Utopia *first (in reality thought)* **which goes on to germinate in active minds. And gradually the carrying out begins. This is** ~~**the hope**~~ *the story* **of our time: railways, ocean liners, telephone, telegraph, aviation, radio, etc... Too often we forget to notice that these examples of modern equipment have, in the last 50 years** *completely* **transformed life on earth.**

City centres, the vital cells of the world, are unusable. They must be replaced. With their wonderful constructions, technology and Architecture can claim the right to take part in history.

Le Corbusier

Conférence Lausanne
18 fev 1924

C3 - 24 6 -

Les révolutions ne se font pas que dans le sang et sur les barricades.

On a assisté dans l'histoire à l'anéantissement d'1 esprit et autre et à l'avènement

Par ex : l'esprit du nord contre le Méditerranéen XI siècle

Conséquence : formes etc. les choses, les villes, les paysages ont changé

nous sommes Comme Sautier dans paquebot.

On peut toutefois à des signes fixer des repères, c'est pourquoi l'EN

Vous avez vu passer la suite hétéroclite des images.

Le Paquebot Paris et le Salon

au moment où a passé la vue de ~~Fontainebleau~~

La Banque americaine et l'architecte

Barbarines

Un fait nouveau formidable, le machinisme, face à 400 siècles

Crée un sentiment nouveau ~~fatalement indispensable~~ imposé et

idéalement humain.

La loi d'économie. exactitude rigueur la ligne juste, le poing juste etc.

~~retrouve les Standarts~~

Le machinisme basé sur la géométrie.

l'homme est basé sur la géométrie

retrouve les Standarts humains. l'homme géométrique Eupalinos Valéry

L'homme a en mains un outillage formidable

il a retrouvé les Standarts. ~~Le machinisme face à 400 siècles~~

La jouissance mathématique. Les arts et la pensée moderne.

Donc Un état de choses nouveau
" " d'esprit "
" mouvement "

Voici un exemple d'esprit nouveau : la maison.

Lecture at Lausanne, 18 February 1924

Facsimile and transcription of the first page of the preparatory notes[27]

Lausanne Lecture
18 Feb. 1924

Revolutions do not only take place with bloodshed and on the barricades.
Throughout history we have witnessed the eradication of one spirit and culture and to the accession [...]
For ex[ample] the influence of the North versus the Mediterranean [in the] XIth century.
Consequences: form etc. things, towns, landscapes changed.

[sketch]

We are like coal trimmers in an ocean liner.
One can however attach certain markers to certain signs, this is the reason for the EN [*Esprit Nouveau*].

You have seen a heterogeneous series of transparencies.
The ocean liner Paris and the drawing room
When I showed the view of Fontainebleau
the American bank and the architect
Barberine
A new wonderful development, mechanization, looking back on 400 centuries of history, creates a new feeling inevitably/imposed/absolutely necessary and ideally human.
The law of economy, exactitude, strictness, the precise line, the correct point etc.

Mechanization is based on geometry.
Man is based on geometry.
Rediscover human standarts [sic]. Geometric man/Eupalinos Valéry
Man has extraordinary equipment in hand; he has rediscovered the standarts.
Use of mathematics. The arts and modern thought.

So a new state of affairs
" " " of mind
" " movement

Here is an example of the *esprit nouveau*: the house

27/FLC C3(6)29, see chapter 2, Fig 29.

Lecture at Lausanne, 18 February 1924

Transcription of stenographic notes taken during the lecture[28]

Ladies and Gentlemen,

An *Esprit Nouveau* [new spirit] that is more powerful than race and stronger than the influence of geographical conditions is passing over all our customs and traditions and is spreading all over the world with clearly defined and unifying characteristics.

These characteristics are [more] universal and human than ever, although the gulf separating the old society from the mechanized society has also never been so wide.

One century (this last century) contrasts with the 400 previous centuries. The machine founded on calculations [...[29]] ensures the coherent system of the laws of physics; the machine imposes its consequences upon our [...[30]] our spirit towards purity [...[31]] between two generations.

We should stop in front of this chasm and think carefully before seeking a way through the confusion of a difficult and widespread crisis.[32]

Revolutions are not only carried out with guns and bloodshed, one can see many examples in history of complete transformations, one can witness the complete destruction of a spirit and the accession of another spirit and another culture; for example, in our country in the XIth century we saw the disappearance of the Mediterranean spirit, driven out by the spirit of the North, we can see the consequences of this accession and, in the order of things that interest us, complete modification of the forms that shaped our surroundings.[33]

Not only have everyday forms been transformed by this spirit, but the consequences have been far-reaching and have affected even everyday objects; the landscape itself has changed.

The follow-on of centuries of work by what we call culture was necessary to rediscover elements of Mediterranean culture, towards which we are once again directing our attention.

I hope you will pardon me this evening, I will frequently be drawing on the board, as I consider that drawing can effectively abbreviate explanations.

Here is a system of forms suddenly introduced at this period, I am talking about the XIth century which gradually expressed itself through a range of special forms replacing this form here:

[Le Corbusier draws on the board, see chapter 2, Fig 29]

You can see that the contrast is not only striking, but in formal opposition; it is a different spirit that completely modifies the old one. In the country where the transformation took place, you can see a site composed of elements like these:

[drawing]

Roof lines set out like this:

[drawing]

[they] confer a truly particular aspect which was then transformed to produce this with a [...] in a fundamentally different system of forms.

These four diagrams show how the smallest detail of our lives can be transformed when one spirit dominates another; I said earlier that even the landscape was tranformed, one can tell that men are not so much made by travel, but that men make their own landscape, lead it, confront it, in the way that corresponds to their ideas, completing it with use of [...] of the same sort whereas beforehand the site was visibly shaped by planting. Here the consequence is certainly less radical.

Then we witness another phenomenon which is that of a predestined march towards murity [sic, read purity] which certainly animates all human

28/FLC C3(6)14-23.

29/The gaps in the typed manuscript can be completed by referring to a page of hand-written notes entitled 'Sorbonne Prague' (FLC C3(8)1), which summarizes the beginning of the lecture. Here: 'engendered by the laws of the world, established in confrontation with the possible wanderings of our minds'.

30/*Ibid.*: 'existence and forcing'.

31/*Ibid.*: 'modifies our surroundings. The distance is enormous, the chasm that is dug today'.

32/In a three-page typed text summarizing this Lausanne lecture, entitled 'programme f[or] Prague; Allendy bulletin; Conférence Corbusier Sorbonne 1924' (FLC C3(8)10-13) this phrase does not appear.

33/*Idem* for this passage from 'for example' onwards.

behaviour. The awareness of these means leads to a quest for the essential that becomes practice, in order to remain in the sphere of architecture.

Here is an example:

[drawing of steeply pitched roof]

In a certain country they make a roof, then the roof evolves under certain influences like this [...]

[drawing of less steep roof and a roof disguised behind a parapet]

and with [...] [...] begins

the difficulties that they try to overcome by going further than the solution; it is this effort that leads to this building of roofs, that has as its effect the creation of the horizontal and the vertical elevations.

I would like to point out in passing and this is in fact the point of this evening's study, that progress, the consequence of science leads us to a system of building that is this:

[drawing of reinforced concrete flat roof]

this section of wall in concrete responds automatically, and in the absence of all technical problems, to a state of mind that appears to identify with the orthogonal formation that we have sought for centuries, where culture has developed in our countries.

This is the force of this technology, which also brings a complete aesthetic revolution, an almost complete scission between all the systems [...] grafted onto the early forms and which could not accept this brutally new system, into which we joyfully step.

Let me quote a special little example which is a very effective indication of these two completely different outlooks that are the very [...] of the present crisis.

This crisis has been a crisis of attitude between generations for centuries and all of a sudden a generation accustomed to seeing the wonders of mechanization.

This example can be expressed in this way:

[drawing]

Here is a country, a beautiful country.

The site has even become famous, houses such as these are built there:

[drawing, see chapter 2, Fig 31, left]

[This is] a place where the last vestiges of romanticism found expression.

On this site with its mountain, there are other mountains with a quite different outline, there is also a generation who regards this mountain only with ennui, then next to it there are mountains with superb profiles reminiscent of certain things, a calm line at the horizon, and in front of this view I am now in the process of building a house that will be like this:

[drawing, middle]

This is a very rough diagram:

[drawing]

I am putting the façade on this side:

[drawing]

Here is the lake, in front of the mountain.

Here is the house turned round [...] which we can no longer see and so on the contrary we look for a landscape where emotion is equivalent to the sort of emotion that animates the creation of this architecture.

You saw a set of images in the slide projection earlier: you saw the ocean liner 'Paris' and then its drawing room, its dining room, its panelling.

When you were shown the Château of Fontainebleau which is nonetheless a thing of beauty, you expressed the feeling of distance that now separates you from this aesthetic ideal and from the feelings that inspired the people who created this building.

I was in Geneva, in completely different surroundings, showing the same set of slides, which provoked a completely different effect, when the view of Fontainebleau was projected, instead of your laughter, there was the customary admiration at the sight of a beautiful thing.

This is to show once again the huge difference [...] ugliness.

You have seen American banks which are beautiful buildings, by a very talented architect. This same architect, in the middle [of an article] publishing his work, prints an invitation, a view of his office. This shows a Renaissance interior with XVth century furniture with turned feet, a suit of armour, cushions, heavy furniture, trimmings. This is an example of the inconsequential nature of men today.

And another example:

I was in the Alps to see one of the most beautiful things that human enterprise can achieve: the dam at Barberine.

I was with a poet who was enthusiastic to discover, at a height of about 2 000 metres, a huge mechanism, made of cables, cranes and iron girders, dominating the chasm to be filled with cement in order to form the dam.

[drawing, see chapter 2, Fig 1]

Human force, force of nature, admiration for the work achieved.

The next day we went to see the engineers; we told them how much we admired their work and they calmly accepted the compliment. After a discussion it came to this, that I managed to make everyone laugh when I expressed my ideas. And when I asked why, they replied: 'But you will destroy the beauty of cities by building skyscrapers.'

These people, who are capable of creating huge grandeur have no understanding of it.

We are faced with an extraordinary thing: mechanization; 400 centuries impose [sic, read oppose] this century, which has succeeded in 100 years in modifying [...] this mechanization [...] in us a feeling of great [...] imposed [...] the ideal that haunts us, a mechanism controlled by laws of technology, greater philosophy, rigour, precise line.

This mechanism, based on geometry, evokes an ideal within us [...] which expresses itself.

Period of regeneration of work by hand.

Man has found the means to free himself of his incapacities and by using his mind to delegate to machines. They carry out the work with surprising conscientiousness.

The mechanism is based on geometry, man can only be aware of himself through geometry, the [...] is not as easy as all that, it provokes enormous reactions.

An example:

Let's leave Paris on the PLM [*Paris Lyon Marseilles railway*] and make our way towards Lyon:

First of all, the station, the rails, the sidings next to each other, dug out of the hillsides, in cuttings.

[drawing]

Man is obliged to establish order in everything he does.

The countryside, a train, 8 to 10 oxen pulling a cart [...] with the feeling of lack of economy that guides this work [...] does not appear in this fashion, appears in fragmentary fashion, we do not see nature as geometrical, man needs geometry; man's first movements included geometry; I was somewhat surprised when I read a wonderful book by Paul Valéry to see [...]

[Le Corbusier reads an extract from *Eupalinos*[34]]

Paul Valéry places geometry at the zenith of human understanding, and a few phrases later:

[extract from *Eupalinos*[35]]

By returning to geometry man is able to rediscover his standard and create works in a spirit that can be a favorable spirit and this use is one of the acts that appear to be the quintessence of modern attitudes, the present [...] leading us towards a mathematical art form [...]

But on the contrary make things that [...] to a rhythm

So we can conclude in this way, that we are in a new state of things, that there is a state of mind and at the present time we are witnessing a general movement of *esprit nouveau*.

This evening I am going to make a demonstration and I will do this by studying the house; please excuse my using for illustration a personal creation made in collaboration with my cousin, Pierre Jeanneret.

The house is a machine for living, a machine for living, it's the [...] for all the functions our work obliges us to carry out, then it is the tranquillity necessary for a sort of meditation, to be able to think.

The practical side is provided by the engineer; there's another side that we could call the [...] and which [...] that we must tune to our senses but first I will raise the question of attitude, beauty and order: deeply human phenomena and that is what we call architecture.

To attain Architecture we must first consider the rational imperatives of what is practical and what is comfortable.

How does one define the sort of *non sequitur* that is architecture, by means of a few factors that are anthropocentrism, that is to say the spatial and the aesthetic means that are the elements of anthropocentrism.

A house is nothing but a shelter provided by doors and windows.

The doors are [...]

The windows [...]

And finally the aesthetic will be provided by the question of the physiology of sensations joining up with the feeling for things [...] from the choice of certain shapes of windows and doors that are paramount (see chapter 2, Fig 30).

The question of anthropocentrism.

A door is a hole for a man [...] making a portico is the opportunity to build something that totally surpasses the scale of the human being and which no longer carries any notion of [...]

The window evolves over time; at the beginning of [...] it was like this:

[drawing, see chapter 2, Fig 35, bottom]

Then it became this:

[drawing]

The Renaissance window, the mullioned window, the Louis XIVth window and then there is no more progress [...] on a human scale.

[...] given in order to arrive at the non-sense that ruled until recently [...] machine for living into machine to impress.

[...] window remains properly established in relation to the height of the rooms; exactly two centuries ago we began to consider comfort [...]

For our present turn of mind encourages us to make ever greater use of the law of economy.

Reconsider the question of the window.

I am no longer obliged to make thick walls to support the arches, I have a *piloti* [concrete post] that is 20 to 30 cm wide.

Complete liberty to say to myself that a man is on his own scale, what does he want: have the widest possible field of vision.

34/'Socrates: [...] Take a style, I say to you, or take a sharp stone, and on some wall, trace any line without thinking. Trace it with one single movement. Are you doing so?
Phaedrus: I am...
Socrates: And what have you done?
Phaedrus: It seems that I have drawn a line of smoke. It moves, breaks, comes back, and ties itself or closes; it gets confused with itself, and presents me with the image of an aimless caprice, with no beginning or end, nor any other meaning except the freedom of my gesture within my arm's span...
Socrates: That is right. Your hand did not know for itself, being at one point, where it would go next. It was compelled, in a confused way, only by the tendency to leave the place where it was [...]'
(Paul Valéry, *Eupalinos* and *L'Ame et la Danse*, with introduction and notes by Vera J. Daniel, London, Oxford University Press, 1967, p. 86.

35/After a description of geometry ('diagrams that are the traces of the movements we can express in few words'), Socrates continues: 'I know nothing more divine, nothing more human, nothing more simple, nothing more powerful' (*Ibid.*, p. 89).

This visual prospect is at his eye height, here is the window that I am called upon to make.

I can see that for several years and in all countries this thing is attractive; I am not saying that I am entirely right, but certainly there is [...] confirmed by the question of economy, the question of aesthetics; the window which is from now on this, is no longer a puncture for light; it created this, that is to say [...] a considerable area of shadow which provokes sadness.

Where there is light we are happy.

This window can provide intimacy, but more sadness than a window like this which [...] an illuminated wall.

Here is the point of anthropocentrism.

This is only a rough indication.

Question of structure [...]

Question of walls [...]

Here is the old wall [...]

Today I replace them with this: you will see several examples of these in the slide show which I will not comment.

Modern walls, reinforced concrete; linking of all the elements whereas the masonry only makes a heterogenous thing.

In front of this wall I observe that I just need to protect myself from the cold and the heat.

A wall like this retains more heat than this:

[drawing]

The temperature never rises very high, but it does fall to 20°.

This wall is fragile, but is not load-bearing, its framework carries itself, the old wall has become simple in-filling.

The present revolution of architecture [...]

The aesthetic revolution that follows on is not a caprice.

All this is rooted in a sheaf of building necessities that create the attitude of architecture.

So at this point another [...] intervenes

The wall no longer bears anything: here I just need to fill in.

Lecture at the Sorbonne, Paris, 12 June 1924

After Le Corbusier's lecture at the Sorbonne, Léandre Vaillant, the formidable decorative arts critic, published the following article (under the pen name of Léandre Vincent). Le Corbusier lost no time in responding.

Léandre Vincent, 'Divagations intempestives' (Untimely ramblings), *Paris Journal*, 20 June 1924[36]

Untimely ramblings
The Romanticism of "Esprit Nouveau"

I went to hear Monsieur Le Corbusier speak at the Sorbonne on architecture and on the "*esprit nouveau*". His presentation was preceded by a pictorial preamble. He organized his slide projections according to the illustration plan established by the journal *L'Esprit Nouveau*. This journal presents a tractor opposite a royal carriage, the bridge over the Hudson opposite Notre Dame Cathedral in Paris, and I know not what. The lecturer replaced the juxtaposition by a rapid succession of contradictory images. However, this intermittence seemed as eloquent as the page layout mentioned above. Its effect on the audience, resolutely sympathetic to the lecturer's argument, was visible and immediate. But while the theoretician was concentrating on his harsh and disdainful analysis of out-dated architectures, of their excess of decoration and their artificial elements, I was carrying out, although with greater cordiality, the same examination regarding his lecture.

After the projection of the first two slides, I was able to classify his system. He doesn't use logic, but a form of stark suggestion. He doesn't prove, he strikes. He advances using regular coupling of antitheses. Antithesis is, like analogy, a philosophical formula used in the search for truth. It is an element of rhetoric: most moving, most effective for dazzling the crowds. Demagogy has no time for syllogism. It thrives in the game of violent contrast.

Indeed, antithesis is the essence of the romantic style. A novel by Victor Hugo is always characterized by the development of an antithesis. The more distant the two terms, the more striking the effect. Example: "Beautiful is Ugly".The series of slides used by M. Lecorbusier [sic] to captivate his audience could have the same title as the prologue of "*Notre Dame de Paris*": "*ceci tuera cela*" ["this will kill that").

Then the architect modifies the rhythm, until then binary – image against image – of his slide show; after a series of illustrations of the same order, three or four, ocean liner, aeroplane, engine, it suddenly shows an isolated and completely different picture: the gallery of the Château of Fontainebleau. This provokes sniggering. Why? Because our understanding of Renaissance architecture and our sense of decoration have withered; they cannot be assimilated by people today? Of course not! This is a nervous reflex to a demonstration of opposites, the result of a psychological calculation that is applicable when needed. Were one to show on screen, after five of six specimens of she-apes borrowed from the Zoo, a figurine by Maillol, or after so many models of sanitary hardware, the Egyptian bread-bearer from the Louvre, the surprise would provoke laughter. You allow the audience to associate similar perceptions, shown in a series, you create inertia, then you break the thread and before the mind can free itself to accommodate the unexpected, laughter erupts! Another form of suggestion.

But here is a picture showing that evidently the length of the ocean liner *France* is greater than the height of the Great Pyramid at Giza and the height of the ship is greater than that of the Arc de Triomphe. Another symptom of the malaise of Romanticism! The pathos of size, the prestige of quantity! For the clear-headed aesthetician, grandeur resides in the rhythm of the relationship between

36/FLC C3(6)38. This is discussed in detail in chapter 2, pp. 69-77.

the elements, it is based on a sense of proportion. The diagram of the huge liner confers no grandeur. A 50 cm study by Maillol (as I have already mentioned him) can have grandeur. The slide projection of a New York *"skyscraper" (in English in the text)* showing off its forty storeys is merely sensationalism – gone cold though, for having been served up so often. And then, it's good on the screen. Do we really see a skyscraper? No more than a pilot flying over a forest would enjoy its shade. The evocation of mass or figures with multiple zeros, the shock effect of fabulous statistics, here we have other methods handed down from erstwhile romanticism to present-day advertising, the last refuge of imagination gone mad. In rhetoric, this use of the superlative overdrive is called hyperbole.

Once the slides have been projected, M. Le Corbusier starts to speak. His delivery is spare, flat, with humorous asides carefully deployed. His dogmatism is that of the sermon rather than the ritual of the mass. No decoration on the roof, nor incense on the altar; he is sententious and cold. But the discourse of this builder is so badly constructed! Is this promoter of impersonal art, of *ne varietur* mass-produced building, not affected by that human frailty, personal pride? For he overturns the fundamental problems of aesthetics and, with childish self-confidence – this is likeable because natural – emphasizes his own experiments and solutions concerning minor details. When he is right – and he is right about some essential questions, such as the huge spiritual impact of geometric symbols – one wishes he were wrong; because his reasoning is shallow. He speaks of the lyricism emanating from simple, rough, prototype forms, of Cézanne's stereometric triad, but he talks about it like Harpagon, the miser serving dinner. Indeed, inspite of the appearance of an algebraic calculation and the reduction to an axiom, he is usually wrong, even when he does not affirm for every argument, that "this does not conform to the *esprit nouveau*", a phrase for excommunication copied from the 'for that is at my pleasure' of the Ancien Régime.

According to him, the machine is our professor of aesthetics. The house that he wishes to build is no more than a "machine for living". "Beauty is created by the function of efficiency. The maximum result from the minimum of means, form determined imperatively by the materials used", such is the teaching of mechanization. The regular workings of mechanical force have as their corollary the production of geometric shapes. From this arises a doctrine of symmetry, balance and stability. At the basis of a construction built according to the spirit of the machine, one finds a form-type, a tectonic dominant or element which is a prefiguration of the whole and determines all the spatial ratios: the "regulating line". At least this is how I understood the lecturer. If we build our dwellings according to the mechanical and economic imperatives they will "ex ipso" follow primary geometric forms. And, as if by the action of some automatic trigger, beauty will appear. You can have the Parthenon whatever your budget, because what is the principle behind the Parthenon? A horizontal resting on a series of verticals; the post and beam. The use of reinforced concrete does away with columns. Their shapeliness is nothing but vain ornamentation. The figures on the pediment – a parasitic growth issuing from a decorative mood unworthy of modern man. Your washroom, vertical walls, horizontal floor and ceiling, is more beautiful than the Parthenon because it is more pure in form. It is a Parthenon. And it is very good of M. Le Corbusier to mention the Parthenon.

And this is where the error shows up; without enlightening the blind. Conformity to function is not beauty itself; it is only a premise of beauty. Beauty starts where function has been achieved or superseded. It is the result of a disinterested play of forms; the creative instinct determines its configuration and reduces resistance to matter. It is active in M. Le Corbusier himself, in spite of his machine fetish and his accountant's taste for mass-production; this instinct pushes him to vary the layout of his basic construction, a model jail, the sunlit and comfortable hell of monotony. Ah, the nameless horror of the working man's mass-produced suburb of London.

But why worry? The builders of the huge metal viaducts laugh in the face of M. Le Corbusier who takes scant notice. They have gone to live in Louis XVIth buildings. Their minds are closed to *esprit nouveau*. At Le Raincy, Auguste Perret has found people to sing a hymn of faith and hope to reinforced concrete.

Long ago Gothic builders succeeded, using the buttress, in building stone houses without interior walls for God, the mind having tamed the stone.

Will the aesthetics of minimum effort put forward by M. Le Corbusier do as much?

But I have to follow him along a road lined with errors. On the blackboard he contrasts formless assymetrical scribbles with regular planimetric forms. He discovers that these are more beautiful than those. Then he takes his square and his circle as bases for three-dimensional figures: cube, cylinder and cone. This is where he quotes Cézanne. Finally he erases the curves, the arcs and the segments of the circles. He will only allow himself to think in right angles and diagonals. He mocks the early town, developed from the nomads' fortified camp, a rampart of chariots. Why, given that the nomads instinctively formed the perfect shape: the circle? It allows the defenders to reach the periphery from the centre at any time. He makes a closed harmonious ground plan. But our pretended theoretician is a fanatic!

A plough, pulled by oxen, glimpsed through the door of a railway carriage, makes him smile. What a waste of time and energy! The aesthetic of slow motion is the great discovery of our time. The cinema, doubling its speed, reaching 32 revolutions per second, can also give us slow motion, the greatest dispenser of lyricism that the machine has created. But the orator from *L'Esprit nouveau* brandishing his square, like Peter the Hermit his cross, has no doubts.

However romantic his lecture appears, his dogma is no more than a new Classicism, but devoid of the grandeurs of earlier classicisms, that of Mastaba, the Temple of Poseidon, of Raphael's "The Disputation of the Sacrament" or Ingres' "The Apotheosis of Homer". For all these classicisms signify royalty. M. Le Corbusier's is slavery.

Le Corbusier, 'M. Le Corbusier répond' (Le Corbusier replies), *Paris Journal*, 3 July 1924[37]

M. Le Corbusier replies

Following the publication of the article "Untimely ramblings" on the subject of M. Le Corbusier's lecture at the Sorbonne, we received this response. We immediately forwarded it to M. Léandre Vincent, who returned it to us with the following letter:

Dear Director,

I invite you to publish M. Le Corbusier's terrible confessions! As long as he sees red, I will be obliged to use green spectacles, according to the theory of complementariness. As soon as he is resigned to show things in a natural light, I will forego the aforementioned spectacles.

Léandre Vincent

Received *Paris Journal*, 20 June 1924, containing "Untimely ramblings" by Léandre Vincent on my Sorbonne Lecture (whose untimely ramblings?).

I am perfectly happy to be in the position of provoking the opposition of your author; the right to criticize is precious and enduring. But I cannot allow him to make me think (in order to "get me") exactly the opposite of what I said. I am sure that *Paris Journal*, a charming and amusing publication that I hold in great esteem, will allow this rectification of the facts, from which your author and your readers will be able to form a clearer and fairer judgement.

I never compared the size of an ocean liner to that of a work of art (to a statue by Maillol). In my film, the synopsis that preceded these images and which was seen by M. Vincent was as follows:

"Powerful and previously unsuspected means have been acquired by a century of science.

Matter is in our hands.

This century of iron is new, looking back on the millennia.

37/FLC C3(6)39.

On every continent, a period of intense labour is beginning.

Mind and spirit communicate between peoples and progress precipitates their consequences."

It was followed by this, the conclusion of the slide projection:

"Man remains breathless.

His heart, which remains the heart of a man, seeks emotion beyond the utilitarian, aspiring to disinterested satisfaction. Violent and radiant poetry emanates from new events.

The heart seeks to tune brutal events to the deep and intimate standards of emotion."

The first synopsis of the film was, "new objects appear, they are surprising, fearless, animated by grandeur, they shock us, upsetting our habits".

And to ensure our advancement, in spite of this momentary confusion, I showed (contrary to M. Vincent's affirmation of my, "harsh and disdainful analysis of out-dated architectures") as peaks of achievement, the Parthenon, Michelangelo's Laurentian Library, another Parthenon, and my film ended with the Orangerie staircase at Versailles and with the Sphinx and the Pyramids:

"Man remains breathless.

...His heart seeks emotion beyond the utilitarian..."

Léandre Vincent has me say: "If we build our dwellings according to the mechanical and economic imperatives they will 'ex ipso' follow primary geometric forms. And, as if by the action of some automatic trigger, beauty will appear."

What I said was the opposite and I affirm this each time I talk about architecture. I wrote this in three chapters in my book *Vers une architecture* [Towards Architecture]: the three main chapters. The following lines appear four times as chapter headings (with the risk of repeating myself, as you can see!).

"Architecture means using basic materials to establish ratios that can provoke emotion.

Architecture is beyond the utilitarian.

Architecture is plastic in nature.

Order, unity of intention, the sense of ratio; architecture manages quantities.

Passion makes drama from inert stones.

Wood and cement are set to work; we use these to build houses, palaces; this is construction. Ingenuity (is) at work.

But suddenly, you touch my heart, you do me good, I am happy. I say: it's beautiful. This is architecture. Art is here.

My house is practical. Thank you, as in thank you to the railway engineers and telephone engineers; you have not touched my heart.

But the walls rise towards the sky in an order such that I am moved. I am aware of your intentions. You were gentle, brutal, charming or dignified. Your stones tell me this. You connect me to this place and my eyes look. My eyes look at something that expresses an idea. An idea that comes to light not through words or meanings but solely through prisms in relation to each other. These prisms are as the light describes them. Their relationship is not necessarily linked to the practical or the descriptive. They are a mathematical creation of your mind. They are the language of architecture. With basic materials, with a more or less utilitarian agenda that you have surpassed, you have established a relationship that moves me. This is architecture."

Then M. Vincent makes me say things about the Parthenon that I have never said and which are serious. (I call my audience to testify). We are not going to confuse God with bidets! (After a caricature of the Parthenon that he attributes to me): "Your washroom, with its vertical walls, horizontal floor and ceiling, is more beautiful than the Parthenon because it is purer in form. It is a Parthenon."

Monsieur Vincent, do you consider me a complete *noc*[38]?

I have always used the Parthenon as the most overwhelming example of architectural beauty. If I can talk knowingly about it, it is because I have taken the trouble (and the pleasure) to go and see it, and I spent four weeks there. I know what it means and how it is made. The end of my book is dedicated to the

Parthenon. I will soon be publishing a book entitled: "The Parthenon" dated 1911. And if the conditions of publication permit, it will be the most humble and the most precise expression of admiration possible for such a monument, when one has had the joy of observing it.

For the record, M. Vincent, this appeared in *L'Esprit Nouveau* and in my book *Vers une architecture*:

"Parthenon. – Here is a machine to move the spirit. We are confronted with the implacable nature of mechanics. There are no symbols linked to these forms: the sensations they provoke are categorical; no need for a key to understand them. Harsh, intense, sometimes the most gentle, very subtle and very powerful. And who found the composition of these elements? An inventor of genius. These rocks were inert and formless in the quarries of Mount Penteli; the person who formed such a composition must have been a great sculptor, rather than an engineer.

For the past thousand years, those who have visited the Parthenon felt that they were observing a decisive moment in the history of architecture.

We are at a decisive moment. At present, while the arts are feeling their way, and where painting for example, is in the gradual process of discovery of a wholesome mode of expression and scandalizes the spectator, the Parthenon provides us with certainty: a lofty emotion of a mathematical nature."

M. Vincent, once again you have made me say the opposite of what I actually said and wrote on the *Series*: a series is a way to relate a standard element to a human scale and to relate it to industrial methods. Using these standard elements, you can assemble "uniformity in the detail, tumult in the ensemble" with maximum variety (this is none other than architecture).

In all good camaraderie, I'll join you in chanting Auguste Perret's canticle of faith and hope at Le Raincy, without really understanding why, in this atmosphere of the lecture hall, we should chant with one heart the canticle of faith and hope.

Then, talking of city planning, you would have us believe that nomads instinctively use the pure form that is the circle, without considering what the circle represents in the modern city. (A fetish, a word, the circle!)

Then finally, here you are glorifying the aesthetics of slowness in relation to a pair of oxen seen from a train. But I was talking about the train!

In a word: I announce a lecture on *red*; you come at it *with green spectacles*. In your eyes, no trace of red in my lecture, on the contrary – only green! So who sold you your green spectacles and why turn criticism (so amusing by the way, whether laudatory or cantankerous) into a report in reverse?

No resentment. Calm indifference. Serenity at least equivalent to that of the aformentioned oxen.

Yours sincerely,

Le Corbusier

38/Le Corbusier's inversion of *con* (arse, idiot) would have been readily understood by his readers. (Translator's note).

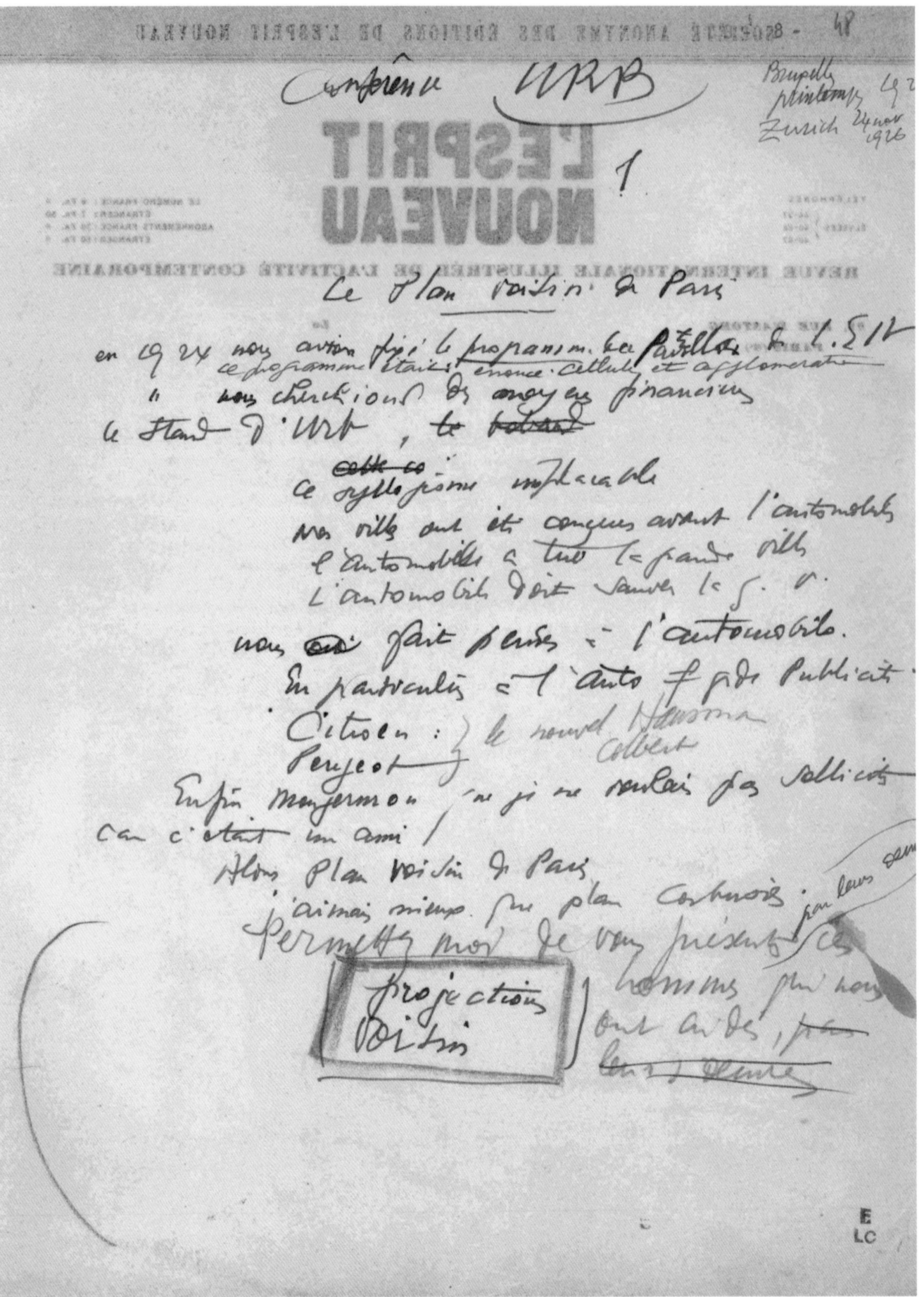

FLC C3(8)48

Lecture at Brussels, 4 May 1926

Preparatory notes (facsimile and transcriptions)[39]

FLC C3(8)46

[page] 1

P[rojection] Voisin aeroplane (New times)
P[rojections] villas Corbu and P[ierre] J[eannere]t
reassure the heart
Terrace, Magne disgraceful
La Roche (then Pessac at the end) Progress interrupted
Léman [Lake Geneva] You are from the corporate
Immeuble-Villas [apartment villas] world and you have
+ view of Hendelot skyscraper been misinformed
[an arrow situates the following argument before the slides "villas Corbu..."]
The Voisin plan
letter from M. Ledoux "if your idea was good..."
I provide a technical/financial/solution
Sellier said: But we haven't got any money
If I give such lectures on Voisin Plan it is to uncover the diamond mine.
"If this were a good idea others would have found it a long time ago", Ledoux
page 2
3
3 b
4
5
6
D[rawing] page 6. 7. 8. 9. 9B. 9C. 9D. 10
P[rojections] city planning (totality) then conclusion 11 and Pessac
P[rojections]

FLC C3(8)47

The Grand B[oulevar]ds
underground
by M. Ledoux
400m A
[sketch]
6 x 400 = 2400
or
[sketch]
2650m
+610m of exits
B

A = slowing down of cars at each crossroads
B = rapid evacuation

A leaves the main boulevards in the present state of traffic congestion
B manages the traffic on the M[ain] B[oulevar]ds

FLC C3(8)48

City Planning Lecture
Brussels Spring 1926
Zurich 24 Nov 1926
[page] 1
The Voisin Plan for Paris
In 1924 we fixed the program for the EN Pavilion.
" the programme was drawn up: cell and appartment.
" we sought financing
the City Planning stand, ~~the tall story~~
this
the implacable syllogism [:]
our towns were conceived before the automobile
the automobile has killed the city
The automobile must save the c[ity]
made us think of the automobile
Particularly the auto? huge advertising
Citroen: } the new Hausmann [sic]
Peugeot: } Colbert
Finally Mongermon whom I did not want to approach because he is a friend/
So, Voisin Plan for Paris
I liked it better than Corbusier plan
Allow me to present/by their
Slides works/ these men who have assisted us,
Voisin ~~by their works~~

FLC C3(8)49

City Planning Lecture
[page] 2
This patronage of the Paris Plan
showed in this way intellectual solidarity
Frame of mind in common: technicality in the/ greatest
precision/
detachment ~~disinterestedness~~ in everything
~~acquired~~ preconceived idea
a certain idealism
(even fairly violent)
(Wege Baumeister)

City planning starts with the road surveyor
the road surveyor applies the formulae
" the rules
consecration of tradition
The present Upheaval demands
other activities than the road surveyor.
The era seems more likely to suddenly produce
outsiders [in English in the original]
t[hat] is to s[ay] that those who apply themselves to other tasks come up against an obstacle everyday at each step.
practical 1
aesthetic 5
sanitary 2
social 3
economic 4
those who are outraged
who shout out their solution
This solution is off the beaten track
it is original, t[hat] is to s[ay]: has an origin
Modern city planning is an exercise in Common Sense.

39/FLC C3(8)46.

URB

3

l'industrie s'est créée sur la taylorisation
taylorisé la circulation, l'hygiène et la beauté,
on fait l'urbanisme d'aujourd'hui
c'est ainsi qui occupé personnellement autrefois
d'art décoratif, j'ai passé architecture
j'occupé d'architecture j'ai passé urbanisme

cheminement rationnel,

inventif
~~rotatif~~ optimiste
de l'idée.

Une idée? une vérité. ça se sème
germe
Etat d'esprit
Unanimité
Réalisation

Exemple Jury d'Urb. Strasbourg. Ex P d N
unanimité finale.

Parlant d'Urb je vais donner des figures
collectives, d

Voici quelques clichés de maisons et d'intérieur

Demain j'analyserai le phénomène architectural

Aujourd'hui: Théorie l'homme semble
rester dehors. Mon point. la cellule
harmonieuse, et liée est la clef de
tout urbanisme, Je ~~viens~~ de Francfort
problème de plan et d'industrie, mais urbanisme
commande
de maison de Stuttgart est prob de plan

ZURICH

FLC C3(8)50

City Planning Lecture
[page] 3

Industry established on Taylorization
Taylorize traffic, sanitation and beauty
is to plan the cities of today
so: previously busy with decorative art, I thought about architecture
and, occupied by architecture, I thought about city planning
a reasonable progression
inventive
~~utop~~ optimist
about the idea
An idea?
A truth; something that can be sown
germinates
State of mind
Unanimity
Carrying out
Example City Planning panel Strasbourg Ex PdN
final unanimity
[in red pencil, lower left, in the margin:]
Slide projection
Talking about Urb[anism] I will give figures
Institutions, of [city planning]
Here are a few shots of houses and interiors
Tomorrow I will analyze the architectural phenomenon
Today: Theory, man seems
to be outside. Not at all. The harmonious and licit cell is the key to all city planning. I have come from Frankfort [sic] problem of plan of house and of industry, but city planning gives
orders
from Stuttgart plan prob[lem]
[these last ten lines are struck through with the indication"Zurich "]

FLC C3(8)51

[page] 3b

I am going to ~~draw~~ show you graphics
then project examples of city plans
Rather arid toil, in appearance at least (because it's fascinating)
But it will seem that I
leave man at a good distance,
man with his heart and his
need for comforts,
that I make him
enter a terrifying mechanism,
Prussian-style barracks
A ~~house~~ [like a]penal colony.
I'm standing up for myself now
energetically.
Man, the individual is
the key to this research, and I am thinking
of him at every instant
And here to prove what I say some
S[lides]: illustrations of houses built in the same frame
of mind

FLC C3(8)52

[page] 3 c
After the slides
architect[ure]
To make a new plan,
a plan,
one needs to know how to live
We do not know how to live
We live badly, false.
It's no good.
Everything must be re-examined.
Proof in city planning: We work
all day like convicts/ workmen
employees
bosses
everywhere there is
overloading
Ingenious Ford suggests 5 days of
production and 2 days of consuming,
of destruction, to create work,
one must forbid work, one must
destroy. This is a pretty
perception. There is matter for revision.
The interruption of work at midday
is a calamity for the city.
It's typical. The quality of work is
bad. The day for men
and for women
a cruxifixion. The home
cannot lawfully exist because
we do not have the time to care for it [?]

FLC C3(8)53

Urb[anism] [page] 4
Reasoning = is the analysis
invention = is synthesis
optimism = strength... divine strength
I always mention it people who are of a
for it is the motor happy nature
for an optimism of the times
collective, a faith
In 1910 trial attempt at city planning
study of current ideas (Sitte)
adaptation
the dull untruth of the inkwell
I cannot finish.
The rumble of war.
idea abandons art, ivory tower
to be aware of the social element
Social
Everything: mechanization
disruption
discouragement
hope
a clear vision
post war: no architecture possible without city planning
no architecture ~~without standardization~~ without industrialization
~~no standardization without industrialization~~
no industrialization = without standardization
no standardization without city planning could provoke
explosive reaction from
the organizers of
the 1925 Exhib

One day a truth is revealed, ~~con~~ digestion of my studies of
1910: the donkeys drew up the town plans
and we are paying for it today

URB

6

Discipline, exactitude

Exactitude = mouvement de la masse
= circulation.

Circulation = l'un des grands problèmes
de l'URB

travail
divertissement
sommeil

et

classement des
catégories de
population

= détails

l'église unie
se couvre
de prières
diverses
qui veut
jouer une partie
exacte
c'est l'urbanisme

1 travail
2 divertissement
3 sommeil

Étude de Laboratoire

Dessin.

Le camp Romain
modèle d'urb

Louis XI

Aigues mortes
Villeneuve les
avignon
monpazier

20 Q = station
d'autobus

cheminement à pied
station de métro

F
LC

FLC C3(8)55

FLC C3(8)54

Urb[anism] [page] 5

Not figurative donkeys
4 legged donkeys (develop)
Ah, this makes us think.
Think about the birth of a town
" " the reason for " "
what a town is
" " city "
City: analysis (develop headquarters)
consequence, the problems are posed because one wishes to rectify, one explains:
why thousands of men of all sorts crowd together
always hurrying
because of the night
discovery of the 24-hour cycle
The ordering of ~~work~~ existence:
work
amusement
sleep
()parenthesis Here is the def[inition] of architecture: light
The speed of communications:
railway
telegraph
telephone
provokes organization
rigorous, exact
Grand army
discipline

FLC C3(8)55

Urb[anism] [page] 6

Discipline, exactness
Exactness = movement of the masses
= traffic
Traffic = one of the main problems of Urb[anism]

Work
Amusement
Sleep
} and { classification of the categories of population

detail = chessboard is covered with various pawns that will play an exact game.
it's city planning

for ex[ample]
[sketch]
1 work
2 amusement
3 sleep

the leaders act
those who think
the scholars
the executives at all levels
Laboratory study
[sketch in green]
[captions of sketch:]

Gothic Louis XI
Roman camp
model of city planning
Aigues Mortes
Villeneuve les Avignon
Monpazier
going on foot 200 = bus stop
subway station

FLC C3(8)56

Urb[anism] [page] 7
densities

[sketch 1]
here there is air
the threshold of the temple
or the forum
or the market
= the centre

Density = [sketch 2]
so
state of things
[sketch 3]
up to 1850

Here is the railway:
people believed in it so little;
antagonism
that stations were situated by chance
but everything pours into the centre
[sketch 4] Congestion
this ~~square~~ orthogonal
obtain [sketch 5] which goes with that
[sketch 6]
and not because of
lots in points

FLC C3(8)57

Urb[anism] [page] 8

Density must remain at Centre
so modify elevation

[sketch 1]
present

[sketch 2]
good

Construct upwards in the centre of cities
Greatly widen the streets at the centre
so destroy the centre
Build a CITY
Horror?
History has never done anything else
~~Voisin Plan~~
~~[Slide] Projections [of City of] 3 Million [inhabitants]s~~
[in pink crayon]

Housing = ~~Rest~~
special urban life
hotels, schools, chancery
Parliaments, theatres
etc...
the corridor street
[sketch 3]
When there is that, Tho[ma]s Cook takes action
break with indents
one gains in surface area. One rises higher
beware
develop
a) apartment
b) palace
parliament
etc.
system of courtyards
the case of Zurich
bank

URB

9

autre chose

en Coupe

habitation

fenêtres sur rue

poussières
bruit

poussière

rue

Aujourd'hui
bien plus
grave

renverse

jamais de cœur

Alvéoles

organisation domestique

jardin

rue

Alvéoles

halls ?

pilotis

Plan Voisin

Esthétique

conclusion

avant
projection

Vie machiniste géométrie amour de

(j'en parlerai demain)

C3 08

10 h

vitesse : nécessité d'horizons

Esprit moderne : espace et ordre

Facteur nouveau
proche } vue d'avion.

œuvre humaine
géométrique

Résumons : Bon-sens organisme : biologie

FLC C3(8)58

FLC C3(8)58

Urb[anism] [page] 9

something else elevation

dwelling [sketch 1] windows to the street
dust dustiness
street noise
Today
much more
serious

overturn [sketch 2] never courtyard

Pigeon-holes [sketch 3] pigeon-holes
or domestic aquisition
hallways? [sketch 4] garden street
pilotis [concrete piers]

Voisin Plan
Aesthetics Conclusion before
projection
mechanized life, geometry, love
(I will talk about this tomorrow)
speed: necessity for horizons
Modern attitudes: space and order

New factor } seen from sky
near } human achievement
geometric

Let us summarize: Common sense organism. Biology*

FLC C3(8)59

[page] 9b

BEWARE! IMPortant
Voisin Plan: I am going to explain the essential point of the
Voisin plan
If it is a measure for an ensemble = diamond
[underlined in green]
If present use = ridiculous total expenditure
Get this understood!!! [underlined in green]

[sketch 1] [sketch 2]
ridiculous expenditure the mine
D [drawing]

~~I'm looking for an economist!~~
Destruction!! ? History has never done
anything else: the centre remains through 4 centuries
and does not move. From Lutetia to Haussmann
(the City)

[sketch 3]
Lutetia
Henri 4 no embankment on the Seine
Louis XIV crisis in 1830 Louvre full of houses
[Louis] XV countryside at Montmartre
Haussmann
Everything changes
rapidly but
10 years are enough f. us to forget.

FLC C3(8)60

[page] 9 c

"Why not enlarge existing thoroughfares?
why destroy?..." etc
Because it is the only economic
and efficient solution

[sketch 1] [sketch 2]
B B B B
expropriation A B
expropriation
similar
or less
for B demands much
(on the existing thoroughfare)
Whereas A only has
little value.
It is sometimes good to provide figures; it is enlightening,
and
contradicts easy concepts
example M Ledoux [underlined in red] his passageways
B[oulevar]ds
see following page [in red pencil]

Increased value must be promoted
The positive solution leads to wealth, whereas the
present bewitchment maintains impoverishment.

FLC C3(8)61

[page] 9 d

We seek
We await/ an economist to provide figures for the
Voisin plan
It is here ~~that~~ that we will find the money
that the garden city solutions demand
(other side of the question): hour of work
hour of rest
M Sellier will not obtain from charity
or from philanthropy the millions needed.
But in the product of a judicious
overall operation, including { techniques
finance
~~a solution is needed~~
To give an idea, for ex. one must not have a
solution that consists of for example making
a pit a/ paying to excavate
b/ " " for disposal
or
making a mound a/ paying to bring materials
b/ " " pile up the materials
We need a *compound* [?] [*English in the original*] solution
with combined result, that pays for itself, that's the only
solution.
My solution that includes a pit and
a mound.
What comes from the pit is used to make
the mound
So Mr Sellier why this hypnotic state
Greater Paris beyond the walls, is nothing but a
mirage, a sweet little dream of cottages and
playgrounds: in fact what we want is little
houses like cottages with dovecotes
And the moment of destiny passes by

UKB · appendice conférence Zurich

après projection

Vous avez été séduits peut-être par le mécanisme harmonieux et raisonnable de l'idée. Mais votre cœur, en face de cette mécanique exacte, vous aurez pensé avec effroi à vous-mêmes, et vous vous serez dit : "Très beau, mais j'aime mieux ne pas en être".

Je voudrais vous rassurer. La conférence de demain a pour objet l'architecture. Et non pas celle des palais qui est celle urgente de ce jour, mais celle de la maison, du logis. Je pourrai demain vous montrer le développement semblable de l'idée au long d'un chemin de raison. Mais vous verrez que l'homme n'est point abandonné en forçat à la mécanique matérielle ou "cérébrale". La mécanique est mise au service de l'homme, l'ordre est mis à disposition de l'homme et lui apporte la liberté. La liberté reconquise est l'objet de nos recherches. Nous sommes aujourd'hui en plein état d'esclavage dans un milieu mort qui nous

FLC

FLC C3(8)62

Urb[anism] [page] 10

Before
slide projections

the Voisin plan
in my book *Urbanisme* I started with
chap. 1 order
then feeling overflows
explain

So having gone to the heart of the analysis and
been aware of the organism of a 1922 city
formulating itself
in fact one had to conclude
s[o] to s[peak] talk to people of today
of things of today
so Paris

Slide projections

FLC C3(8)63

Urb][anism] appendix lecture
[page] 11 Zurich

after slide projections

You may perhaps have been persuaded by
the harmonious and reasonable mechanism
of the idea. But in your heart,
faced with this exact mechanism you
may have thought fearfully of yourself
and you will have said to yourself: "Very beautiful, but
I don't want to be part of it."

I would like to reassure you. The lecture
tomorrow has architecture as its subject.
And not the architecture of palaces because there is no
urgency for that at present, but
of the house, the dwelling. Tomorrow
I will be able to show you similar development
of the idea along
a path of reason. But you will see
that people are never abandoned to
become slaves to material or ~~spiritual~~
cerebral mechanics. Mechanics are
to serve the people, order is for
the benefit of people and brings them
freedom. Freedom reconquered is
the object of my research. Today we are
in a full state of slavery in dead surroundings
that stifle us.

FLC C3(8)65

Conclusion [page] 11

How to believe in such a solution?
Who to ask for opinions?
~~The error~~ Confusion reigns coming
either from divergence of opinion, or from ignorance, or
from mischievous antagonisms.
In this way Magne
All this programme Slide P[rojections] 2 rotunda
was that of Urb[anism] Pavilion
EN pavilion
Silence of Mr Magne
More than that, a warning
against the anti-French tendancies – The Terrace
shameful Slide P[rojections]
Stopping progress Auteuil terrace
You are from the corporations
You are told lies
through passion and ignorance

Here is M. Bonnier on a committee
water will not rise, the reservoirs
of Paris
Let us imagine a committee of financiers, bankers
Aug[uste] Perret: skyscraper periphery gardens in centre
Aug[uste] Perret, in passing, but concluding
his lecture: "reinforced concrete not for houses"
This is an opinion
Aug[uste] Perret grand practitioner. Blériot war 1908
and reinforced concrete small houses:
with steel one can construct the Brooklin [sic] bridge but
not automobiles
" railway lines but not loco[motives]
" locos, but not the mechanic's stopwatch etc.

Here is Pessac and Standardization of windows, beams,
stair industrialization teams
production cost
comfort
diversity
aesthetics
modern happiness
Slide P[rojections] Pessac
Paris expects from the era
Slide P[rojections] How will public opinion be informed
unless by lengthy individual effort.
I have submitted the voisin plan to you in order that public opinion may judge it

Lecture at Brussels, 26 June 1958

Preparatory notes (facsimile)

1

Conférence Bruxelles
Pavillon France 26 juin 58

Prologue

Ce que je vais exposer ici pourra être considéré comme subversif par quelques uns. Une espèce d'ouverture aux horizons, (je dis bien aux horizons) va être proposée, un élément d'urbanisme, un facteur de solution!

Solution à quoi? à une impasse! A un monde en crise aigüe de mutation. ~~On~~ tourne la page? Ou, ne la tournera-t-on pas? On refuse de la tourner? Il y a longtemps qu'elle est tournée!

Les heures de crises sont celles où 2 termes seulement sont présents devant nous — deux extrêmes, les deux pôles de n'importe quelle question. Il est bon, il est nécessaire de connaître ces deux rivages, ces 2 limites, ces deux arrêts, ces deux butées. Mais le ruisseau, la rivière de vie, le fleuve de vie — coule entre ces deux rives, ~~tantôt~~ s'approchant de l'une, ~~tantôt~~ de l'autre, ~~tantôt~~ attirée vers, tantôt ~~rejeté~~ rejeté par. A chaque minute, la situation est variable; mais par groupement, adhésion, ~~solidarité~~ s'établit un courant ~~tantôt~~ allant à gauche et tantôt à droite: la tâche de chaque jour: il faut avancer, il faut passer!

Le vol d'avion sur les estuaires des grands

2/ fleuves d'Asie ou d'amérique nord ~~et~~ sud, invite à une ~~méditation~~ : en fin de compte, vous le verrez, ~~tout~~ arrive à la mer
Mais comment, et dans quel état?

à chaque jour
J'ai parlé de la Vue d'Avion
jusqu'ici : ~~vue~~ vue à vol d'oiseau
nous avons aujourd'hui la vue d'avion
occasion admirable de déchiffrer, de découvrir la leçon de la nature.

Je continue ~~parler~~ d'avion
formidable perturbation
apportera

un exemple : Bogota de Colombie.

1947 1920 Cie Allemande
4 siècles de silence de 300 000 habitants
à 3 000 mètres d'altitude
sur l'équateur presque.

Dans une ville carré espagnol qui fut romain
qui fut grec
" égyptien
etc etc

ville d'un UN étage de maison (de colonisation)
= solitude
silence
isolement

1er Etape : des hommes ~~partent~~ sortent, vont.
il fallait 20 jours = aujourd'hui Deux heures
p Baranquilla.

2me Etape des hommes viennent
des hommes d'avion = l'homme exact, idoine qui appelle à lui l'homme exact d'ailleurs : de N York, de Londres, de Paris, Rome Berlin. etc. etc

3

Ainsi des problèmes sont - en 1942, à échelle universelle, tous les esprits sont conjugués ..... entre les 2 rives !!!

Des solutions apparaissent

méthode. Par ex. l'Ascoral pendant l'"occupation"

11 sections
22 comités (en tapinois)
→ un examen du domaine bâti
pendant 1 année totalement consacrée à

un examen de l'homme et de sa condition.

○ Des actes allant du dedans au dehors

○ Des thèses

○ une doctrine

Doctrine = fruit de méditation d'une vie

placée sur le banc d'essai sans relâche

ici Ascoral : désintéressé totalement hors de la contingence immédiate des matériaux

pas de commandes
pas de cas d'espèce
pas d'argent dans le circuit

alors une = trajectoire

→ voici :

C3 - 10 128

4

Chasseurs et pêcheurs

une époque cruciale : découverte des graminés

1ère étape (séparation de la forêt / la clairière | les graminés
= les travaux collectifs
puis

2° étape (répartition et partage individuel

puis à nouveau :
3ème étape (= ~~travaux~~ entreprise d'intérêt commun
(les travaux)
~~collectif~~
de bien public

Ne fais pas ici de politique !

je dessine :

C3- 10 129
le bourg
New York
Paris
les ceintures militaires jusqu'en .... 1914 ou !
XIX siècle l'industrie
la ville tentaculaire
= 2 établissements humains
habiter
travailler
!!!
FONDATION LE CORBUSIER PARIS

FLC C3(10)129

le machinisme
les "unités de grandeur conforme"

les 3 établissements

1/ l'unité d'exploitation agricole de grandeur conforme

2/ la cité linéaire industrielle

3/ la ville radio concentrique des échanges : a/ marchandises b/ idées c/ gouvernement/

3

1

2

3

écoles théâtre

N°3

unités d'habitation grandeur conforme

avec services communs

= le prolétariat

les 24 heures solaires

cité industrielle linéaire dénoue impasse villes tentaculaires

= la nouvelle unité : industrielle

N° 2

4

tentaculaire

classement et contacts →

1 2 3

= occupation du territoire par les travaux de la civilisation machiniste

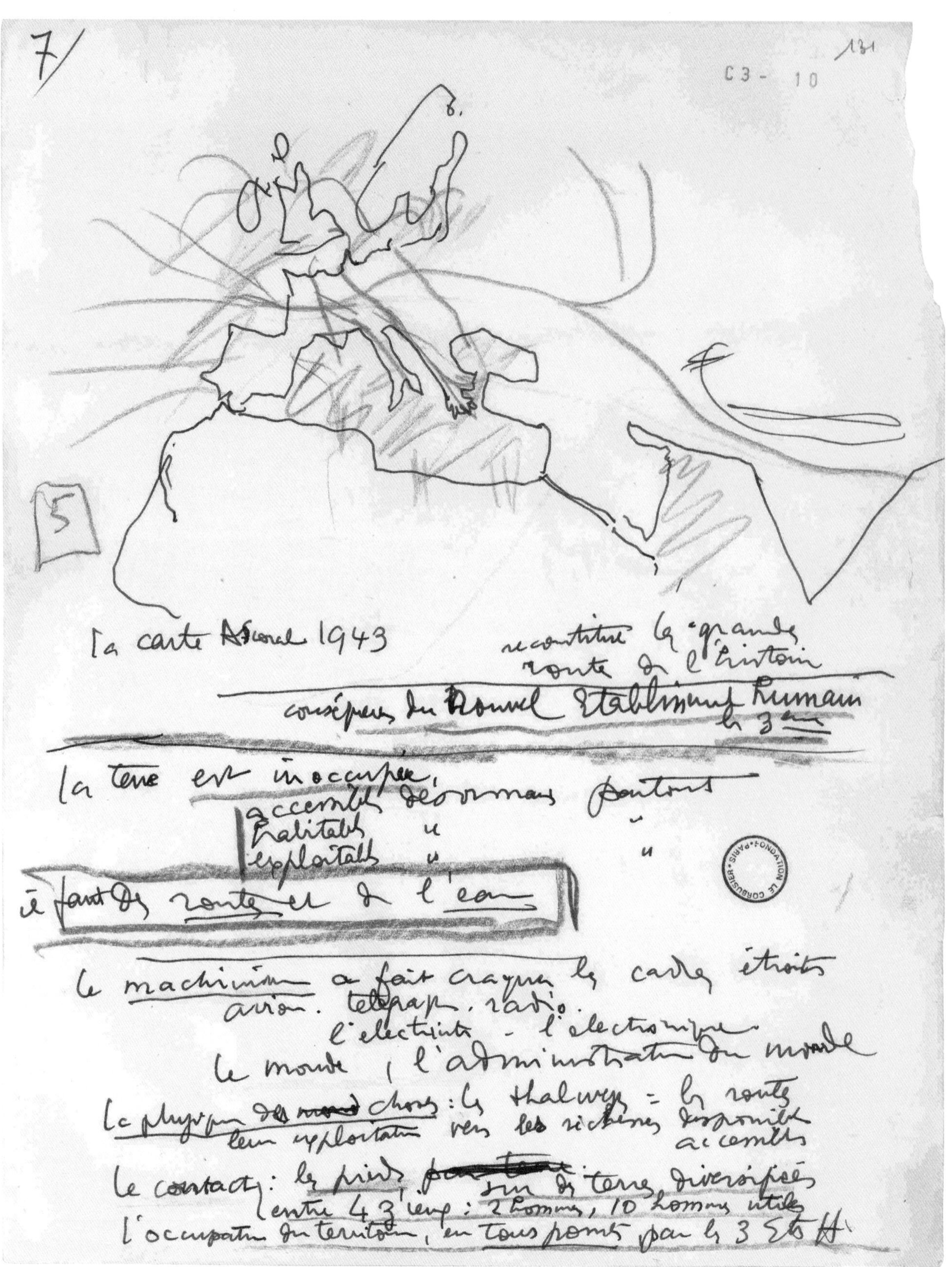
7/
131
C3- 10
5
la carte Ascoral 1943
reconstitue les grandes routes de l'histoire
conséquences du Nouvel Etablissement humain les 3
la terre est inoccupée, accessible désormais partout
habitable "
exploitable "
il faut des routes et de l'eau
le machinisme a fait craquer les cadres étroits
avion. telegraph. radio.
l'electricité - l'electronique.
le monde, l'administration du monde
la plupart des choses : les thalwegs = les routes
leur exploitation vers les richesses disponibles accessibles
le contact : les pieds sur des terres diversifiées
entre 4 3 temps : 2 hommes, 10 hommes utiles
l'occupation du territoire, en tous points par les 3 Ets H.

FLC C3(10)131

les 3 Etabl. Humains
= Solution offerts aux gouvernements

s'aident
s'associent
additionner tant de moyens
hommes
et
outillage.

l'entreprise des grands travaux d'équipement
d'une civilisation indubitablement machiniste

binôme | individu / collectivité | harmonieux

condition de nature retrouvées
(échelle humaine)

l'industrie s'empare du bâtiment

ingénieurs
et
architectes

= 2 mains unies, serrées
les 10 doigts
2 fois 5 doigts
2 mains

une ~~seule~~ idée une

climats, races, coutumes
diversité adorable
raison, amitié, fraternité

idées exposées nées dans
ce pays de France si
plein de tous les songes, [place essentielle d'un continent]
si plein de ~~to~~ l'histoire, si ardent, si vif
toujours. Laissez-moi, dans ma totale responsabilité
et en plein risque vous avoir affirmé que ces choses

point rêverie, mais sève du temps présent

Lecture at Brussels, 26 June 1958

Transcription of typescript derived from the recording of the lecture, rewritten by Le Corbusier on 31 March 1959.[40]

Text for the lecture on 26 June 1958
by Le Corbusier in Brussels, corrected on 31 March 1959

Occupation of land by
the Three Human Establishments
of the machine civilization:
– the unity of Agricultural Activity
– the linear city of industrial transformations
– the radioconcentric city of exchange:
government, ideas, merchandise

The ideas I am about to expound here may be considered subversive by some. I am offering a sort of opening of horizons – a city planning event, a component of the solution. Solution to what? To the dead-end of a world in serious crisis. We turn the page (or do not turn it!); refuse to turn it.... It was already turned a long time ago: the banks have been breached !

A time of crisis is when only two outcomes are under discussion – two extremes, the two poles of any subject. It is a good thing, it is necessary to know about the two banks of a river, the two shores – these two limits or these two aims. But the stream of life, the river of life, the flow of life run between two banks, sometimes close to one, sometimes close to the other, attracted "towards"... repulsed "by"... The situation varies by the second. And yet one must go forward, one must get through...

Flight by aeroplane over the big rivers of Asia or North or South America is available to the observer, leading him to meditate; this admirable mechanism for mobility and balance, that is instantaneous every time, increases his possibilities; ceaseless conflict, struggle, disasters or harmony. In the end, as you shall see, everything goes into the sea, but how and in what state?

[On large sheets of paper, with charcoal and coloured chalk, Le Corbusier draws two lines closely following the bed of a big river seen from the sky. See chapter 3, Fig 10] It is the season when the water is low; the water follows strange, unexpected paths; it seeks its way (it must get through!) making meanders, gentle or sharp turns, leaving empty spaces that will become its bed in the future.

We are observing essential phenomena: here age-old ground worn away by erosion; over there, on the contrary, sands deposited and spread out gently to form vast alluvial plains. But these deposits are of different types and strange shapes are formed by the path of the waters.

....

[another diagram] Here is the sea, the plain, the mountains. The waters evaporate to form travelling clouds, carrying rain or snow, transporting the sea to the plain or the hills, watering, fertilizing the earth, creating reserves of solidified water for the summertime, glaciers that the sun will distribute over the plains. A masterly cycle, presenting itself for our admiration and inspiring us to use our minds to work out generous cycles too.

Every day of our lives creates a necessity to seek and find a solution; in one simple phrase, to find the way through. It is easier to espouse an extreme: left or right: "one must take sides! one must commit" is what we hear! Life obeys far more subtle and differentiated rules.

xxx

40/FLC U3(8)307-324. In fact, Le Corbusier substantially rewrote the transcripts of the lecture. Compare this text with the recording (pp. 235-243).

The aeroplane has allowed us to philosophize. In its material form it has also generated the mobility which, by radically changing the modern world, has placed us on the threshold of an immense and universal mutation.

An example: Bogotá in Colombia, a town built by Spanish colonials on the "Spanish square" plan (which had already been used in Ancient Rome, Greece and even Egypt), had been a sleepy place for the last four centuries, remotely situated on the Equator and at an altitude of 3,000 metres in the Andes. A journey of 20 to 25 days was needed to reach the (Caribbean) sea to embark on a ship. Nobody embarked! The town was closed in on itself with its university and its bishopric, its one-storey houses and its bullock carts in the streets. After 1918, a German company brought some old aeroplanes to an airport. From that time onwards one could reach the port in two hours; it took one day to get to New York; and two days for Paris, London or Berlin. People were transported – people going to see and to seek, bringing back with them other people coming to see and to seek. The men who left, those who arrived, transported in a flash by air travel are, in both cases, men of quality – "the exact man" from Paris or London etc... Intensity, initiative, information, study and construction took over the place that until then had been left to itself. Problems were set, solutions were offered by the meeting of minds: movement, mobility, decision, activity...

xxx

In Paris, in the years 1942-1943 (during the Occupation) during the difficult time where some of us didn't even have one square centimetre that needed planning, or one cubic centimetre needing architecture, the alternative was to await the return of better days or to seize the opportunity of this empty time to try to "see clearly". ASCORAL was founded [*Assemblée de constructeurs pour une rénovation architecturale*]. It was composed of eleven sections and sub-sections including all the different building trades[a]; they met twice a month (discreetly) which obliged your humble servant to chair twenty committees per month, so that every minute of the year was used for the thorough exploration of built-up areas. For none of us, (and I mean not for a single one of us) was there before us, or on the table, either one single order, or any money, or even the slightest hope that some reward might come to us. Our intentions were pure, our ideas clear, our conversations fruitful. The result was positive.

What confuses the perspective or clips the wings of the imagination and is in opposition to vision and therefore to solutions, is the idea of quick money.

So we were able to examine man and his condition. We set problems, constructed theses and established a doctrine from the fruit of our meditations – meditations which for some of us had been nourished by life-long research and experimentation. Experimentation is a lucky chance to be grabbed by the hair when success or failure, discovery, a revelation or a lesson crosses one's path...

I am going to show you the product of one of our harvests, a discovery from 1942 which has ripened as much in our minds as in contemporary events. It is a reading of a situation, it is a proposition, it is also a valid and perhaps providential position that can be adjusted to the extraordinary fluidity that has taken hold of the modern world. A world in the process of opening to healthy, strong, brave, constructive enterprise and that brings material realities in its wake. A world dispensing with the demons of discord because it is opening the book at the blank page of the second era of mechanization: the era of harmony...

So here we have, and they can be organized, the three human establishments of the civilization of the machine.

Since time immemorial, men's labours were directed towards only two establishments:

a/the Unit of agriculture controlled by the pace of oxen or horses. Units adjoining each other covered the arable land, in a network of polygonal or orthogonal surfaces.

b/The second: the radioconcentric town of exchange established at crossroads or in situations dependent on topography: a hamlet, a village, a town. The exchange was in the form of merchandise, ideas or commandment. The volume of merchandise was insignificant; the riches of the East arrived by camel train;

a/Note: General Ideas; '*Savoir habiter*' (knowing how to live); Science of Housing (equipment, standardization); Industrialization; Health Equipment; Work (agriculture, industry, exchange); Ethics and Aesthetics; Enterprise; Synthesis of Major Art Forms.

ships on return from the shores of America or Asia brought gold, rare cloth and spices.

The shape of these units of exchange was radioconcentric. The pace of the horse or the speed of the wind in the sails set the equation relative to time.

xxx

Industry was born of steam, unexpectedly, and has developed over the last hundred years through feeling its way forwards.

It has destabilized the modern era, creating an obstruction in the way of our present undertakings.

[Le Corbusier continues with a drawing, see chapter 3, Fig 13]: Here is the intersection of two roads, here is a small town, here is a city – Paris for example; we are in a continental area. Here are two earth tracks arriving at the seashore; they join up with two or three maritime routes. A harbour city, New York for example.

Railway lines have been added; they go to faraway places, or come from them.

I am drawing the hexagon shape of France: Paris here, connected to its seaports, connected to other capital cities. It gives the impression of being one of the most well-organized towns, organized over the centuries. Today it is in a critical state; it is threatened at all levels.

Here is another drawing showing a small town that has become a city surrounded by fortifications (protection in war time), medieval fortifications or Renaissance but that does not matter. Here are new fortified surrounds, ever more extensive enclosing the old roads from the country and leading them towards an urban destiny, bringing the destiny of their route into the town: road to Spain or to Italy – the way to the South, to the North, to the East or to the West intersecting in the very centre of the city, the very centre of the capital. The old fortified surrounds are gradually demolished to form boulevards.

And now, taking a purple chalk, I am drawing the first examples of industry in the XIXth century; then with blue the residential areas needed to accommodate the labour force of the factories and workshops. Finally, round the perimeter of this dysfunctional product of the XIXth century, I am drawing the circles for the satellite towns of present-day city planning. And I say, here are our cities, our chronically sick cities, here are the tentacular towns, mistakes that have had criminal and inhumaine results, that have provoked the "Great Wastage" where the labour, nerves and activity of modern societies are worn to exhaustion.

And here we reach deadlock.

Because transport has progressed from the pace of the horse to the wheel of the locomotive, to the wheel of the subway and the automobile. Transport's shameless liberation, alas!

On the drawing of this small town that has become a tentacular city during the present century, I am using black chalk to draw a cross.

I am denouncing the iniquity: industry has set up a new human establishment: the industrial city. This must be linear rather than radioconcentric.

This is the formulation of a fact, a solution and also a task: the great, urgent task of the machine civilization: the invention and the building, in all the countries of the world, of linear-industrial-cities.

Let us define the linear industrial city:

Natural ressources are delivered by roads, waterways and railways.

Manufactured products are distributed by roads, waterways and railways.

The road is the origin of society.

Waterways by river or by sea developed slowly (canals and harbours) until the use of steam power.

The railroad was developed – the "rail way" – in the XIXth century. The locomotive changed everything, leading the way into modern times. Let us remember that under the Second Republic (second half of the XIXth century) a leader of the government declared in parliament: "Never will a railroad be able to connect two towns..."

Let us consider topography: in principle[b], roads, waterways and railways all follow the "water incline" – the "*thalweg*" a universally adopted technical term (the way along the valley). The three different ways tend to follow the same route. They can therefore be combined.

This combined supply system for the linear industrial cities demands the purpose-built construction of the three ways by road, rail and water, intended specifically for the transport of materials and products.

The organization of today's mature modern industry is based on "Standard-size Units": different, successive, linked operations making up the production "line", a new phenomenon in the workplace. These "units" are animate elements acting in accordance with their own perfect biology. They are set out at a practical distance from each other along the linear industrial city, on one side only of the three combined ways, and by virtue of a simple decision, organize a favourable run of consequences.

The arrival of resources and the departure of products demonstrate the new methods: transhipment to replace connection. You are aware of the congestion on the ground and the problems for buildings caused by forks and junctions on railway lines – the costly operations of unloading and loading of merchandise for transport by waterway. During the ASCORAL discussions of 1943 (section V: WORK) we summoned the delegates of various big companies and we asked them: "Do you see any objection to the systematic use, by each standard-size industrial unit, of the 'transhipment' of products and materials?" Their reply was favorable. Transhipment, enjoying *a priori* "standard-size" packaging, includes the installation of a travelling crane and rational handling across the waterways, roadways and railways, perpendicular to these ways and above them, entering the factory, going through it and coming back to the three ways to place the products in the waggons, trucks or boats. This method is part of the second era of the machine civilization, under the sign of harmony: quantities, proportion, etc...

At the other end of the industrial unit (standard size) are the administrative offices and social services, the workers' and executives' entrance. Where do these people come from? They come on foot from their dwellings, a quarter of an hour's walk away and situated right in the countryside.

You know that factories have ceased to be infernos (as in the XIXth century). Plans for "green factories" have appeared (Bata and in the U.S.A) and operate with perfect efficiency. We built the cartridge factory at Moutier-Rozeille in the Creuse region in 1940, for Mr Dautry, Armaments Minister. The green meadows came right up to the workshop windows; the personnel and the workers arrived for work via the top of the building, through closed-in corridors leading to their cloakrooms and toilets, and then descended directly to their places in the machine rooms. The raw materials were brought by rail and followed their own specified route; the goods being manufactured followed cement trackways across the factory floor, functioning in the same way as the cardiac system...

Then there was the debacle and that arrested everything...!

What is a dwelling exactly? If you would like to enjoy calm and privacy with your family, to live in peace and quiet and to benefit from the designed "natural conditions" that are available thanks to modern technology, then be part of a group of two thousand individuals, with one single entrance; create 400 or 500 homes; install the efficient grouping of four elevators each carrying 20 people. Build to a height of fifty metres, to a length of one hundred and fifty metres, to a width of twenty-four metres. Inside the building create seven horizontal superimposed streets evenly distributed over the height. You won't meet anyone in the inside streets (an elevator in motion, 20 people, 7 streets, 3 people per street – two going to the left, one to the right... The second elevator will always arrive in a street that is already empty). Glass covers thousands of square metres, in all, the east, south and west façades. With so much glass and light, establish the control of the sun with a loggia at both ends of the appartment. Every day and at any time, let one thousand two hundred people (for example at Nantes-Rezé) enter over a bridge (over the water) that is only 1 metre 83 centimetres wide; this is the one and only pedestrian access point at the

b/Note: (Industries installed for geological reasons above mineral deposits are an exception to this rule.)

Nantes Unit. Your high density suggests you acquire 2 to 3 hectares of land for 1,500 to 2,000 inhabitants; the nearest neighbour will be 200 or 300 metres away. If you were in a horizontal garden city, in so-called "family" houses, your neighbours would be 10 metres away. And in Marseilles, in a town where most of the inhabitants live in streets that are only ten or twenty metres wide, and behind closed shutters, the Boulevard Michelet Unit has recreated the conditions of nature: on one side, each dwelling opens on to the sea and the islands through fifteen square metres of windows, and on the other side on to the mountain through 7 1/2 square metres of windows (and vice versa). A Homeric view from every dwelling that can enter every heart. In Berlin at Charlottenburg, on the Olympic hill, the tall meadow grass runs right up to the stilts. 2,000 inhabitants and one doorway. At Briey-en-Forêt, the building site for the new Unit has started right in the middle of the woods, accompanied by birdsong. At Meaux, five Units will house ten thousand inhabitants, in a "Green Town" , the automobile completely separated from the pedestrian, sports facilities at the foot of the housing, nursery schools on the roof-gardens, school-rooms on the ground, the clubs for children and young people on the lawns, etc., etc... The market is inside each Unit (as in Marseilles) on the 7th floor; a clientele of 2,000 mouths is ensured of the healthy and honest organization of food supplies.

Ladies and Gentlemen, when it is all finished, here is the bill: you will have built on stilts (one single entrance). The land is unoccupied under the stilts. Your building will have covered 10% of the land leaving 90% as park. The roof is an (adorable) garden.

90% garden
10% free-standing stilts
10% roof garden
Total: 110% land available

I have sometimes proposed this calculation to my audience during lectures. The arithmetic is implacable! People scratched their heads to make sure they were not dreaming!

The dwellings in the linear industrial city could be "radiant dwellings". Father, mother and children will be able to live in natural surroundings. Social services, perfect sanitation, complete silence (yes!): the "SUN – SPACE – GREENERY" of the Athens Charter drawn up at the CIAM [*Congrès International d'Architecture Moderne*] have been achieved. Cinemas, sports facilities, libraries, childrens clubs and others are part of the "housing equation". "The housing equation" is individuals – collectives in partnership and harmony: Marseilles, Nantes, Berlin, Briey-en-Forêt are living examples.

Such fighting, such struggles! Such fighting, such atrocities, such cruelty, such stupidness barred the way.

[Mr Le Corbusier picks up his coloured chalk again, see chap. 3, fig. 14]: I'm drawing the road in red (red because it will be the track for the speeds of machines and the tool of the category always present in any society: the "awkward customers"). The vast majority of people are content with the drone of daily routine. Here the routine is "sun-space-greenery" and walking has replaced today's forms of transport and the waste that is its result.

Here the "awkward customers" can have ideas, pursue their ideas; they have material or intellectual ambitions, need a qualification, etc., etc... Here they are going off along the red road, on the left or on the right, on scooters, by car, by express bus, sometimes in the evening, definitely at the weekend, to see a friend or friends, to find the training or study they need, or the leisure activities that can mould the character towards a sense of elite. Where are they going? To a radioconcentric-exchange centre, to the right or to the left of their home, a centre that has been standing at the crossroads for centuries, that is written into the strictness of the topography and the geography, that is full of ancient wisdom, or full of modern liveliness. Living, moving, thinking! University courses, evening or Saturday technical classes, libraries and theatres, exhibitions. At a hub for exchange of ideas: modern times, the second period of the machine civilization (in harmony) has begun, has created its tools, with respect:

for people
for natural order
for the beauties of nature
with tireless curiosity for scientific resources
with the need for friendship
Civilization that could be placed
under the sign of "the Outstretched Hand"
" The Outstretched Hand"
to receive
and to give
at the time when the modern world
bursts with infinite and unlimited,
intellectual
and
material riches

The three routes to the linear industrial city, by water, land and rail, cut us off from the adjacent countryside. But only on one side. On the other side there is uninterrupted access between the residential areas of the linear city and life in the country.

Farming is suffering from the enormous impetus of the machine age. The agrarian mode of existence has been shattered and diluted; it has a tendency to try to establish new groups, and is actively seeking a new form, a form based on the scale of the tractor and the metalled road. We have seen this with our own eyes: we are turning the page... we are refusing to turn it... it was already turned a long time ago...!! The farmer, as citizen of the machine civilization, is at the dawn of a new adventure and a new way of managing the age-old lands to render the riches of the motherland accessible.

....

I am here to present you with a truth loaded with promise: the new human establishment of our machine society (the linear industrial city) is volunteering to resolve the deadlock of towns, countryside and transport.

If you are prepared to admit that this (new) point of view is valid, here in a continuous charcoal line on this fourth large sheet of white paper, is the result of its application:

I am drawing France, Spain, Italy, Greece, Germany, England, the Scandinavian countries, Switzerland; here are the vast territories of the Eastern countries; here are the Muslims from the Atlantic to the Himalayas with Gibraltar, Suez, the Persian Gulf; here is India. And here is Africa – the huge poetic continent – and here are the yellow peoples. I am drawing this continuous line to show the form and to locate movement between the linear industrial cities. This line moves and connects; it does not block. When it touches the sea it is taken over by a maritime route. The whole round earth is part of the action.

During the war, in the days of ASCORAL, we called in a geographer, of the sort we call "human geographers" because their task is to study the realities of the planet in relation to the presence of people. "Sir, here are our three human establishments, particularly, here is the youngest, the linear city of industrial transformations. Could you situate the valid lines of movement on the maps of France and of Europe?" He came back to us with a map of Europe with the title "Ascoral map of Europe 1943" which was extended and revised to become the Unesco Europe-Asia-Africa map eight years later.[c]

Cross-wise: from Le Havre to Marseilles, from Amsterdam to Marseilles, from Hamburg to Trieste and Salonika, from Danzig to Odessa, from Leningrad to Moscow Tashkend [sic].

Length-wise: from Nantes or La Rochelle to Strasbourg, Augsburg, Vienna, Moscow, etc; – Budapest, Belgrade and the Black Sea, etc... The linear industrial cities rediscovered the old thoroughfares imposed by the permanence of geography, the caravan trails, the silk and jade roads, the Chad route.

An anecdote in passing: in 1910, with a rucksack and a companion we walked from Prague to the Danube and in seven months, crossing countryside

c/Published at the request of Unesco, printed in volume five of Le Corbusier's *Oeuvres Complètes*, 1946-1952, edited by Girsberger.

and towns we reached Asia Minor (this journey was the most important part of my study of architecture). In the Bazaar at Stambul [sic] (the vast and extraordinary bazaar at Stambul), I bought a pottery statuette for five francs. For forty years I searched in vain to discover the origin of this strange – and unknown – object. Shortly after the Liberation of France, I received a book from Marcel Griaule, from the Musée de l'Homme in Paris, on the civilization of Chad that he had just discovered in the equatorial forest thanks to an old wooden airplane that had allowed him to fly above the vegetation and observe its informative characteristics. In the book there is a reproduction of a pottery head of a woman (the only example of an unknown statuary); and this was the origin of my complete statue bought forty years previously; mine had covered the trails of Chad, the Sudan and the Nile, arriving one day in the Bazaar at Stambul...

The paths that carried merchandise, raw materials and migration are ill-fated routes, blocked nowadays by political, administrative and military barriers that have become ineffective: they are now opening up to the harmonization of the modern world.

Horizons are opening!

The Three Human Establishments will be able to assist governments in helping each other, forming partnerships, uniting men's means, undertaking major civil engineering projects for an undoubtedly machine-orientated civilization, the binary "individual-collective" unit located in "natural conditions", rediscovered on a human scale.

Industry is taking over building – engineers and architects united, hands joined, one right hand, one left hand, facing each other and fashioning the whole structural achievement of modern times.

This call for solidarity addressed to builders has the right to be made. I say: two hands clasped, united, ten fingers, twice times five fingers; two hands, one single idea; climate, races, customs; friendship, fraternity. Here I have set out ideas born of the country that is France, so full of history, and always with the same thirst for life. Let me take full responsibility and all the accompanying risks, to assure you that all this is not day-dreaming but belongs in the flow of rising sap of the present day.

The problem is to recover land in order to occupy it with the projects of the machine civilization; the land is vacant, or badly used; everywhere there are vast deserted areas. The two main imperatives for occupying the land are road construction and water mains. Two major contemporary tasks. They are right in line with contemporary technical possibilities.

....

And with the ricochet effect, our towns will be put back in order and our lives saved.

....

While you have been watching I have made these four large-scale drawings in black and in colour. They contain the substance for possible and opportune decisions. I pick up my charcoal again to dedicate them to my friend Malraux whose life also launched him along the test track of the human condition. May these drawings be used like Gobelins or Aubusson hangings (but on drawing paper) on the adminstrative walls of one of the offices where the fates of men or societies are sometimes decided.

LE CORBUSIER

31.3.59 Text rewritten from a tape-recording of Le Corbusier's lecture delivered on 26 June 1958 in the auditorium of the French Pavilion at the Brussels International Exhibition.[41]

41/This recording was broadcast on the French radio station France Culture, in the programme *Métropolitains* on 3 March 1995. The sound recording is archived at the Institut national de l'audiovisuel (DLR 19950303 FCR 18; original n° 430D583). The recording lasts 58 minutes.

Lecture at Brussels, 26 June 1958

Transcription of the recording[42]

– Le Corbusier: What I am going to explain in this lecture may be considered as subversive by some people. A sort of opening... can everyone hear me?
– Some listeners: No.
– Le Corbusier: No? Well, what can be done? Are there any electricians in the audience? [laughter] No, but you see, I'm speaking loudly, I'm speaking normally; I can't speak any louder. And if the electricity is not working, I'm very sorry. Tell me if that is better? Yes... yes...
– Listeners: Yes.
– Le Corbusier: Right, I have to stand here and I am going to draw over there, it won't be easy. What I am going to explain here may be considered subversive by some. A sort of opening on the horizons – and I mean on the horizons – is going to be suggested. An element of city planning, a factor of the solution. Solution to what? To a dead-end, to a world in a serious crisis of mutation. We turn the page (or we don't turn it!). It has already been turned for a long time!

A time of crisis is when only two conclusions are available to us, two extremes, two poles of any problem. It is good, it is necessary to be familiar with the two riversides. But the brook, the river of life, the flow of life run between these two banks, sometimes closer to one, sometimes to the other, sometimes drawn "towards" , sometimes pushed away "by". At every instant, the situation is different, but through grouping, adhesion or solidarity a current is formed that goes sometimes to the left, sometimes to the right. The task of each day is the necessity of moving forward, getting through...

A bird's eye view over the estuaries of the great rivers of Asia or America – North or South – is an invitation to meditation. In the end, as you will see, everything flows to the sea, but how and in what state? [Le Corbusier moves towards his paper in order to draw. He moves the microphone.] One moment, please, I am going to put this... No, it's very funny really... [laughter from the audience]

I am drawing... Wait, I'm drawing all over the place... [laughter]

I'm drawing the bank of something, and another bank; it's the bed of a river seen from an aeroplane. The riverbed, during the rainy season is there and fills with water. There's no question about it, both banks are occupied. At mid-season, in the between-seasons, the water follows certain strange, unexpected paths, it's seeking its way. Here it's meandering, making islets, making bends and... I am going to do this again... I do this if necessary, sometimes to the left, sometimes to the right. [sound of the pencil on the paper] First of all here you will see the essential thing of the permafrost strata attacked by erosion. Here, on the contrary, opposite we have sands that have slowly built up as alluvial deposits, haven't we? [he moves away from the microphone] and you will see, when the rains start to fall, you will see places where there are sorts of violent currents in the... in the... er... rocks that are being eroded, natural rocks, and others making complicated courses.

This is the story of an atmospheric cycle. It can be shown with this diagram. You have the sea (with or without an accent) [*Le Corbusier is referring here to the identical pronounciation of mer = sea and mère = mother, translator's note*], the plain, the mountains and you have a necessary equilibrium charged with relativity, charged with counterweight, which means that here you have water evaporating in droplets [sound of the pencil tapping on the paper to make dots] which create clouds, which create storms, which make winds, lightning, and the water that flows down from the mountains and comes down again to the sea.

But it is this cycle and the way it is expressed here that shows you the range of difficulties, the range of possible solutions. The opportunity presented by a day as it passes and time as it passes. Here you have the [T of day??], it's the first of the month, there it will be the first of the second month... the third month, and every day of your life you will be under the obligation, you will find it necessary... having to find, to seek and to find a solution.

42/This recording was transmitted on the France Culture radio channel, as part of the *Métropolitains* weekly radio programme edited by François Chaslin, on 3 March 1995. In its transmitted form, the recording is 58 minutes long. It is conserved at the Institut National de l'Audiovisuel (DLR19950303 FCR18). The original recording on disk is also archived at the INA (No 430DS83).

– Er... [another interruption] I don't know if you can hear me.
– Listeners: Yes.
– Le Corbusier: Yes, alright?

Until now we had the bird's eye view. Old drawings, old engravings bore the indication "bird's eye view". We now have the view from the aeroplane which is a wonderful opportunity to decode, to discover the lessons of nature. The aeroplane is creating huge disruption, as well as bringing hope for a solution.

An example, Bogotá, in Colombia. Bogotá was at an altitude of three thousand metres, on the Equator, in a sad, serene landscape, quiet, dead – well, dreary... it was dreary. After the 1918 War, a German company, which had some old aeroplanes well past their prime, had an idea, saying to themselves: we'll make an airport out there on the rock-hard turf – they brought out special grass – and we're going to build an airport and bring meat to the country. And what happened? Until then and for the past four centuries, to get from Bogotá to the Caribbean, to Barranquilla, it took twenty to twenty-five days, and with an aeroplane it took two hours. On the strength of that, everything changed. On the strength of that, life took hold of the place that had been abandoned to its solitude until then, and such is... and problems arose there as they were arising elsewhere. There, the problems were absolutely clear. Bogotá had been a one-storey town – built to a height of one storey – and now had the possibility of becoming a skyscraper town, didn't it? And indeed, between these two extremes, the solution became apparent.

I also want to say this, it's that when things like this happen, one can see a method appearing, one can see why it's useful to introduce a method in order to achieve a definition, a doctrine, a formulation of the something that is there, facing one. We architects had the opportunity in Paris during the Occupation, in 1942, 1943, when for some of us, for those of us, there was not a single cubic centimetre to build, not a single square centimetre of city planning, zero absolutely zero, we had the possibility of waiting for time to pass or for things to come back, or the possibility of saying to ourselves that we would use this unexpected and extraordinary staging-post to see things clearly. And at that point we founded a group, a small group, l'Ascoral – *the Assemblée de constructeurs pour une rénovation architectural* – which allowed us... us to have eleven study groups which met twice a month – that made twenty-two committees every month – and as there were no orders, no money, no network, ideas were clear, conversation was fruitful and results were positive. I say this and I maintain what I say, what clips the wings and shackles the progress of solutions is base interest, immediate gain, submitting to the interest for money that deprives research of its possibility for momentum which is a thing, the thing one should expect. [He removes a sheet of paper] I... I am going to quote the result, the reading of a result, the result of an interesting reading from... from a professor from Dijon whose name escapes me, who has written a wonderful history of the French countryside, and who has shown that men in the past were hunters and fishermen and that they could not have been anything else. They fed themselves with their hunting and their fishing, they had weapons to use for these activities, they weren't wonderful weapons, but that is how they spent their time and they didn't have banquets every day. And these men were relentless individualists. One day, we don't have a definite date, they discovered grasses – grasses means wheat. We tend to forget these things; we can't imagine that there was a time when there wasn't wheat, and consequently no bread, consequently a whole part of the nourishment necessary for the body didn't exist, did it, and an entire trade, a professional activity, didn't exist, and that was farming. So how was it possible to sow the grain in the arid soil? It wasn't possible so they... didn't plough because there were no machines, those things had not yet been imagined, so they removed the stones from a clearing, everywhere where there were clearings, they took away the stones, extended the clearing, according to the necessity of the slopes, facing the sun, etc., to obtain land that could be ploughed, that could one day be sown, and they sowed wheat and to do this... men had to work together. That's the first stage. [Rustle of paper]

Then came the time when they said to themselves: we don't need to be bothered with being together any more, we'll share all the fruits, and they shared them out, and this society became individualist and still is.

And now when a new phenomenon appears, that of mechanization which has been... which is the result of various sets of circumstances and which now comes from there... has allowed working the land under entirely new auspices, hasn't it, with machines, I had the opportunity to see it this morning from a helicopter flying at a height of one hundred metres or one hundred and fifty metres, and one can see the plains of Picardy planted out in an admirable way, sown like a garden tended by angels – it's amazing, isn't it? – machines that have done it, but for the moment they have created a real malaise, haven't they? They have removed the inhabitants from the land, farms have become obsolete, the [?] likely to fall into ruin, falling down and lands deserted. [Sound of organ music] So here we have this thing that is before us, it's the problem, one of the problems where the common good plays a part: projects for the common good. The words means exactly what they should mean and there is no question of searching for another meaning, to find consequences to the situation that have no reason to be; from a professional like myself, the point is to find projects for the common good, is it not?

Now I am going to make a little incursion into... the state of things, into the birth of cities, into the present state of the countryside and show you that they have both got to a stage, one of terrible congestion, i.e. the tentacular city, and the other of tragic desertion, i.e. the countryside. And this state of things today can give rise to admirable possibilities for solutions.

But let us start by drawing here [see chapter 3, Fig 13]. Here are two crossroads. Here is a town... [sound of microphone being moved] Good heavens... it's heavy! Here is a town, a beach; this is the sea, this is the ocean. [sound of pencil on paper] Here is a city created at some point and developing; it's New York, for example, with its street leading towards the Far West, isn't it, Broadway, it's a street that remains on course across all the obstacles in the town, with routes coming here by water and roads leaving overland via various junctions. Here for example we have a characteristic adventure, the hexagon shape of France with Paris in a place that is connected... connected to other capitals, connected to its frontiers, to the seaports, connected to everything... everywhere connected to useful places. And being the expression of one of the best organized cities, the most beautifully organized cities that have existed right up to the present. Nowadays it is in a critical state. Here is another drawing showing you this... this small town that became a city surrounded by... surrounded by fortifications of various sorts, either mediaeval, very high towers, aren't they, with crenellations, etc., or those of the Renaissance, er, anyway that doesn't matter, and the surrounding walls, successive, to a height of... of a city, whether it's a French or a European one, or one in any place where there has been development of towns over the centuries. And now here we have the ancient centre of the city, with its surrounding circles, which are no longer fortifications but thoroughfares, that is to say boulevards... boulevards. The word boulevard – unless I am mistaken, I could be – comes from *Bollwerk*, which means, er... defence, fortification, doesn't it? And so you see appearing, and I'll use a purple chalk if I've got one here, I don't know, it's barely visible... I'll use purple, to situate from the XIXth century onwards, like so, to situate the first appearances of industry which I can draw anywhere with... the growth of the city, with its quarters, residential quarters that I will show in blue for example... in brown... these residential quarters, these successive residential zones, successive, etc. And then the escape routes... miraculous towards the exterior, aren't they, satellite towns... which are an absolutely disastrous miracle for the future of cities – a complete illusion because the... the roads continue to serve all these... these diverse radiating elements, don't they? Living conditions develop at the same time as the industrial centres, so either... either in rings... in satellite rings, or in general rings and gradually you have tentacular cities which are the most chronically sick aspects and... deadly aspects of the cities of the present time, are the tentacular cities. Now you see in the tentacular cities on every continent, you see radiating railways too, don't you, taking people at four, five, six o'clock in the morning, taking them to the centre and then putting them in buses, subways, making them to and fro so much that this to and fro is certainly the most tragic waste of our modern times. There are people who find advantage in this; some people say it's wonderful, we're making tyres, we're making buses, we're making cars, we're making subways, we're making trains, rails, beams, joists in wood or concrete, we're making work for the... for the... *wattmans*, for the drivers, for the road-menders, for maintenance, etc. One day I had a conversation with Burleigh in New York, he was one of Roosevelt's right-hand men, he said to me, you are completely right; we have so lost ourselves in this situation that we use 52% of the activity of our country to pay for the wastage. I said to him, that is half of people's work and I drew another circle for the occupation of the daily hour, saying that men in our present society pay... spend four hours a day to pay for the waste in our system. But then, I cannot expand on all these circumstances for you.

But then concerning... [Sound of the microphone being moved] Concerning the countryside, it was the... the village... the village with its church, its little municipal building, when it had one, a church etc., the family farm sometimes, that depends on the type of agriculture and on the people er... which became, which could still be run with the price of labour being affordable before the twentieth century but which today has become completely impossible – and it is useful to explain why, but the countryside has been deserted. During [Le Corbusier moves the microphone again] those times, technology was developing and in these towns, in these towns the residential question could be solved by the creation of vertical communes – with no political element of course – the commune created around the hearth, around the family, around the 24-hour solar cycle of daily life, of everything, of whoever and whatever the ideas of anybody, it's there... the 24-hour solar cycle which is the fundamental key to the life of all beings on earth must be respected and the malformation of the tentacular city has no respect for the solar cycle or for its status in the countryside. The solar cycle can regain its equilibrium in the creation of units each housing 2000 individuals, if you wish. I am going to make you shudder, but it doesn't matter, these 2000 individuals are, can go in and out through one single entrance, and as they go in and out, and having elevators available to distribute the inhabitants to the inside streets at the various levels, and being 50 metres high in order to provide lodgings that are all in natural surroundings, in the countryside, in the hills, on the plain, in the meadows, on the lawns, mountains wherever you like. And so this thing that was, that is the vindication of a way of life, of the privacy of a home where each person can feel free, being totally independent from his neighbours, whom he neither sees nor hears, is immersed in natural surroundings; for so many years this appeared to be a paradox but it has now become self-evident. I can't give you all the details, I'm sorry, but I would ask you simply to believe that what I am talking about is not a Utopia. Things are based on the sun of course, the sun that shines, that determines which way the buildings face, the greenery that surrounds the buildings, which are 200, 300, 400, 500 metres one from the other, laid out in such a way that each appartment receives the rays of the rising sun and the setting sun coming through, through the whole appartment... You have a state of affairs here that is possible because of technology and what is this technology? It is the technology of the structure that means it can be done very easily, of the industry that... you are in the French pavilion, in a model, in a structural model that is perfectly relevant, isn't it? The structural art that has [?] given the order, it's... It is just my age of seventy years, isn't it, and now... now sound-proofing is making its entrance into the realities of building, sound-proofing which is a new science, a science that is as exact as the science of electricity, or chemistry, or physics, is it not? Er... that mathematics should allow total silence between neighbours, through a party wall only a few centimetres thick, I'm not dreaming, am I? I'm talking about things that have been achieved, checked and experienced, am I not? Well, with this phonic insulation, and the benefit of vertical placing... that I can draw in this way... putting a vertical system in place here... and horizontal branches like so... you have elevators that can carry twenty people and then distribute them over five or ten inside streets with two or three people or one person per street, you never see anyone, you have the perfect technical solution to the problems facing society. And faced with the scandalous, shameful and disgusting chaos that is the ubiquitous slum, you have the certainty of absolute innovation, that technology can offer. I am not a prophet in this, I am... I'm talking about the past, it exists. It's been done, hasn't it? And so, you see for example in a thing like this... you have here... the automobile track, the automobile track, the automobile road which goes through one place, and that's enough, and you have the pedestrian track, the street for pedestrians that follows completely different routes, passing underneath the housing... wait a moment, excuse me, we can't see the colours properly at all here, and I'm getting confused between the yellow and the red, it's not my fault and I'm only using red here... And so you have, for example, an experiment which is personal for me, at the moment, it's in Meaux, in a town that for four centuries had eighteen thousand inhabitants with its cathedral and all sorts of charming and lively things, I have a plan... where city planning, architecture, housing, etc... and all the useful technology provides accommodation for 30000 inhabitants in 15 units, with three kilometres of streets and that's all. The automobile kilometre. All the rest without anyone, child, elderly person, nor anyone of any age having to meet an automobile. This isn't verbiage, it's reality. So you now have alongside the new aspect of the residential unit, you have what was... what can happen from the point of view of work, that... it's living... and so you from the point of view of work, you have, for example, this New York, so... that I outlined, which is somewhere over there, which is here, which is composed of pointed skyscrapers like so with... 300 metres, or like this, isn't it, then little houses roundabout, and then others like this, then etc... isn't it? With a... a spiky aspect, absolutely sublime and discouraging, discouraging, it's very beautiful, its extraordinary, we can have great fun visiting it all, can't we? But in the meantime, it's a sign of... a mixture of things, a signal of inconsequence... tragic, and... and with this we can contrast what has been done for the United Nations, and if you will pardon me, I have my part of responsibility, but there I am... It's this, it's that the road is here, the road that is here is like this with... with houses filling in all this, the street is here, with only cars, and the buildings are here inside, with trees all around and the access points taking the cars at low speed and into the car park. So then... the other achievement, and these buildings can be 200 metres high, accommodate... 3,000, 5,000, even 10,000 employees in optimal conditions of efficiency and comfort... I'm not saying that this has been achieved in New York, because I have a little personal resentment concerning New York, don't I? But that means I do not consider everything has been done in the best possible way in the best of worlds. But in the end, you have there, if I finish my drawing, I am going to finish with... the trees are here, all around, aren't they, inside... you have what we can call the radiant City, the green City, that is to say a... an entirely new attitude towards the city... and its resources. This could be extended to cover research that... is endless, needing constant verification, but we will not have the time this evening.

I would like to take you directly to the conclusion of this presentation by showing you how this state of affairs... prophetic below [?], and already carried out, reality, and here an already outmoded inferno, how it... men's projects are now able to use any sort of land, and how, with recognized ways of using the land, it will be possible to combine architecture, city planning and all the imaginable technology.

So I have here three drawings to show you [see chapter 3, Fig 14], because I am going to talk to you about the three human establishments and I am going to make a fundamental observation: until now there have been two human establishments, there is the unit of agricultural activity, I presented it newborn, developing and dying, and there is the unit of exchange, the radio-concentric city of exchange, that has become the tentacular city. As for technology, the ordering of things leads us to import... to introduce into the industrial system the third human establishment, which is the linear city of industrial transformations. That is what I wish to explain... and it carries... carries with it the complete solution.

We have the first... the first modern agricultural institution, don't we? Here for example we have an agricultural co-operative, with a grain silo, workshops, machines, etc... We have the... that's the equipment... Here we have the dwelling, which can be in a chosen place or anywhere, it doesn't matter, anyhow the chosen place or the dwelling will not be to rebuild dilapidated old farms and already defunct, deceased equipment but things of today. Near the... near the machines you will have the roads that will lead to the fields, the new crops, extensive crops to scale with the machines, orchards, and then pasture, there where it lies. There are places near the forest, near the meadows, aren't there, with stables and the... the hay, and the fodder etc... That is the agrarian reform that has been outlined in every country, gradually by continuing research, hasn't it? It's... You have America who started with machines which made us... which made us laugh. Gigantic machines, fantastic where they... they... shaved the wheat, and then it came out in bags at the back, didn't it, already in bags. We thought it was very comical, exaggerated, and now, well, we have managed to do these things very well. It's not the result of... of an America or whatever, it's the result of mechanical advance. And it's the... the too narrow... the too wide division of the land, isn't it, in the countryside that now prevents sowing, harvesting, and creates the rural exodus. It is necessary to form groups, and here we are without my having to insist on... a type of grouping of lands. But above all I would like to show you the... the essential thing that is the classifying of the three units. I will draw here, always at a cross-roads: an ancient fortified town, and... and I will surround it, not with development itself, of no consequence... but within I will indicate the places where there are theatres, universities, evening classes, workshops etc...

And inside we find... it's the radioconcentric city for exchange, I am going to note that here, the radioconcentric city for exchange, and I would draw your attention to the fact that it has always existed at cross-roads, I started this evening with a drawing of this type, but with ... now... much greater precision, it's the government, if there is one, the.. thought, merchandise.

There, and there, and there... the radioconcentric place of exchange. And now let us move on to civilization. I wrote that: a civilization... a machine civilization, it used to be... in the past a very unpleasant term. Machine. But not at all: we are witnessing a period of industrial transformation. What do we need for industrial transformation? We need raw materials and we need manufactured products that leave the factory. Raw materials that arrive, don't they? So we need roads, what sort of roads are there? There are... it's beautiful at night [?]... There's the way, the waterway, there's the land route... There's the iron way; the railway. One has always been there. The land route dates from the time of men, it is already a construction, the railway is relatively recent. There's a fourth route, it's the air route, and ... and it has a different destiny, it passes over everything, it's another thing all together. These are routes that are attached to the ground. They are the arrival roads that generally follow the talweg, the... geography shows us that water follows the water incline. That's a bit repetitive. That the land route travels where water travels because that is the passage, and then the route of the railway generally went that way too, allowing itself the liberty at a certain point to cross the water incline, joining two inclines with a tunnel. However this is still in the talwegs. So... you can now accept that the industrial phenomenon consists in installing... these industrial establishments... that I will describe as standard-size. Designed differently to those designed by the generally accepted method. All living beings, all organisms proceed from the inside to the outside, don't they? They have internal organs, that's biology. And a factory has its biology, just as a house should have its biology, just as... a living being should have its established biology. And so, here is the arrival of the merchandise, connecting is no longer via connections, the connections, the contacts are via transhipment. That is very important. It is something new to be taken into consideration. I'll put transhipment, not connections. Because connections waste floor space, er... paralyze everything, whereas the conn... the... transhipment means merchandise can cross the three "ways" but never causes an obstacle. So next I am going to draw a route that I call the red route, it's the high-speed route which is here and which will come this way, and will go from... from a cross-roads where there is a radioconcentric city, to another cross-roads, and... this red route is there to establish rapid contact with what I call the alternative, the alternative... it is the opposite of the day-to-day activity, taking place every 24 hours, and it has... as a means... as... an object, to connect here, by roads, to connect with other roads that are here, and which satisfy the conditions of residence, it's... little villages for those who like that kind of thing, but in the end, they may well soon decide against the estates, the housing estates, and others where you will find large standard-size units, designed like this, like this, etc... with sports grounds, swimming pools, there are as many sports grounds as needed, aren't there... and the 24-hour contact, it's here [?]. There... so just think, this is why it is necessary to define what I call the standard-size units. Earlier I showed you standard-size units, for 2,000 inhabitants, to create vertical residential communes. In the workplace... apart from the little workshop of the wheelwright, or the little mechanic who will one day become Louis Renault and Company, that's an exception, there are, in the industry of the country, the industry bosses who have big orders and who must provide all the produce for the whole country, and who need standard-size units, that is to say to [set up?] production lines, they need a certain number of workers, a certain amount of raw materials, a progression... a daily progression, don't they? Which makes up a standard-size unit, that can be clearly formed and occupy a certain surface... as I have indicated here. The workers, the administrative staff, all the... participants in these standard-size units can easily live at... at walking distance from their work, can't they? To find here, deep in the countryside, all the benefits of the sun, the earth, and contact with nature. So if I draw, if I finish this drawing, let's say that among the... clients for the 24-hour cycle, most people only want one thing and that is to be with their family, with their children, their wife, etc... their relatives, there are a few, what I would call the awkward customers, people of my sort if you like, who would say but I... I want to go and study, I want to go... to go to classes, I want to go to the theatre, I want to go and see things that are out of the ordinary, participate, even perform at the theatre if need be, this person has the direct route to go intermittently, that's what I should have written, I wrote something wrong here, intermittent... well I thought I had written that... intermittent, isn't it? The intermittent people here, who are going there to find, in the radioconcentric places, there where the exchanges that have come, you see here, by the routes from the other sides, and that are fed by substance. This gives you a... an attitude towards land use in the country, that I am going to transcribe with my last drawing, which will be this. I am going to put a city here... a linear industrial city...

How... wait a moment... linear city... oh my goodness! Oh dear, we can't see a thing! A linear industrial city with its units, you will notice one thing, and that is I have put each one of them, I've put them all on the same side of the ways. With this simple common sense decision, it will be forbidden to cross over in the other direction. Why? Because if we allow crossing over everything will be disrupted, and all the nonsense will start all over again with the traffic problems. So here, it's only on one side, but never mind, they just need to be installed where it's necessary, and... There we are... So now I am drawing the... the radioconcentric cities of exchange where there is the early hub or if the agglomeration is by chance a recent one – it's possible – where there is the hub here, and beside it as I said, the buildings intended for leisure, education, even government, yes... if government is part of the arrangement in that particular place. And here, another radioconcentric city, which is here, with the same conditions, what can be the... the distance, perhaps... (it looks like a drunkard, my drawing...) So here I have the third one, and the drawing continues, the routes continue, and they can arrive here like this. You see here in the green zones... the green reserves, where there are agricultural units adapted for the use of machines, aren't there? And in here, you will have the residential estates, here, like this... with standard-size residential units, which are here... which are like this, which are there, etc... I'm drawing them here... There, I've finished, you can see now...

The reading of situations... I'll use green crayon again to show that all this is in the middle of the countryside, all this isn't it? And my final drawing will be on the remaining piece of paper, to show you that the abomination I described at the beginning, that is to say the tentacular city, with its ring roads, with its horrors, its deadlock, atrocious... And I assure you, if you are not afraid of getting a headache, take a helicopter and go, do... go to Paris in a helicopter, you'll see the Paris suburbs, choose a grey morning like today, it's more typical, you'll see the abomination, the terrible disorder, of these things, won't you? And, we have the... the factories, I'll show them in red, the dwellings in purple, etc... are the tentacular cities that are like this, swollen up with all sorts of things, and on top of it all five million... five million inhabitants, aren't there? Or twelve or ten, or twelve, it's your choice, London or New York, maybe? And faced with this, you're in deadlock. I'll tell you about an exchange I had with one of my very good friends, who is in an important position, with... with enormous responsibilities in today's world, I said to him one day: "Listen old chap, who is ever going to give the order to demolish the Paris suburbs?" The Paris suburbs. He said: "You... you..." what did he say? He said... must... "Don't talk nonsense!" And so I said: "Right, I say it can't go on like this, and that it is going to be necessary to order the demolition of the Paris suburbs." That is to say, to find the way of getting through, to create the... as I have drawn them here, the linear cities with residential areas, with residential areas in... being part of... Yes, there... a residential area here, isn't it? And the... the countryside being like this, and... allowing more space here in... the green zones, this and that, and if you would even like me to finish my drawing because this is where I started, with the map of France and of Paris, I would say that we will have these routes that will come to empty Paris of its overflow and its congestion, the... the main roads will be like this, there and... over here, greenery will be able to grow in place of the slums, the city retrieves possession of its ground, and large positive structures will align themselves with real and useful attitudes towards monuments, the past could be preserved... as much as desired, easily, and honoured, whereas now a large part is in a shameful state, it is... it is like a pauper, and so my drawing will be completed like this: I am going to show you these... these tentacular cities that find a solution, and here... the three human establishments occupy the land in harmony – harmoniously. And I put = by = increased value, increased value of the land, the cities and the countryside = I really want to write this for you: = life and an exclamation mark at the end!

Because it's a profitable transaction! I still have another little drawing for you, but I will follow... I've finished... I thought it was the last one, but there is still one more. You have seen... you have seen the routes in the talwegs; I told you that the third human establishment, the industrial city for transformation was the solution for the use of the land by the projects of the machine civilization. I am going to do a horrible thing and you will see. I am drawing France, Spain, Italy, Greece, the Black Sea, here, there are countries that... as we are in Belgium, Flanders, the Netherlands, Jutland, here er... Norway, here... England... Scotland, Ireland, here... Russia, here Asia Minor, here Gibraltar, Algiers, Tripoli, Suez, the Persian Gulf, oil, India, 4000 years of civilization, Asia etc... Africa here, Somalia etc...

I have never been active in politics, and I never want to be, it's not one of my talents. As you see, I'm busy with really interesting activities, and I don't want to do politics. And what I am about to draw isn't political. Except that I would say... during the Occupation I asked a human geographer to... I asked him to... I said: Here is the theory of the three human establishments, how do they fit into the map of Europe? And so that I don't er... leave anything out, I should start by drawing the people of the sea, shouldn't I? Who come and go. Here everything one needs too, there, here, isn't there? The early navigators, the earliest, even here there is all that, it's all the same idea, and now the land route. And so let's start with the one we know, shall we? So you could have that one, and there might be that one, you've got... you've got this one coming in, haven't you? Here you have roads coming in to... this, and you have some that come from here, to Odessa. You have some that go over there, er... to the Caucasus, that are going to Persia, going to the foot of the Himalayas, going to China, aren't they? They are... that are going to Moscow if need be, to Saint Petersburg, wherever. Here you have them for the Spanish countries, they are er... almost insular countries, special in a way, like Italy, but which will sort themselves out perfectly well on their own, for example... in Piedmont they know how to run first class industries, don't they, and the Spaniards are not a sleepy country, they will do it too, won't they? All this will be done and so you see... that the necessity, the... the installation – I'm going to put a bit of blue for the sea, to finish the picture – so you will see that the routes of the machine civilization, so... are traced across the continents, joining up with the eternal routes from China for example, the Jade route, coming... across Asia and Europe. China and from Chad. Where there are all sorts of age-old interests that are... conjugated in there, that go through here, that come this way, that come here, don't they? That come down there, and that go over there. We... people, when they went on foot, covered huge distances across all the continents carrying rocks, or... or weapons, or not much of anything, merchandise in small quantities. The routes... which are the regular passage for merchandise, raw materials, work, can lead the world towards an effort for harmonization.

I don't know if I'm supposed to give you a closing word here, maybe... The three human establishments offer a solution to governments... to assist each other, to join forces and to pool the means of labour and equipment. The project of public works for an undoubtedly mechanized civilization, the individual-collective binomial working in harmony, natural settings rediscovered and to a human scale, industry taking charge of building, collaboration between engineers and architects. Two hands united, clasped together, ten fingers, twice times five fingers, two hands, one idea, one single idea: climate, race, customs, adorable diversity, reason, friendship, fraternity, here the ideas presented were born in France, a country where blood [?] is so varied... so full of history, so ardent, always so full of life. Allow me, in the face of all risks, to assume complete responsibility for stating that all this is no daydream, but the rising, living sap of the present.

[Applause]

The index does not comprise the appendix.

Anon. *La Renaissance des Cités 1916-1935*. Paris.

Baird, George (1974). "Documents: Karel Teige's *Mundaneum* and Le Corbusier's *In Defense of Architecture*, 1933", *Oppositions*, no. 4, pp. 79-108.

Barthes, Roland (1977). "Rhetoric of the Image." In: *Image, Music, Text*. Edited and translated by Stephen Heath. New York: Hill and Wang. Pp. 32-51.

Benton, Tim (2004). "Pessac and Lège revisited: standards dimensions and failures", *Massilia* (Barcelona), vol. 2, pp. 64-99.

Benton, Tim; Peter Carl, et al. (2003). *Le Corbusier and the architecture of reinvention*. London: AA Publications.

Benton, Tim; Christopher Green, William J. R. Curtis, Colin Rowe, Kenneth Frampton, Adrian Forty, Sunand Prasad and Judi Loach (1987). *Le Corbusier, architect of the century: a centenary exhibition organized by the Arts Council of Great Britain*. London: Arts Council of Great Britain.

Budry, Paul (1930). "De l'Architecture considérée comme un des Beaux Arts", *Aujourd'hui* (Lausanne), no. 19, p. 1.

Cingria-Vaneyre, Alexandre (1908). *Entretiens de la Villa du Rouet*. Genève: A. Jullien.

Colomina, Beatriz (1988). "L'Esprit Nouveau: Architecture and Publicité." In: *Architecture-Reproduction*. Edited by Beatriz Colomina and Joan Ockman. New York: Princeton Architectural Press. Pp. 24-55.

Columbia University School of Architecture (1970). *Four great makers of modern architecture: Gropius, Le Corbusier, Mies van der Rohe, Wright. The verbatim record of a symposium held at the School of Architecture, Columbia University, March-May, 1961*. New York, Da Capo Press.

Durand, Jacques (1970). "Rhétorique et image publicitaire", *Communications*, no. 15, pp. 70-95.

Eliel, Carol S. (2001). *L'Esprit Nouveau: Purism in Paris 1918-1925*. Los Angeles: Los Angeles County Museum of Art, in association with Harry N. Abrams, New York.

Exposition universelle et internationale de Bruxelles (1959). *Entretiens et conférences donnés à l'Auditorium du Pavillon de France d'avril à octobre 1958*. Dijon: Commissariat général de la section française.

Ferry, Jules (1868). *Les Comptes fantastiques d'Haussmann*. Paris: Armand Le Chevalier.

Frampton, Kenneth (1979). "Le Corbusier and l'Esprit Nouveau", *Oppositions*, no. 15-16, pp. 12-59.

Gabetti, Roberto and Carlo Maria Olmo (1975). *Le Corbusier e L'Esprit nouveau*. Turin: G. Einaudi.

Garnier, Tony (1917). *Une Cité industrielle. Etude pour la construction des villes*. Paris: Editions Vincent, Fréal & Cie.

Gobineau, Joseph-Arthur Comte de (1853-55). *Essai sur l'inégalité des races humaines*. Paris: Firmin Didot.

Gubler, Jacques (1977). "Les identités d'une région", *Werk-Archithese*, vol. 6, pp. 3-8.

Jeanneret, Charles-Edouard and Amédée Ozenfant (1925). *La peinture moderne*. Paris: Editions Georges Crès et Cie.

Le Boeufle, René and Paul Guadet (1923). "Les Hangars à dirigeables de Villeneuve-Orly", *L'Architecture*, vol. XXXVI, no. 15, pp. 215-218.

Le Corbusier (1926). *Almanach d'architecture moderne; documents, théorie, pronostics, histoire, petites histoires, dates, propos standarts, apologie et idéalisation du standart, organisation, industrialisation du bâtiment*. Paris: Editions Georges Crès et Cie. (Reprint 1987. Paris: Editions Connivences.)

Le Corbusier (1926). "Architecture d'époque machiniste", *Journal de Psychologie normale et pathologique*, vol. XXIII, pp. 17-42.

Le Corbusier (1959). *L'art décoratif d'aujourd'hui*. Paris: Editions Vincent, Fréal & Cie. English edition: *The decorative art of today* (1987). Translated and introduced by James I. Dunnett. London: Architectural Press.

Le Corbusier (1925). "L'Esprit Nouveau en Architecture", *Bulletin de L'Ordre de l'Etoile de l'Orient*, pp. 24-54.

Le Corbusier (1928). *Une maison – un palais. A la recherche d'une unité architecturale*. Paris: Editions Georges Crès et Cie.

Le Corbusier (1964). *Œuvre complète. Vol. 3: 1934-1938*. Zurich: Les Editions d'Architecture (Artemis). English edition: *Complete works. Vol. 3: 1934-1938* (1994). Basel, Berlin, Boston: Birkhäuser Verlag.

Le Corbusier (1930). *Précisions sur un état présent de l'architecture et de l'urbanisme avec un prologue américain et un corollaire Brésilien suivi d'une température Parisienne et d'une atmosphère Moscovite*. Paris: Editions Georges Crès et Cie. (Reprint 1960.) English edition: *Precisions on the present state of architecture and city planning* (1991). Translated by Edith Schreiber Aujame. Cambridge, MA: MIT Press.

Le Corbusier (1925) *Urbanisme. Collection de "L'Esprit Nouveau"*. Paris: Editions Georges Crès & Co. (Reprint 1966. Paris: Editions Vincent, Fréal & Cie.)

Le Corbusier (1966). *Vers une architecture*. Reprint of the 1925 edition. Paris: Editions Vincent, Frèal & Cie, 1966. (Revised and enlarged edition 1977. Paris: Arthaud.) English edition: *Toward an Architecture* (2007). Translated by John Goodman from the 2nd edition, 1928 printing. Los Angeles: Getty Research Institute Publications.

Le Corbusier (1964). *La ville radieuse; éléments d'une doctrine d'urbanisme pour l'équipement de la civilisation machiniste*. Paris, Genève, Rio de Janeiro: Editions Vincent, Fréal et Cie. English edition: *The radiant city: elements of a doctrine of urbanism to be used as the basis of our machine-age civilization* (1967). Translated by Pamela Knight, Eleanor Levieux, Derek Coltman. London: Faber.

Le Corbusier, Norbert Bézard, et al. (1945). *L'Urbanisme des trois établissements humains*. Paris: Editions Denoël. (Reprint 1959. Paris: Editions de Minuit.)

Le Corbusier and Clive Entwistle (1947). *Concerning town planning*. London: Architectural Press.

Le Corbusier and N.V. Philips' gloeilampenfabrieken Eindhoven Netherlands. (1958). *Le poème électronique, Le Corbusier. Pavillon Philips pour l'Exposition universelle de Bruxelles, 1958*. Paris: Editions de Minuit.

Le Corbusier, Stanislaus von Moos and Fondation Le Corbusier (1997). *Album La Roche*. New York: Monacelli Press, in association with Fondation Le Corbusier, Paris.

Loyer, François and Hélène Guéné (1987). *Henri Sauvage – Les immeubles à gradins*. Liège: Pierre Mardaga.

Mauclair, Camille (1930). *La Farce de l'art vivant II: Les Métèques contre l'art français*. Paris: Éditions de la Nouvelle Revue Critique.

Mauclair, Camille (1933). *La crise du panbetonisme integral; L'Architecture va-t-elle mourir?* Paris: Editions de la Nouvelle Revue Critique.

Michels, Karen (1985). "Le Corbusier: poème électronique: die Synthèse der Künste im Philips Pavillon, Weltausstellung, Brussel 1958". *Idea: Jahrbuch der Hamburger Kunsthalle*, vol. 4, pp. 147-163.

Passanti, Francesco (1993). "Le Corbusier et le gratte-ciel: aux origines du plan Voisin". *Americanisme et modernité: l'ideal americain dans l'architecture*. Edited by Jean-Louis Cohen and Hubert Damisch. Paris: EHESS and Flammarion. Pp. 171-189.

Passanti, Francesco (1987). "The skyscrapers of the Ville Contemporaine", *Assemblage* 4, pp. 52-65.

Perelman, Chaïm (1982). *The realm of rhetoric*. Translated by William Kluback. Notre Dame, IN; London: University of Notre Dame Press.

Pérez Oyarzún, Fernando and Le Corbusier (1991). *Le Corbusier y Sudamerica: viajes y proyectos*. Santiago: Ediciones ARQ.

Poole, Cynthia Anne (1997). *From private to public: Le Corbusier and the House-Palace 1926-1928*. Ph. Thesis. School of Architecture. London: University of Westminster.

Robrieux, Jean-Jacques (1993). *Eléments de rhétorique et d'argumentation*. Paris: Dunod.

Roth, Alfred (1927). *Zwei Wohnhäuser von Le Corbusier [pseud.] und Pierre Jeanneret*. Stuttgart: F. Wedekind & Co.

Sauvage, Henri (1922). "Les Tendances de l'architecture moderne", *L'Amour de l'art*, pp. 333-334.

Senger, Alexander von (1928). *Le cheval de troie du bolchevisme*. Bienne: Les Editions du Chandelier.

Senger, Alexander von (1928). *Krisis der Architektur*. Zurich, Leipzig, Stuttgart: Rascher.

Smet, Catherine de (2005). *Le Corbusier, architect of books*. Translated by Deke Dusinberre. Baden, Switzerland: Lars Müller Publishers.

Société française des urbanistes (1923). *Où en est l'urbanisme en France et à l'étranger?* Edited on the occasion of the Congrès international d'urbanisme et d'hygiène municipal de Strasbourg. Paris: Léon Eyrolles.

Tsiomis, Yannis (2006). *Le Corbusier; conférences de Rio*. Paris, Flammarion.

Turner, Paul Venable (1977). *The education of Le Corbusier*. New York, London: Garland Publishing.

Valéry, Paul (1989). "Eupalinos; or, The architect" and "Dance and the soul". *Dialogues Vol. 4* (Bollingen Series XLV). Translated with a preface by William McCausland Stewart. Reprint. Princeton, NJ: Princeton University Press.

Von Moos, Stanislaus; Françoise Dueros and Tim Benton (1987). *L'Esprit Nouveau. Le Corbusier et l'Industrie 1920-1925*. Exhibition catalogue. Zurich: Museum für Gestaltung.